Software Engineering Design

Theory and Practice

Titles in the
Auerbach Series on Applied Software Engineering
Phillip A. Laplante, Pennsylvania State University, Series Editor

Software Engineering Design: Theory and Practice
Carlos E. Otero
978-1-4398-5168-5

Ethics in IT Outsourcing
Tandy Gold
978-1-4398-5062-6

The ScrumMaster Study Guide
James Schiel
978-1-4398-5991-9

**Antipatterns: Managing Software Organizations and People,
Second Edition**
Colin J. Neill, Philip A. Laplante, and Joanna F. DeFranco
978-1-4398-6186-8

Enterprise-Scale Agile Software Development
James Schiel
978-1-4398-0321-9

Requirements Engineering for Software and Systems
Phillip A. Laplante
978-1-4200-6467-4

Building Software: A Practioner's Guide
Nikhilesh Krishnamurthy and Amitabh Saran
978-0-8493-7303-9

Global Software Development Handbook
Raghvinder Sangwan, Matthew Bass, Neel Mullick, Daniel J. Paulish,
and Juergen Kazmeier
978-0-8493-9384-6

Software Engineering Quality Practices
Ronald Kirk Kandt
978-0-8493-4633-0

Software Engineering Design

Theory and Practice

Carlos E. Otero

CRC Press
Taylor & Francis Group
Boca Raton   London   New York

CRC Press is an imprint of the
Taylor & Francis Group, an **informa** business
AN AUERBACH BOOK

CRC Press
Taylor & Francis Group
6000 Broken Sound Parkway NW, Suite 300
Boca Raton, FL 33487-2742

© 2012 by Taylor & Francis Group, LLC
CRC Press is an imprint of Taylor & Francis Group, an Informa business

No claim to original U.S. Government works

Version Date: 20120420

International Standard Book Number: 978-1-4398-5168-5 (Hardback)

Visit the Taylor & Francis Web site at
http://www.taylorandfrancis.com

and the CRC Press Web site at
http://www.crcpress.com

This book is dedicated to my wife, Kelly,

children Allison, Amanda, Michael, and Ashley,

and parents Angel L. Otero and Lydia E. Rivera.

Contents

Chapter 9

Jacob Somervell

Preface

This book is the result of an effort that I began in 2010 at the University of Virginia's College at Wise to create a course in software engineering design consistent with the 2004 IEEE/ACM curriculum guidelines for undergraduate programs in software engineering (SE). In a broad context, the recommended topics for undergraduate SE programs include design concepts, design strategies, architectural design, detailed design, human–computer interface design, and design evaluation. As a former industry practitioner, I learned first-hand the difference between hearing or "learning" about these topics and developing the necessary skills to apply them in a way that adds value to some development team, program, project, or business. With that in mind, I set out to compile material that I could use (from previous industry experience) to help students become proficient in designing software-intensive systems. Throughout the process, many of the original examples considered dry or hard to follow by students were replaced with new problem domains (e.g., gaming systems) that helped students assimilate the concepts better. Because of the "hands-on" approach required to master these concepts, the teaching style evolved to emphasize both theory and practice. The theory portion was used to present acceptable general design principles or a body of design principles to explain successful software systems' designs. The practice portion provided the avenue for transforming design theory into skills that can be employed directly to real-life industrial settings. The knowledge and experience gained from these efforts have been captured in this textbook, which can be useful for both industry practitioners and students in software engineering, computer science, and information technology programs.

INTRODUCTION

This book provides an introduction to the essential concepts employed by software engineers who design large-scale, software-intensive systems in a professional environment. It bridges the gap between industry and academia by providing students with a comprehensive view of software design using industry-proven concepts for designing complex software systems. Its unique blend of theory and practice provides both students and industry practitioners with key concepts that are immediately relevant to today's software designers. The book contains examples, review questions, and chapter exercises carefully selected to bring real-world problems into a classroom environment. More importantly, it incorporates an effective learn-by-doing approach that allows students to transform design theory into the skills required to design complex software systems. The book starts by providing a general overview of software design, including the fundamentals of software design, the importance of studying software design, and different practical concepts used for designing software.

As part of the introductory material, the software engineering process is covered briefly to provide the context in which software design takes place and a formal top-down design process is presented. The top-down approach consists of several design phases and activities that occur at varied levels of detail/abstraction, including the software architecture, detailed design, and construction design. As part of the top-down approach, detailed coverage of applied architectural, creational, structural, and behavioral design patterns is provided and a collection of standards and guidelines for structuring high-quality code is presented. The book also provides techniques for evaluating software design quality at different stages and much needed coverage of management and engineering leadership for software designers. This provides software engineers with the necessary management, ethical, and leadership knowledge required to build products for the public domain. The book also provides coverage of the software design document and other forms of documentation important during the design of software systems. Collectively, the book comprehensively introduces students and practitioners to software engineering design and provides the knowledge required to emerge and succeed as tomorrow's professional design leaders.

USE AS A TEXTBOOK

The textbook provides a comprehensive (sophomore-level) introduction to required concepts in software design. When used as textbook, instructors are encouraged to visit the textbook website to download slides, the solutions manual, and other exercises developed as part of the ongoing effort to improve education in software engineering design. The material presented in the book's 10 chapters can be easily extended to 16 weeks, especially when covering the topics of design patterns. A recommended approach includes conducting microdesign reviews, where students (or student groups) design, implement, and present their work regularly, while other students evaluate, critique, and provide peer-review comments. Because of the nature of the topics covered, students are expected to meet the following prerequisites:

- Introduction to Programming (with object-oriented language)
- Data Structures and Algorithms
- Introduction to Software Engineering

Ultimately, the most important feature of software designs is their applicability to build software; therefore, the course should require students to implement a large portion of the designs created as part of the course. A recommended approach (when possible) is to adopt a unified modeling language (UML) modeling tool capable of forward and reverse engineering and use the textbook as a guide for creating and assigning design problems centered around the topics discussed throughout the book, since they are essential to all software engineering students from ABET-accredited programs.

Acknowledgments

Many people have contributed to this effort in one way or another. First, I would like to thank Dr. Jacob Somervell from the University of Virginia's College at Wise, and Dr. Luis Daniel Otero from Florida Institute of Technology for providing the material for Chapters 9 and 10, respectively. Your work made the overall product complete, and many students and practitioners will benefit from your contributions. I also thank Dr. Ira Weissberger from Harris Corporation for his contribution on the section on software design documentation in Chapter 5 and Stefan Joe-Yen from Northrop Grumman Corporation for his contribution to the architectural patterns chapter. I would also like to thank the reviewers and staff at Taylor & Francis—in particular John Wyzalek—for their help throughout this long process. Finally, and most importantly, I thank my wife, Kelly, and children Allison, Amanda, Michael, and Ashley, for their sacrifices, patience, and support.

About the Author

Carlos E. Otero, PhD, is assistant professor in the College of Technology and Innovation at the University of South Florida Polytechnic (USFP). Prior to joining USFP, Dr. Otero worked as assistant professor of software engineering in the Department of Mathematics and Computer Science at the University of Virginia's College at Wise, where he created the software engineering design course for Virginia's first and (at the time of writing) only ABET-accredited BS in software engineering.

Prior to his academic career, Dr. Otero spent 11 years in the private industry, where he worked as design and development engineer in a wide variety of military computer systems, including satellite communications systems, command and control systems, wireless security systems, and unmanned aerial vehicle systems. Currently, he continues to consult with industry in the areas of requirements engineering, software systems design and development, quality assurance, and mobile systems engineering.

Dr. Otero received his BS in computer science, MS in software engineering, MS in systems engineering, and PhD in computer engineering from Florida Institute of Technology in Melbourne. He has published over 25 technical publications in scientific peer-reviewed journals and conferences proceedings. He is a senior member of the IEEE, a science advisor for the National Aeronautics and Space Administration (NASA) DEVELOP program, an active professional member of the Association for Computing Machinery (ACM), and a member of several journal editorial boards in technology and engineering.

1

Introduction to Software Engineering Design

CHAPTER OBJECTIVES

- Understand software design from the engineering perspective
- Understand the importance of software design in developing complex products
- Understand the issues that make software design challenging
- Understand the software design process and differentiate between its activities
- Become familiar with software design principles, considerations, and strategies

CONCEPTUAL OVERVIEW

Software design is an indispensable phase of the software engineering process for creating and evaluating software models that guide the construction effort for developing high-quality software systems on time and within budget. Conceptually, design is the process of transforming functional and nonfunctional requirements into models that describe the technical solution before construction begins. To achieve this, the concept of software design, its activities, and tasks must be well understood so that a problem-solving framework for designing quality into software products can be established. In today's modern software systems, there are numerous design principles, processes, strategies, and other factors affecting how designers execute the software design phase. When equipped with the proper design foundation knowledge, an understanding of the designer's roles and responsibilities can be acquired, allowing designers to become effective in designing large-scale software systems under a wide variety of challenging conditions. This chapter presents the fundamental concepts of software engineering design, within context, and provides the motivation for the rest of the book.

ENGINEERING DESIGN

Design is an integral part of every engineering discipline. Airplanes, bridges, buildings, electronic devices, cars, and many other products of similar complexity are all designed. In civil engineering, designs are used to specify detailed plans for developing physical and naturally built environments, such as bridges, roads, canals, dams, and buildings. In electrical engineering, designs are used to capture, evaluate, and specify the detailed qualitative and quantitative description of solutions for telecommunication systems, electrical systems, and electronic devices. In mechanical engineering, designs are used for analyzing, evaluating, and specifying technical features required to construct machines and tools, such as industrial equipment, heating and cooling systems, aircrafts, robots, and medical devices. In all other engineering disciplines, design provides a systematic approach for creating products that meet their intended functions and users' expectations. Formally, Dym and Little (2008, p. 6) define engineering design as

> A systematic, intelligent process in which designers generate, evaluate and specify designs for devices, systems or processes whose form(s) and function(s) achieve clients' objectives and users' needs while satisfying a specified set of constraints.

Design is a lengthy and complex process requiring significant investments in time and effort. So why conduct design in engineering disciplines? There are many possible answers to this question, stemming from simple common sense to more complicated ones involving professional, ethical, social, and legal implications. From the commonsense perspective, products of such complexity are hard to create, are costly to change, and, when built carelessly or incorrectly, can significantly impact human life. When working toward the creation of complex products, teams must organize in a disciplined manner, and a systematic approach needs to be employed to carefully ensure that products are built to meet their specifications. Consider the construction of a bridge that spans over a body of water and is required to support a particular weight, to maintain access to watercrafts navigating underneath, to withstand expected wind speeds, and to provide other features such as sidewalks—all while being bound by a schedule and budget. The successful construction of such a bridge is a nontrivial task and requires years of experience, formal education, and large teams collaborating together to achieve the construction goals. If constructed incorrectly, reconstructing the bridge can skyrocket from its original construction cost; worse yet, if defects are undetected, the bridge could collapse, resulting in the catastrophic loss of human life. Similar to the construction of the bridge, teams engineering other products, such as airplanes, watercrafts, medical devices, and safety-critical software systems, share comparable challenges, and failure of these products can also result in catastrophic events. In an engineering environment, before product construction begins, the design of products needs to be carefully and extensively planned, evaluated, verified, and validated to ensure the product's success. This is mainly achieved through design.

ENGINEERING PROBLEM SOLVING

Throughout the design process, designers are constantly engaging in problem-solving activities that are fundamental to all modern engineering projects. In a broad sense, engineers can be characterized as specialized problem solvers. Their work requires them to identify, evaluate, and propose solutions to complex problems (in particular domains) under tight project constraints. In some situations, engineers tackle problems that have never been solved before, creating challenges to meet not only functional aspects of products but also their established schedule and budget. Before engaging in more concrete design topics, a formal discussion on problem solving is necessary to identify fundamental concepts that are well understood by successful designers; these serve as basis for establishing a holistic problem solving framework that can be employed any time during design.

To become a good designer, engineers must be good problem solvers. This may require years of experience solving problems in a particular domain. In many cases, experience allows engineers to reuse already proven solutions across separate but similar problems. In other cases, where unsolved problems are encountered, designers are required to "think out of the box" and carefully craft a systematic approach for solving the problem in an acceptable manner, which may require problem classification, identification of the solution approach and type of adequate solution, and identifying the overall strategy for reaching its solution. In a general sense, problem solving during design occurs in three different states (Plotnik and Kouyoumdjian 2010):

- Initial state
- Operation state
- Goal state

Through these states, designers employ several techniques and strategies to create a landscape suitable for problem solving. The initial state is where problems are formulated and interpreted. In some cases, achieving full understanding of the problem is a problem itself. Once problems are well understood, designers move to the operational state, where thinking about the problem occurs and viable solutions come to light. Once an appropriate solution is identified, evaluated, and validated, designers move to the goal state, where a final solution to the problem is found, marking the end of the problem-solving process.

TABLE 1.1

Problem Classification

Problem	Description
Well-defined	Problem with clear goals and known constraints
Ill-defined	Problem with undefined or ambiguous goals and unknown constraints
Wicked	Problem with no definite solution; not understood until after the formulation of its solution

Initial State

Design problems are not all the same; they vary in size, complexity, and, based on these characteristics, the amount of time and effort required for their solution. In some cases, it quickly becomes evident that certain problems are harder to solve than others. When this determination is made, the strategy for the solution approach is adjusted to account for the additional complexity. Being able to differentiate between types of problem is crucial in helping designers account for the amount of effort, time, and risk associated with the solution approach. Therefore, an important problem-solving skill involves identifying and classifying the type of problem encountered, which includes *well-defined*, *ill-defined*, and *wicked problems*, as presented in Table 1.1 (Giachetti 2010).

Well-defined problems have clear defined goals and their constraints are well understood. This makes scoping the problem, proposing a solution approach, and arriving at the solution easier than with other types of problems, such as ill-defined and wicked problems. Ill-defined problems are problems where the mere interpretation of the problem is a problem itself; they are ambiguous with undefined goals and require more time and effort to clarify and interpret the problem to arrive at a solution. In some cases, with additional effort, ill-defined problems can be transformed into well-defined problems. Finally, wicked problems are problems where no single problem formulation exists. There may be many acceptable formulations of the problem and no definite solutions, and solutions are not deemed correct or incorrect but good or bad (Giachetti 2010). In many cases, wicked problems can lead to contradictive goals that need additional resolution before the problem solving can occur. When contradictive goals are present, providing a solution to one part of the problem results in the inability of solving other parts of the problem. In these types of problem, optimal solutions are hard to find, requiring additional struggle and collaborative brainstorming. Also, evaluation of alternative designs may require advanced techniques to determine the best course of action, which tends to require more time. In many cases, the solution to wicked problems is not known until after the problem is solved.

Operational State

The operational state of problem solving is where thinking about the problem solution takes place. It requires employing multiple techniques for problem solving such as using metaphors, decomposing problems into smaller, less complex problems (i.e., divide and conquer), reusing solutions (e.g., patterns), and so forth. In all of the techniques, designers

FIGURE 1.1
The nine-dot puzzle.

are expected to exhibit a "think outside the box" mentality to be able to solve complex problems. This requires shifting the mental model from a conventional approach to unconventional methodology where solutions to complex problems may arise from thinking in ways that deviate from conventional wisdom. For example, consider the popular nine-dot puzzle illustrated in Figure 1.1 (Kershaw and Ohlsson 2004).

The requirements for solving the nine-dot puzzle problem are as follows:

1. Draw four straight lines to connect all dots.
2. The pencil cannot be lifted from the paper once the line-drawing process begins.
3. No lines can be retraced.

Before moving on, think about this problem and attempt to provide a solution. At first, this may seem difficult because of the tendency of fixing the mental process to operate on the assumption that lines should begin and end on a dot. This *functional fixedness* limits the ability to find solutions based on objects having a different function from their usual ones (Plotnik and Kouyoumdjian 2010). In the case of the nine-dot puzzle, for some, functional fixedness makes it awkward or even impossible to propose solutions that involve lines going past the dots, which is what is required to solve this problem. To increase the chance of overcoming functional fixedness, problems need to be attempted several times and considered from many different viewpoints and unusual angles (Plotnik and Kouyoumdjian). Overcoming functional fixedness is critical for designers attempting to provide solutions at the operational state of problem solving.

Thinking about the Problem

Different types of thinking take place when finding solutions to problems. For example, when learning about a problem for the first time, problem solvers may begin by asking questions, which allows them to think about many different alternative solutions; as the problem-solving process moves forward, problem solvers can begin narrowing down the possibilities and think about the single best solution to the problem. These types of thinking are known as *convergent thinking* and *divergent thinking* (Table 1.2).

Both convergent and divergent thinking have significant roles in solving engineering problems. In many cases, problem solvers begin using divergent thinking with different levels of abstraction, and each level provides finer-grained solutions to the problem until convergent thinking can be employed to solve it.

TABLE 1.2

Types of Thinking

Type	Description
Convergent thinking	Type of thinking that seeks to find one single solution to a problem
Divergent thinking	Type of thinking that seeks to find multiple solutions to a problem

TABLE 1.3

Types of Problem Solution

Problem	Description
Algorithm	Fixed set of rules that lead to the solution of a problem
Heuristic	Rules of thumb (or procedure) that may or may not lead to the solution of a problem

Problem Solution

In many cases, determining the type of solution required for a given problem can reduce wasted time and effort spent in attempting to find a single, optimal solution. In such cases, designers can elect to seek approximate solutions—as opposed to optimal solutions—that are appropriate and acceptable for meeting project constraints. Determining the type of solution for a given problem can reduce time and budget required for building the system. Two types of solutions are *algorithms* and *heuristics*, as presented in Table 1.3.

Algorithms are step-by-step procedures for finding the correct solution to given problems. Algorithms do not normally involve subjective decisions or rely on intuition or creativity to find solutions (Brassard and Bratley 1995). For some types of problems, using algorithms to find solutions can be unrealistic, especially in time-driven, practical engineering problems. In these cases, heuristics provide a realistic approach for finding good approximations of the solution. In some cases, heuristics can lead to optimal solutions; in others, they can lead to solutions that are far from optimal or no solution at all (Brassard and Bratley 1995). Algorithms and heuristics are both used heavily in the design of engineering systems and determining their appropriateness for solving particular problems is essential to meeting other project demands.

Goal State

The goal state represents the final state of problem solving. It is where adequate solutions to given problems are determined. For many engineering problems, reaching the goal state is a nontrivial task that requires careful attention to all important aspects of the problem. The concepts of initial, operational, and goal state can be fused together to create a holistic problem-solving framework adequate to solving engineering problems at all stages of the development effort. The approach consists of the following tasks:

- Interpret problem
- Evaluate constraints
- Collaborative brainstorming

- Synthesize possibilities
- Evaluate solution
- Implement solution

The first task of the problem-solving approach involves *interpreting the problem*. This is where problem information is received and processed; problem classification is identified (e.g., well-defined, ill-defined) and activities are performed to formulate the problem. Interpreting the problem is a task performed during the initial state of problem solving. During the initial state, identification of stakeholders—persons, groups, or organizations that have direct or indirect stake in the problem and its solution—is essential. Once the problem is formulated, the *evaluate constraints* task is used to identify external problem constraints, which are negotiated, integrated, and used to set the bounds on the solution landscape. Once the problem and constraints are well understood, *collaborative brainstorming* can begin among problem solvers and stakeholders. During collaborative brainstorming, problem solvers use mostly divergent thinking to come up with alternative solutions that may bring to light new knowledge, which can trigger a transition back to the problem interpretation task. Once a set of acceptable solutions is identified, problem solvers *synthesize possibilities* to form the acceptable proposed solution to the problem. During this task, problem solvers shift from divergent thinking to convergent thinking to propose the best-known solution to the problem. The solution is shared and *evaluated* by everyone involved in the problem-solving process. Flaws in the solution may trigger a transition back to the collaborative brainstorming task; otherwise, implementation begins. *Collaborative brainstorming, synthesize possibilities*, and *evaluate solutions* are all tasks performed as part of the operational state of problem solving. During implementation, the proposed solution is executed until the problem is solved, which is a task performed during the goal state of problem solving. Together, these tasks are combined with other problem variables to provide a holistic approach to problem solving (Harrell, Ghosh, and Bowden 2004), as presented in Figure 1.2.

As seen in the figure, inputs are items that require processing during problem solving. Inputs come from many different sources and are interpreted and formulated for particular problems. They drive all activities by specifying the overarching need that promotes the execution of the problem-solving tasks. Constraints are external properties that come inherent with any problem and limit the solution approach. Outputs are the expected outcome in problem solving. In many engineering projects, merely coming up with the solution to a given problem is not enough, since the solution needs to be documented, formatted, decorated, specified in graphical model format, or placed under configuration management. Outputs coming out of the problem-solving process need to meet the appropriate standards as defined by the developing organization. The development organization may also set standards for activities, controls, and resources, which all impact problem solving. These variables are presented in Table 1.4.

Activities are internal tasks determined by the development organization that must be followed when solving problems. These are intended to help manage the problem-solving approach and may include review activities at different stages of problem solving, including preliminary and detailed stages, status reports, and documentation, which all impact the

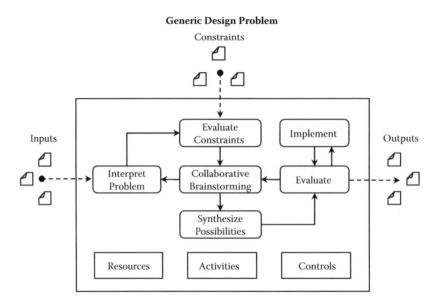

FIGURE 1.2

Holistic approach to problem solving.

TABLE 1.4

Problem-Solving Process Variables

Phase	Description
Activities	One or more tasks identified and required to solve the problem
Resources	Means by which activities are performed
Controls	Internal properties of the organization that place bounds on the solution, or the solution process, for the problem

time required to solve the problem. Controls, on the other hand, are internal constraints set by the development organization that limit the possible solutions so that they align well with the organizational goals and current practices. These controls can dictate when and where problem solving takes place, selection of strategies, permitted tools, personnel allowed to engage in problem solving, and measures for quality control. Finally, resources are the means by which activities are performed, which include people, software, and hardware, and their availability, which all impact problem solving. Together, all of these variables mix together to define the problem-solving landscape, which must be considered when tackling engineering problems.

Skill Development 1.1: Using the Holistic Approach in Problem Solving

Use and document all the steps of the holistic problem-solving approach presented in Figure 1.2 to solve the following problem. If possible, do this exercise as a team. The problem specification is as follows: there are six equal matches; connect each match to form four equilateral triangles. When done, explain how functional fixedness played a role in preventing you from arriving at the solution to this problem.

SOFTWARE ENGINEERING DESIGN

In the previous sections, design was introduced as a systematic and intelligent process for generating, evaluating, and specifying designs for devices, systems, or processes. To support this process, the problem-solving skill was identified as an essential ingredient for designing complex products. These discussions provided a general perspective on the importance of these concepts in the engineering profession. As in other engineering disciplines, design and problem-solving are crucial to the development of professional, large-scale, software systems. Software systems are highly complex, difficult to create, costly to change, and—depending on the software product—critical to human safety. Similarly to other engineering disciplines, designs in software engineering are used to identify, evaluate, and specify the structural and behavioral characteristics of software systems that adhere to some specification. Software designs provide blueprints that capture how software systems meet their required functions and how they are shaped to meet their intended quality. Formally, software engineering design is defined as

(1) The process of identifying, evaluating, validating, and specifying the architectural, detailed, and construction models required to build software that meets its intended functional and non-functional requirements; and (2) the result of such process.

The term software design is used interchangeably in practice as a means to describe both the process and product of software design. From a process perspective, software design is used to identify the phase, activities, tasks, and interrelationship between them required to model software's structure and behavior before construction begins. From a product development perspective, software design is used to identify the design artifacts that result from the identified phase, activities, and tasks; therefore, these products by themselves, or collectively, are referred to as software design. Design products vary according to several factors, including design perspective, language, purpose, and their capabilities for evaluation and analysis. For example, designs can be in architectural form, using architectural notations targeted for specific stakeholders. These types of design can be presented using block diagrams, Unified Modeling Language (UML) diagrams, or other descriptive form of black-box design documentation. In other cases, design can be in detailed form, where a more white-box representation of the system is used to model structural and behavioral aspects. These can include software models that contain class diagrams, object diagrams, sequence diagrams, or activity diagrams. Other design products include models that represent interfaces, data, or user interface designs. Due to the many ways software design is used in practice, a common pitfall in software engineering projects is to associate design with a particular type of design artifact, therefore neglecting other forms of design or the activities required to create complete and correct software designs. Collectively, both process and products, including all variety of design products, are considered software design and are essential in most professional software projects.

WHY STUDY SOFTWARE ENGINEERING DESIGN?

On February 25, 1991, a software error on the Patriot missile defense system operating during operation Desert Storm caused it to fail to track and intercept an incoming Scud, which resulted in the death of 28 Americans (GAO, 1992). In 1996, a software error caused the Ariane 501 satellite launch to fail catastrophically, resulting in a direct cost of approximately $370 million (Dowson 1997). The software error that caused Ariane 501 to fail could be attributed to its software design. Similarly, the literature is swamped with many examples of disastrous results of software-based products. The reason for many of these disasters is that developing high-quality software on time and within budget is a daunting task. From the outset, the landscape for software development projects is plagued with a variety of challenges that increase complexity in software projects. Software design plays an integral part in managing the complexity and the challenges encountered in any software development effort.

During the software design phase, the system is decomposed to allow optimum development of the software; requirements are mapped to conceptual models of the operational software; roles are assigned to software teams on the same or remote sites; well-known interfaces for software components are created; quality attributes are addressed and incorporated into the design of the system; the user interface is created; the software's capability is analyzed; function and variable names are identified; design documentation goals are established; and the foundation for the rest of the software engineering life cycle is established. Given its impact on the creation and management of software products, mastering software design becomes essential to successfully engineer software products. The reasons for studying software engineering design can be described using a product development perspective and a project management perspective.

Reasons for Studying Software Design in Product Development

From the product development view, studying software design is important because designs form the foundation for all other software construction activities. Software designs allow software engineers to create models that represent the structure and behavior of the software system. Through these models, the main components and their interconnection for the solution are identified. Characteristics of quality code, such as modularization, cohesiveness, and coupling, are all born in the design phase. For complex tasks, abstractions and encapsulation are used in software design as means to provide a systematic approach for problem solving. In addition, software designs are reusable; therefore, they can be applied to different projects to provide ready-made solutions to common problems. Software design also provides the means to evaluate and incorporate the quality attributes necessary for software systems. Therefore, issues such as performance, usability, portability, and security can all be addressed early on in the development project. These benefits are carried over to all other subsequent phases of the software development life cycle and have direct impact on the implementation, testing, and maintenance phase.

Reasons for Studying Software Design in Project Management

Managing software projects characterized by changing requirements, tight schedules, cost constraints, and high expectations for software quality is tough. Among these, requirement changes are common drivers for all other project characteristics. This means that, as requirements change, projects should expect some impact in their cost, schedule, and quality. In some cases, requirement changes can easily translate to extended schedules and increased cost; in others, where schedules are not extended, requirement changes translate to decreased software quality. Good software design can minimize (or counter) the effects of requirements volatility in managing software projects. From the management's point of view, software design is important because it helps accommodate changes to the requirements or system updates, therefore minimizing impact on schedule, cost, and quality. In addition, good software design increases efficiency in human resource allocation tasks. By decomposing the software into independent units, resources can be assigned to software components so that they can be built in parallel in the same or different construction sites, therefore having significant impact on software schedules and cost. By compartmentalizing the design, the effects of unwanted employment attrition (i.e., employees leaving the company) can also be minimized, since new employees need only to take on the individual design component assigned to that employee. Good software designs provide an efficient mapping of customer requirements to software solutions, therefore facilitating requirements tracing throughout the design. Having a strong grasp on software design helps management abstract project tasks and acquire better appreciation of the work to be done. Overall, having a strong grasp in software design helps management improve the project planning, organization, staffing, and tracking and provide overall guidance for the project.

SOFTWARE DESIGN CHALLENGES

Today, the software design phase has evolved from an ad hoc and sometimes overlooked phase to an essential phase of the development life cycle. Furthermore, the increasing complexity of today's systems has created a set of particular challenges that makes it hard for software engineers to meet the continuous customer demand for higher software quality. These challenges have prompted software engineers to pay closer attention to the design process to better understand, apply, and promulgate well known design principles, processes, and professional practices to overcome these challenges. Some of the major challenges include requirements volatility, design process, quality issues (e.g., performance, usability, security), distributed software development, efficient allocation of human resources to development tasks, limited budgets, unreasonable expectations and schedules, fast-changing technology, and accurate transformation from software requirement to a software product. A brief discussion of these challenges is presented next.

Design Challenge 1: Requirements Volatility

A major reason for the complexity of software projects is the constant change of requirements. When designed properly, software can be modified or extended easily; however, when designed poorly, modifying software can become overwhelming and lead to all sorts of complex problems. Unlike the development of computer hardware, bridges, houses, or mechanical parts, software's very own nature allows itself to change to provide different or new functionality to systems. This same trait that makes software so desirable is what makes it also so complex. Although much effort is put into the requirements phase to ensure that requirements are complete and consistent, that is rarely the case; leaving the software design phase as the most influential one when it comes to minimizing the effects of new or changing requirements. Requirements volatility is challenging because they impact future or current development efforts. This forces designers to create designs that provide solutions to problems at a given state while also anticipating changes and accommodating them with minimal effort. This requires designers to have a strong understanding of the principles of software design and develop skills to manage complexity and change in software development.

Design Challenge 2: Process

Software engineering is a process-oriented field. Software processes allow engineers to organize the steps required to develop software solutions with schedule and cost constraints. Therefore, at the core of every software development company, there should be a sound, well-understood, and consistent process for software development. Processes can also be developed and customized for particular phases of the software engineering life cycle. In the design phase, software processes involve a broad set of activities and tasks that bridge the gap between requirements and construction while adhering to a set of project-specific (or company-specific) constraints. These activities include common ones, such as architectural and detailed design, as well as other supporting activities. These supporting activities include establishing a design review process, defining design quality evaluation criteria, evaluating design reuse, establishing design change management and version control procedures, adopting design tools, and allocating resources. In many cases, a company's design process is not well established, is poorly understood, or is approached with minimalistic expectations that ignore aspects that are essential to executing a successful design phase. Focusing design efforts on creating independent software products, such as a simple class diagram or user interface, while ignoring other design activities may create complexities later on during system's test and maintenance. The design process is challenging because essential design process activities are often overlooked, done in an ad hoc manner, or simply not done at all. In many cases, a well-established and well carried out design process serves an indication of future project's success.

Design Challenge 3: Technology

Software is meant to be everywhere. From health-care systems and education to defense and everyday ubiquitous devices, software is required to operate on a massive and always evolving technology landscape. Besides the operating environment, the technology for designing and implementing today's software systems continues to evolve to provide improved capabilities. Examples of these include modeling languages and tools, programming languages, development environments, design patterns, and design strategies. As new technologies emerge, software engineers are required to assimilate and employ them all at the same time. In some cases, emerging technologies do not completely replace old ones. Some software systems are required to interoperate with old legacy systems designed with older design methodologies. This results in software designers employing different design methodologies and technologies, all on the same software system. In other cases, design models need to be derived from existing code, modified, and made interoperable with newer technologies. This technology-driven aspect of the design phase creates a demand for capable software designers that can assimilate new technology quickly and effectively to succeed at designing software. The technology aspect of software design is challenging because it is fast and ever-changing; therefore, designers must keep abreast of the latest advances and become proficient in the application of these advancements while maintaining rooted in legacy technology.

Design Challenge 4: Ethical and Professional Practices

Designers create blueprints that drive the construction of the software. During this creation process, designers are required to determine how design decisions affect the environment and the people that use the software. In many cases, the software development process is traditionally carried out under tight schedule constraints. Inherently, all phases of the development life cycle suffer from this, including the design phase. This creates external pressures that can lead designers to deviate from the normal design approach to meet these demands, which can have catastrophic consequences. No matter how tight deadlines are, how much animosity exists within the design team, or how much other external/personal factors are brought into the design phase, software designers must exhibit strong ethical and professional practices to ensure that the systems they build are of highest quality and that all design considerations are properly evaluated. In many cases, this requires designers to exert strong leadership skills to influence and negotiate with stakeholders, motivate the design team, and lead the design process to accomplish the project's goals. Designers are also responsible for enforcing ethical guidelines during the design process; evaluating the social impacts of their designs in the public domain or in safety-critical systems; and to follow the appropriate professional practices to ensure success in the overall system. The ethical and professional practices aspect of software design are challenging because designers are constantly faced with numerous pressures from stakeholders that influence designers' decisions, most of which have consequences of social, ethical, or professional nature.

Design Challenge 5: Managing Design Influences

Designs are shaped by many different influences from stakeholders, the development organization, and other factors. These influences can have cyclical effects between the system and its external influences, such that external factors affect the development of the system and the system affects its external factors (Bass, Clements, and Kazman 2003). Managing these influences is essential for maximizing the quality of systems and their related influence on future business opportunities. Of specific importance are design influences that come from the system stakeholders and its developing organization.

Stakeholders

Designing software is a nondeterministic activity. If given the same task to different designers, different solutions will be proposed, each of them being perfectly acceptable (McConnell 2004). Now add to the mix the multitude of influences that come from different stakeholders, and you can easily get a variety of design alternatives for meeting a variety of stakeholders' concerns, all conflicting with each other. This creates a challenge when trading off design alternatives that meet all stakeholders concerns. Making such design trade-offs is difficult, especially on large-scale design efforts. Consider a project with multiple customers, each with conflicting goals affecting design decisions. In such projects, creating a design that sacrifices some desired customer capability but provides other desired properties, such as quick time-to-market, reliability, or lower cost, can lead to the development of a high-quality system that maintains acceptable levels of satisfaction among stakeholders. This is an example of how stakeholders affect design decision, and the design, in turn, influences the stakeholder goals (Bass et al. 2003). Managing stakeholders' influences is challenging because it requires designers to exert a high-level of communication, negotiation, and technical skills to ensure that design decisions are made to accommodate all concerns without negatively affecting the project.

Development Organization's Structure

The development organization's structure influences the development of software products, in particular, the design of those products. As example, consider the case of distributed software engineering. In today's global market, more and more cases of distributed software development are taking place. A wide variety of reasons exist for developing software at different sites. Consider companies that have sites in multiple states, where various levels of domain expertise are found at different sites. Or consider the case of software engineers resigning, creating a gap in the development team that is hard to fill with local resources. Finally, consider companies that simply want to reduce cost by hiring software engineers from different countries. These and many other reasons exist for having development across site boundaries. In each of these cases, the structure of the development's organization makes it complicated to, for example, coordinate design efforts, evaluate and discuss design alternatives, conduct peer reviews, and manage version control. In these cases, designers need to consider not only technical aspects of the design but also the distribution of employees, organizational goals, resource availability, and so forth. Designs that support integration of distributed expertise across sites can introduce capabilities for building new software products that could not be engineered otherwise. This in turn can influence the developing organization to target new areas of businesses, therefore allowing the software design to influence its business goals. Managing the influences of the development organization is challenging because it requires designers to span out of the technical domain to have a keen interest on the organization as a whole.

CONTEXT OF SOFTWARE DESIGN

In today's modern software systems, software design plays a key role in the development of software products; however, it is only one phase of the complete software engineering life cycle. To understand how design fits within the whole software engineering process, it is necessary to provide the appropriate context so that clear distinctions can be made between the different life cycle phases and an appreciation of the importance of software design activities and tasks can be acquired. For this reason, an overview of software engineering and its life cycle is required. Software engineering is defined by the IEEE (1990, p. 67) as

(1) The application of a systematic, disciplined, quantifiable approach to the development, operation, and maintenance of software; that is, the application of engineering to software.
(2) The study of approaches as in (1).

The fundamental software engineering life cycle phases include requirements, design, construction, test, and maintenance, as presented in Table 1.5.

The requirements phase is where stakeholders are identified and customer needs, wants, and the (often overlooked) nonfunctional requirements are determined (Laplante 2009). During this phase, requirements are analyzed in their raw form to address issues such as requirements that don't make sense, contradict each other, or are incomplete, vague, or just wrong (Laplante 2009); requirements are classified and prioritized; and the specification of the software system, which typically results in the production of a document, or its electronic equivalent is reviewed and validated (Abran, Moore, Bourque, and Dupuis

TABLE 1.5

Fundamental Software Engineering Phases

Phase	Description
Requirements	Initial stage in the software development life cycle where requirements are elicited, analyzed, specified, and validated
Design	The requirement's specification is used to create the software design, which includes its architecture and detailed design
Construction	Relies on the requirements' specification, the software architecture, and detailed design to implement the solution using a programming language; a great deal of design can also occur at this phase
Test	Ensures that the software behaves correctly and that it meets the specified requirements
Maintenance	Modifies software after delivery to correct faults, improve performance, or adapt it for a different environment

2005). Once the requirements for the system are specified, designing the system takes place, which is the main topic of this book.

The construction phase begins once the design phase has been executed and all requirements can be traced to a section of the software design models. The construction phase is where designs are implemented using the programming language of choice. In this phase, code is generated according to a style guide. In addition, the code is unit tested, debugged, and peer-reviewed; programming errors are detected, tracked, and resolved; code is managed by using change management and version control software; and, finally, code is prepared for delivery using a predefined set of conventions for formatting. The construction phase is tightly related to the design phase and in some cases (typically on smaller projects) the line dividing both phases can be hard to identify. There are several reasons for this, the main one being that detailed designs can be directly translated to code; therefore, software engineers tend to design and code at the same time. In other cases, where design and construction are clearly delineated by the process, it is common for some construction tasks, such as identifying appropriate class, function, and variable names, to be performed during detailed design. Finally, because many discoveries made well into the construction phase give rise to functionality that requires design work, engineers must iterate back and forth between construction and design activities. Once all the design artifacts are implemented with programming and all assigned requirements can be validated through execution of code during unit testing, the construction phase is complete.

The testing phase is typically the final step before the software goes out the door. The main purpose of the testing phase is to verify and validate the software to ensure that it meets the predefined functions and level of quality defined in the software requirement's phase. Formally, the IEEE (1990, p. 76) defines testing as

(1) The process of operating a system or component under specified conditions, observing or recording the results, and making an evaluation of some aspect of the system or component. (2) The process of analyzing a software item to detect the differences between existing and required conditions (that is, bugs) and to evaluate the features of the software item.

The software testing phase serves as a gateway between product development and product release. Therefore, verification and validation efforts need to be made to ensure that the software meets the specification and the integrity of the software can be assured under normal and harsh conditions. It is important to note that no desired quality attribute can be verified during testing if it hasn't been designed into the product first. Therefore, even though testing is typically credited for ensuring product quality, design is fundamental in supporting a successful testing phase. Once software is delivered, the maintenance phase begins to implement corrections, adaptations, or improvements to the software. Corrections are typically made on a smaller scale to rectify faulty behavior or output of the software. These typically do not require design work. However, for adaptations or improvements, design work may be required to accommodate the changes. Together, all phases of the software engineering life cycle work together to define the functions that the software must provide, to transform these functions into technical solutions, to implement those solutions, and to validate their implementation and ensure the quality of the system throughout future versions.

SOFTWARE DESIGN PROCESS

In the previous section, the design phase was briefly mentioned as a means for determining its place within the software engineering process. However, as it will be seen, the design phase incorporates many activities and tasks conducted by different teams and typically managed by personnel other than designers. This requires a formal process to ensure that the design phase is conducted properly and that it addresses all the concerns identified for the software system being built. Many processes exist to carry out phases, activities, and tasks throughout the software engineering life cycle, including the unified process (UP), Scrum, and the dynamic systems development method (DSDM) (Pressman 2010). What follows is a discussion on the software design process in terms of the fundamental activities and tasks required to build software products. These activities and tasks are essential and typically built into other formal processes such as the ones already mentioned. The hope is that by placing more emphasis on the fundamental activities and tasks and less on particular process approaches readers can obtain a more concise and understandable coverage of the topic.

In today's professional software engineering landscape, software engineers are being asked to build larger and more complex software systems in the same or different sites. Therefore, both design processes and artifacts are increasing in complexity. This means that it is not enough to know how to model structural and behavioral aspects of the system in the design phase, but it is also essential that software designers know about the particular process (e.g., UP, Scrum) required to manage, create, and control software design activities. Sommerville (2010) defines a software process as a set of activities that lead to the production of a software product. Similarly, a software design process is a set of activities and controls that specify how resources work together for the production of software design artifacts. The software engineering body of knowledge identifies two major activities for software design: software architecture and detailed design (Abran et al. 2005). These are the essential activities for managing the complexity involved in developing large-scale software systems. However, numerous other important activities are required for supporting the creation of architectural and detailed designs. Therefore, when planning and identifying an appropriate software design process, the effort required for these activities needs to be considered. In addition, because of the emphasis that some forms of design place on construction, the detailed design activity process can be modified to explicitly present the construction design activity that addresses design issues encountered during the construction phase. With this in mind, a holistic approach to software design, which includes architecture, detailed and construction design, management, and documentation, is presented in Figure 1.3.

As seen in the figure, software architecture is the first activity conducted in the design process. Architectural designs are elaborated through detailed designs, which are further elaborated through construction designs. All of these design activities need to be documented, and the process for design and documentation needs to be managed. Figure 1.3 also presents a necessary differentiation between the software design phase and the distribution of its activities throughout the software engineering life cycle. In some cases, the architectural design activities can begin during the analysis activity of the requirements

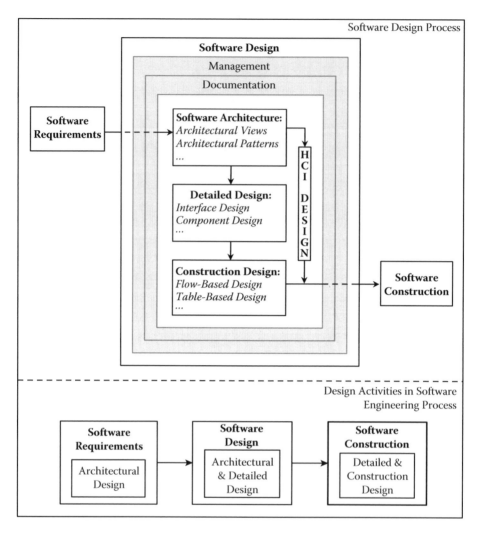

FIGURE 1.3
The software design process and design activities during the SWE process.

phase and span through the design phase; in others, it begins after the requirements are specified and validated. In a similar fashion, the detailed design activity can start at the project's design phase and span through the software construction phase. These scenarios are highly project dependent; therefore, following to a strict waterfall-like process for software development is impractical for all but the simplest software applications.

Software Architecture

The software architecture activity corresponds to a macrodesign approach for creating models that depict the quality and function of the software system. It provides black-box models used to evaluate the system's projected capabilities as well as its expected quality, all from multiple perspectives. Therefore, architectural designs allow different stakeholders, with different backgrounds and expertise, to evaluate the design and ensure that the software architecture is addressing their concerns. For example, from the systems engineering perspective, architectural designs can provide information about the physical deployment of the system, including subsystems located at different locations, the artifacts executing in the subsystems, and how the system as a whole communicates. From the configuration management perspective, architectural designs can provide information about the hierarchy of files in the file system and how these files are interconnected to build and deploy the software system. From the software engineering perspective, different architectural designs can help decompose the software and define the major structural components of the system, identify interfaces between the components, map the requirements to them, evaluate concurrency issues, and provide overall insight into the design solution. A major benefit of architectural designs is their capacity to evaluate high-level concerns from stakeholders that deal mostly with nonfunctional requirements (e.g., performance, usability, security). For these purposes, architectural designs serve as important communication, reasoning, and analysis tools that support the development and growth of the systems (Bass et al. 2003). Software architecture lays the foundation for all subsequent work in the software engineering life cycle.

Detailed Design

The detailed design step begins after the software architecture is specified, reviewed, and deemed sufficiently complete for detailed design to begin. The detailed design activity builds on the software architecture to provide white-box design elements of the structure and behavior of the software system and in many cases is the last major effort before software construction begins. Detailed design is the activity that deals with refining the software architecture to reach a point where the software design, including architecture and detailed design, is deemed sufficiently complete for construction to begin. Whereas the software architecture places a major emphasis on quality (nonfunctional requirements), the detailed design activity places a major focus on addressing functional requirements of the system. In object-oriented systems, the detailed design activity is where components are refined into one or more classes, interfaces are realized, relationships between classes are specified, class functions and variable names are created, design patterns are identified and applied, and, if applicable, design tools are configured for code generation. Two major tasks of the detailed design activity are *interface design* and *component design*.

Interface Design

Interface design refers to the design activity that deals with specification of interfaces between components in the design (Sommerville 2010). Interface design can be focused on specifying the interfaces used internally within software components or externally across software components. In both cases, interfaces provide a standardized way for specifying how services are accessed and provided by software components. Interface design allows subsystems to be designed independently and in parallel; therefore, it is typically one of the first tasks performed as part of the detailed design. Other forms of interface design specify communication between systems, for example, custom binary or Extensible Markup Language (XML) messaging specifications used for communication between two or more subsystems through the network.

Component Design

During architecture, the software system is decomposed into logical components that abstract required system functions. During detailed design, these logical components are refined and their interactions are modeled to verify the validity of their structural composition. The execution of the detailed design activity requires a shift from the macrodesign approach to the microdesign approach to further decompose and refine system components into one or more fine-grained elements, functions, and data variables required for supporting the internal structure and behavior of components that meet assigned roles during the software architecture activity. Component design refers to modeling the *internal structure and behavior* of components—which includes the internal structure of both logical and physical components—identified during the software architecture phase. During this activity, fine-grained components are derived from the architecture, and their internal structure and behavior are designed. Components are not limited to object-oriented systems; therefore, component designs can be realized in many ways. In object-oriented systems, the internal structure of components is typically modeled using UML through one or more diagrams, including class and sequence diagrams. When modeling the internal structure of components, several design principles, heuristics, and patterns are used to create and evaluate component designs.

Construction Design

The idea of the detailed design activity is to get as close to the solution as possible without beginning the construction phase. In many cases, in object-oriented systems, this amounts to identifying classes, their attributes and functions, and interrelationships with other classes. These tasks are done while abstracting and deferring details of implementation to the construction phase. In some cases, however, implementing complex software functions identified during the detailed design activity requires additional design work to ensure they work properly and maintain the quality standards sought during the software architecture activities. In these cases, construction design is necessary. Construction design is not a new concept. Many other authors have proposed it as an important design activity. For example, McConnell (2004) specifies five levels of software design; one of them, being at the lowest level, deals with internal routine design. Similarly, Fox (2006) identifies a form of low-level design that fills the gap between detailed design and programming and deals with issues such as operation specification, including operation name, parameter types, and return types among others. Other authors, such as Meyers (2005), have highlighted the importance of designing code at low levels, during construction. Construction design is the last design activity—typically conducted during the construction phase—required to support the system's quality attributes, such as performance, maintainability, and testability.

Human–Computer Interface Design

The human–computer Interface (HCI) design activity is where general principles are applied to optimize the interface between humans and computers. Visual designs have a major role on the success or failure of software systems. Systems that meet functional requirements but that are not usable cannot succeed. The HCI design activity can be executed in parallel to the software architecture or detailed design activities. In some cases, HCI design is considered an architectural task, while in others it is considered a detailed design task. Regardless of where HCI design fits within design processes adopted by specific organizations, it is a major design activitiy that requires careful attention. The major concerns of the HCI designs may include the evaluation and use of modes, navigation, visual designs, response time and feedback, and design modalities, such as forms and menu-driven. HCI designs directly influence the quality of any system and are essential to understanding and addressing the factors that affect the overall usability of the system. Many design principles and evaluation techniques exist to succesfully design user interfaces.

Software Design Documentation

Similar to the specification activity of the requirements phase, software design documentation, also known as software design description (SDD), plays a big role in professional, large-scale, or software-intensive systems. Its importance is specified by the IEEE (1998, p. iii) as follows:

> SDDs play a pivotal role in the development and maintenance of software systems. During its lifetime, a given design description is used by project managers, quality assurance staff, configuration managers, software designers, programmers, testers, and maintainers. Each of these users has unique needs, both in terms of required design information and optimal organization of that information. Hence, a design description must contain all the design information needed by those users.

SDD should include the necessary information that properly captures the design of the system. As part of this activity, other issues such as tools for generating design documents, validation, and configuration management must be addressed. The software design documentation activity typically begins at the design phase and continues throughout the lifetime of the software system.

Software Design Management

Management plays a big role in software engineering projects. Griffin (2010, p. 5) defines management as

> A set of activities (including planning and decision making, organizing, leading, and controlling) directed at an organization's resources (human, financial, physical, and information), with the aim of achieving organizational goals in an efficient and effective manner.

In the design phase, management refers to the set of activities required to efficiently create and implement quality design artifacts, within schedule and budget constraints. This definition encompasses a broad set of activities that are particular to specific organizations. However, at the core of every organization's management activities, quality is a focal point. The quality of software designs can be assessed in various ways. From the management's perspective, quality of software designs can be evaluated in terms of cost and scheduling. From the engineering point of view, quality in designs can be evaluated using a set of well-known design principles as well as modeling and evaluating the quality attributes that the software must exhibit, which are specified via nonfunctional, quality requirements. From the configuration management's perspective, design quality can be achieved through change management processes that control how designs are created, modified, and improved. In large-scale software projects, software design management is essential to plan, organize, staff, track, and lead the activities required to carry out successfully the software architecture and detailed design steps.

ROLES OF THE SOFTWARE DESIGNER

From the discussions provided so far, it should be evident that designers are not all equal. In many design efforts, designers have different roles, with different titles and responsibilities that focus on specific design problems of the software system. There are many factors in place that determine the designer's role, including an engineer's work preference, experience, and capabilities. When studying software design, it is important to understand how these roles differ, the type of work performed, and capabilities required to perform the activities required of each role. In some cases, software designers are heavily involved in the requirements and construction phases; therefore, they must have expertise not only in design but also in requirements engineering and software construction. In other cases, a clear organizational delineation exists, allowing designers to focus on their area of expertise. A list of typical designer roles is presented in Table 1.6 (Giachetti 2010).

TABLE 1.6

Typical Roles in Software Design

Designer	Description
Enterprise architect	Designs the enterprise's strategy, processes, information, and organizational structure
Software architect	Designs software systems using a black-box modeling approach; concern is placed on the external properties of software components that determine the system's quality and support the further design of functional requirements
Component designer	Focuses on designing the internal structure of software components identified during the software architecture phase; has strong programming skills
User Interface designer	Designs the software's user interface; skilled in determining ways that increase usability of the system
System engineer	Designs systems using a holistic approach, which include designing how software and hardware collaborate to achieve the system's goals

Systems Engineer

The systems engineer designs the overall development process of systems as a whole, including processes for development of both the software and hardware that are part of the system. As a specialization of system engineering, software systems engineers design software at the system level; in many cases, the work performed by software systems engineers is similar to that of a software architect. Systems engineers work closely with customers to provide a holistic view of systems, their interfaces, and the distribution of requirements to subsystems. Software systems engineers are typically experts in the problem domain, and, depending on the type of system (e.g., embedded, web), they also develop expertise on other nonsoftware-related parts, such as hardware, communications, and avionics. This is essential at all phases of the software development process, since they must be able to communicate with other engineering disciplines, such as electrical, mechanical, and civil. In this role, designers have typically accumulated experience in other design roles, such as software architecture, component design, and in some cases construction. In addition to technical skills, systems engineers are required to have strong leadership skills to ensure the successful system development.

Software Architect

The software architect is in charge of designing the software architecture. Software architects can be found under a wide variety of titles, such as software lead, senior software engineer, or principal software engineer. Regardless of the title, software architects have extensive experience architecting systems that meet their intended requirements. Experience is typically acquired while moving up through the ranks, from software programmer all the way up to software architect. Software architects have strong leadership skills and are required to be skilled in initiation, communication, and negotiation. They also need to have a keen understanding of the developing organization to determine ways software systems can influence the organizational business goals and increase new business ventures leveraged from existing architectures. Other skills beneficial to software architects include project management skills.

Component Designer

Component designers are highly noticeable during detailed and construction designs, since they are typically the ones constructing the software. Therefore, they have strong programming skills and a strong foundation in design principles. For object-oriented component designers, strong object-oriented skills including knowledge of design patterns are essential. Component designers create both static and dynamic models of the software system at levels appropriate to drive construction; these include (when applicable) UML class diagrams and sequence diagrams. They have deep knowledge and understanding of the software requirements assigned to them; they are knowledgeable about other tools that support the design and development effort, such as modeling tools, integrated development environments, forward and reverse engineering, and configuration management. When designing at the component level, component designers have a full understanding of style guides for the project, since they dictate naming, spacing, and commenting conventions and other aspects that shape the structure of code. Component designers devise construction designs as needed and are proficient at creating effective unit tests that verify the quality of their product developed. Finally, component designers need to be comfortable scheduling and conducting peer reviews and accepting feedback and evaluating it objectively to improve their designs.

SOFTWARE DESIGN FUNDAMENTALS

Within the design process, many principles, considerations, and strategies help designers execute the software design process in an effective and consistent manner. For the most part, these help designers manage and simplify problems, consider the impacts of their proposed solutions, and establish a foundation for decision making during design. In this context, design principles refer to knowledge matter that has been found effective throughout the years in multiple projects on different domains. Design principles are applicable on most design projects; therefore, their use is expected to help achieve high-quality designs. On the other hand, design considerations are recommendations that help designers in the design process; they may or may not be followed. Finally, design strategies consist of tactical approaches in which design principles and considerations can be employed to drive the design process. These concepts are further discussed in the next sections.

General Software Design Principles

Throughout the history of software engineering, many design principles have emerged to become fundamental drivers for decision making during the software design process. These design principles are used as a basis for reasoning and serve as justification for almost all design decisions. They also provide designers with a foundation from which other more sophisticated design methods can be applied (Pressman 2010). These principles are not specific to any particular design strategy (e.g., object oriented) or process, so they are fundamental to all software design efforts and can be applied during architectural, detailed, and construction designs. The principles include (Abran et al. 2005):

- Modularization
- Abstraction
- Encapsulation
- Coupling and cohesion
- Separation of interface and implementation
- Sufficiency and completeness

Modularization

Modularization is one of the most important (and perhaps oversimplified) design principles in software design. Modularity allows software systems to be manageable at all levels of the development life cycle. That is, the work products of the requirements, design, construction, and testing efforts can all be modularized to efficiently carry out the operations. In the design phase, modularization is the principle that drives the continuous decomposition of the software system until fine-grained components are created. Modularization plays a key role during all design activities, including software architecture and detailed and construction design; when applied effectively, it provides a roadmap for software development starting from coarse-grained components that are further modularized into fine-grained components directly related to code. If applied properly, modularization can lead to designs that are easier to understand, resulting in systems that are easier to develop and maintain. Efficient modularization can be achieved by following and applying the principles of *abstraction* and *encapsulation*. With proper modularization, software systems can be decomposed into modules that allow the system's complexity to be manageable and allow the system to be efficiently built, maintained, and reused.

Abstraction

While the principle of modularization specifies what needs to be done, the principle of abstraction provides the guidance as to how it should be done. Modularizing systems in an ad hoc manner leads to designs that are incoherent, hard to understand, and hard to maintain. To modularize intelligently, a thorough understanding of abstraction is required (Liskov and Guttag 2010). Abstraction is the principle that deals with creating conceptual entities required to facilitate problem solving by focusing on essential characteristics of entities—in their active context—while deferring unnecessary details. When abstraction is applied, the level of detail required to think about a problem is adjusted to productively modularize a system; this allows for the creation of coherent entities that can be used to represent their possible variations in the problem's context and domain. The principle of abstraction can be applied iteratively at multiple levels during the design phase. At the software architecture level, abstraction helps during the identification of software components and their interfaces. At the detailed design phase, abstraction helps identify the entities, functions, and interfaces required to realize the component's provided services. At the construction level, abstraction helps in the further design of functions identified during detailed design. In all of these, abstraction is used to facilitate problem-solving by deferring details to later stages. The principle of abstraction can be classified as (Pressman 2010):

- Procedural abstraction
- Data abstraction

Procedural abstraction is a specific type of abstraction that simplifies *behavioral operations* containing a sequence of steps or other procedural abstractions. For example, consider a client–server application in which the client sends data to the server through the Internet. In this case, the *Send* procedural abstraction can be used to denote a series of operations, for example, retrieving the server's information (e.g., Internet Protocol [IP] address, port number), opening a connection, sending the message, and closing the connection. On the other hand, data abstraction is used to simplify the *structural composition* of data objects. Using the previous example, the *Message* data abstraction can be used to represent various messages with different attributes, such as the message's ID, content, and format. The definition of all of these properties can be deferred to later stages. Abstraction is fundamental for managing complexity in all activities of the software design phase.

Skill Development 1.2: The Abstraction Principle

The world is full of abstractions; without abstractions, communicating with our peers would be much more difficult. As an exercise, look for the nearest rectangular object that contains a knob and (maybe) a keyhole; if the object is blocking an entrance, change the state of the object so that it no longer blocks the entrance. Summarize this scenario by coming up with two abstractions: one data and the other procedural to increase communication with peers. When done, create a list of four other abstractions that surround you, and provide an abstraction as well as the detailed object description that would be required if the abstraction is not used. Ensure that there are two data abstractions and two procedural abstractions.

Encapsulation

In previous sections, modularization is presented as principle for decomposing monolithic systems into manageable units. While abstraction provides the principle for guiding the decomposition of the systems based on behavior and data, encapsulation provides the principle for enhancing the efficiency of the collaboration among modularized units. Encapsulation is the principle that deals with providing access to the services of conceptual entities (e.g., modules, components) by exposing only the information that is essential to carry out such services while hiding details of how the services are carried out. While abstraction is employed to find conceptual entities, encapsulation enforces that abstracted entities communicate between each other using a "need to know only" basis. When evaluated this way, the abstraction design principle helps create the modules and the encapsulation design principle enforces efficient communication between them. These principles are all essential in achieving efficient modularization. The relationship among modularization, abstraction, and encapsulation is presented in Figure 1.4. As seen, after the principle of abstraction is applied, the encapsulation principle is used to hide irrelevant details from the abstraction. In Figure 1.4, the shaded region corresponds to information that is irrelevant to other modules, while the white region corresponds to access points that modules can use to interoperate.

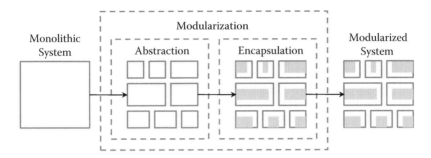

FIGURE 1.4
The modularization, abstraction, and encapsulation principles.

Coupling

Similar to abstraction and encapsulation, coupling and cohesion are design principles that lead to efficient module creation by emphasizing on the degree of dependency and belonging of modules, respectively. Formally, the IEEE (1990, p. 22) defines coupling as

> The manner and degree of interdependence between software modules.

Like all other design principles discussed so far, coupling can be applied during software architecture, detailed design, and construction design to measure the degree of dependency of design units, such as an architectural subsystem, a class in a detailed design's class diagram, or a function in code. In other words, the coupling principle can be used to determine how much an architectural subsystem depends on other architectural subsystems, how much a class depends on other classes, and how much a function depends on other functions. When measuring coupling, the number of dependencies between design units does not tell the whole story, since the nature of the dependencies plays an important role in decision making. For example, design units can depend on well-defined and stable interfaces, common data structures, and internal structure of other design units. It is not hard to support the idea that dependencies on well-defined and stable interfaces are less troublesome than dependencies on the internal structure of other design units. Three common types of coupling are

- Content coupling
- Common coupling
- Data coupling

Content coupling represents the most severe type of coupling, since it refers to modules that modify and rely on the internal details of other modules. *Common coupling* refers to dependencies based on a common access area, such as a global variable (IEEE 1990). When this occurs, changes to the global data area causes changes in all dependent modules. This type of coupling results in lesser severity than content coupling; however, it shares many of the undesired effects as content coupling. Finally, *data coupling* refers to the type of dependency in which design units communicate with each other only through a set of data parameters. Unlike content coupling, data coupling does not depend on the internals of other design units, and unlike common coupling it provides more control over the form of dependency. When dependency between modules relies on data parameters that are globally inaccessible, design units are shielded from undesired changes to the data by other design units. In all cases, a high degree of coupling gives rise to negative side effects. For example, as coupling increases, reusability and manageability of the design units decrease since errors or changes to the independent unit propagate to all dependent units. In other cases, when coupling increases, so does the complexity of managing and maintaining design units. Other types of coupling include *control coupling, hybrid coupling,* and *pathological coupling* (IEEE 1990).

Cohesion

While coupling gives insight to a design unit's degree of dependency, cohesion provides insight into its strengths. The IEEE (1990, p. 17) defines cohesion as

> The manner and degree to which the tasks performed by a single software module are related to one another.

Cohesion measures how well design units are put together for achieving a particular purpose and can be classified based on the measurement approach as

- Functional cohesion
- Procedural (or sequential) cohesion
- Temporal cohesion
- Communication cohesion

Functional cohesion measures a design unit's strength by the degree to which its tasks, operations, or subunits all contribute to perform a single function. When the function to be performed has a single logical meaning, functional cohesion can be seen as a form of logical cohesion. A highly functionally cohesive module is one whose internal details work toward achieving the same function. Functional cohesion is the most typical type of cohesion. *Procedural cohesion* measures the strength of a design unit by the degree to which its tasks work procedurally (in steps) to achieve the unit's purpose. Therefore, functional and procedural cohesion are not mutually exclusive; that is, modules can exhibit both high functional and procedural cohesion. *Temporal cohesion* measures strength by the degree to which all tasks in a design unit are performed at specific times. Consider a design unit responsible for carrying out the initialization of a system. This unit may be responsible for performing a power-on self-test that may include memory tests, file system checks, and communication checks. These are all different functions but need to be executed at the same time during initialization; therefore, the unit is temporally cohesive. Finally, *communication cohesion* measures a unit's strength by the degree to which its tasks produce or consume the same data.

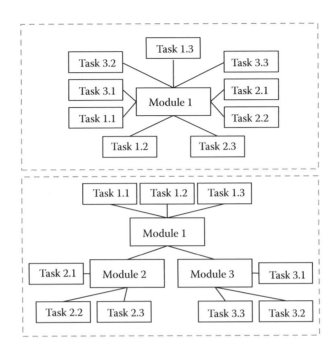

FIGURE 1.5
Example of principles of coupling and cohesion.

Cohesion provides an important principle that measures how much design units that are grouped together actually belong together based on different criteria. Cohesion can also be seen at different levels of the design process. During the software architecture activity, logical and communication cohesive modules are typical, whereas, during the detailed and construction design activities, functional, procedural, and temporal cohesiveness are more expected. In all cases, highly cohesive modules increase reusability. An example of the cohesion and coupling principles is presented in Figure 1.5. As seen in the top part of the figure, *Module 1* performs three unrelated different tasks (i.e., Task 1, Task 2, and Task 3), each requiring three independent subtasks. For example, *Task 1* requires three different subtasks, denoted by the labels *Task 1.1*, *Task 1.2*, and *Task 1.3*. As seen, *Module 1* has dependencies to nine different unrelated tasks, which can translate to a high degree of coupling and low degree of cohesion. The bottom part of Figure 1.5 shows how the system is decomposed into three more cohesive units, each with lower coupling than the original approach. In this case, the system is transformed to a modular system with higher cohesiveness and lower coupling. With this transformation, *Module 1* now has five dependencies and stronger functional cohesion. *Modules 2* and *3* have lower coupling than *Module 1* (both in its original and improve form) and are highly cohesive.

Separation of Interface and Implementation

The principle of separation of interface and implementation deals with creating modules in such way that a stable interface is identified and separated from its implementation. This design principle should not be confused with encapsulation. During encapsulation,

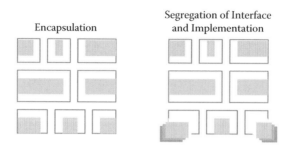

FIGURE 1.6
Principle of segregation of interface and implementation.

interfaces are created to provide public access to services provided by the design unit while hiding unnecessary details, which include implementation. While encapsulation dictates hiding the details of implementation, the principle of separation dictates their separation, so that different implementation of the same interface can be swapped to provide modified or new behavior. Figure 1.6 presents these concepts.

As seen, the bottom design units have separated interfaces; therefore, varied implementations can be employed without changes to a unit's interface and, subsequently, to dependent units. There are many benefits from this principle, including increased extensibility, reusability, and maintainability. Since implementation is compartmentalized, new capabilities can be added simply by including a new variation of the implementation without changes to old implementations. Also, in this way specific implementations can be reused.

Completeness and Sufficiency

The principles of completeness and sufficiency deal with efficient module creation. *Completeness* is a characteristic that measures how well design units provide the required services to achieve their intent. For example, during the detailed design activity, a communication class can be considered complete for a particular application if it provides services for establishing and terminating connections, sending and receiving messages. Missing any of these services would render the class incomplete. On the other hand, sufficiency measures how well design units are at providing only the services that are sufficient for achieving their intent. Consider the same communication class, which can include services for logging statistics, visualization of network activity, or any other capability applicable to the communication task. Although these capabilities enhance the class' service list, the class is considered sufficient by providing the required services of opening/terminating connections, sending, and receiving messages. That is, these sets of services are sufficient to achieve the unit's required functions, nothing more and nothing less.

Practical Software Design Considerations

Design principles are well-known throughout the software engineering community and are applied in one way or another in most projects. However, other considerations need to be made to provide the appropriate context in which these principles can be successfully applied for developing high-quality software systems. These considerations are discussed in the next sections.

Design for Minimizing Complexity

Design is about minimizing complexity. Every decision that is made during the design phase must take into account reducing complexity (McConnell 2004). In fact, the majority of design principles (e.g., modularization, abstraction, encapsulation) are meant to reduce complexity in one way or another. By doing this, details of the problem solution can be pushed further down the process, where they can be appropriately handled. As another example, consider HCI design: it is all about reducing complexity for the user. Finally, code design is about reducing complexity for other developers maintaining the software. As rule of thumb, when faced with competing design options, always choose the one that minimizes complexity.

Design for Change

As stated before, software will change; therefore, design with extension in mind. There are numerous reasons for this; for example, customers who like the software may want to extend its functionalities. On the other hand, customers who are discontent with the software may want to replace or remove functionality. In other cases, hardware changes may trigger a software change; advances in communications may cause software to change; or, simply, newer, better software technology becomes available triggering a change of software that introduces no new functionality but a more maintainable development technology that is supported by current practices. In any case, software will change; therefore, its very own nature requires software designers to plan for the future. A variety of techniques is available during the detailed design phase to achieve this.

Software Design Strategies

Throughout the years, a wide variety of strategies for designing software has been proposed. Some of these include structured design, object-oriented design, aspect-oriented design, data component-based design, and data structure-based design. Two popular strategies are discussed in the following sections.

Structured Design

In a broad context, structured design refers to any disciplined functional design approach where software systems are decomposed into independent, single-purpose modules, using an iterative top-down approach. The main focus of structured design is on the functions that systems need to provide, the decomposition of these functions, and the creation of modules that incorporate these functions. Structured design approaches are typically employed after structured analysis, where the main purpose is to derive a structure chart (i.e., software architecture) from data flow diagrams. Structured design introduced many benefits; for instance, by decomposing the system into independent, single-purpose modules, programs were simpler to understand, manage, code, debug, and reuse (Stevens 1981). However, structured design does not address the issues of data abstraction and information hiding and "is largely inappropriate for use with object-based and object-oriented programming languages" (Booch 1994, p. 22).

Object-Oriented Design

Unlike structured design, which focuses on functional decomposition of systems, object-oriented design focuses on object decomposition. Formally, the IEEE (1990, p. 51) defines object-oriented design as

> A design strategy in which a system or component is expressed in terms of objects and connections between those objects.

Objects provide numerous capabilities that make them desirable for efficiently designing software systems. For example, objects are capable of maintaining state information and provide services that can be used independently or relative to the object's state. Therefore, they are naturally good building blocks for creating good abstractions. Object-oriented designs also provide capabilities for inheritance and polymorphism, which provide various advantages when designing complex and large-scale software systems. Inheritance allows designers to create families of objects capable of reusing each other's interfaces or interfaces with implementations. While inheritance allows objects to inherit interfaces and implementations, polymorphism allows objects to change the behavior of inherited interfaces. Numerous design methods based on objects have been proposed. Today, the UP provides a popular framework for object-oriented software engineering using UML.

CHAPTER SUMMARY

Designs in software engineering are used to identify, evaluate, and specify the structural and behavioral characteristics of software systems that adhere to some specification. Software designs provide blueprints that capture how software systems meet their required functions and how they are shaped to meet their intended quality. Formally, software engineering design is defined as the process of identifying, evaluating, validating, and specifying the architectural, detailed, and construction models required to build software that meets its intended functional and nonfunctional requirements and the result of such a process. The term software design is used interchangeably in practice as means to describe both the process and product of software design. Throughout the design process, designers are constantly engaging in problem-solving activities that are fundamental to all modern engineering projects; therefore, they can be characterized as specialized problem solvers.

To ensure that all problem considerations are incorporated when solving design problems, a holistic problem-solving approach must be adopted, including all relevant concerns. Software design provides numerous advantages from both product development and process; however, many challenges must be considered and addressed before software designs can lead to complete and sufficient software models. In today's modern software systems, numerous design principles, processes, strategies, and other factors affect how designers execute the software design phase. When equipped with the proper design foundation knowledge, an understanding of the designer's roles and responsibilities can be acquired; allowing designers to become effective in designing large-scale software systems under a wide variety of challenging conditions.

REVIEW QUESTIONS

1. What is software engineering design, and why is it important?
2. What are the three states of problem solving? Describe each and explain how they apply to design problems?
3. What are two types of thinking employed during problem solving? Provide an example of how they are applied to design problems.
4. What is the difference between well-defined, ill-defined, and wicked problems and how these problems can affect software design?
5. What is the difference between an algorithm and a heuristic? Give examples of how both approaches can be applied during the design phase?
6. What is the holistic approach to problem solving? Explain.
7. How does design fits within the software engineering life cycle? Explain.
8. What are the major activities of the software design phase, and how do they differ from one another?
9. List and explain the challenges faced in software design.
10. Why is important to emphasize on documentation and management activities during design?
11. Compare and contrast the following: interface design, user interface design, and construction design.
12. What are the different roles of software designers? How do they differ?
13. Explain the difference between procedural and data abstraction.
14. What is content coupling, and how does it differ from other forms of coupling?
15. Explain in detail the concept of cohesion.
16. What do completeness and sufficiency mean?
17. What is the difference among the principles of modularization, abstraction, encapsulation, and separation of interface and implementation? Provide an example of each.
18. Compare and contrast the structured design strategy with the object-oriented design strategy.

REFERENCES

Abran, Alain, James W. Moore, Pierre Bourque, and Robert Dupuis. *Guide to the Software Engineering Body of Knowledge—2004 Version—SWEBOK*. Los Alamitos, CA: IEEE Computer Society Press, 2005.

Bass, Len, Paul Clements, and Rick Kazman. *Software Architecture in Practice*, 2d ed. Boston: Addison-Wesley, 2003.

Booch, Grady. *Object-Oriented Analysis and Design with Applications*, 2d ed. Santa Clara, CA: Addison-Wesley, 1994.

Brassard, Gilles, and Paul Bratley. *Fundamentals of Algorithmics*. Upper Saddle River, NJ: Prentice Hall, 1995.

Dowson, Mark. "The Ariane 5 Software Failure." *ACM SIGSOFT Software Engineering Notes*, March 1997.

Dym, Clive L., and Patrick Little. *Engineering Design: A Project-Based Introduction*. Hoboken, NJ: Wiley, 2008.

Fox, Christopher. *Introduction to Software Engineering Design: Processes, Principles, and Patterns with UML2*. Boston: Addison Wesley, 2006.

Giachetti, Ronald E. *Design of Enterprise Systems: Theory, Architecture, and Methods*. Boca Raton, FL; CRC Press, 2010.

Griffin, Ricky W. *Management*, 10th ed. Mayfield Hts, Ohio: South-Western College Pub, 2010.

Harrell, C., Biman K. Ghosh, and Royce O. Bowden. *Simulation Using Promodel*. New York: McGraw-Hill, 2004.

IEEE. "IEEE Recommended Practice for Software Design Descriptions." 1998. http://ieeexplore.ieee.org/xpl/freeabs_all.jsp?arnumber=741934.

IEEE. "IEEE Standard Glossary of Software Engineering Terminology." IEEE, 1990. http://ieeexplore.ieee.org/xpl/freeabs_all.jsp?arnumber=159342.

IEEE/ACM. *Software Engineering 2004*. August 23, 2004. Available at: http://sites.computer.org/ccse/SE2004Volume.pdf (accessed September 22, 2010).

Kershaw, T. C., and S. Ohlsson. "Multiple Causes of Difficulty in Insight: The Case of the Nine-Dot Problem." *Journal of Experimental Psychology: Learning, Memory, and Cognition* 30:3–15, 2004.

Laplante, Phillip A. *Requirements Engineering for Software and Systems*. Boca Raton, FL: Auerbach Publications, 2009.

Liskov, Barbara, and John Guttag. *Program Development in Java: Abstraction, Specification, and Object-Oriented Design*. Boston: Addison-Wesley, 2000.

McConnell, Steve. *Code Complete*, 2d ed. Redmond, WA: Microsoft Press, 2004.

Meyers, Scott. *Effective C++: 55 Ways to Improve Your Programs and Designs*, 3d ed. Boston: Addison-Wesley, 2005.

U.S. General Accounting Office. (GAO). *Patriot Missile Defense: Software Problem Led to System Failure at Dhahran, Saudi Arabia*. Washington, DC: U.S. Government Accountability Office, 1992.

Plotnik, Rod, and Haig Kouyoumdjian. *Introduction to Psychology*, 9th ed. Wadsworth Publishing, 2010.

Pressman, Roger S. *Software Engineering: A Practitioner's Approach*, 7th ed. Belmont, CA: McGraw-Hill, 2010.

Sommerville, Ian. *Software Engineering*, 9th ed. Boston: Addison Wesley, 2010.

Stevens, Wayne P. *Using Structured Design: How to Make Programs Simple, Changeable, Flexible and Reusable*. Hoboken, NJ: John Wiley & Sons, 1981.

2

Software Design with Unified Modeling Language

CHAPTER OBJECTIVES

- Understand the role and importance of Unified Modeling Language (UML) in software design
- Become familiar with UML's common structural and behavioral diagrams
- Understand the relationship between structural UML models and code
- Understand how to model concurrency with UML

CONCEPTUAL OVERVIEW

Communication is an essential, critical skill for engineers. Throughout a project's life cycle, software engineers spend a great deal of time and effort communicating with stakeholders, among themselves, and with the computer via programming languages. By unifying the communication language, so that it is appropriate for stakeholders, software engineers, and translation to programming languages, a more efficient design process can be executed and better framing of design problem and their solutions can be achieved to account for all intricacies that are present throughout the design process. Unified Modeling Language (UML) provides the mechanisms for creating detailed models that portray a system's design. By providing a visualization method for complex design concepts, communication is enhanced at all phases of the software development life cycle. This chapter presents the fundamental concepts of UML to establish a common frame of reference for discussing important design concepts throughout the rest of the book.

WHAT IS UML?

The Unified Modeling Language is a visual language with an extensive set of features appropriate for designing software systems across a broad set of application domains. It is the result of years of collaborative work spent in devising a unified approach for modeling software systems. The first efforts focused on unifying three popular modeling methods: the Booch method (devised by Grady Booch); the object-oriented software engineering (OOSE) method (devised by Ivar Jacobson); and the object modeling technique (OMT) method (devised by James Rumbaugh). The goals of this unification project were specified by Booch, Rumbaugh, and Jacobson (2005, p. xvii) as follows:

1. To model systems, from concept to executable artifact, using object-oriented techniques
2. To address the issues of scale inherent in complex, mission-critical systems
3. To create a modeling language usable by both humans and machines

The development of early UML versions generated interest among the software engineering community, resulting in the creation of UML consortium supported by numerous influential organizations, such as Microsoft, IBM, Oracle, and Rational. This collaboration resulted in UML 1.0, which after revisions was adopted by the Object Management Group (OMG) in 1997 as UML 1.1 (Booch et al. 2005). Since then, UML has evolved through many versions that improve capabilities for efficient analysis, design, and implementation of software systems of varying complexity. In 2005, a major revision of UML 1 was proposed and adopted by the OMG as UML 2.0. At the time of writing, UML 2.3 provides the latest specification (UML 2.3 Superstructure 2010). Formally, UML can be defined as a visual language for specifying, analyzing, and documenting design elements essential for modeling and building software system. To provide an organized methodology for creating models that address different stakeholders' concerns, UML defines different modeling diagrams and provides a classification scheme that delineates clearly between the static and dynamic nature of software systems, as seen in Table 2.1.

Every diagram in UML belongs to one of the classes presented in Table 2.1. Throughout the rest of the chapter, UML diagrams fundamental for modeling systems from both structural and behavioral perspectives are presented, and their capabilities for addressing issues of different concerns from different levels of abstractions are examined.

TABLE 2.1

Classification of UML Diagrams

Classification	Description
Structural	Concerned with capturing and specifying static elements and their interrelationships required for supporting the solution to a given problem, within a given context
Behavioral	Concerned with capturing and specifying the dynamic behavior and the inherent complexities present in the behavioral aspects of software systems

WHY STUDY UML?

UML 2.3 provides 14 different types of diagrams that can be used for modeling structural and behavioral aspects of software systems. Since software systems vary across a large set of application domains, not all 14 diagrams are required or used in any given project. For example, real-time systems may employ the use of UML timing, state, and communication diagrams to model behavior and real-time constraints related to real-time systems. Distributed systems may employ sequence diagrams for modeling time-ordered sequence of operations among components and deployment diagrams for modeling distributed aspects of the systems. Finally, object-oriented systems—which can also be distributed or real-time systems—may rely heavily on class and object diagrams to model class hierarchies and particular instances of their interaction. Even though not all diagrams are used in system modeling efforts, it is important to identify a common set of diagrams that provide appropriate avenues for modeling essential activities during the software development process. Therefore, the study of UML becomes important so that the modeling capabilities of particular diagrams are well understood and applied in practical efforts. The two main reasons for studying UML include

- The UML enhances system analysis and specification.
- The UML enhances communication.

Modeling software is essential to developing high-quality, large-scale, and software-intensive systems. The UML is important because it provides well-known and widely accepted means for modeling complex systems. Through UML, a common approach can be used for analyzing, evaluating, and specifying systems at all levels of abstraction during requirements, design, and construction. After systems are specified at one level of abstraction using UML, the models are transferred downstream for subsequent, finer-grained analysis, evaluation, and specification. This process continues until the software is constructed and ready for testing and verification. Throughout this process, UML is the main tool for transferring knowledge and enhancing communication among stakeholders, including customers, designers (i.e., architects, component, and construction), programmers, and managers. By providing the means for visualizing complex system concepts, it becomes easier to reason about the problem at hand, therefore increasing communication during the problem-solving process. The UML's visualization capabilities enhance communication greatly throughout, especially when creating documentation deliverables, such as the software design document, which lives long after the development effort is complete.

THE UML'S FUNDAMENTALS

The UML is an extensible and flexible language that can be used to model almost any aspect of today's modern software systems. Given the rich set of modeling features provided by

TABLE 2.2

UML 2.3 Common Classifiers

Classifier	Description
Use case	Classifier used to model a single required system behavior; represented with icons of elliptical shape
Component	Represents a modular and replaceable part of the system; modeled using a box with the keyword <<component>> and optional component icon on the top right corner
Class	Classifier used to model a type in terms of operations, attributes, relationships, and other semantics; modeled with a rectangular box
Active class	Classifier used to model a class that owns an independent flow of execution and can initiate control activity; modeled as a class with double lines on each side
Interface	Classifier that models the set of operations that specify the services provided by a class or component; represented as stereotyped classes or using the ball-and-socket notation
Node	Classifier used to model a physical element (e.g., computer), its processing capabilities, and other semantics; modeled using a cube
Artifact	Classifier that models a physical deployable information element (e.g., *.exe, .dll, script, etc.*); modeled using a rectangle with the keyword <<artifact>>

UML, its application can become confusing at times, resulting in model inconsistencies that can hinder communication during the development effort. The built-in flexibility in UML is essential for modeling systems with disparate capabilities; therefore, understanding its fundamental building blocks is necessary for employing the built-in flexibility to model a wide variety of software systems. The UML building blocks are grouped as follows:

- Classifiers
- Relationships
- Enhancing features

Classifiers are structural things that represent conceptual or physical elements of a model (Booch et al. 2005). They are typically the main elements of UML models, and each type of UML diagram has a specific type of classifiers so that not all classifiers are relevant to all UML diagrams. A list of common UML classifiers is presented in Table 2.2.

Classifiers provide designers the capability of defining the structure for achieving some desired system feature. This capability allows designers to visualize the structural design of systems, provide analysis, and make design improvements, all at design time. Structural designs are good for evaluating logical relationships in software design; however, they are limited when it comes to evaluating the system's behavioral aspects—that is, modeling and evaluating the manifestation and behavioral aspects of classifiers once the system is executed. For this purpose, UML provides techniques for representing almost all classifiers as manifested entities. For example, structural classes can be modeled as behavioral (executing) objects; the behavior of active classes can be modeled using active objects; components can be modeled as component instances; use cases can be modeled as use case executions; and nodes can be modeled as node instances (Booch et al. 2005). The

TABLE 2.3

Common Types of UML Relationships

Relationship	Description
Dependency	Dashed line (typically directed with a stick arrow) used to model the relationship between two UML elements indicating that changes to one element affect the other
Association	Line used to model the relationship between two UML elements indicating that a connection exists between associated instances at run time; associations can be directed using a stick arrow
Generalization	Line with a hollow arrowhead used to model the relationship between two UML elements indicating that one element (i.e., the child) inherits features from another (i.e., the parent)
Realization	Relationship between two UML elements indicating that one element realizes a specified interface; modeled using a dashed line with hollow arrowhead

TABLE 2.4

Common UML Mechanisms for Enhancement

Mechanism	Description
Notes	Mechanism for adding descriptive information to UML elements and diagrams; modeled using a rectangle with a dog-eared corner and can be connected to a design element using a dashed line
Stereotypes	Mechanism for extending UML by adding information that gives existing UML element a different meaning, therefore creating a semantically different element for modeling application-specific concepts; modeled as existing UML elements with the <<stereotype>> mechanism (e.g., <<subsystem>>)
Tagged Values	Mechanism for adding new properties to a stereotype; modeled by adding the tagged value in the form of *property = value* to existing stereotyped UML elements (e.g., *data rate = 5 Mbps*)
Constraints	Mechanism for specifying constraints to design elements; associated with specific design elements in the form of {*constraint description*} (e.g., {secure line})

usefulness of modeling classifiers (and their behavioral counterparts) is maximized when defining and visualizing the interconnections that exist among them. A list of UML common relationship types is presented in Table 2.3.

The UML is required to provide enough flexibility to allow designers to enhance and evolve the fundamental building blocks so that they become appropriate for modeling particular systems. Therefore, it provides the means for enhancing and extending classifiers, behavioral manifestations, and relationships through common extension mechanisms. These extension mechanisms allow designers to redefine UML elements so that they can represent domain-specific concepts. Also, extension mechanisms allow detailed design information to be captured and specified in the models. The common mechanisms for enhancing UML are presented in Table 2.4.

Together, classifiers, relationships, and enhancement mechanisms provide powerful constructs for evaluating both *structural* and *behavioral* design elements that interact and collaborate with each other, provide the means for evaluating design alternatives, and provide the sufficient information to build the software system.

TABLE 2.5

UML 2.3 Structural Diagrams

Diagram	Description
Component	High-level; used to model the software as group of components connected to each other through well-defined interfaces and thus said to be replaceable within its context
Class	Used to model software as a set of classes, including their operations, attributes, and their mutual relationships
Object	Used to model an instant snapshot of the life of an object during execution, including its state and attribute values
Deployment	Used to model the physical realization of software systems, including physical nodes where software is deployed, interfaces between nodes, software artifacts executing on nodes, and the manifestation of software components within the software artifacts
Package Diagram	Diagram used to model the division of software as a set of packages, including the relationships between packages

STRUCTURAL MODELING

Structural modeling is concerned with capturing and specifying structural elements and interrelationships required for supporting the solution to a given problem, within a given context. Structural models are static in nature, since they model structure and not behavior; therefore, they provide the main avenues for evaluating design decisions that directly support functional requirements as well as desired quality attributes, such as modularity, portability, and maintainability. A list of common UML structural diagrams is presented in Table 2.5.

Other structural diagrams include *composite structure* and *profile* diagrams. As seen, each structural diagram addresses a particular system concern; therefore, the set of classifiers and relationship employed varies from diagram to diagram. Understanding the capabilities and goals of each structural diagram is important for determining the selection of effective constructs that are appropriate at particular levels of abstraction during system design.

COMPONENT DIAGRAMS

A component represents a modular part of a system that encapsulates its contents and whose manifestation is replaceable within its environment (UML 2.3 Superstructure 2010). For this reason, component diagrams can be used to decompose systems and represent their structural architecture, from a logical perspective. Components can be modeled using an external black-box view or internal white-box view. With the black-box view, components encapsulate their internal structure; therefore, collaboration with other components is achieved through well-defined interfaces. These interfaces can be classified as *provided* or *required* interfaces. Provided interfaces are used by other external components to interact with the component providing the interface. Required interfaces are those the

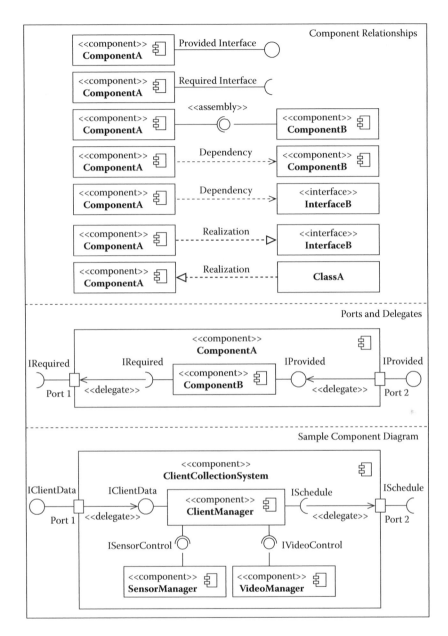

FIGURE 2.1
Overview of UML component diagram.

components need to realize a component's function. Modeling component interfaces in UML can be achieved using two distinct notations: the *ball-and-socket* notation or the *dependency* and *realization* relationships, as seen in Figure 2.1.

Figure 2.1 shows the basic component relationships and examples of component diagrams. As seen, the basic notations for modeling components are *components*, *assembly connectors*, and *provided/required interfaces*. The notations presented in Figure 2.1 are used to model components using an external, black-box view; however, components can also be designed using an internal, white-box view, not presented in Figure 2.1. When using the black-box approach, components use the *ports* and *delegates* concepts to model how components interact with other (external) components and how the responsibility for realizing external requests are delegated throughout parts of components. As seen, ports are used to model access points for allowing the external environment to access the components' services and for allowing components to interact with their external environment. Delegation connectors are used to model the link between the external provided interfaces of a component to the realization of those interfaces internally within the component (UML 2.3 Superstructure 2010). Similarly, delegation connectors model the link between internally required interfaces to ports requiring the interface from external components.

Figure 2.1 presents a design element for devising a logical representation for the software architecture of a sensor collection system. The system includes a client collection node that is decomposed into *ClientManager*, *SensorManager*, and *VideoManager*. The client subsystem requires a collection schedule, which provides the information necessary for activating sensor and video nodes to begin collection. The client subsystem makes this information available to other nodes upon request. As seen, the *ClientManager* component requires a collection schedule, which is delegated to Port 2; this interface requires external components to provide the collection schedule using the *ISchedule* interface. In addition, the *ClientCollectionSystem* component provides status information to external components via Port 1 using the *IClientData* interface. The responsibility of realizing the *IClientData* interface to provide status data is delegated to the *ClientManager* component so that all requests received at Port 1 can be handled by the target component.

Logical versus Physical Components

The UML 2.3 Superstructure Specification supports the specification of both logical and physical components and describes them as substitutable units that can be replaced at design time or run time (UML 2.3 Superstructure 2010). This, combined with the previous usage (in UML 1.x) of components, creates confusion among designers. Although UML 1.x and UML 2.x components can look the same in UML, the context in which they are used should make the distinction between physical and logical components evident. For this reason, a thorough discussion is needed.

Logical components are used from a logical perspective, while physical components are used from a deployment perspective, which in UML 2.0 can be modeled as *artifacts*. Logical components are components that can be replaced at design time. For example, the internal structure of a software system may be composed of three logical components: the UI component, the business logic component, and the database component. Each of these has well-known interfaces that allow them to be replaceable at design time. By having well-known interfaces, the internal design of components (e.g., the UI component) becomes irrelevant to other external components (e.g., the business logic component). Logical components specify the decomposed structure of software; they exist in the context of the logical design of the software system.

On the other hand, physical components are components that exist within the context of deployment; they are distinctively different from logical components in that they are independently deployable units that reside on their own and provide services to other physical components or software applications. They provide stable interfaces that allows them to be replaceable at run time, for example, JavaBean components, EJB components, and .NET components, which can be deployed independently through a jar file, ear file, and DLL file, respectively (Qian, Qian, Fu, Tao, Xu, and Diaz-Herrera 2009).

Using components to denote logical units (as opposed to physical units) is new to UML 2.0; therefore, they provide modeling features that are specially fitting for designing logical elements of the software architecture. In previous versions of UML, components were reserved exclusively for modeling physical entities deployable within a system and replaceable at run time. Now, UML supports the specification of both logical and physical components, together with the artifacts that implement them and the nodes on which they are executed (UML 2.3 Superstructure 2010). This new paradigm allows designers to model physical deployment aspects of components using the *artifact* classifier deployed on a *node* (Booch et al. 2007).

CLASS DIAGRAMS

Class diagrams exist at a lower level of abstractions than component diagrams. That is, whereas component diagrams serve well to modularize the system, they do not have a direct translation from model to code. Class diagrams have direct translation to object-oriented programming languages. In simple terms, class diagrams are models consisting of classes and relationships between classes necessary to achieve a system's functionality. Therefore, whether a detailed class diagram is made or not, the resulting object-oriented code will always reflect some class design. This characteristic of class designs results in a two-way relationship between class diagrams and code, which allows designers to generate code from class diagrams (i.e., code generation or forward engineering) or to generate class diagrams from code (i.e., reverse engineering). This makes class diagrams the most powerful tool for component designers to model the design characteristics of object-oriented software before the construction phase.

Class diagrams vary in complexity, ranging from diagrams with a few classes with simple relationships to diagrams with many classes interconnected via elegant and efficient relationships. Class diagrams are perhaps the most important UML diagrams for object-oriented component designers. To effectively model object-oriented software, designers need to have an understanding of the basic class constructs, relationships, and the direct mapping that result from model to code.

Classes

A class is the specification of a type, nothing more, nothing less. For a class to be useful to software programs, objects of that class need to be instantiated during the program's execution. Instantiation is the process of manifesting a class in the computer's memory. A single class specification can be manifested in the computer's memory during program execution as multiple objects, their specific values for each having operations and relationships with other objects. Classes are the building blocks of object-oriented systems; therefore, being able to model classes in an efficient and reusable way is essential. In UML, a class is modeled with a rectangular shape with three main compartments, namely, the name, attribute, and operation compartments.

Name Compartment

The name compartment is reserved for the class name and its stereotype. A class name is a string value that uniquely identifies a class from other classes in the system. Class names can be qualified to show the package that they belong to in the form of *Owner::ClassName*, where *Owner* refers to the package that owns the class and *ClassName* refers to the class name. UML classes can be enhanced to convey more information by using stereotypes. Stereotypes are displayed above the class name using the format <<stereotype>>. Commonly used stereotypes for classes include the <<interface>> and <<utility>> stereotypes. The <<interface>> stereotype is used to model interfaces, which specify the services of a class. The <<utility>> stereotype is used to model a class that has no instances but instead represents a named collection of class-scoped (i.e., static) attributes and operations.

Attribute Compartment

Attributes are named properties used to specify the information required by objects to carry out their intended function or to represent the object modeled by the class. The attribute compartment is reserved for specifying the class attributes, including their name, type, and other properties, such as visibility and scope. Attribute names, similar to class names, are string values that uniquely identify one attribute from all other attributes. The attribute type specifies the type of data appropriate for the attribute, for example, integer, string, or double. Typically, the attribute compartment is used to specify primitive types, whereas attributes that result as consequence of relationships with user-defined types are kept from the attribute compartment; these are modeled using the appropriate UML relationship with a label containing the attribute's name. The attribute's visibility specifies policies on how attributes are accessed by clients. In UML, visibility can be set to the types represented in Table 2.6.

The scope of an attribute can be specified to be class-specific (i.e., static) or object-specific, which allows each individual object to have individual copies that help keep track of attribute values independently.

TABLE 2.6

Common Visibility Types in Class Diagrams

Visibility	Symbol	Description
Public	+	Allows access to external clients
Private	−	Hides private members or operations from external clients
Protected	#	Allows access internally within the class and to derived classes
Package	~	Allows access to entities within the same package

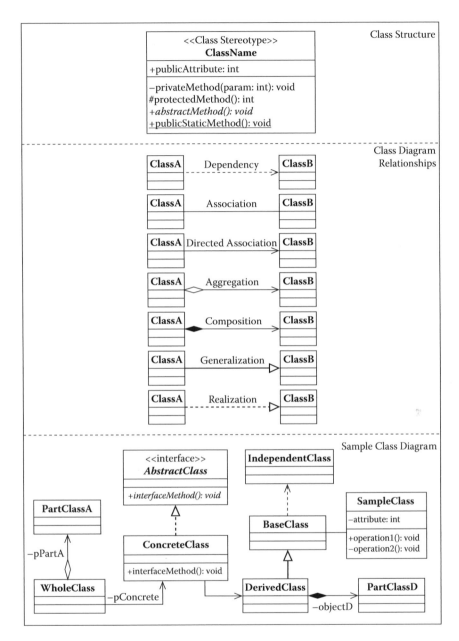

FIGURE 2.2
Overview of class diagram.

Operation Compartment

Operations are services provided by classes. The operation compartment is reserved for specifying the class operations, including their name, return type, parameters, and other properties, such as visibility, scope, type (e.g., abstract), and constraints, as seen in Figure 2.2.

The class concept is easier to understand for most programmers, since it directly maps to code in object-oriented languages. An important aspect of modeling software with class diagrams is the understanding of how classes modeled in the design translate to code.

Listing 2.1: C++ Code Generated from SampleClass Designed in Figure 2.2

```
class SampleClass {

public:

  // Methods in this section are made public.
  void operation1() {

    // Code here.
  }
private:

  // Methods and attributes in this section are made private.
  void operation2() {

    // Code here
  }

  // Private attribute.
  int attribute;
};
```

UML, as a universal language, provides the appropriate mechanisms to allow designers to model almost any aspect of modern object-oriented programming languages. Therefore, when modeling UML classes, it is important to understand what decisions made at design time result in code. As an example, consider Listing 2.1, which presents C++ code for the *SampleClass* designed in the Sample Class Diagram section of Figure 2.2.

As seen, generation of code from UML *SampleClass* results in the manifestation of UML class as code; both versions (i.e., code and UML class drawing) of the *SampleClass* design element convey identical information. The same UML class can be used to generate code in other programming languages as well. For example, Listing 2.2 presents the manifestation of UML *SampleClass* class design using the Java programming language.

Relationships

Classes that do not collaborate with each other may not accomplish much. Therefore, depicting the relationships among classes is an essential part of class diagrams. UML relationships can be used to model the connection between UML classes in a class diagram. The UML relationships identified in Table 2.3 can all be used in class diagrams to provide connections appropriate to model relationships found in object-oriented systems. Similar to the modeling of classes, it is essential for designers to understand how UML relationships translate to code. Since UML is programming language-agnostic, some of the relationships that have different meanings in the modeling domain will translate with no difference in the code domain.

Listing 2.2: Java Code Generated from SampleClass Designed in Figure 2.2

```java
class SampleClass {

  // Public method.
  public void operation1() {

  }

  // Private method.
  private void operation2() {

  }

  // Private attribute.
  private int attribute;
}
```

Listing 2.3: C++ Code Generated for UML Dependency Relationship

```cpp
// The dependency relationship can result in code as a #include.
#include "IndependentClass.h"

class DependentClass {

  // Other attributes.
  // Other operations.
};
```

Dependency

In a class diagram, the dependency relationship, rendered as a dashed line and stick arrow, is used to model the relationship between two UML classes. Dependency models the relationship that indicates that changes to one class affect the other. In C++, dependency relationship may translate to a *#include* statement, as seen in Listing 2.3.

Association

Associations are *structural* relationships; that is, they affect the structure of UML classes. In a class diagram, associations are modeled with solid lines connecting two classes, as seen in Figure 2.2 from BaseClass to SampleClass. This structural relationship indicates that a connection exists between associated instances at run time. Associations are bidirectional by default. When using bidirectional associations, classes on each end of the association are structurally modified to provide navigation to their associated classes, providing

---

Listing 2.4: C++ Code Generated for UML Association Relationship

```cpp
#include "PartClassA.h"
#include "ConcreteClass.h"

class WholeClass {

  // Code here...

private:

  // Association relationship.
  ConcreteClass* pConcrete;

  // Aggregation relationship.
  PartClassA* pPartA;
};
```

---

objects of one type ability to navigate to objects of another type and vice versa. Navigation can be limited to one-way by modeling the association relationship with a directional arrow. When this is the case, only the structure of one class is modified to provide navigational capabilities to the other. In C++, the structural modification resulting from using associations is presented in Listing 2.4. As seen, the association from WholeClass and ConcreteClass may translate to a pointer type.

Aggregation

Aggregation is a specialized form of association to denote a whole–part relationship. That is, aggregation can be seen as association with special semantics for modeling that one object is part of another. This added semantic is purely conceptual, and its use is constrained to design time; that is, forward-engineered aggregation relationships may translate to code in the same way that associations are translated. Therefore, aggregation is used to increase the communication language at design time. Aggregation is modeled using an association line with a hollow diamond at one end. Similar to association, aggregation can be made directional, as seen in Figure 2.2. When aggregation is used, the class connected to the diamond part of the aggregation arrow is said to be the whole, and the one connected to the arrow is the part. As seen in Listing 2.4, aggregation may not be differentiable from association in code, since both associations and aggregation can translate the same way in code.

Composition

Object composition is a specialized form of aggregation used to model ownership relationship. Similar to aggregation, object composition models a whole–part relationship;

Listing 2.5: C++ Code Generated for UML Composition Relationship

```cpp
// Object composition requires this dependency.
#include "File.h"

class EventLogger {

  // Code here...

private:

  //The Object Composition Relationship.
  File _file;
};
```

however, unlike aggregation, composition provides deeper semantics to indicate that the lifetime of the part is owned by the whole. Therefore, when the whole object goes out of scope, so does the part. In UML, object composition is modeled similarly to aggregation, but instead of using a hollow diamond a solid diamond is used. In code, object composition can be manifested in different ways. For example, Listing 2.5 presents the forward engineering (using C++) of some designed EventLogger class, which is used to log events in a system.

As seen, the EventLogger will own at run time an instance of the File class; therefore, once the EventLogger goes out of scope, so will the instance of the File class. This relationship can be translated differently in C++, via pointers. Listing 2.6 presents the forward engineering of the EventLogger class with a different manifestation of the object composition relationship.

As seen, object composition is achieved using a different approach that creates and destroys the _file object. It is important to emphasize once again that UML is a flexible language; therefore, forward engineering of UML models can be realized differently by different tools and different programming languages. For example, association, aggregation, and object composition can all look different in other object-oriented languages, such as Java and C#, which have no pointer notation.

Generalization

Generalization is a relationship that denotes inheritance; that is, one (child) class inherits the structure and behavior of another (parent) class. Child classes can reuse services provided by parent classes, override these services, or add entirely new ones. In class diagrams, generalization is modeled using a solid line with a hollow arrowhead connecting two classes, as seen in Figure 2.2. Generalization always translates to code as inheritance, as seen in Listing 2.7.

Listing 2.6: C++ Code Generated for UML Composition Relationship

```cpp
#include "File.h"

class EventLogger {

  // Constructor.
  EventLogger() {

    // Instantiate the message object during initialization.
    _file = new File;
  }

  // Destructor.
  ~EventLogger() {

    // Because of UML composition relationship, once the this object
    // goes out of scope, so does the _file object.
    delete _file;
  }

private:

  // Object composition via pointers.
  File* _file;
};
```

Listing 2.7: C++ Implementation for UML Generalization Relationship

```cpp
#include "BaseClass.h"

// Generalization results in inheritance.
class DerivedClass : public BaseClass {

  // Code here...
};
```

Realization

Whereas generalization allows classes to inherit a parent's class interface and behavior, realization allows classes to inherit the interface. Realization is used to model a contract relationship in which one class specifies an interface contract and another buys into that contract. When realization is used, classes that realize interfaces are required by contract to provide implementations for those interfaces before objects of those classes can be instantiated. In UML, realization is modeled using a dashed line with a hollow arrowhead

---

Listing 2.8: C++ Code Generation for Interfaces

```cpp
class Gps {

public:

  // The interface method to obtain latitude information.
  virtual double getLatitude() = 0;

  // The start interface method.
  virtual double getLongitude() = 0;
};
```

Listing 2.9: C++ Implementation for UML Realization Relationship

```cpp
#include "Gps.h"

// SimulatedGps realizes the Gps interface.
class SimulatedGps : public Gps {

public:

  // The interface method to obtain latitude information.
  double getLatitude() {

    // Generate a sample latitude and return.
  }

  // The interface method to obtain longitude information.
  double getLongitude() {

    // Generate a sample longitude and return.
  }
};
```

---

connecting two classes. In code, realization can translate in different ways depending on the target programming language; however, the semantics remain the same. In the code context, an interface is the collection of public methods that define the services provided by class. In C++, interfaces are created using pure virtual methods as seen in Listing 2.8. As seen, the Gps class is made up of two pure virtual methods, which means that objects of the Gps class cannot be instantiated; the Gps class is typically referred to as an interface to define a common set of services, in this case, global positioning system (GPS) services.

Similar to all other relationships discussed so far, the realization relationship translates different in different languages. In C++, the realization relationship translates identical to the generalization relationship. As seen in Listing 2.9, the forward engineering

---

Listing 2.10: Java Code Generated for Interfaces

```java
interface Gps {

  // The interface method to obtain latitude information.
  public double getLatitude();

  // The interface method to obtain longitude information.
  public double getLongitude();
}
```

Listing 2.11: Java Code Generated for UML Realization Relationship

```java
class SimulatedGps implements Gps {

  // The interface method to obtain latitude information.
  public double getLatitude() {

    // Generate a sample latitude and return.
  }

  // The start interface method.
  public double getLongitude() {

    // Generate a sample longitude and return.
  }
}
```

---

of the `SimulatedGps` class results in inheritance with provided methods for both interface methods.

`Gps` services can be realized by different `Gps` classes differently; for example, one derived `Gps` class (e.g., `HardwareGps`) may realize the `Gps` interface by providing code that interfaces with specific hardware to obtain actual readings for latitude and longitude. Another derived `Gps` class (e.g., `SimulatedGps`) can realize the `Gps` interface by providing code that simulates latitude and longitude readings in case the `Gps` hardware is not available. By designing such framework (i.e., `Gps` interface, `HardwareGps`, and `SimulatedGps`) clients can create their designs relying on using the `Gps` interface; by relying on a well-defined interface, objects of type `HardwareGps` or `SimulatedGps` can be swapped without ever having to change the client code.

Interfaces and the realization relationship are so essential to object-oriented systems that modern languages include keywords to support this relationship. In Java, the forward engineering of the `Gps` interface translates to an interface, as seen in Listing 2.10.

The forward engineering of the realization relationship in Java results in a `class` that `implements` and interface. Listing 2.11 presents the forward engineering of the realization relationship for the `SimulatedGps` class in Java.

Skill Development 2.1: Modeling Structure with Class Diagrams

Using pencil and paper, create the class diagram that models the following relationships. Class B inherits from class A. Class B is directionally associated with class F and has a special whole–part relationship with class C, so that when B goes out of scope, so does C. Class B has another whole–part relationship with class D, which depends on interface E. When class B goes out of scope, D remains active as an object during run time. Both classes G and H realize the E interface. When done, replace the class names A, B, C, D, E, F, G, and H with names that represent types appropriate for these relationships. Discuss your results with your peers.

DEPLOYMENT DIAGRAMS

Deployment diagrams are structural diagrams used to model the physical realization of software systems. They provide the means for visualizing the environment in which software executes and how different entities communicate with each other to achieve the systems' functions. Deployment diagrams provide a static holistic view of the software system, from the deployment perspective, by providing avenues for modeling and specification of the physical nodes, software artifacts, and the interrelationship among them.

A node is a computational resource that host software artifacts for execution (UML 2.3 Superstructure 2010). In UML, nodes are named classifiers modeled as a cube. Nodes can be associated with other nodes to model the communication path between them; these communication paths can be enhanced with stereotypes, multiplicity, and other adornments to further specify their properties and constraints. For example, in Figure 2.3, communication paths are enhanced by specifying the communication protocol (e.g., Transmission Control Protocol/Internet Protocol [TCP/IP], Universal Serial Bus [USB], and ZigBee).

In addition, multiplicity is used to model the number of elements connected to other elements. As seen, there is a plurality of sensor nodes connected to the embedded client computer via the ZigBee wireless protocol. This deployment diagram also models the optional use of mobile devices in the system; that is, the embedded client computer may or may not have mobile devices interfacing to it. Nodes can also be modeled as hosts by including the components that execute in the node and their manifestation as artifacts.

Artifacts are used to model physical units of information that form part of the software system, such as binary executable files, configuration files, and scripts. Artifacts are modeled using the <<artifact>> keyword and can be related to nodes, components, and other artifacts using the dependency relationship, as seen in Figure 2.3. Artifacts that collaborate with other artifacts can be modeled using the dependency relationship. To model the deployment relationship, artifacts are connected to nodes using the dependency relationship with the <<deploy>> stereotype. When connected this way, it is said that the artifact is deployed on the node connected to the other end of the dependency relationship. When necessary, the

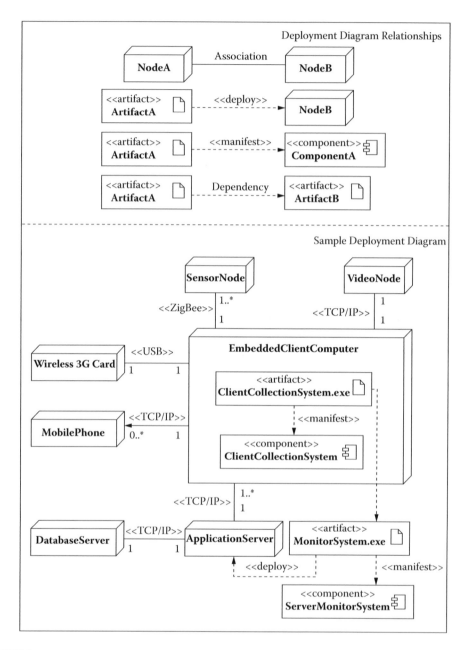

FIGURE 2.3
Overview of UML deployment diagram.

manifestation of components (designed in component diagrams) on a target node can be modeled using the dependency relationship from the artifact to the component with the <<manifest>> stereotype.

Together, the concepts of nodes, relationships, and artifacts can be used to create deployment diagrams that include the physical nodes where software is deployed, communication paths between nodes, software artifacts executing on nodes, and the manifestation of software components within the software artifacts, as seen in Figure 2.3.

TABLE 2.7

UML 2.3 Behavioral Diagrams

Diagram	Description
Use case diagram	Used to capture, specify, and visualize required system behavior (i.e., requirements)
Sequence diagram	Used to capture, specify, and visualize system interactions with emphasis on the time-order sequence of messages exchanged
Communication diagram	Used to capture, specify, and visualize system interactions with emphasis on the structural order of entities participating in the message exchange
State machine diagram	Used to capture, specify, and visualize system behavior as a set of discrete states and the transitions between them
Activity diagram	Used to capture, specify, and visualize system behavior; provide mechanisms for modeling that includes conditional statements, repetition, concurrency, and parallel execution and thus can be used at many different levels of abstraction, from modeling business work flows to code

BEHAVIORAL MODELING

Structural modeling is essential to evaluate, characterize, and visualize the structural design of software systems from various perspectives. These static diagrams provide good avenues for analyzing properties that are the direct result of structural designs, such as their ability to meet functional requirements, reusability, and maintainability; however, they are not adequate for modeling the inherent complexities present in the behavioral aspects of software systems. For this reason, behavioral diagrams are necessary to models and specify the dynamic aspects and evaluate the quality attributes related to the system behavior. To this end, UML provides several diagrams that can be used to model important behavioral aspects of software. These are presented in Table 2.7.

Table 2.7 does not present an exhaustive list of UML behavioral diagrams. However, these diagrams can be used to model almost any behavioral aspect of modern software systems, and their use is ubiquitous in practical development efforts. Therefore, their understanding and applicability must be well understood. Other diagrams, such as timing and interaction overview diagrams, are not covered here.

USE CASE DIAGRAMS

Use case diagrams are behavioral diagrams used to capture, specify, and visualize required system behavior. The main elements of use case diagrams are actors, use cases, and the relationships connecting them together. Actors are entities used to model users or other systems that interact with the system being modeled (i.e., the subject); that is, operators using the system, sensors providing information, and a client computer in a client–server system can all be modeled as actors. Use cases are entities used in use case diagrams to

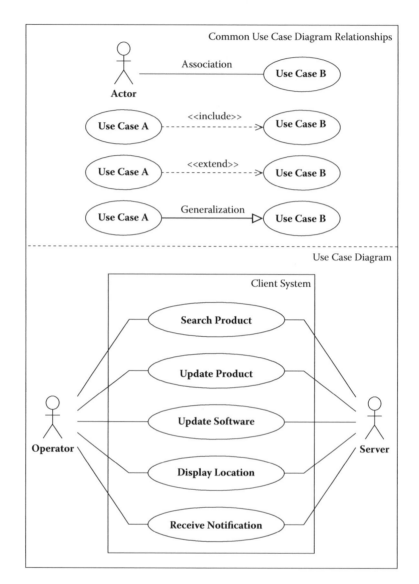

FIGURE 2.4
Sample UML use case diagram and common relationships.

specify the required behavior of a system. Therefore, they provide the means necessary to capture, model, and visualize the requirements of a system.

Use case modeling provides an avenue for presenting a holistic view of the system to be designed and increasing communication among stakeholders before more detailed approaches to design can begin. For example, Figure 2.4 presents a use case diagram for a client–server system. The system interacts with both an operator and server and is required to provide the operator with the capability for searching for a product, updating the product, displaying the location of the product, and receiving notifications from the server. In addition, the client system is required to check for software updates. Collectively, these use cases, together with the actors and relationships, capture the requirements of the system and provide a context for the development of the client system. In UML, use cases are modeled using a named ellipsis and actors as stick figures, as seen in Figure 2.4.

As seen, the association relationship is used to model the link between actors and use cases; however, other relationships, such as <<include>>, <<extend>>, and generalization, can be used to include, extend, and generalize, respectively, other use cases. In addition, a system boundary is used to delineate the boundaries of the client system within context of other relevant actors. Use case diagrams provide a valuable means for establishing a framework for eliciting requirements, identifying major system functions, and specifying the context of the subject being modeled.

Skill Development 2.2: Modeling Behavior with Use Cases

Consider what you think the five most important functions that your home personal computer system needs to provide. Using pencil and paper, create a use case diagram that depicts the personal computer system, its five major functions, and the interaction between you and the computing system. For one of the created use cases, create a list of detailed steps that you think the computer needs to do internally to achieve the specified behavior.

INTERACTION DIAGRAMS

Interaction diagrams exist at lower levels of abstraction than use case diagrams and can be used extensively during the complete life cycle of software projects. At the architectural (system) level, interaction diagrams can be used for modeling interactions among software components; during detailed design, they provide interaction modeling capabilities among objects at run time; and at the construction level they can be used to model collaborative algorithms that include conditional and repetition structures, such as loops. Interaction diagrams are popular because they provide avenues for modeling complex interactions among software units together with the messages exchanged and the type of the exchange. By modeling the interactions required to realize a particular system function, designers can determine if current structural diagrams are adequate to support the system; this gives designers the ability to model interactions for which the capability of the structural design to meet its functional and quality requirements may be in question. In these cases, interaction diagrams can serve as validation tool before construction can begin. In many situations, interaction diagrams can reveal many important issues related to the overall quality of the system (e.g., performance). Two types of interaction diagrams are

- Communication diagrams
- Sequence diagrams

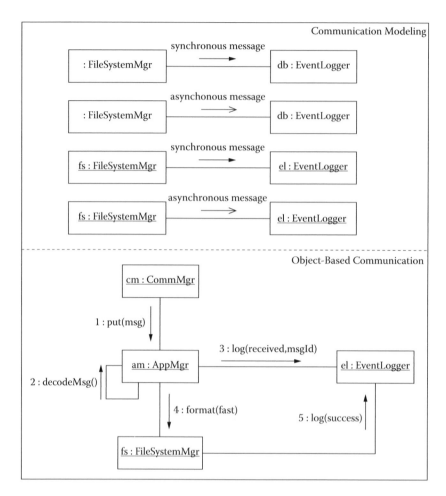

FIGURE 2.5
Sample UML communication diagram.

Communication Diagrams

Communication diagrams are behavioral diagram used to capture, specify, evaluate, and visualize system interactions with emphasis on the structural order of entities participating in the message exchange. When using communication diagrams, entities can be modeled as *objects* representing instances of classes or as *roles* representing prototypical instances of other entities, such as classes and components (Booch et al. 2005). Both objects and roles can be connected to model the exchange of messages using links or connectors, respectively. As seen in Figure 2.5, a role is modeled using a named box (similar to a class) without underlining the role's type. In addition, roles can be named or anonymous, as seen in Figure 2.5. On the other hand, objects are modeled using similar notation, but the name of the object is underlined. In many practical situations, designers are interested in modeling how roles interact with each other to model a system behavior and not on how individual objects interact. For these situations, roles provide the appropriate modeling entity. When using roles for modeling behavior, they can be connected using a solid *connector* line to represent a prototypical connection between roles. Similarly, when using objects, their connection is made using *links*, which represent an instance of an association (Booch et al. 2005). Connectors and links look exactly alike and differ only semantically.

To model the message exchanges in communication diagrams, messages in the form of arrows are used. Two common types of messages include synchronous and asynchronous messages. Synchronous messages—modeled using a solid arrowhead—are used to model interactions in which both sender and receiver work in lock-step to achieve an operation. Asynchronous messages—modeled using a stick arrow—model interactions that are carried out by receivers independently from the sender. That is, upon sending an asynchronous message, the sender continues working while the receiver carries out the message request. The main elements present in communication diagrams, together with sample object-based communication diagram design, are presented in Figure 2.5.

The communication diagram presented in Figure 2.5 models a system receiving a message to initiate a file system format. As seen, the "cm" object sends a message to the application manager object "am," which decodes the message, logs the receipt of the message by sending a message to the event logger object "el," and initiates a format by sending a message to the file system manager object "fs." Once finished formatting the file system the "fs" object logs an event. All messaging in the communication is done synchronously using links.

Sequence Diagrams

Sequence diagrams are behavioral diagrams used to capture, specify, and visualize system interactions with emphasis on the time-order sequence of messages exchanged. Sequence diagrams are closely related to communication diagrams. Therefore, many of the modeling techniques are the same; that is, sequence diagrams include objects, roles, synchronous, and asynchronous messages. Sequence diagrams put emphasis on the time order of messages by introducing a lifeline and activation bar. Lifelines are modeled with the object/role connected to a vertical dashed line that represents the lifetime of the object/role. Typically, objects/roles in a sequence diagram are aligned from left to right, depending on the order in which messages are sent. Once a message is sent, the activation bar is rendered on the object's lifeline to model the relative processing time that results from the message exchange. Asynchronous and synchronous messaging are modeled similar to communication diagrams, and return messages can be modeled using a dashed line with a stick arrow. Figure 2.6 presents an equivalent sequence diagram for the formatting operation modeled with a communication diagram in Figure 2.5.

Concurrency in Interaction Diagrams

In previous sections, the discussion on messaging in interaction diagrams eluded the topic of concurrency. When using the synchronous mode of communication, an implication is not made as to the presence of independent flows of execution; however, the same is not true for asynchronous communications. As explained before, the asynchronous mode of communication provides the ability to model independent flows of execution, since the

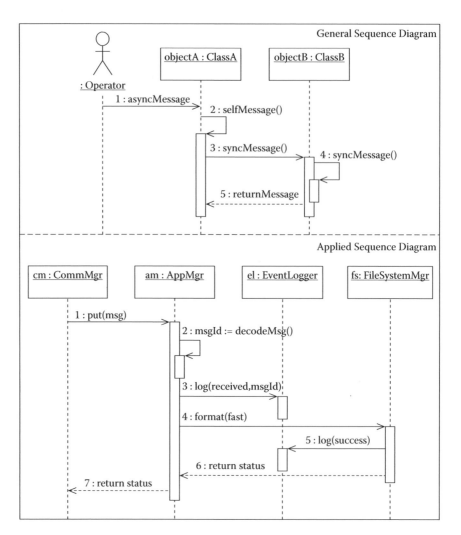

FIGURE 2.6
UML sequence diagram.

sender of an asynchronous message continues on executing while the receiver carries out the work requested. Typically, independent flows of executions are manifested as multiple processes or threads. When applications are multiprocessed or multithreaded, concurrency issues arise when they execute in parallel (or pseudo-parallel) with each other. Therefore, it is important to model concurrent design issues so that their impacts are well understood before construction begins.

Concurrent designs require designers to decompose applications into multiple processes or threads to meet performance (e.g., usability, throughput) requirements. Processes can execute concurrently with other processes, while threads can execute concurrently with other threads (within the same process). The importance of modeling concurrent designs up front is often overlooked in many design efforts; that is, too much concurrency can end up degrading the systems while insufficient concurrency results in decreased systems throughput (Booch et al. 2005). Developing these systems requires skills typically acquired through

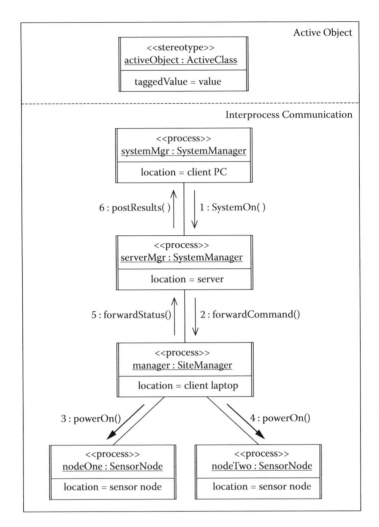

FIGURE 2.7
Sample UML interprocess communication.

experience; therefore, novice designers are encouraged to create concurrency models and when possible to have more experienced personnel review them.

UML provides the necessary mechanisms to model independent flows of controls, such as processes or threads, using the concept of an *active object* within sequence and communication diagrams. Active objects are represented in UML as an instance of an active class with certain concurrency semantics to aid in the synchronization of interactions among independent flows (Booch et al. 2005). Models that include active objects can be used to reason about quality issues that deal with concurrency, communication, and synchronization. An example of a concurrent system is presented in Figure 2.7 using a communication diagram.

In this diagram, objects are modeled as active objects by adding double lines to the left and right side of the object's rectangle. This denotes independent flows of execution and ability to initiate control activity. The model is also enhanced by using the location *tagged value* to specify the location of the running processes.

The model in Figure 2.7 relies on active objects, asynchronous and synchronous messages, to properly model the interprocess operations in a multiprocess distributed system. As seen, the system is composed of five processes executing in different locations, namely, the client PC, server, client laptop, and embedded sensor nodes. The model uses asynchronous messages, from the client PC to the server and from the server to the client laptop, to communicate to initiate a power on sequence of the embedded sensor nodes. This makes sense because of the nature of a distributed system. Remember that asynchronous messages allow the sender to continue operation (and not block) waiting for the message response. In this case, the client PC will send a *systemOn* message to the distributed system and continue serving operators without waiting for a response to come back. Communication between server and client laptop is done in a similar fashion; however, communication between the client laptop and embedded sensor nodes occurs in synchronous fashion. That is, once a *systemOn* message is received, the client laptop will synchronously power up sensor node one; control returns back once the power up operation is complete, at which point it can initiate the power on message to sensor node two. When both sensor nodes are up, status is returned asynchronously from the site manager to the system manager.

Concurrent designs that work on the same data are tougher to manage, since they can lead to errors that are hard to find during construction. When this happens, access to shared sections of data needs to be designed properly and carefully to ensure the integrity of the data. To this end, UML provides synchronization properties that can be used to constrain the model so that it supports concurrency by controlling the way multiple flows of execution access critical sections of code. These are presented in Table 2.8.

The *Sequential* synchronization property specifies that no concurrency management mechanism is associated with an operation. With sequential access, concurrency conflicts may occur, so clients that rely on the operation need to coordinate so that only one invocation occurs at any given point. The *Guarded* property specifies that the operation can be invoked from multiple independent flows simultaneously, but only one flow of execution is allowed to commence; other independent flows are blocked until the execution of currently executing operation, under the currently executing thread, is complete. When using the *Guarded* synchronization property, it is the responsibility of the designer to ensure that concurrency issues, such as starvation and deadlocks, do not occur. Finally,

TABLE 2.8

UML Synchronization Properties

Synchronization	Description
Sequential	No concurrency management mechanism are associated with the operation.
Guarded	Concurrency management mechanisms are in place so that operations can be invoked from multiple independent flows simultaneously; each call waits for the previous one to finish execution.
Concurrent	Multiple invocations may occur simultaneously, and all of them may proceed concurrently.

the *Concurrent* synchronization property specifies that multiple invocations may occur simultaneously and that all of them may proceed concurrently. *Concurrent* synchronization is achieved in languages with built-in support for concurrency, such as Java with the use of the `synchronized` property. All three of these properties can be modeled as *constraints* to fully specify the behavior of concurrent systems.

CHAPTER SUMMARY

UML is a visual language with an extensive set of features appropriate for designing software systems across a broad set of application domains. The current version of UML (2.3) provides 14 diagrams for structural and behavioral modeling of software systems. These diagrams support software design during architectural, detailed design, and construction design activities. Since UML has been designed with flexibility in mind, it is important to understand how the its fundamental building blocks (i.e., classifiers, relationships, and enhancing features) can be used to model systems of disparate capabilities and domains. While some UML diagrams provide modeling concepts that are too abstract for direct translation to code, others are not. Therefore, it is essential that designers understand how these models translate to code and how they are used to model quality attributes. By providing a unified communication language for software design, UML is appropriate and efficient for capturing and conveying information that can be evaluated by many stakeholders including customers and software engineers alike, resulting in a more efficient design process.

REVIEW QUESTIONS

1. What is UML, and why is it important in software design?
2. What are the two main classifications for UML diagrams, and how do these differ from one another?
3. List and explain two important reasons for software designers to study UML.
4. In UML context, what are classifiers? Provide examples of classifiers.
5. What are the main relationships used in UML diagrams? Provide examples of each.
6. List and explain the main mechanisms for extending UML.
7. What is structural modeling?
8. Compare and contrasts the following:
   a. Component diagram
   b. Class diagram
   c. Deployment diagram

9. Explain the following relationships, and show how they are modeled in component diagrams:
    a. Provided and required interfaces
    b. Assembly connector
    c. Delegates
10. What is a UML artifact? How are artifacts different from components?
11. List and explain the main compartments of UML class.
12. What are the possible types of visibility that can be used in items of class diagrams? Explain.
13. In a class diagram, what is the difference between the following relationships:
    a. Generalization vs. realization
    b. Aggregation vs. object composition
    c. Dependency vs. association
14. How can the manifestation of software components in a deployed environment be modeled in UML? Explain.
15. In a UML deployment diagram, what is a node?
16. Compare and contrasts the following:
    a. Use case diagram
    b. Sequence diagram
    c. Communication diagram
17. What is the difference between synchronous and asynchronous messages?
18. Explain how concurrency issues can be addressed using UML.
19. Compare and contrasts the following:
    a. Sequential synchronization
    b. Guarded synchronization
    c. Concurrent synchronization

CHAPTER EXERCISES

1. Consider the software design of a car in a racing game. Use a software modeling tool to identify the major components of the car, define the component's interfaces, and connect all components the way you think provides the best design for developing the car. Create a list of design factors that influenced the final car's design and the benefits provided by your approach. When done, ask a peer to do the same and compare your approach and final results.

2. Use the component design created in Exercise 1 to design the classes required to support the component's interfaces and provided services. Create a list of design factors that influenced the final car's design and the benefits provided by your approach. When done, ask a peer to do the same and compare your approach and final results.

3. Create a UML class diagram containing the following information.

Class Name		Operations			Attributes			Relationships
Name	*Type*	*Return*	*Name*	*Visibility*	*Return*	*Name*	*Visibility*	Inherits from ClassZ and uses aggregation with ClassT
ClassA	Class	void	operation1	public	char*	x	private	
		int	operation2	private	bool	y	protected	
ClassB	Interface	void	operation3	public				Depends on ClassA and is associated with ClassO using a directional association
		void	operation4	public		None		
ClassC	Class		none			None		Realizes ClassB and is composed of ClassA

4. Matt and Alice are starting a bed-and-breakfast in a small Virginia town. They will have three bedrooms for guests. They want a system to manage the reservations and to monitor expenses and profits. When a potential customer calls for a reservation, they will check the calendar, and if there is a vacancy they will enter the customer name, address, phone number, dates, agreed upon price, credit card number, and room number. To facilitate reservations, the system needs to print weekly schedules, including available rooms, their locations, price, and special rates. Reservations must be guaranteed by one day's payment. Reservations will be held without guarantee for an agreed upon time. If not guaranteed by that date, the reservation will be dropped. Create a UML use case diagram using a system boundary for this system.

REFERENCES

Booch, Grady, Robert A. Maksimchuk, Michael W. Engle, Bobbi J. Young, Jim Conallen, and Kelli A. Houston. *Object-Oriented Analysis and Design with Applications.* Upper Saddle River, NJ: Addison-Wesley Professional, 2007.

Booch, Grady, James Rumbaugh, and Ivar Jacobson. *The Unified Modeling Language User Guide.* Santa Clara, CA: Addison-Wesley, 2005.

Qian, Kai, Xiang Fu, Lixin Tao, Chong-Wei Xu, and Jorge L. Diaz-Herrera. *Software Architecture and Design Illuminated.* Sudbury, MA: Jones & Barlett, 2009.

"UML 2.3 Superstructure." Vers. 2.3. Object Management Group. May 2010. Available from: http://www.omg.org.

3

Principles of Software Architecture

CHAPTER OBJECTIVES

- Understand the role of software architecture within the software design phase
- Become familiar with architectural tasks and problem solving during architecture
- Understand the importance and role of architectural views in software architecture
- Become familiar with the software architecture process
- Become familiar with the concept of architecture evaluation

---

CONCEPTUAL OVERVIEW

The software architecture activity corresponds to a macrodesign approach for transforming software requirements into design elements that support quality and functions of software systems. During software architecture, perspectives appropriate for modeling particular concerns are identified and design elements created to address those concerns. These design elements present systems from different perspectives, thus providing stakeholders, with different background and expertise, the means to evaluate the appropriateness of architectural decisions for supporting the construction of the desired system. The software architecture activity places emphasis on systems' quality and therefore provides the earliest means for ensuring that identified quality goals are evaluated and incorporated into the design before moving on to more detailed design and construction work. The software architecture lays the foundation for all subsequent work in the development process and serves as an important communication, reasoning, and analysis tool for developing and maintaining software systems.

WHAT IS SOFTWARE ARCHITECTURE?

In a broad context, software architecture refers to both the process and design products required to systematically build software systems that meet their intended functions and quality. Of course, such broad definition of software architecture leaves out many of the details that make architecture essential in designing today's complex software systems. To understand the meaning and importance of software architecture, it helps to examine how other engineering disciplines employ architectural designs to build complex systems with demanding functional and quality requirements. Consider the role of architecture in civil engineering, where designing and building structures such as houses, bridges, and high-rises is a nontrivial task. In these cases, architectural designs are used to specify the overall appearance of physical structures. When examined closer, it becomes evident that this broad definition is insufficient to describe to actual role of architecture in the process of building these systems, which involve far more than structural appearance. Architectural designs must also specify a variety of quality properties that make structures functional, safe, and economical. This requires architects to incorporate design alternatives that consider a wide variety of factors (e.g., social, aesthetic, and cost) supporting the needs of stakeholders, including the people who use these physical structures.

In software engineering, architects work to create the overall design elements appropriate for supporting efficient refinement and construction of software systems. However, as in the previous discussion, architectural designs in software engineering involve far more than structural composition. They must also address numerous quality properties (e.g., performance, usability, and maintainability) that combine together to produce software systems that meet the quality expected by their stakeholders. To address these numerous concerns, software architects create different models of the software system, each addressing the system design from different perspectives. From the structural, logical perspective, the software architecture should address the needs of downstream designers and developers by decomposing the software (in an efficient manner) and defining the major components of the system, identifying their interfaces and interrelationships, and providing support for both functional and quality attributes of the system. From the configuration management perspective, the architecture should provide information about the hierarchy of files in the file system, their interrelationships, and the process for building one or more versions of the software system. From a systems engineering perspective, the architecture provides information about the physical deployment of the system, including the location of distributed subsystems, their interfaces and interrelationship, and specification of communication protocols between them. Other architectural perspectives exist for addressing various concerns that stakeholders may have and should be considered and designed for during the software architecture activity. Since the nature of stakeholders varies greatly in software systems, the perspective used to model the structure and behavior of software systems varies as well. Therefore, it is almost never the case that a single design element, from a single perspective, can represent the software architecture, especially for large-scale software intensive systems. In these cases, the collection of design elements and their detailed descriptions help form the software architecture. Formally, software architecture is defined as

> The foundational software design activity that evaluates and translates software requirements (both functional and non-functional) into a collection of design elements that specify structural and behavioral aspects of the major components of the system, together with their provided quality, and interrelationships required to support the detailed design and construction of software systems; and the product resulting from such activity.

From this definition, a few things are of interest and need further explanation. First, as *foundational design*, software architecture provides the groundwork essential for meeting functional and nonfunctional requirements. The architectural design foundation provides the necessary structure for achieving quality throughout subsequent phases of the software engineering life cycle. This suggests that architecture is not an optional design activity or an activity performed as a means of documenting software systems long after they are implemented. Although deriving and documenting a system's software architecture from its implementation in legacy systems provides an excellent avenue for capturing and transferring knowledge about the system's design, new development efforts should approach software architecture as a forward engineering activity that leads to the implementation of systems and not as a reverse engineering mechanism for documentation. Second, software architecture provides abstractions for software *requirements* in the design domain, so that design elements, components, and alternatives all derive from requirements. This suggests that as part of the architectural effort architects must be proficient in activities related to requirements engineering. Third, by specifying that architecture is a *collection of design elements*, it is implied that software architectures are composed of multiple structures and that no one structure can fully describe the software architecture (Bass, Clements, and Kazman 2003). Fourth, as a design activity that deals with the *major system components*, it is suggested that software architecture works at a distinct level of abstraction that differs from other forms of design, such as detailed design. This means that architectural work focuses on the major components—which become the units of system composition—and the properties and services that these components exhibit and provide to other components. This clearly delineates architectural efforts from other detailed design efforts. Fifth, a sometimes overlooked or underappreciated piece of the software architecture definition is its *support for detailed design and construction*. Even though architects do not need to be proficient with particular programming languages, they benefit greatly from having proficiency with general programming design concepts, so that their architectural designs provide sufficient avenues for efficient construction of the system. Finally, software architecture *supports*—as opposed to ensures—the achievement of quality goals; that is, software architecture cannot single-handedly provide the work necessary for achieving the desired quality properties of the system. Since work performed during subsequent activities and phases significantly shapes the system's quality, software architecture can play only the initial (indispensable) role of establishing the design quality framework for the rest of the development process.

WHY STUDY SOFTWARE ARCHITECTURE?

Architectural designs identify the necessary elements—and attributes of those elements—that support detailed design and construction efforts. These design elements are presented in context for examining how well the system as a whole collaborates to meet its intended functions. In many cases, this includes the modeling of other nonsoftware elements (e.g., physical nodes) that play a key role in assessing the system's capabilities for achieving a desired quality goal. An understanding of architectural modeling capabilities is essential in problem solving, since they provide the means to overcome *functional fixedness* early on in the development process by allowing designers to model and evaluate the same problem from different perspectives. Benefits from studying software architecture are also evident in numerous aspects of both product development and management. From the product development perspective, studying software architecture is important for creating an efficient bridge between the software requirements phase and the detailed design phase. Having extended knowledge of software architecture provides architects with a wider pool of design alternatives, some of which have been proven successful in previously developed and similar systems. In these cases, architects can reuse structural design elements and interconnections and their responsibilities and can gain insight into their quality properties, all based on previously used architectures. This provides quick insight into the system's or individual component's ability to meet quality expectations. Besides aiding in product development activities, studying software architecture also enhances project managers' activities because it helps dictate units of planning, scheduling, and budget; it helps establish inter-team communication channels, configuration control, and file system organization; and it helps manage the integration, test, and maintenance efforts (Bass et al. 2003).

KEY TASKS IN ARCHITECTURAL DESIGN

Defining the structure of software systems requires consideration of many project-specific aspects and how those aspects relate to the organization's goals. Therefore, examining the business impact of architectural decisions in the organization is a major task of software architects (Bass et al. 2003). This requires a holistic approach that considers all factors that help shape the system in an efficient manner. Some of the key tasks that need to be performed during the software architectural design effort include

- Identifying stakeholders concerns
- Identifying appropriate architectural views
- Identifying architectural styles and patterns
- Identifying influences of architectural decisions in organization
- Identifying the system's major components and interfaces
- Evaluating and validating the architecture
- Establish policies for ensuring architectural design synchronicity

Identifying Stakeholders' Concerns

Stakeholders are persons, groups, or organizations that have a direct or indirect stake in the system. They include systems engineers, software engineers, hardware engineers, project management, customers and their representatives, testing teams, quality assurance teams, and members of the configuration management team. The list of stakeholders and the ability to manage them from an architectural design's perspective varies in magnitude and complexity per project. An important job of the software architect is to ensure that the software to be developed addresses stakeholders' concerns. Stakeholders' concerns provide high-level information about desired characteristics of the software system. Therefore, a key factor in the architectural design activity is identifying and understanding the different ways stakeholders influence the system and how they interact with each other. These concerns need to be elicited and captured before any design effort can begin. Stakeholders' concerns (e.g., requirements) are the driving force behind architectural decisions and can influence both product and processes, may be functional or quality in nature, and may have different levels of abstraction. During project inception, stakeholders' concerns are captured and specified in a clear and consistent manner to define the expected functions and quality of the software system. An essential characteristic of the specification of concerns is their ability to provide verifiable specifications, which are used as evaluation criteria for all architectural design activities. Therefore, when identifying stakeholders' concerns, additional effort is required so that they are understandable, achievable, and consistent with all other identified concerns from all other stakeholders.

Identifying Appropriate Architectural Views

Software architects work hard to create designs that achieve all functional and quality features expected from stakeholders. In complex software systems, there can be a multitude of stakeholders with myriad backgrounds, all shaping the way the system development is approached based on their perception of what the final product should be. Different perceptions significantly influence the way these stakeholders evaluate the system's design and determine the appropriateness of the design to meet their goals. For this reason, architectural designs must support different architectural views used to evaluate the design from a particular stakeholder's perspective. By providing different architectural views of the system, communication among stakeholders is enhanced during new or ongoing development or during a system's maintenance phase. These architectural views provide designers the ability to address concerns using a perspective and design elements well suited for analyzing and evaluating the particular problem. By using appropriate views, architectural design can be placed in context to yield better modeling and evaluation capabilities. Therefore, the result of any architectural effort must contain design solutions that address one or more viewpoints specific to the problem at hand.

Identifying Architectural Styles and Patterns

The concepts of architectural styles and patterns are fundamental to the efficient creation of software architectures. Architectural styles and patterns provide an overall strategy for designing a family of software systems. They provide generic, reusable architectural solutions, documented in a way that is easily understood and applied to new problems requiring similar architectural features. For this reason, identifying architectural styles and patterns is one of the first decisions that software architects make. This decision has long-lasting effects on all subsequent design and construction efforts. Decisions based on architectural styles and patterns benefit from years of documented experience that highlight the solution approach to given problems, from the advantages of these approaches, and from gaining understanding of the consequences of designing the system with a particular style. Today, numerous architectural styles and patterns have been documented, so software architects need to identify and determine the appropriateness, benefits, and consequences of choosing a particular style or pattern for their system's design.

Identifying System Interfaces

Interface identification and definition compose another essential task of the software architecture activity. Interfaces are defined for components residing within single physical nodes within a single process space, for components residing within a single node in different process spaces, or for components residing in separate processes distributed across a network. Interface definition may include the definition of stable interfaces such as abstract classes in object-oriented environments. When using a structured design approach, identifying internal interfaces can result in determining the set of services required by each architectural component to collaborate with all other architectural components. These identify the major access points for architectural components together with the communication rules that must be followed during the detailed design activity. Having well-defined interfaces allows the software system to evolve gracefully with time when existing capabilities are modified or new capabilities are added to the system. Defining the interfaces between components that reside in different nodes may include specifying messaging structures, protocols, and other communication mechanisms for allowing communication across distributed components. These can include identification of physical medium, data-link protocols, network and transport protocols, messaging specification, and application-level protocols. Identification of external interfaces can significantly impact a system's ability to support its identifying quality properties.

Identifying Impact of Architectural Decisions in Organization

During the architectural design activity, software architects are required to make decisions that support the efficient development of the software system within bounds placed by the organization mission and goals. These restrictions are company-specific and in many cases appear outside the scope of architects' work; nonetheless, these restrictions need to be considered and are typically manifested in software architectures. For example, consider the case of software system decomposition. From a pure logical standpoint, decomposition is made to define units of manageable complexity that can be evaluated, built, and maintained. These criteria are typically used as basis for system decomposition; however, in practical applications, other key organizational issues need to be addressed to determine the right granularity of components when decomposing a system. When approached this way, architectural decisions are driven not only by common design principles discussed in Chapter 1 but also by other organizational and project-specific factors, such as stakeholders' concerns, resource availability, resource location, schedule, and budget. These factors drive architectural decisions to create design solutions that are appropriate for meeting both product and organizational requirements, therefore bridging the gap between the business organization and its technical products.

Impact on Customer Base

Decisions made during the architectural activity affect not only subsequent activities in the software life cycle but also stakeholders, especially customers. When faced with competing alternatives, each benefiting one customer more than others, architects have to find ways to make decisions that accommodate each customer and minimize overall customer dissatisfaction. In these cases, software architects must be skilled at predicting, verifying, and validating the effects of their design decisions. This issue is further complicated by the presence of quality requirements. The problem with quality attributes is that they typically contradict each other. This property of quality attributes is described in detail by Gorton (2011, p. 37):

> Quality attributes are not orthogonal. They interact in subtle ways, meaning a design that satisfies one quality attribute requirement may have a detrimental effect on another. For example, a highly secure system may be difficult or impossible to integrate in an open environment.

Software architects are constantly faced with the challenging task of determining the effects of individual design alternatives, identifying conflicting design solutions, negotiating systems' features among stakeholders, and verifying and documenting the final architectural solution, all of which impact the customer base.

Impact on Budget and Schedule

Architectural designs provide project management with more concrete representations of the effort required to build the software system. Specifically, they provide the best source of information for creating or reevaluating schedules and cost so that they reflect realistic and achievable milestones. Once schedule and budget are established, other attributes of the project can be fine-tuned to meet the established goals. For example, architectural designs can highlight inadequacy in resources required for completing the system on time and within budget. In these cases, architectural designs are used as concrete justification for requesting more resources early on in the project life cycle. In cases where adding resources is infeasible, architectural designs can help justify reevaluation of the strategy, which requires decision making in all aspects of the project, such as schedule, budget, or make versus buy decisions. These adjustments based on architectural designs impact the development organization's budget and schedule and are necessary to manage risks, to maintain customer satisfaction, and to ensure the project's success.

Impact from Resource Availability

The previous section introduced human resource availability as an impacting factor in the development project. However, architectural decisions are also affected by other different forms of resource availability. Resource availability, such as employees, software, and hardware, can all prompt adjustments to the architecture. Architectural designs that take into account human resources can maximize employee efficiency throughout the detailed design and construction phase. By taking into account employee availability, location, and team composition, work can be compartmentalized and developed in parallel. Employees that are distributed across different sites can prompt the creation of components with well-defined interfaces that can be developed independently and integrated into the system with minimal effort. Hardware availability can also prompt adjustment in the software architecture. In cases where hardware availability is essential to the development and test of software, the architecture may be adjusted to provide simulation components that can be used to move the development effort forward in case hardware is unavailable. In these cases, construction and test can continue until the hardware becomes available. At any point, the simulation component can be swapped easily for the real hardware component without changes to the overall architecture or software. The same approach can be employed for other software resources that are essential to the development of the system.

Identifying the System's Major Components and Interfaces

A major task performed during the software architecture activity involves decomposing systems into manageable component units. In doing so, it is important to identify the interfaces that these components use to collaborate with each other. Components and interfaces are identified during system decomposition; however, the nature of these significant elements varies according to the perspective used for system decomposition. In the broad context of system decomposition, identifying the major components and interfaces may involve, for example, logical components, physical nodes, files, or directories, and physical or logical interfaces required for these components to interoperate with each other. Examples of identifying logical and physical components and their interfaces are presented in Chapter 4.

Evaluating and Validating the Architecture

Consider designing a large-scale, secure, high-performing, distributed system composed of multiple nodes, each with usable interfaces, all while emphasizing the system's testability and maintainability. In addition, the system needs to be built using a joint approach among three organizations in separate geographical locations. For such development efforts, an unsuitable architecture is a recipe for disaster. Therefore, software architecture evaluation and validation are essential tasks of the software architecture activity. In most cases, failure to evaluate and validate the architecture significantly impacts the effort and cost incurred to develop the system. Typically, defects found during earlier stages of the development life cycle (e.g., architecture) take much less effort to correct than if found at later stages, such as during the testing phase (Clements, Kazman, and Klein 2001). For this reason, it is essential to evaluate and validate the suitability of the architecture to meet its intended purpose before attempting to construct the system. Evaluation and validation can focus on components, subsystems, or the entire system, depending on how the architecture is structured and the requirements placed on the system. In all of these cases, evaluation and validation ensure that architectural components and the architecture itself are sufficiently complete to support the expected services and quality of those services.

Introducing Policies for Design Synchronicity

A most often overlooked issue in software design efforts is the concept of design synchronicity. Design synchronicity is a measurement of the degree of how well the software system's implementation reflects its software architecture and detailed design. In many cases, design synchronicity reflects the quality of the software process in place; in others, it reflects the organization's capability for monitoring and controlling processes throughout. The software architecture establishes the foundation required for subsequent design and construction work to meet the system requirements (including quality requirements). Therefore, unmanaged deviations from the software architecture during detailed design and construction can reshape the properties of the system and affect its overall capability to meet requirements. For any software architecture effort to result in successful implementation of a system, all subsequent phases and activities (i.e., detailed design and construction) must be synchronized with the software architecture. Therefore, designers and programmers need to work closely and communicate to ensure that the detailed design and software implementation are consistent with architectural decisions. In addition, project managers need to set processes in place to support design synchronicity throughout the software development life cycle, which is difficult for large-scale multiyear efforts or for projects entering the maintenance phase.

Skill Development 3.1: Key Tasks in Architectural Design

A building architect is hired to design an indoor sports complex with capacity of 3,000 people. The building will be used to host sports, concerts, and other major activities. The initial design consists of a futuristic building with single door for both entrance and exit. The building's design is technically sound and can even withstand major natural disasters common to the area. Create an exhaustive list of stakeholders, and identify the concerns they may have and how they can be addressed in the proposed building's architectural design. Do any of the identified key tasks of software architecture apply to this problem? Explain.

PROBLEM SOLVING IN SOFTWARE ARCHITECTURE

In Chapter 1, a generic model for problem solving was introduced based on inputs, constraints, and outputs, where each input problem is interpreted and carefully formulated, is evaluated against its external constraints, and is ultimately processed, evaluated, and documented. Different instances of this problem-solving model can be created for particular activities in the design process, such as the software architecture activity. During software architecture, the problem-solving landscape can be characterized by a particular set of inputs, constraints, and outputs common to architectural problems encountered during the design effort. These properties can be consistently defined for most architectural design efforts; therefore, it becomes essential for software architects to understand the types of inputs, constraints, and outputs expected during architectural problem solving. Using the holistic problem-solving approach presented in Chapter 1, the generic problem-solving model is modified to account for common properties present during the software architecture activity and is presented in Figure 3.1.

As seen in the figure, typical inputs present during the software architecture activity include requirements, system goals, and scenarios. These are interpreted and carefully formulated as part of the requirements engineering (RE) phase; however, it is not uncommon for software architects to perform RE activities, since requirements may not be well understood or defined or new requirements may be created as knowledge of the system is acquired throughout the design phase. These inputs are interpreted and evaluated against the architectural and project constraints, are transformed through collaborative work into architectural design products, and are evaluated and documented—typically as part of the software design document—as architectural design elements for future activities or phases in the development life cycle.

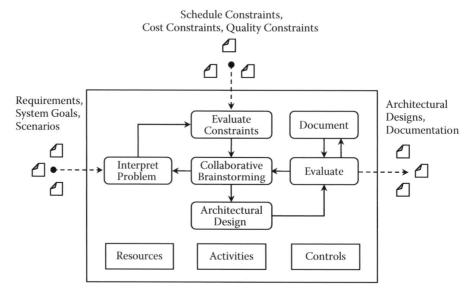

FIGURE 3.1
Holistic architectural problem-solving model.

Inputs

The most typical inputs encountered in problem solving during the software architecture activity are requirements and system goals, which both can be represented using scenarios. These inputs are elicited from stakeholders and provide the driving forces behind all problems and solutions devised during the architectural design activity. Requirement inputs must have certain characteristics so that they can be well understood by designers. Bad or misunderstood requirements lead to problems that are hard to solve or solved incorrectly. In some cases, requirement input can be incomplete, misleading, or inconsistent; in others, they may specify unverifiable or unachievable capabilities, which makes problem solving difficult or impossible at times. In these cases, requirement input results in ill-defined or wicked problems, which are hard to solve. On the other hand, system goals, which establish a high-level desired capability, need to be transformed (when possible) into requirement form so that they are appropriate for problem solving. Before any problem solving can occur during architecture, issues with requirements, system goals, and scenarios need to be resolved so that the proper problem interpretation and formulation can be made. Therefore, careful attention needs to be placed when interpreting inputs so that their correct solution can be integrated into the design and evaluated and validated appropriately. These tasks belong mostly to the requirements phase; however, in many cases it is common for software architects to iterate back and forth from requirements to design.

Constraints

Whereas inputs define the problems that need solutions during the architectural design activity, constrains specify bounds identified for their proposed solutions. At the architectural design level, typical constraints include schedule, budget, and process constraints. Besides constraints derived from nonfunctional requirements, other constraints include specific platform constraints (e.g., embedded, mobile, web), constraints from existing and reused architectures, constraints on new technology (e.g., cloud-based solutions), incorporating commercial of-the-shelf (COTS) products, and numerous other constraints placed on both product and processes. During architectural problem solving, architects must be quick to learn technology aspects of product constraints and also must have a keen sense of project management aspects to account for both schedule and budget constraints when decomposing the major software components of the architectural design. Other characteristics of the software project may give rise to constraints placed on the architectural design process. For example, process constraints may dictate the type of architectural designs required, the views supported by the architecture, and other supporting activities required to meet constraints placed on the architectural design process.

Outputs

Problem solving during architectural design should lead to further understanding of the major structure and behavior of software systems. Therefore, outputs consist of design elements and descriptions that differ from other forms of design, such as detailed design. Outputs during the architecture activity are in the form of black-box solutions, which require refinement in subsequent design work. In many cases it is difficult to delineate between where an architectural design solution ends and its respective detailed design solution begins. From the logical perspective, architectural solutions need to account for the necessary components and interfaces required to achieve functional requirements and to support its quality requirements. Once architectural solutions can account for these criteria, details of implementation can be deferred to detailed designs.

The output of problem solving during the architectural design activity is essential to producing a high-quality software system. Problem solutions during software architecture need to be evaluated and documented accordingly so that they can be used in future design and construction work. The documentation format varies from project to project and from organization to organization. Typically, solutions found during the architectural design activity are documented in the form of diagrams, documents, or a combination of the two. They can contain analysis and documentation for major design decisions, the concerns and stakeholders related to the problem, design trade-offs, identified conflicting goals, prioritization schemes, design synchronization plans, and a mapping of requirements to the architectural solution. This information can be incorporated into an official architectural design document that is maintained independently or incorporated into the official software design document, which is completed, reviewed, and approved after completion of the design phase. Regardless of the documentation format, solutions to problems during the architectural design activity must be understandable, complete, and sufficient to support the detailed design phase.

SOFTWARE ARCHITECTURE PROCESS

The architectural design activity involves many problems that need to be solved before the software architecture is created and the development effort can move forward. Each problem solved during architecture helps address a particular concern and has an associated set of inputs (e.g., requirements), constraints, and desired output. Outputs of the architectural problem-solving process produce design elements of the software architecture, and the collective set of elements is combined to form the software architecture. Therefore, problem solving during architecture forms part of a broader process for creating software architectures. On a larger scale, the process for creating software architecture can be executed using the following tasks:

- Understand and evaluate requirements
- Design the architecture
- Evaluate the architecture
- Document the architecture
- Monitor and control implementation

UNDERSTAND AND EVALUATE REQUIREMENTS

Software architects spend a great deal of time working with software requirements. Even after requirements are specified, software architects find themselves going back and forth between requirements and design to clarify them, correct them, or completely revise them. In some cases, software architects are completely immersed in the requirements process, playing a key role in specifying the requirements of the system. For this reason, software architects need to understand RE, the discipline within software engineering that is concerned with the systematic approach to requirements specification, mainly through the following activities (Abran, Moore, Bourque, and Dupuis 2005):

- Elicitation
- Analysis
- Specification
- Validation

Together, these activities are performed to express the needs and constraints placed on the software system, which provides the foundation for all architectural and subsequent design and construction work. Understanding RE and how the fundamental activities relate to designing software architectures provides architects with a different dimension for designing successful systems by filling gaps or making appropriate corrections to the software specification before committing to a particular design solution.

Elicitation

Elicitation is the requirement activity that deals with identifying stakeholders, with uncovering what the customer needs and wants, and with determining the (often overlooked) nonfunctional requirements (Laplante 2009). Elicitation begins by identifying all *sources* of information that can be used to generate requirements. Sources of information vary from project to project and can provide bias information to shape the system in a way that addresses their particular needs. Sources of information also come from a variety of backgrounds; therefore, the use of *techniques* that are effective in extracting important information from a variety of sources with different expertise and background is essential.

Requirement Sources

Software requirements originate from many different sources. In some cases, requirements may originate from one source with an overall strategy and consistent vision for the system, which makes analyzing, specifying, and validating requirements more manageable. In most large-scale software efforts, requirements originate from many different sources with similar but inconsistent visions for the system. In these cases, identifying and managing these sources becomes a nontrivial task that requires additional time and effort. Some of the most common sources of requirements include (Abran et al. 2005):

- Stakeholders
- Goals
- Domain knowledge
- Operational and organizational environment

Multiple stakeholders view the system differently and provide different input and constraints for the system. Having an increased number of stakeholders causes almost every aspect of requirements elicitation to be more complex. Particularly, having a greater number of stakeholders increases the goals for the system. System goals can specify desirable aspects of the business, process, or product and are typically referred to as quality attributes. When goals are identified, they must be evaluated and (if possible) transformed into nonfunctional (quality) requirements. Nonfunctional requirements can be used to place constraints on the devised solutions so that they support acceptable levels of quality, as defined by stakeholders (Abran et al. 2005). As mentioned before, an essential characteristic of requirements (both functional and nonfunctional) is their ability to provide verifiable specifications. By transforming goals to nonfunctional requirements, they can be used not only for decision making during architectural, detailed, and construction design but also as evaluation criteria during system test, after the system is designed, constructed, and unit tested. A list of common quality attributes with descriptions is presented in Table 3.1.

Domain knowledge provides an essential source for requirements since it provides details of how the system should behave and help determine obscure functions that the

TABLE 3.1

Common Quality Attributes for Software Systems

Quality	Description
Usability	A goal that seeks to minimize the degree of complexity involved when learning or using the system
Modifiability	A goal that seeks to minimize the degree of complexity involved when changing the system to fit current or future needs
Security	A goal that seeks to maximize the system's ability to protect and defend its information or information system
Performance	A goal that seeks to maximize the system's capacity to accomplish useful work under time and resource constraints
Reliability	A goal that seeks to minimize the system's failure rate
Portability	A goal that seeks to minimize the degree of complexity involved when adapting the system to other software or hardware environments
Testability	A goal that seeks to minimize the degree of complexity involved when verifying and validating the system's required functions
Availability	A goal that seeks to maximize the system's uptime
Interoperability	A goal that seeks to maximize the system's ability to collaborate with other software or hardware systems

system needs to provide in special cases. This knowledge is obtained through the design and development of similar systems or through involvement in the development effort under different disciplines, such as hardware, test, and management. Finally, the operational and organizational environment can be used as a source for requirements common to software product lines within the organization to maintain consistency among all products developed in the organization.

Elicitation Techniques

Different stakeholders view systems differently, based on their specific background and specialization. When eliciting information from different stakeholders, it is sometimes difficult to compile a consistent set of requirements, since needs from stakeholders may contradict each other. Therefore, effective elicitation techniques are required to gather and consolidate a consistent set of requirements for the system. Some of the most common techniques for requirements elicitation include (Abran et al. 2005):

- Interviews
- Facilitated meetings
- Observation
- Scenarios

Interviews and facilitated meetings are both common techniques for requirement elicitation. During interviews, meetings are scheduled individually with different stakeholders to bring forth their particular needs and gain understanding of their particular expectations for the system. On the other hand, facilitated meetings are performed with a group of stakeholders to bring forth a collective vision and to gain more insight into the overall expectations of the system. Typically, facilitated meetings include a moderator, the design team, and peer reviewers (including stakeholders). By eliciting requirements in a collective fashion, details that affect different stakeholders can be identified, negotiations can be made, and collective resolutions can be achieved. Information from both interviews and facilitated meetings needs to be carefully documented, further elaborated, and iteratively refined until a solid grasp of the system needs is acquired.

In many cases, stakeholders are unaware or cannot articulate desirable system features. When this occurs, observations of similar systems can help capture desired functions of the system behavior under particular (nonobvious) conditions. This information can be learned to gain insight into a particular system behavior, quality, or interaction and used to generate appropriate requirements for the system. When systems are hard to specify, observation allows both engineers and stakeholders to effectively conceptualize and transfer knowledge required to yield important system information; however, in some cases it can be intrusive, expensive, or impossible.

Finally, a popular approach to eliciting requirements is through scenarios. Scenarios are popular because they allow software architects to create and present to stakeholders *storylines* about different behaviors that the system is expected to provide. These storylines are born out of perceived expected behavior by the software architect and refined and validated through stakeholders' reviews. Scenarios provide a valuable means for establishing a framework for eliciting requirements, identifying major system functions and details of the software, and providing initial insight in the required testing of the software. In Unified Modeling Language (UML), scenarios can be grouped by use cases, as presented in Chapter 2. For each use case, one or more scenarios—one for the main flow of events and others for alternate scenarios—are created to document the expected system behavior and deviations from its main flow of events. Scenarios represent instances of use cases; therefore, there exists a one-to-many relationship between use cases and scenarios. Since there are no universal methods accepted as standard for formatting and capturing scenarios, scenarios can be created as paragraphs, numbered list, tabular or graphical form, or any other convenient form that is appropriate for systems analysis and knowledge transfer. Table 3.2 contains a sample scenario for the *Search Product* use case presented in Chapter 2.

Scenarios provide an effective method for eliciting the system's functions and serve as excellent communication avenue between stakeholders and engineers. They also provide an effective method for identifying quality information that can lead to the creation of nonfunctional requirements. By presenting a particular quality attribute within context, stakeholders can get a better appreciation of how it relates and affects the system. For example, as seen in step 3 of the search product's main scenario, a statement of performance is initially brought forth for evaluation and (if necessary) modification to specify the actual expected performance of the system. In this example, the scenario helped identify an important quality of the system, and, if required, prototypes can be developed to further evaluate the adequacy of the desired performance.

Skill Development 3.2: Eliciting Requirements Using Scenarios

Use any of the other remaining use cases presented in Figure 2.4, and create a detailed scenario description including steps, operator actions, and system actions. After completing the task, can you think of any quality requirements that can be derived from the scenario? Explain. Lists the steps that would you consider taking after completion of the scenario to ensure that requirements derived from the scenario are incorporated into the system.

Analysis

In the analysis activity, requirements are analyzed in their raw form to address issues such as requirements that are contradicting, incomplete, vague, or just wrong (Laplante 2009). During analysis, software architects spend a great deal of time evaluating each requirement to determine its impact on the system design as well as its impact on all other identified requirements. Analysis allows architects to clear the air in regards to what needs to be

TABLE 3.2

Main Scenario for Search Product Use Case

UC-00-Search Product Main Scenario

Description: This scenario describes the main flow of operations for requesting a product search with the server system.

Actors: Operator, Server System

Preconditions: The client and server system have been initialized.

Requirements: MCR-001, MCR-002

Alternate scenario: UC-10-Invalid Search, UC-11-Connection Failure, UC-12-Response Timeout

		Revision History	
Date	**Version**	**Description**	**Revised By**
9/17/2010	1.0	Initial scenario creation	John Doe

	Description	
Step	**Operator Action**	**System Action**
1	Operator enters valid product ID and clicks on the search button.	*Validates the data.* Retrieves server's communication information from config file.
2		Establishes a connection with the server system and sends product request data to the server.
3		Waits a maximum of 3 seconds for a server response.
4		.
		.
5		Response received and product information is displayed.
6		*Save response data* in file system and ask user to search for another product.
7	Operator clicks the cancel button to finish searching for products.	

Notes

For details of data validation and saving response data to file system see use cases UC-05 and UC-06 respectively.

Approval Signatures

Software engineer:

Stakeholder(s):

Quality auditor:

done before devising more detailed designs. Software architects may be required to carry out important tasks, such as

- Requirement classification
- Requirement prioritization
- Requirement negotiation
- Conceptual modeling

Requirement classification refers to the activity and process required for identifying the nature of each requirement. Classification is important in determining the relative

TABLE 3.3

Common Criteria for Requirement Classification

Criteria	Description
Functional vs. nonfunctional	Classification that differentiates between requirements that specify the functional aspects of the system versus the ones that place constraints on how the functional aspects are achieved
Product vs. process	Requirement placed on the system product versus requirements placed on the process employed to build the product
Imposed vs. derived	Requirements imposed by stakeholders versus requirements that are derived by the development team

importance of each requirement and can serve as a driver for prioritization of work units and negotiation and trade-off throughout. Common criteria for classifying requirements are presented in Table 3.3.

Prioritization of requirements is done to help identify the most important functions of the software system. When done properly, prioritization can help refine the projected schedule by determining which requirements (or component carrying out these requirements) need to be developed first or can help identify different builds of the software system, which can be designed, developed, and deployed at different times. Prioritization also helps during requirement negotiation when conflicts between requirements are identified during analysis. When this occurs, negotiation takes place among stakeholders, and resolutions to conflicts are made while taking into account requirement priorities. Finally, an integral task of the analysis activity is conceptual modeling. Conceptual models are created to further identify the requirements by understanding their context, discovering the bounds of the software system, and conceptualizing how the system interacts with its environment. In many projects, conceptual modeling is where architectural design begins, since system decomposition is essential to developing effective conceptual models.

Specification and Validation

Specification is the activity of the requirements phase where the results of elicitation and analysis are formally captured and documented in an appropriate format for the use and review of all stakeholders. The format of the specification varies depending on the developing organization or project; however, it is typically produced as a document or its electronic equivalent (Abran et al. 2005) and is referred to as the software requirements specification (SRS). When specifying requirements, it is important that each requirement exhibit certain characteristics desired for designing successful systems, including the following:

- Specific
- Correct
- Complete
- Consistent
- Attainable
- Verifiable

Once requirements are specified and the SRS is created, validation can occur. Requirements validation is the process of ensuring (through well-known techniques) that the SRS provides a complete and correct representation of what the stakeholders need (Laplante 2009).

Specific

Requirements need to be specified in a clear, concise, and exclusive manner. Clear requirements are not open to interpretation; unclear or ambiguous requirements lead to incorrect designs, incorrect implementations, and deceptive validation during test. Concise requirements are brief and to the point and are therefore easier to understand. Finally, exclusive requirements specify one, and only one, thing, making them easier to verify. Consider the following statements:

- The software needs to provide an easy-to-use interface; that is, it must be usable.
- Speed is a concern; therefore, the software should operate with high performance.
- Software evolution is a concern; therefore, the software shall be testable and maintainable.

These statements provide important information to begin thinking about what the customer wants and expects from the software system. However, in their current form, the statements are too generic to use as a basis for design, construction, and verification of software systems. For example, a console-based user interface may be highly visible for the system's developers but not its customers or intended users. Alternatively, the system's technical developers may interpret speed as the system responding to received message within 5 milliseconds; anything above would be considered an infeasible solution. Designing the system based on this interpretation may entail sacrificing other functions that may be important to customers and users, when all the while customers and intended users perceived speed as receiving responses within 2 seconds. When left unresolved, statements like these become a major reason for the failure of the project. Examples of specific requirements are presented in Table 3.4.

TABLE 3.4

Example of Specific and Nonspecific Requirements

Specific	Requirement
No	The software shall search the database.
Yes	The software shall search for a product using the product ID.
No	The software shall be secure.
Yes	The software shall authenticate users with user ID and password.
No	The software shall be secure and fast.
Yes	The software shall authenticate users with user ID and password. Server acknowledgment message shall be sent within 1/2 second from the time a request is received.

TABLE 3.5

Example of Correct and Incorrect Requirements

Correct	Requirement
No	The software shall require users to log on using a unique combination of user ID and password.
Yes	The software shall require users to log on using a user ID and password.
	The software shall require users to log on using a valid e-mail address.

Correct

Requirements need to be correct in the sense that they must accurately describe a desired system function. Similar to ambiguous or unclear requirements, specifying incorrect system functions leads to a chain of incorrect solutions in subsequent development phases. In some cases, correctness of requirements is easily identified; in others, it is not. To illustrate this problem, Laplante (2009) presents an example based on requirements for a computer security system for which it requires users to log on using a *unique combination* of user ID and password. In this case, when users attempt to log on using an already existing user name or password, the system is required to reject the attempt, therefore giving insight into someone else's logon information. Incorrect requirements, when left unchecked, can lead to incorrect or undesired behavior, such as the vulnerability found in the computer security system described above. Examples of correct and incorrect requirements are presented in Table 3.5.

Complete

Requirements should be complete both individually and as collective set. This means that each requirement should be specified thoroughly so that it absolutely describes the functions required to meet some need. Collectively, requirements need to provide complete specification of the software's required functionality in the SRS. Incomplete requirements lead to incomplete designs, which in turn leads to incomplete construction of the software system. Requirements that are complete help clarify questions during construction and testing by providing the information necessary to disambiguate or prevent misinterpretations of required functionality. Consider requirements for a software system that supports generation of product reports. An example of an incomplete requirement created for this system is presented in Table 3.6. As seen, determining incomplete requirements is not always an easy task.

As seen, the first requirement presented in Table 3.6 specifies the system's function to generate product reports; this is a good requirement in the sense that it specifies a function

TABLE 3.6

Example of Complete and Incomplete Requirements

Complete	Requirement
No	The software shall generate product reports.
Yes	The software shall generate product reports consisting of product description, picture, and price. Product reports shall be in PDF format.

that the system must perform. However, when additional information is available, this requirement becomes incomplete when this information is not specified and is necessary for providing the correct function that meets a particular stakeholder's need. Consider the case where products have vast amounts of information, such as color, dimensions, store location, history, and other product information. Generating reports containing all product information may be undesirable if the intended reporting function requires only the product's description, picture, and price. In this case, making requirements as complete as possible improves the efficiency of the construction and verification phases. Consider another case where there is a need for a client system to interoperate with two existing legacy servers by sending and receiving messages back and forth using two different (already existing) messaging specifications. A requirement that fails to specify a mandate to interoperate with both existing servers supporting both messaging specification may easily lead to client systems that are unable to interoperate with one of the servers, therefore rendering the client unusable for the system in mind. Completeness is hard because it is not always obvious or it is sometimes too difficult to determine when information is missing (Laplante 2009).

Consistent

Requirements are consistent when they do not preclude the design or construction of other requirements. When they do, individual requirements or the SRS as a whole are referred to as inconsistent. Inconsistent requirements are hard to resolve, since they almost always originate from different stakeholders' needs. When this occurs, negotiation and trade-offs need to occur to consolidate the requirements and provide a consistent specification. Requirements can also be inconsistent due to incorrect requirements. In these cases, requirements are made consistent easily by removing them from the SRS.

Attainable

Requirements that are unattainable serve no purpose. Attainability is a property that spans many different characteristics of the software system, including product characteristics such as functionality as well as project characteristics such as cost and schedule. When specifying requirements, it is important to evaluate their attainability under both cost and schedule constraints. Examples of attainable and unattainable requirements are presented in Table 3.7. As seen, although it is nice to develop software without platform limitations now or in the future, verifying this requirement is impossible since it is unattainable.

TABLE 3.7

Example of Attainable and Unattainable Requirements

Attainable	Requirement
No	The software shall execute on all future operating systems.
Yes	The software shall execute on the Microsoft Windows 7 platform.

TABLE 3.8

Example of Verifiable and Unverifiable Requirements

Verifiable	Requirement
No	The system shall maximize communication speed.
Yes	The system's data rate shall be no less than 1 Mbps.

Verifiable

Perhaps the most obvious desirable characteristic of requirements in practical applications is their verifiability. Requirements that cannot be verified cannot be claimed as met. Inability to verify requirements points to a serious flaw early on in the development project, since requirements are the driving force of all software development activities. In some cases, verifying requirements can include a complex and costly task. Typically, requirements that are unclear or ambiguous lead to unverifiable requirements. Before engaging in any design or construction work, all requirements in the SRS must be evaluated and analyzed for their verifiability. Examples of verifiable and unverifiable requirements are presented in Table 3.8.

Skill Development 3.3: Requirements Engineering

Consider the use case models created as part of Skill Development 2.2 that show the five most important functions that your home personal computer system needs to provide. Create a list of requirements (three per characteristic) for the computer system that meet the following characteristics: specific, correct, complete, consistent, attainable, and verifiable. Share the list of 18 requirements with a peer, and have him or her explain to you what the requirements specify. Is your understanding of the requirements consistent with that of your peer?

DESIGNING THE ARCHITECTURE

In a typical waterfall model for software development, once the software specification (i.e., SRS) is validated, the architectural design effort can begin. In practical applications, following a strict waterfall model is rarely productive, since new knowledge acquired during the development process forces iterative approaches between requirements and architectural design. As discussed in previous sections, architectural designs can begin as early as the analysis activity of the requirements phase, where conceptual models of the system are devised. In either case, be it during requirements or design, designing architectures require the selection of particular perspectives for design that are appropriate for describing the system to be developed. To this end, several models have been created that suggest popular views that are useful in the design of most systems. These models propose addressing the system's architectural design from perspectives that are common to most software

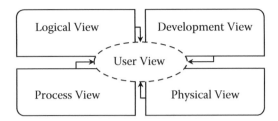

FIGURE 3.2
4+1 view model for software architecture.

systems and provide designers with a structured approach for modeling the architecture of software-intensive systems. Two popular models are Kruchten's (1995) 4 + 1 view model and Siemens' 4 views model (Hofmeister, Nord, and Soni 2000).

The 4 + 1 View Model

In 1995, Philippe Kruchten published an influential paper that proposed modeling software architectures using different perspectives; each perspective provides avenues for addressing problems from different angles, and, when combined, the set of models created from each perspective helps form the software architecture. Kruchten's model concentrated on four main views: *logical*, *process*, *development*, and *physical*. Modeling systems from each view requires addressing design problems of different natures, such as problems that deal with the logical system structure or problems that deal with dynamic, concurrency system issues. To ensure consistency among all four views, the user's perpective is captured through several key use cases. Today, Kructhen's 4+1 view model, presented in Figure 3.2, is used as a basis for the rational unified process (Bass et al. 2003).

The 4+1 model provides an adequate framework for modeling the architecture of most software systems. However, adoption of the model varies from organization to organization, and from project to project. For example, when concurrency is not an issue, modeling the system from a process view makes little to no sense. Similarly, for systems that reside in one node and in which the physical properties of their deployment are not of concern, modeling them using the physical view provides little to no benefit. Typically, all software systems benefit from the logical view; therefore, designs elements from this view should be incorporated into the software architecture.

User View

The user view of a software system represents the behavior that the system exhibits to its users. Specifically, the user view depicts how users interact with the system and how the specific sequences of inputs and outputs occur during software operation. Users represent anyone who interacts with the software system, such as operators, software testers, analysts, and quality. As part of this view, UML use case models can be used to drive scenarios that provide storylines and to promote consistency among all other models. The scenarios created can help capture important system functions and discover new knowledge that drives architectural design decisions. The user view also provides an effective source of information for verifying and validating system functions, after the system is built. In addition to UML use cases, UML activity diagrams can be used to flush out important user interactions that are important during architectural design (Pressman 2010).

Process View

The process view of a software system represents the dynamic or behavioral aspects of the software system where the main units of analysis are processes and threads. Using this view, software systems are decomposed into processes and threads to address design issues that deal with the dynamic flow of control between architectural elements, such as concurrency, distribution, system's integrity, fault tolerance, and other nonfunctional requirements (Kruchten 1995). Since analysis using the process view is behavioral in nature, behavioral UML diagrams can be used efficiently to address issues pertinent to the process views. Particularly, UML sequence and communication diagrams, together with the active object notation (presented in Chapter 2), can be used to evaluate, analyze, and characterize the system's capabilities from the process perspective. This view is necessary for projects that need to meet *performance* and *availability* requirements by modeling aspects of concurrency, distribution, and fault tolerance.

Physical View

The physical view of a software system represents the deployment aspects of software systems where the main elements of analysis are nodes, connections between nodes, and maps of software artifacts to nodes. The physical view focuses on modeling of elements that directly affect quality requirements, such as *availability*, *performance*, and *scalability* (Kruchten 1995). For example, consider a case where system quality is measured in part by the availability of the system. That is, systems are perceived as low quality when they fail to provide a specified behavior. In this case, availability can be addressed via redundancy of processors or complete nodes, which both can be depicted using UML deployment diagrams. The identification of redundant nodes using the physical view requires downstream design and development to think about techniques for identifying faults and swapping between primary and redundant nodes when necessary to support the system's availability. Similarly, aspects that affect system performance must be addressed using the physical view. When performance is measured with throughput, the physical view of systems must identify the elements that directly impact this metric, such as required bandwidth between a client and server.

In some applications, modeling system deployment may require one or more UML deployment diagrams. Different deployment diagrams may be necessary to model different deployment configurations of the same software system, for example, deployments of software systems in testing environments or in different locations where deployment configurations may differ. In each case, the physical view provides insight into necessary elements that directly affect the perceived quality of the software system. An example of the physical view of software systems is presented as a deployment diagram in Chapter 2.

Development View

The development view of software systems represents the software development configuration aspects of the software system, where the main units of decomposition are actual physical files and directories. The development view is used to analyze the system from the perspective of how logical components map to physical files and directories. These analyses can be employed to address concerns that deal with ease of development, reusability, constraints imposed by tool sets, allocation of work to teams, cost evaluation and planning, monitoring the project's progress, portability, and security (Kruchten 1995). In UML, architectural elements resulting from analyzing systems from the development's perspective can be documented using package diagrams in combination with components and class diagrams as well as notes, tagged values, and constraints to enhance the meaning of the diagrams. This way, components can be mapped to the hierarchy of files in the file system, and their interrelationships and process for building one or more versions of the software system can be carefully specified.

Logical View

The logical view of a software system is used to decompose systems into logical components that represent the structural integrity that supports functional and nonfunctional requirements. Examples of architectural design elements using the logical view are presented in Figure 2.1. Using this view, the static structure of the system can be modeled using high-level diagrams to decompose, abstract, and encapsulate the services that the system needs to provide to its users. By using these diagrams, the major components, their interfaces, and their associations with all other components are identified. Architectural logical designs exist at a higher level of abstraction than detailed designs and can be modeled using box and line diagrams, UML component diagrams, package diagrams, or class diagrams. Architectural logical designs provide the building blocks for detailed design; therefore, they are indispensable in the architectural design of software systems.

Skill Development 3.4: Designing with Architectural Views

As seen, views are used to present the system from particular perspectives so that design elements particular to that perspective can serve as tool for evaluating a desired property of the system. Using the logical view, the system's reusability can be evaluated; through the physical view, the system's availability can be examined; and the process view can be used to evaluate the system's performance. Consider the architectural design of two systems: a banking information system and a safety-critical medical system. For each system, come up with appropriate views—feel free to come up with ones other than those presented in this chapter—and how they could help address particular concerns in each. Discuss and justify your results with peers.

Components and Connectors

In Chapter 2, components were presented to depict units of the logical architecture. Conceptually, a component is an entity that encapsulates some functionality and provides services through well-known interfaces. By definition, then, components can be replaceable by other components that provide equal interfaces. Components are building blocks that exemplify the general design principles of abstraction, encapsulation, and modularization presented in Chapter 1. Prior to UML 2.0, the concept of components was different in that it denoted specifically a physically deployable unit, which limited the use of the component entity in architectural diagrams. However, this is not the case in the current version of the UML, so the component concept can be used to model logical, modular parts of a system.

Components do not exist in isolation; they are part of a logical architecture that depicts interactions with other components. In some applications, interactions between components are far more complicated than what UML's typical relationships (e.g., association, dependency) can reflect. In these systems, the proper identification and description of such interactions can have a profound impact on quality requirements. For this reason, the concept of a *connector* is devised. A *connector* is an architectural entity that abstracts the complexities of the interactions between components. Therefore, connectors can represent interaction between components as simple procedure calls, shared data access, or more advanced mechanisms such as remote procedure calls (Taylor, Medvidovic, and Dashofy 2009). Together, components and connectors can be used as fundamental building blocks for large-scale software architectures.

Designing Logical Architectural Elements Using Data Flows

There are many approaches for designing logical architectures. These approaches are typically associated with the overall design strategy selected for a given product. For example, when using the structured design strategy, a disciplined approach is employed to decompose systems into independent, single-purpose modules, using an iterative top-down approach. The main focus of structured design is on the functions that systems need to provide, the decomposition of these functions, and the creation of modules that incorporate these functions. Structured design approaches are typically employed after structured analysis, where the main purpose is to derive a structure chart (i.e., logical software architecture) from data flow diagrams (DFDs). A popular approach for creating structure charts includes employing transform analysis (Pressman 2010). When using transform analysis, the flow of data through the system is analyzed using DFDs to derive data transformations (i.e., functions) required to generate the system's outputs. Initially, a level 0 DFD is used to represent the initial context of the system. As the DFD is refined, further levels of the DFD are produced to expose further transformations of different scope. This refinement process is iteratively done until all transformations are identified and grouped into components to form the logical architecture of the system.

Designing Logical Architectural Elements Using Styles and Patterns

In the 1990s, the software engineering community began paying attention to recurring architectural solutions in terms of specific elements and their relationships. These solutions were known as architectural styles and patterns; these terms are used interchangeably throughout (see Chapter 4). Architectural patterns provide the means for software architects to reuse architectural design solutions in different projects. Buschmann, Meunier, Rohnert, Sommerlad, and Stal (1996) introduced a catalog of architectural patterns that conveyed fundamental structural organization for software systems, including predefined components, their responsibility, and rules for specifying the relationship between them. Together, these architectural patterns serve as a blueprint for designing elements of the logical architecture of particular groups of systems. The application of architectural patterns to the development of software systems occurs at the highest level of abstraction in the design process. Since they are used to create architectural elements, they do not describe the detailed design of the system and therefore cannot be directly translated into code. Identifying patterns at the architectural level (and designing around them) improves the quality of the final system by reducing the design of logical architectural elements to a collection of interacting components whose expected behavior is well understood. Examples of architectural design elements using architectural patterns are presented in Chapter 4.

Designing the Process Architecture

Whereas logical elements of the software architecture model static, structural aspects of the software system, process elements model how elements interact to evaluate certain aspects of the software's quality, such as concurrency. In software systems, concurrency is achieved mainly though multithreading or multiprocessing the system. Multithreading or multiprocessing applications introduce concurrency issues that require careful analysis to ensure that architectural designs account for effective synchronization techniques. Concurrent designs that work on the same data are tougher to design and manage since they can lead to software errors that are hard to find (e.g., race conditions) and increase the complexity of the software development effort. To fully understand and model issues such as performance, one must have some understanding of the universal mechanisms in place when software applications execute. Although *code has no place during the software architecture activity*, every software architect must understand how the modeling of process elements affects the downstream work performed during construction. For this reason, an unconventional learning approach involving code in the study of software architecture to introduce important architectural concepts and present the process view of software architecture is employed. This understanding is essential when modeling parts of the software that will affect its process quality.

Processes

Processes and threads are fundamental units of execution in today's modern software systems. They are created, managed, and terminated by the operating system. A process is a unit of software execution, that is, a program in execution. When you execute software, for example, an executable (.exe) file in Windows, a process is created by the Windows operating system. This process has some unique characteristics that distinguish from other processes. Whenever a process is created, the operating system creates a process control block (PCB) with information required by the operating systems to schedule and manage the process. This information can include the program counter, process state, registers, and stack. In single-processor systems, the operating system uses this information to switch between different processes while maintaining the integrity of all processes. This switching, known as a *context switch*, requires saving the information from a PCB of the active process and loading a PCB of the new process into memory to continue execution. A context switch is pure overhead, since the processor's time is spent doing management tasks rather than useful work for the software system; however, it enables *concurrency*. These operations happen so quickly that programs executing are perceived as executing concurrently. In single-processor systems, this pseudo-concurrency allows designers to model the system with concurrency in mind. In multiprocessor systems, processes are scheduled for execution in more than one processor, so actual concurrency is achieved. In either case, concurrency is used to increase the *performance* of the software system. Software systems, especially distributed systems, can be designed as systems of multiple processes executing on the same or different networked computing platforms. Multiple processes are used to leverage off the operating system to achieve concurrency of operations and increase the system's performance. That is, modern operating systems provide scheduling mechanisms that allow multiple processes to execute concurrently to maximize CPU usage.

Threads

Threads, sometimes called lightweight processes, are similar to processes in that they allow code to be compartmentalized in a way that they are schedulable as independent flows of control by the operating systems. In most modern operating systems, threads execute within a single process in a one-to-many fashion—that is, one process can contain one or more threads. Threads, therefore, can be thought of as small, schedulable, and sequential program units executing (typically) within a process. Processes that execute with only one thread can be described as sequential, or serial, which means that the commands in the programs are executed in turn so that a specific command is executed only after the previous command is finished. In single-threaded applications, if one statement halts waiting for some computer resource (e.g., input–output resource), the execution of the program blocks until the resource becomes available and execution can continue. For example, consider the code in Listing 3.1.

In the Windows operating system, when the code in Listing 3.1 is compiled and built, a file with an .exe extension is created. When this file is executed, a process is created with one thread, whose body of execution is defined by the `main` function. In this case, the operations in the main thread will execute sequentially until the return operation is encountered, at which point the operating system destroys both thread and process and the program is finished. Since there is only one independent flow of execution (i.e., one thread),

---

Listing 3.1: C++ Code for Single-Threaded Application

```cpp
#include <iostream>

using namespace std;

int main( int argc, char* argv[] ) {

   // A number to be guessed.
   const int THE_NUMBER = 10;

   // User input.
   int number;

   // Display message to user.
   cout<<"Guess a number from 0-100:\n";

   // Block waiting for user input.
   cin>>number;

   // Display results to user.
   cout<<"Your guess is "<<number<<", actual number is "
       <<THE_NUMBER<<endl;

   // End of program.
   return 0;
}
```

---

the program will halt at the `cin>>number` line until a number followed by the `return` key is entered as input. This is true because the `cin>>` line results in a *blocking call* to the operating system; that is, the main thread will block execution until input is provided. While blocking, the program wastes execution time in the sense that it is not utilizing the processor for achieving other necessary application-dependent tasks. When the thread is blocked, the process can accomplish nothing else, since there is only one flow of execution.

When multiple threads execute, multiple independent flows of control exit, so that if one is in a *blocking state* others can continue executing. To achieve this, the operating system needs to execute context switches to manage the program execution among the different threads in pseudo-concurrent fashion at the expense of causing similar but reduced overhead as the ones described with processes. By allowing the executing software to perform other activities while waiting for some resource, its performance may be enhanced. Consider Listing 3.2 for a number-guessing game where the executing software counts until user input is received and then determines if the input (i.e., guessed number) matches the counted number.

When this program executes, a single process is created, and its main thread is executed. As the main thread executes sequentially, a `counter` object of `ThreadCounter` type is created. The `ThreadCounter` type abstracts the creation of another thread that is started by calling the object's `count()` method, which results in an independent flow of

---

Listing 3.2: C++ Code for Concurrent Number-Guessing Game

```cpp
#include <iostream>
#include "ThreadCounter.h"

using namespace std;

int main( int argc, char* argv[] ) {

  // User input.
  int number;

  // Create the thread counter object.
  ThreadCounter counter;

  // Start the counter.
  counter.count();

  // Display message to user.
  cout<<"Guess a number from 0-100:\n";

  // Block waiting for user input.
  cin>>number;

  // Stop the counter.
  counter.stop();

  // Display results to user.
  cout<<"Your guess is "<<number<<", actual number is "
    <<counter.current()<<endl;

  // End of program.
  return 0;
}
```

---

execution created tasked with counting. This allows the main thread to continue executing sequentially while the counter thread counts. The main thread will block waiting for user input (via `cin`) while the counter thread continues to count, therefore introducing concurrency into the software. Once user input is received, the main thread terminates the counter thread and displays the results. This process is presented in Figure 3.3 using a sequence diagram with active objects relying on synchronous and asynchronous messages. Notice that once the counter threads calls its `start()` method, it counts and does nothing else until it is finished counting, which is triggered by the `stop()` method. This is modeled using the synchronous message to self.

The code presented in Listing 3.2 serves as a good example for introducing the concept of concurrency in a simplified manner. Concurrency issues are always amplified when data need to be shared among concurrent flows of executions. In these cases, correct

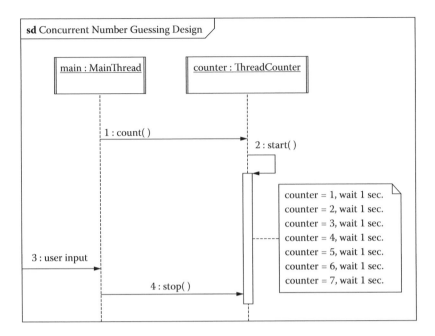

FIGURE 3.3
UML design for concurrent guessing game.

synchronization mechanisms need to be in place to ensure the proper execution of the software system. Consider the case of a communication system receiving messages concurrently through two different interfaces. Upon receiving messages, the system updates its message count statistic and continues on to process each message. Listing 3.3 presents the code for the MessageStatistics type used to abstract services for managing message statistics.

As seen, the MessageStatistics type has an interface method to increment the number of received messages throughout the system. Since the system requires concurrency, each independent flow of message processing is carried out using two different threads; therefore, it is assumed that a base Thread class exists that abstracts the creation and management of threads, providing a simplified interface that contains start() and stop() methods to execute and terminate the thread. In addition, the Thread base class provides an abstract method run() used by derived classes to provide the implementation of the thread's main (entry) function and an isActive() method to determine if the thread should continue executing or not. With such framework in place, the code for the SerialReceiverThread class, used to receive messages through the serial communication interface, is presented in Listing 3.4.

As seen, the class is configured with a reference to an object of type Message-Statistics, which is used to update the message count once a serial message is received. Similarly, the EthernetReceiverThread class is designed to be a thread that waits for incoming messages via the Ethernet interface, as presented in Listing 3.5.

As seen, this class is also initialized using a reference to a MessageStatistics object, so that both serial and Ethernet threads rely on the same data structure to update message statistics. Consider what happens when objects of type SerialReceiverThread and

---

Listing 3.3: C++ Code for Specification of the MessageStatistics Type

```cpp
class MessageStatistics {

public:

   // Use constructor to set messageCount = 0;

   // Method to increment number of received messages.
   void increment() {

      // A message has been received, increment the current count.
      _messageCount++;
   }

   // Method to return the current number of messages received.
   int count() {

      // Return the number of messages received.
      return _messageCount;
   }

   // ...
private:

   // Variable used to keep track of the number of messages received.
   int _messageCount;
   // ...
};
```

EthernetReceiverThread are both initialized using the same object instance of the MessageStatistics class, as illustrated in Listing 3.6. Once instantiated, both threads start to receive messages via their respective interfaces. The main thread simply waits until all expected messages are received.

The main problem with Listing 3.6 can be traced to the critical section of code inside the increment() method of the MessageStatistics class. A *critical section* is a code segment that makes changes to common variables, such as the _messageCount. This makes software more challenging to design and evaluate since the integrity of the data inside the critical section needs to be preserved. Since there are no safeguards to ensure the proper synchronization of multiple threads when updating the _messageCount variable, both threads may attempt to update the message count at the same time, therefore resulting in unpredictable results that may hinder the system's integrity. To illustrate this point, consider the assembly (lower-level) code generated to increment the _messageCount variable, as seen in Listing 3.7.

Using a disassembly tool, it can be seen that the _messageCount++ written in C++ requires three assembly lines of code: one to move the current value of _messageCount

Listing 3.4: C++ Code for the Serial Message Processor Thread Class

```cpp
class SerialReceiverThread : public Thread {

public:
  // Constructor.
  SerialReceiverThread(MessageStatistics& stats) {

    // Save the statistics object for later use.
    _stats = &stats;
  }
protected:

  // Thread's main function.
  virtual void run() {

    while( isActive() ) {

      // Wait for a message via the serial interface.
      // Once a message is received, increment count in the stats
      // object.
      _stats->increment();

      // Process received serial message.

    } // end while loop.
  } // end run() method.

private:

  // The pointer to the stats object.
  MessageStatistics* _stats;
};
```

to the accumulator eax register; one to increment the value; and the last one to move the results back from the eax register to the address referenced by the _messageCount variable in C++. When executed concurrently, both threads of execution will execute the operations. However the order in which they are executed cannot be guaranteed; that is, the order can be interleaved in some arbitrary fashion. Consider the interleaved order of execution among the two threads—each receiving messages at the same time—presented in Table 3.9.

After execution, the value of _messageCount is incorrectly set to 1, when it should be 2, since two messages were received. This phenomenon is known as a *race condition* and occurs when two processes or threads operate concurrently on the same data and the outcome of the execution depends on the particular order in which the access takes place. This example shows the importance of designing and evaluating architectural elements using the process view, which provides the appropriate perspective for detecting such

Listing 3.5: C++ Code for the Serial Message Processor Thread Class

```cpp
class EthernetReceiverThread : public Thread {

public:

  // Constructor.
  EthernetReceiverThread(MessageStatistics& stats) {

    // Save the statistics object for later use.
    _stats = &stats;
  }
protected:

  // Thread's main function.
  virtual void run() {

    while( isActive() ) {

      // Block waiting for a message via the serial interface.
      // Once a message is received, increment count in the stats
      // object.
      _stats->increment();

      // Process received Ethernet message.

    } // end while loop.
  } // end run() method.

private:

  // The pointer to the stats object.
  MessageStatistics* _stats;

};
```

cases. When these cases are detected, guards in the design can be introduced to protect the integrity of such critical sections of code. In UML, such design evaluations and decisions can be captured using the synchronization properties such as *Sequential, Guarded*, and *Concurrent* presented in Chapter 2. These properties place constraints in process models to support concurrency by controlling the way multiple flows of execution access critical sections of code. The *Sequential* synchronization property specifies that no concurrency management mechanism is associated with an operation, such as in the case of the existing increment method in Listing 3.3. With sequential access, concurrency conflicts may occur, so clients that rely on the operation need to coordinate so that only one invocation occurs at any given point. The *Guarded* property specifies that the operation can be invoked from

Listing 3.6: C++ Code for Concurrent Application

```cpp
// Code to demonstrate the critical section concept in concurrent
programs.

#include <iostream>
#include "SerialReceiverThread.h"
#include "EthernetReceiverThread.h"
#include "MessageStatistics.h"

using namespace std;

int main( int argc, char* argv[] ) {

  // Number of messages received.
  int messagesReceived = 0;

  // Number of messages expected.
  const int MESSAGES_EXPECTED = 10;

  // Create the object to keep track of message statistics.
  MessageStatistics msgStats;

  // Create the thread to receive messages via serial interface.
  SerialReceiverThread serial(msgStats);

  // Create the thread to receive messages via Ethernet interface.
  EthernetReceiverThread ethernet(msgStats);

  // Start receiving messages through both interfaces.
  serial.start();
  ethernet.start();

  while( msgStats.count() < MESSAGES_EXPECTED ) {

    cout<<"Messages received: "<<msgStats.count()<<endl;

    // if flag set, exit loop.

    // Blocking call. Wait one second before checking again.
    sleep(1000);
  }

  // Stop receiving through serial interface.
  serial.stop();

  // Stop receiving through Ethernet interface.
  ethernet.stop();

  // End of program.
  return 0;
}
```

Listing 3.7: Sample Assembly Program to Increment _ `messageCount`

```
; Move contents of _messageCount to eax register.
mov eax, dword ptr [_messageCount (417140h)]


; Add one to the number in eax.
add eax, 1


; Copy the result from eax to _messageCount.
mov dword ptr [_messageCount (417140h)], eax
```

TABLE 3.9

Interleaved Execution in Concurrent Designs

Time	Source	Operation	_messageCount
T_0	Thread 1	mov eax, dword ptr [_messageCount (417140h)]	0
T_1	Thread 1	add eax, 1	0
T_2	Thread 2	mov eax, dword ptr [_messageCount (417140h)]	0
T_3	Thread 2	add eax, 1	0
T_4	Thread 1	mov dword ptr [_messageCount (417140h)], eax	1
T_5	Thread 2	mov dword ptr [_messageCount (417140h)], eax	1

multiple independent flows simultaneously, but only one flow of execution is allowed to commence; other independent flows are blocked until the execution of a currently executing operation, under the currently executing thread, is complete. When using the *Guarded* synchronization property, it is the responsibility of the designer to ensure that concurrency issues, such as *starvation* and *deadlocks*, do not occur. Finally, the *Concurrent* synchronization property specifies that multiple invocations may occur simultaneously and all of them may proceed concurrently. Concurrency is achieved in languages with built-in support for concurrency, such as Java, with the use of the `synchronized` property. To resolve the issue of concurrency caused by the `increment()` method, the *Guarded* synchronization concept can be modeled and manifested in code by ensuring that the critical section of code that increments the _messageCount is mutually exclusive to both threads of execution. This can be achieved by employing a mutually exclusive (*Mutex*) object, typically provided by the operating system. The code from Listing 3.3 is modified using pseudo-code to support concurrency, as seen in Listing 3.8.

The concepts presented in Listings 3.3, 3.4, 3.5, 3.6, and 3.8 can all be summarized using two simple UML designs, as seen in Figure 3.4.

The concepts presented so far are essential for understanding how the process view of software architecture is used to evaluate and design for performance in software systems. These concepts play a key role in designing systems that meet *performance* and *availability* requirements by modeling aspects of concurrency, distribution, and fault tolerance.

Listing 3.8: C++ Code for Guarded Implementation of the `increment()` method

```cpp
// Method to increment number of received messages.
void increment() {

  // Access Mutex. If unavailable, block until it becomes available.

  // If you are here, it means that you have access to the Mutex. Once
  // in possession, no other thread of execution can gain access to the
  // Mutex, therefore this critical section of code is protected.

  // Increment the message count.
  _messageCount++;

  // Release the Mutex. The next thread waiting for the Mutex will gain
  // access to it, therefore gaining protected access to the critical
  // section of code.
}
```

EVALUATING THE ARCHITECTURE

Architecture evaluation is the process of determining how well suited architecture is for developing a system that meets both its intended functional and quality requirements. From a functional perspective, architectures need to introduce the appropriate abstractions for the services that the system is required to provide. The functional properties of the architecture can be evaluated using the identified logical components, assigning requirements to them and modeling the interactions required among components to support all functional requirements. On the other hand, evaluating the architecture's ability to support expected system quality requires more effort to ensure that the proposed architecture provides a good approach for a system's development. Evaluating architectures for their provided quality requires the investigation and breakdown of quality goals to attributes that are adequate for evaluation. The architectural evaluation determines the appropriateness for supporting these quality features and can be used for determining their relative importance and how they impact other quality attributes supported by the architecture. This information, in turn, is used to evaluate different proposed architectures and to prioritize quality goals so that design trade-off among stakeholders can occur. Ultimately, the evaluation process is performed until a solution that is sufficiently complete and acceptable for all stakeholders is found. Although there is no universally accepted methodology for analyzing and evaluating software architectures, the architecture trade-off analysis method (ATAM) approach (Bass et al. 2003) provides a rigorous and proven methodology for such endeavors.

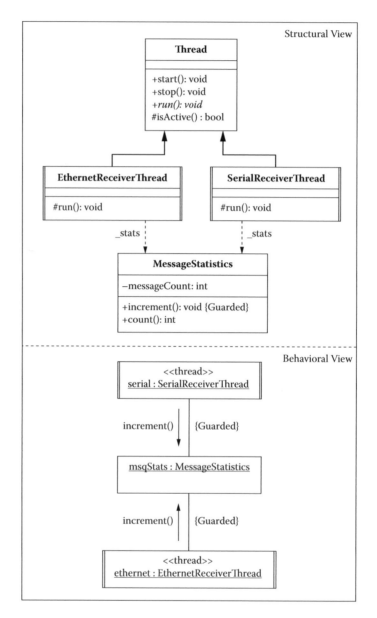

FIGURE 3.4
UML concurrent design for communication elements.

CHAPTER SUMMARY

The software architecture activity corresponds to a macrodesign approach for transforming software requirements into design elements that support quality and functions of software systems. Formally, software architecture is defined as the foundational software design activity that evaluates and translates software requirements (both functional and nonfunctional) into a collection of design elements that specify structural and behavioral aspects of the major components of the system, together with their provided quality and interrelationships required to support the detailed design and construction of software systems and the product resulting from such activity. To accomplish all of this, software architects must be familiar with activities from the requirements engineering discipline so that inputs to the software architecture activity can be well understood and formulated in such a way that supports the design and development of the software system. To address the concerns from multiple stakeholders, architects model architectural elements using different views, which may be prescribed by popular view models, such as the 4+1 view model. All systems use the logical view to identify and structure the major components, assign responsibility to them, and model their interactions. In some cases, architectural styles and patterns can be used to provide architectural (logical) solutions to common architectural problems. All architectural elements designed from all particular views form the software architecture, which can be used to establish the initial framework for the quality of the system. Since architecture alone cannot guarantee the quality of the system, processes need to be in place to ensure that architectural decisions made to address quality concerns are maintained throughout the development life cycle. The software architecture lays the foundation for all subsequent work in the development process and serves as an important communication, reasoning, and analysis tool for the development and maintenance of software systems. Once complete, the detailed design activity can begin.

REVIEW QUESTIONS

1. What is software architecture, and how does it differ from other forms of design?
2. How can software architecture affect both product development and product management activities?
3. List and explain the common tasks performed during software architecture.
4. What are the common input, constraints, and outputs found during architectural problem solving?
5. Why is it important for software architects to be familiar with the discipline of requirements engineering?
6. What are the four main activities performed during requirements engineering? Explain.
7. List and explain four common quality attributes for software systems.
8. What are the essential characteristics that requirements must exhibit when specifying requirements? Provide an example of each.
9. What are architectural views, and why are they important in software architecture?
10. Explain Kruchten's (1995) 4+1 view model.
11. What are architectural styles and patterns, and why are they important in software architecture?
12. What are the following concepts, and how do they relate to the process architecture of software systems?
    a. Process versus threads
    b. Blocking calls

    c. Race condition

    d. Critical section

13. In UML, what synchronization properties are available to constraints process models that support concurrency? Explain each.

CHAPTER EXERCISES

1. Select a problem of interest and write a statement of work that describes the overview of the problem. Use this statement of work to generate a list of requirements for the system and to explain how each requirement meets the desired characteristics of requirements. Once the list of requirements is defined, complete the following steps:

    a. Determine at least two views appropriate for this problem.

    b. Using a UML modeling tool, create design elements appropriate for each view.

    c. For each design element, write a paragraph describing how the design element help address particular concerns for the system.

    d. Assume that portability and performance have been identified as new quality attributes for the system. Integrate these into the design. Note that you will have to make assumptions to complete this step. Make sure that you document all assumptions.

    e. Evaluate how all assumptions, identified requirements, and quality attributes are supported by the resulting architectural elements. Create a report that documents the result of the evaluation process.

REFERENCES

Abran, Alain, James W. Moore, Pierre Bourque, and Robert Dupuis. *Guide to the Software Engineering Body of Knowledge—2004 Version—SWEBOK*. Los Alamitos, CA: IEEE Computer Society Press, 2005.

Bass, Len, Paul Clements, and Rick Kazman. *Software Architecture in Practice,* 2d ed. Boston: Addison-Wesley, 2003.

Buschmann, Frank, Regine Meunier, Hans Rohnert, Peter Sommerlad, and Michael Stal. *Pattern-Oriented Software Architecture: A System of Patterns*. West Sussex, UK: Wiley, 1996.

Clements, Paul, Rick Kazman, and Mark Klein. *Evaluating Software Architectures*. Santa Clara, CA: Addison Wesley, 2001.

Gorton, Ian. *Essential Software Architecture*. Heidelberg, Germany: Springer, 2011.

Hofmeister, C., R. Nord, and D. Soni. *Applied Software Architecture*. Boston: Addison-Wesley, 2000.

Kruchten, Philippe. "Architectural Blueprints—The "4+1" View Model of Software Architecture." *IEEE Software* 12, no. 6 (1995): 42–50.

Laplante, Phillip A. *Requirements Engineering for Software and Systems*. Boca Raton, FL: Auerbach Publications, 2009.

Pressman, Roger S. *Software Engineering: A Practitioner's Approach,* 7th ed. Chicago: McGraw-Hill, 2010.

Taylor, Richard N., Nenad Medvidovic, and Eric M. Dashofy. *Software Architecture: Foundations, Theory, and Practice*. Hoboken, NJ: Wiley, 2009.

4

Patterns and Styles in Software Architecture

CHAPTER OBJECTIVES

- Understand the concept of architectural styles and patterns
- Understand the importance and role of architectural patterns in architectural designs
- Identify, understand, and apply the major types of architectural patterns
- Understand the quality benefits associated with using different architectural patterns

---

CONCEPTUAL OVERVIEW

During software architecture, designers spend a great deal of time devising architectural solutions that provide the necessary components and interfaces to achieve system requirements. At the architectural level, common patterns have emerged that describe elements of the system together with their interrelationships and quality characteristics. These patterns allow designers to quickly and systematically identify structural characteristics of systems (or subsystems) and provide the means for examining interactions and the proposed quality of the system. During the past decade, many styles and patterns for software architecture have been researched and published. Many of these patterns have been identified in pattern catalogue books; some of these are common design patterns in enterprise-level systems, while others address specific needs such as distributed systems. This chapter explores several well-established architectural patterns and examines the problems they are designed to address, together with their exhibited quality attributes. Identifying and designing using architectural patterns can improve the efficiency of the development process and the quality of the final system.

ARCHITECTURAL STYLES AND PATTERNS

As seen in Chapter 3, software systems need to be carefully architected and evaluated from various perspectives to properly address multiple concerns that affect the quality of the end product. Modeling systems from each view requires addressing design problems of different natures, such as problems that deal with the logical system structure or problems that deal with dynamic, concurrency system issues. In all cases, it is essential to identify the necessary components and interfaces (at the right granularity) and the responsibility of each component and to model behavioral interactions among them before moving on to detailed design. Of particular interest is the logical architecture of software systems, since it includes system decomposition into logical components that are refined throughout the design phase and ultimately implemented during construction. From this perspective, it is important to use past experience with logical decompositions together with their interfaces when designing today's software systems. To this end, the concepts of *architectural styles* and *architectural patterns* have emerged as mainstream approach for achieving (mostly logical design) reuse at the architectural level. These concepts are fundamental to the efficient creation of software architectures by providing an overall strategy for designing families of software systems. They provide generic, reusable architectural solutions, documented in a way that can be easily understood and applied to new problems requiring similar architectural features. Decisions based on architectural styles and patterns benefit from years of documented experience that highlights the solution approach to given problems, the benefits of these approaches, and the consequences of designing the system with a particular style.

Today, the terms *architectural styles* and *architectural patterns* are used loosely to refer to similar concept. The fuzzy line that may exist among them can be a source of confusion, which shifts the focus away from the true importance and role of both concepts in designing today's complex software. Since numerous architectural styles and patterns are documented today, a brief history of the concepts is required to consolidate the terms and provide a consistent approach for applying them throughout the rest of the chapter.

History of Architectural Styles and Patterns

In 1977, Christopher Alexander presented a language intended to help individuals, or teams of individuals, design quality structures of different sizes, shapes, and complexities (Ishikawa, Silverstein, Jacobson, Fiksdahl-King, and Angel 1977, p. x). This language—born out of experience—had at its core entities called patterns. According to Alexander et al.:

> Each pattern describes a problem which occurs over and over again in our environment, and then describes the core of the solution to that problem, in such a way that you can use this solution a million times over, without ever doing it the same way twice.

Alexander's work resulted in a catalogue of 253 patterns, each describing in detail the essential information required for documenting the patterns. Each pattern's description included a picture of the pattern, the context of the pattern, the problem that it attempts to solve, evidence for its validity, solution for the problem, and related patterns among others (Alexander et al. 1977). Together, these patterns formed a language for use during the design and construction process. Although Alexander's work on patterns appears relevant and appropriate for the software engineering profession, it actually referred to patterns found in the design of buildings and towns.

Alexander's work significantly impacted the field of software engineering. Even though his patterns dealt with design quality in buildings and towns, it inspired computer scientists to answer the same types of questions about quality in object-oriented designs. In the early 1990s, the software engineering community began researching and finding recurring high-level problem solutions in terms of specific elements and their relationships; these were originally referred to as architectural styles (Clements, Kazman, and Klein 2001). Architectural styles provided the means for software architects to reuse architectural design solutions in different projects. In 1995, Gamma, Helm, Johnson, and Vlissides—better known as the Gang of Four (or GoF)—embarked on a similar quest to find and document detailed object-oriented solutions successfully applied more than once in different systems. Their influential work focused on a finer-grained set of detailed design patterns and resulted in the creation of a catalogue of 23 patterns, commonly known as design patterns. In 1996, the work of Buschmann, Meunier, Rohnert, Sommerland, and Stal (1996) meshed the work of styles and patterns by providing a set of well-known architectural styles documented using a pattern-like approach (Clements et al. 2001). In their original work, Bushman and colleagues indicate that patterns and styles are essentially the same thing by stating (Buschman et al. 1996, p. 395):

> Every architectural style can be described as an architectural pattern.

Today, the terms architectural styles and architectural patterns are used to convey fundamental structural and architectural organization for software systems. Other authors, such as Bass, Clements, and Kazman (2003) and Qian, Tao, Xu, and Diaz-Herrera (2009), consider both concepts to be the same thing. Throughout this chapter (and the rest of the book), the terms architectural patterns and architectural styles are used interchangeably to denote architectural solutions for software systems that occur at the highest level of abstraction in the design process. The concern of the work presented in this chapter is to understand not how to document specific architectural solutions but how and when to apply a particular pattern and the quality attributes these patterns provide. Architectural patterns do not describe the detailed design of the system and therefore cannot be directly translated into code. However, they are appropriately used as basis for system decomposition and for analyzing the structure of systems in principled manner, which is essential to constructing high-quality systems.

Architectural Pattern Classification

The choice of applying architectural patterns for designing some architectural element depends on the particular system type, requirements, and desired quality attributes. These characteristics help guide the choice of selecting one particular pattern over another. In some cases, several recognized patterns can all meet the identified characteristics of the system, therefore leaving the design team with the decision of choosing the most appropriate pattern for the design. In other cases, various architectural patterns can be used in combination to collectively provide the appropriate architectural solution that best fits the identified system type, requirements, and quality attributes. Since architectural patterns are found at the highest level of system decomposition, they are too abstract to yield a concrete system design; therefore, they are not tied to a particular system implementation but can be associated with types (or families) of systems so that their solution can be reused across systems of the same type. For example, a data-centered type of system can employ architectural patterns that provide the logical design that reflects various components interacting with a main component where data are hosted. The architectural pattern for such a system would include the structural entity that manages the data, components that perform work on the data, their data-centered interrelationships, and the quality of those components for providing the application-specific structure for the data-centered software system. As another example, consider the design of a distributed software system with components that communicate and collaborate across the network. In such cases, architectural patterns that support these components and their interrelationships in a distributed manner can be employed to define the overall strategy of the distributed systems. A list of common types of systems appropriate for classifying architectural patterns is presented in Table 4.1.

For large-scale systems, a single architectural pattern is inadequate for describing all the interactions of the complete system. In these cases, several patterns may be required to aid in the composition of architectural designs of the system and subsystems. That is, at the highest level, the logical design of a distributed system can incorporate an architectural pattern fitting of such system; however, at finer levels of abstraction, the system can include in its logical architecture other patterns that address other nondistributed system issues. Consider, for example, both distributed and data-centered systems already discussed. The overall architectural logical composition may include an architectural pattern that includes client and server components collaborating in distributed fashion. When further refined, the architectural design of the server's logical composition may employ an architectural pattern appropriate for data-centered systems, while the design of the client's architectural

TABLE 4.1

Type of Software Systems for Classifying Architectural Patterns

Type	Description
Data-centered	Systems that serve as a centralized repository for data, while allowing clients to access and perform work on the data
Data flow	Systems oriented around the transport and transformation of a stream of data
Distributed	Systems that primarily involve interaction between several independent processing units connected via a network
Interactive	Systems that serve users or user-centric systems
Hierarchical	Systems where components can be structured as a hierarchy (vertically and horizontally) to reflect different levels of abstraction and responsibility

composition may employ an architectural pattern appropriate for data-flow systems. All of these issues are architectural, and different design elements addressing these concerns throughout the system are required to form the software architecture. This way, architectural patterns are combined to describe the complete layout of a system. In the rest of the chapter, common architectural patterns for each of these major system types are presented and examined. The central features of the pattern and the problems addressed are shown along with a summary of the benefits and limitations of each pattern.

DATA-CENTERED SYSTEMS

Data-centered systems are systems primarily decomposed around a main central repository of data. Therefore, typical responsibilities found in components of data-centered system include a centralized data manager and various worker components. The data manager component controls, provides, and manages access to system data, while worker components execute operations and perform work based on the data. The communication in data-centered systems is characterized by a one-to-one bidirectional communication between workers and data manager components. That is, worker components do not interact with each other directly; all communication goes through the data manager. Some considerations for these systems are data manipulation, communications protocols, transactions and recovery (also known as roll-back), and security. Examples of data-centered systems include expert systems, which interact with a database management system for storing and retrieving knowledge information. An example of an architectural pattern for data-centered systems includes the blackboard architectural pattern.

Blackboard Pattern

The blackboard architectural pattern decomposes software systems into components that work around a central data component to provide solutions to complex problems. These components work independently of each other to provide partial solutions to problems using an opportunistic problem-solving approach. That is, there are no predetermined, or correct, sequences of operations for reaching the problem's solution. Each component provides solutions that build upon the problem's current state, which is defined by the collective set of solutions provided by the blackboard's components. The access to the central data component can be made through direct memory reference, procedure calls, or database query (Taylor, Medvidovic, and Dashofy 2009). Other forms of access to the data central store may require complex and distributed remote method invocations, which may prompt designing blackboard systems as part of a broader architectural pattern. Nevertheless, this data-driven and opportunistic problem-solving approach is typical in the development of expert systems (Buschmann et al. 1996).

Using the blackboard architectural pattern, systems can be broken down to include a common repository where data and solutions to particular problems reside (i.e., the blackboard), a controller, and various agents that work to refine and further solutions to arrive at an acceptable solution. The blackboard architectural pattern resembles the approach a group of scientists would employ to solve a complex problem. Consider a group of scientists at one location using a blackboard (chalkboard, whiteboard, or electronic blackboard) to solve a complex problem. Assume that to manage the problem-solving process among scientists, a mediator controls access to the blackboard. Once the controller assigns control to the blackboard, a scientist evaluates the current problem's state as presented in the blackboard and, if possible, advances its solution before releasing control of the blackboard. With new knowledge obtained from the previous solution attempt, control is assigned to the next scientist who can further improve the problem's state. This process continues until no more progress can be made, at which point the blackboard system reaches a solution. Similar to this example, the blackboard architectural pattern identifies specialized agents that independently contribute to a problem's solution. Together, one or more agent components, the controller component, the blackboard component, and their interrelationships form the essence of the blackboard architectural pattern, as presented in the box-and-line diagram in Figure 4.1.

Consider the application of the blackboard architectural pattern for the design of a university software system that manages student registrations. Registrations are managed based on course availability, students' course history, and students' work schedule.

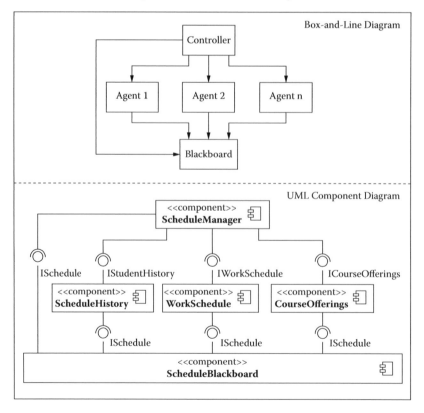

FIGURE 4.1
The blackboard architectural pattern.

TABLE 4.2

Architectural Components for Students Scheduling System

Component	Description
ScheduleManager	Manages access to the ScheduleBlackboard and controls the problem-solving process
StudentHistory	Knowledge source for students' history, including course and other preferences
WorkSchedule	Knowledge source for students' work schedule
CourseOfferings	Knowledge source for university's course offerings
ScheduleBlackboard	Central data store where elements of the solution space are stored

Acquiring each independent piece of information may require the system to interface with other systems with, for example, particular messaging protocols and interfaces. The current state of students' schedule is managed in a central component, housed with a database system containing the schedule details. To update schedules, the student scheduling system needs to interface with these external systems to retrieve information pertinent to create an optimized student schedule. In addition, future implementations of the scheduling system may include other information pertinent to the problem; therefore, the logical architecture needs to provide flexibility for incorporating new specialized agents capable of further improving the scheduling generation capabilities. Using the blackboard architectural pattern, the following components are identified in Table 4.2 and presented in Figure 4.1 using the Unified Modeling Language (UML) component diagram.

The *ScheduleManager* corresponds to the controller component of the blackboard architectural pattern seen in the box-and-line diagram of Figure 4.1. The *StudentHistory*, *WorkSchedule*, and *CourseOfferings* components correspond to the worker agents prescribed in the blackboard architectural pattern, which work independently to contribute to the problem solution by addressing a particular part of the problem and injecting their results back into the main data repository component. Finally, the *ScheduleBlackboard* corresponds to the prescribed blackboard component from the blackboard architectural pattern, which manages and controls access to the current state of students' schedules.

Assuming the design configuration presented in Figure 4.1, the solution approach to generate a schedule that *maximizes* both the *number of courses* taken and *work hours* (subject to some constraints) can be devised as follows. First, the *ScheduleManager* component initializes all other components, including agents and *ScheduleBlackboard* components. Once components in the blackboard system are initialized, the *StudentHistory* component is activated to search for a particular student's course history and retrieves information regarding courses left to complete a particular degree, the student's preference between day and night courses, and their preference between face-to-face and online courses. This information is stored in the *ScheduleBlackboard* component and is used to generate the first version of the student's schedule. Next, the *ScheduleManager* activates the *CourseOffering* component to search for the particular semester's course offering, including courses offered online, within the university system, from local and remote branch campuses. This may require the *CourseOfferings* component to have the capability of interfacing with different distributed information systems. The course offering information is used to modify the original schedule to include a schedule that reflects the student's preference fused with the course offerings. That is, if the student prefers face-to-face night courses, the *CourseOffering* component will combine this information to propose the schedule most appropriate for meeting these preferences. After the *CourseOfferings* component releases control of the *ScheduleBlackboard* component, the *ScheduleManager* activates the *WorkScheduler* component to determine the student's federal work-study schedule, which is accessible through the university system. Assuming the student's work schedule includes alternatives for various shifts, the *WorkScheduler* component evaluates the current state of the scheduling problem stored in the *ScheduleBlackboard* and determines the best shift based on the current schedule. When doing this, the *WorkSchedule* component may modify the schedule by removing classes that conflict with the most desirable and proposed work schedule. After releasing control of the *ScheduleBlackboard*, future iterations of the problem-solving process may include the *CourseOffering* component filling the gaps in the master schedule by selecting different classes that may or may not be of the student's preference but result in the schedule that maximizes both the number of courses taken and work hours. This process, as presented in Figure 4.2, can be repeated many times until the process is complete

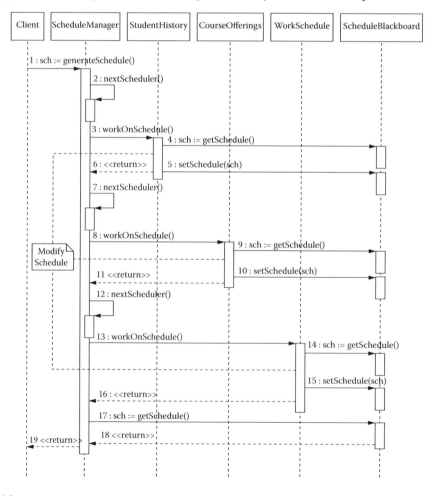

FIGURE 4.2
Interactions among components in the blackboard architectural pattern.

TABLE 4.3

Quality Properties of the Blackboard Architectural Pattern

Quality	Description
Modifiability	Agents are compartmentalized and independent from each other; therefore, it is easy to add or remove agents to fit new systems.
Reusability	Specialized components can be reused easily in other applications.
Maintainability	Allows for separation of concerns and independence of the knowledge-based agents; therefore, maintaining existing components becomes easier.

and the schedule provides the best possible solution. Because the number of agents can vary, the solutions provided by blackboard systems are (typically) nondeterministic and vary depending on the number of agents and the available information.

As seen, each component in the system abstracts the process and capabilities for acquiring information necessary for carrying out work to improve the solution from their particular standpoint. By abstracting each agent's work, the details employed inside the component, such as interprocess communication with external or distributed sources of data, protocols, messaging interfaces, and others, can be separated from the overall system design. Also, as seen, interactions between workers and the blackboard are limited to retrieving and injecting new knowledge to the blackboard. This way, changes to one agent component do not affect other agents or the blackboard components.

The major benefits of using the blackboard architectural pattern include its modifiability, reusability, and maintainability. These quality properties come as a result of compartmentalizing knowledge sources and establishing a standard method for using the blackboard. Since each agent needs to know only how to communicate with the blackboard, new agents can be introduced without much effort to improve the system's capabilities. Also, by compartmentalizing knowledge sources, changes to the system are also compartmentalized; therefore, changes to one agent do not affect other agents in the system. Finally, compartmentalization of agents supports easy reuse in future systems. The list of quality properties associated with the blackboard architectural pattern is presented in Table 4.3.

An important element to consider when applying *any* architectural pattern, including the blackboard, is their deployment aspect. Going back to the example with the scientists, it was explicitly stated that they were located in the same room, in front of the blackboard. However, scientists can be distributed all over the world, collaborating via electronic avenues. Similarly, blackboard systems and other systems based on architectural patterns discussed in this chapter may be distributed through the network, in which case describing the nature of their connectors becomes important. This would be presented using an architectural design element from a deployment perspective.

Skill Development 4.1: The Blackboard Architectural Pattern

Consider the existence of the new *HolidaySchedule* software component that can retrieve information regarding the university system's holiday schedule. This includes information regarding operation hours during, for example, holidays and spring break.

Using pencil and paper, redraw Figure 4.1 to include this component. How can such a component be used in the student's schedule blackboard system to further increase the number of hours worked? Using Figure 4.2 as context, how much effort and how many architectural changes would be required to add this new component to the system? Discuss this problem with a peer.

DATA FLOW SYSTEMS

Data-flow systems are primarily decomposed around the central theme of transporting data (or data streams) and transforming the data along the way to meet application-specific requirements. Therefore, typical responsibilities found in components of data-flow systems include worker components—those who perform work on data—and transport components, which transmit data among worker components. The worker components abstract data transformations that need to take place before passing data streams forward in the system, such as encryption, decryption, compression, decompression, and changing data format form binary to Extensible Markup Language (XML). The transport components abstract the management and control of the data transport mechanisms, which could include interprocess communication, socket-based communication, and serial interfaces. Together, these components combine to form architectural elements of data-flow systems. The data transformation and transport in data-flow systems can entail transporting and transforming data among different components within a single node or between nodes in distributed fashion. Data-flow systems provide the means for data transformation to take place in series or in parallel fashion, which helps the system improve performance by adding concurrency to the system. Other considerations for these system include modifiability, security, and reusability of worker components capable of performing complex operations. An example of an architectural pattern for data-flow systems is the pipe and filter architectural pattern.

Pipe and Filter Pattern

The pipe and filter architectural pattern decomposes software systems into components that carry out two major functions: processing and transforming data and transferring data between components. Components responsible for processing and transforming data are referred as filters, while components that transfer data between components are referred as pipes. Together, these components are combined in various ways to create families of related systems that process streams of data (Buschmann et al. 1996). The pipes and filters architectural pattern is commonly seen in data-flow systems, where data inputs need to be transformed into data output through a series of computational or manipulative components (Pressman 2010). The structure of the pipe and filter architectural pattern is often presented using a box-and-line diagram, such as the one in Figure 4.3. As seen, systems

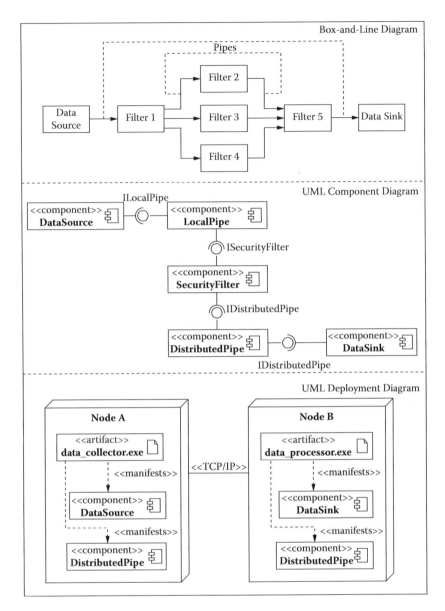

FIGURE 4.3
The pipe and filter architectural pattern.

based on the pipe and filter architectural pattern require a data source, one or more filter components, and a data sink, all connected via filters.

Using the box-and-line diagram presented in Figure 4.3, the flow of operations of pipe and filter systems can be described as follows. Initially, the *DataSource* component produces data and sends it to the *Filter 1* component through a *Pipe*, denoted by an arrow flowing out of the *DataSource* component and into *Filter 1*. The *Filter 1* component processes the data, transforms it, and outputs the transformed data to three other filters for further processing. At this point, three independent and concurrent data transformations occur and their results sent to *Filter 5*. This process continues until the final formatted output is sent to the *DataSink*.

TABLE 4.4

Architectural Components for Distributed Signal Processing System

Component	Description
Data source	Produces real-time video or audio streams
Local pipe	Mechanism for transferring video or audio data streams locally from data source to security filter
Security filter	Transforms data streams by encrypting flow of data
Distributed pipe	Mechanism for transferring encrypted data streams wirelessly (e.g., Satellite Communications [SATCOM]) from local site to remote site; provides the logical connection between data source and data sink
Data sink	Destination component where data streams are stored for later review

When using the pipe and filter architectural pattern, the software system consumes and processes input data incrementally, in separate filters, instead of consuming and processing all of its input data at once. This allows the system to become more efficient, mainly by achieving low latency, which can be achieved through parallel processing (Buschmann et al. 1996). Also, by segregating the processing components and abstracting the data transferring process, processing and computations can be performed across process boundaries or across node boundaries. In these cases, the pipe and filter architectural pattern can exist within another architectural pattern for distributed systems. That is, several computers, executing different processes, can work together to process input data, transform the data, and generate the desired output data.

Consider the design of a signal processing system that operates on real-time video or audio streams and is designed to collect data, encrypt it, and forward it for further processing. This process can be repeated for various steps of data processing; however, for simplicity, the number of pipes and filters is limited to present the concept in a concise manner. Using the pipe and filter architectural pattern, the components in Table 4.4 are identified.

Together, these components work to collect video and audio data streams, to encrypt them, and to transmit them to a remote location, where data can be further processed and distributed. The pipe and filter logical architecture for the real-time collection system is presented using the component notation in Figure 4.3. As seen, the component notation is used to model and abstract the major functions identified for the system; however, it may still be difficult to envision the actual system simply by viewing the logical distribution of components. Consider the following flow of operations. Once data become available at the *DataSource* component, they are transferred locally to the *SecurityFilter* component using the *LocalPipe* component. At the *SecurityFilter* component, the data stream is transformed using encryption and is transferred to the *DataSink* component using mechanisms provided by the *DistributedPipe* component. In this case, the *DistributedPipe* component abstracts the details of transferring data across the network, since the *DataSource* and *DataSink* are hosted on different nodes; therefore, a deployment view is necessary to properly characterize the system. As seen in the deployment diagram in Figure 4.3, the *DataSource* and *DistributedPipe* components are manifested in *Node A,* while the *DataSink* and (another) *DistributedPipe* components are manifested in *Node B*. The manifestation of

TABLE 4.5

Qualities of the Pipes and Filter Architectural Pattern

Quality	Description
Extensibility	Processing filters can be added easily for more capabilities.
Efficiency	By connecting filters in parallel, concurrency can be achieved to reduce latency in the system.
Reusability	By compartmentalizing pipes and filters, they can both be reused as is in other systems.
Modifiability	Filters are compartmentalized and independent from each other; therefore, it is easy to add or remove filters to enhance the system
Security	At any point during data flow, security components can be injected to the work flow to provide different types of security mechanisms to the data.
Maintainability	Allows for separation of concerns and independence of the filters and pipes; therefore, maintaining existing components becomes easier.

the *LocalPipe* and *SecurityFilter* components is omitted for simplicity; however, they would be presented in *Node A*. This example shows how using different architectural views can enhance the understanding of the true architecture of a system.

The presentation of the pipe and filter system using component diagrams is appropriate since the piping mechanisms entail more advanced mechanisms than a simple method call to another component. However, the same knowledge can be conveyed using a box-and-line diagram or other non-UML diagram approach. The problem with using a simple box-and-line diagram is that it becomes difficult to capture or abstract the work required to realize the work required by the pipe (or connector). When components are identified during the software architecture activity, they are slated for refinement during detailed design work, therefore providing an explicit and manageable unit of design work. By modeling complex pipes as components, the details of their work are abstracted, and future planned work for providing the details of such abstraction can be integrated into the designs and construction schedule, similar to any other component in the system.

The pipe and filter architectural pattern can be applied to a problem of smaller scope where both pipe and filter components reside within a single node and communicate using simple method calls or using simple mechanisms provided by the operating systems, such as message queues. In other cases, creating a customized pipe, such as the *DistributedPipe* presented earlier, may require additional work. Filters can be designed as multiple components manifested by as single process or by multiple independent processes executing within a node and communicating through common inter-process pipe mechanisms. Typically, once the pipe and filter framework is in place, numerous filters can be added (serially or in parallel) to provide additional capabilities. The major quality properties associated with pipes and filter systems are presented in Table 4.5.

Skill Development 4.2: Designing with the Pipes and Filter Architectural Pattern

Using pencil and paper, complete the design for Node B required to distribute the audio and video feed. Once the data reach the data sink, all data need to be decrypted, compressed, and stored in the file system—operations that can take a long time due to the expected massive amounts of data. In addition, data need to be prepared for viewing in real-time using a web server and client PCs and provided to a client (non-web page) application hosted on a mobile phone. In all of these, efficiency is the most important characteristic of the system so that the quality of audio and video is appropriate. Assuming that there are no resource constraints, also draw a deployment diagram to helps support the required efficiency of the system. How does the pipe and filter pattern help in meeting efficiency expectations?

DISTRIBUTED SYSTEMS

Distributed systems are commonly known as systems decomposed into multiple processes that collaborate through the network. These systems are ubiquitous in today's modern systems thanks to wireless, mobile, and Internet technology. In some distributed systems, one or more distributed processes perform work on behalf of client users and provide a bridge to some server computer, typically located remotely and performing work delegated to it by the client part of the system. Once complete, results are typically returned back to clients for viewing and further processing. Other distributed systems may be composed of peer nodes, each with similar capabilities and collaborating together to provide enhanced services, such as music-sharing distributed applications. These forms of distributed systems are well-known in the sense that their deployment architecture typically entails multiple nodes. However, with the advent of multiple CPU architectures, distributed architectures are also relevant to software that executes on a single node with multiprocessor capability. The main concerns for distributed systems may include performance, reliability, availability, security, and interoperability. Some examples are Internet systems with web services and high-performance scientific computing projects such as the Search for Extraterrestrial Intelligence (SETI) program or the Large Hadron Collider (LHC) at CERN. In such systems, multiple processors that may reside on different physical machines or in different concurrent processes on a single machine cooperate to solve the tasks required of the system. Common architectural patterns for these systems include

- Client–server
- Broker

Client–Server Pattern

The client–server architecture is a popular architectural pattern present in today's modern systems. It decomposes software systems into two main components: the client and the server. These components are manifested as individual processes that can be distributed over the network or within a single node. Client–server systems are not determined merely by separating processes or by distributing processes across the network but by having one

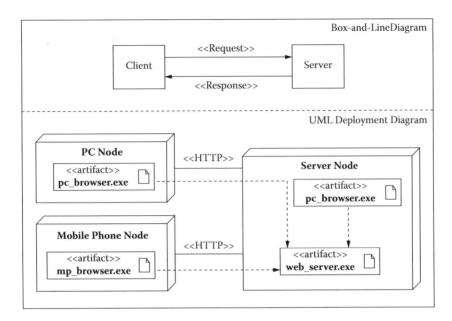

FIGURE 4.4
The client–server architectural pattern.

process, the client, depend on the services provided by another process, the server. The most pervasive example of a client–server system today includes the web browser client and the web server. When searching for a particular site using the web browser client, a connection is made to the server, a request is sent and received by the server, and the server processes the requests and sends a response back to the client. Note that this is also true regardless of the location—which can be on the same node as the server— of the web client, as long as it can connect to the server. In addition, web browser clients are not very useful without the services provided by the server; therefore, they are dependent on the server. Figure 4.4 presents the client–server architectural pattern.

Client–server systems are particularly useful for distributed systems with a large client base, since they provide localization of data in one central place. Therefore, making updates or adding new information in once central place is all that it is needed for a multitude of clients to receive this information. The quality attributes associated with client–server systems are identified in Table 4.6.

TABLE 4.6

Qualities of the Client–Server Architectural Pattern

Quality	Description
Interoperability	Allows clients on different platforms to interoperate with servers of different platforms
Modifiability	Allows for centralized changes in the server and quick distribution among many clients
Availability	By separating server data, multiple server nodes can be connected as backup to increase the server data or services' availability
Reusability	By separating server from clients, services or data provided by the server can be reused in different applications

Servers can abstract the services—and the details of providing those services—provided by the host platform, therefore creating a window for clients to interoperate with the host platform. When done properly, this allows interoperation between systems of different platforms. Client–server systems can also lead to highly modifiable systems. Consider a corporate web-based intranet system, where modifying or adding completely new system capabilities may require creating the necessary server code, including a new hyperlink to the existing corporate portal, and deploying the modified code to the production server. Once deployed, everyone in the corporate network would have instant access to the modified system. Also, by separating the client application from the server data, client–server systems allow designers to render multiple views of the same data; clients can be improved or replaced independently of the resources needed to perform computations on the data; multiple clients can share the resources of a server allowing for increased efficiency; or the user interface can be replaced completely, allowing specialized clients to consume and perform additional processing on the data for further processing.

Broker Pattern

The broker architectural pattern provides mechanisms for achieving better flexibility between clients and servers in a distributed environment. Consider the client–server example presented in Figure 4.4. In the typical client–server architectural pattern, clients directly access services of servers, which may require them to establish direct connection (e.g., Transmission Control Protocol/Internet Protocol [TCP/IP]) or employ other interprocess communication mechanisms for communicating with the server. This result in a higher degree of coupling between clients and servers, which leads to complexity for systems expected to evolve by providing services from different servers hosted at different locations. In some cases, client terminals need to be able to access services from multiple servers without knowing their actual locations or particular details of communication for accessing those services. This leads to systems with increased interoperability and flexibility.

The broker architectural pattern decreases coupling between clients and servers by mediating between them so that one client can transparently access the services of multiple servers. Instead of accessing servers directly, clients access their functionality via a broker component, which locates appropriate servers, forwards requests, and relays responses (including exceptions) back to clients (Buschmann et al. 1996). With this mechanism in place, clients can request services as if they were provided locally on the same node as the server, when they are in fact being provided in distributed fashion over the network by different nodes. The main participants in the broker architectural pattern are presented in Table 4.7, and examples of modeling broker systems are presented in Figure 4.5 using box-and-line, UML components, and UML deployment diagrams.

In the box-and-line diagram presented in Figure 4.5, it can be seen that broker components can interoperate with other brokers, so that if a service requested by a client is accessible through a separate broker this communication can be established to provide clients additional services. For example, *Client 1* may forward a request to *Broker 1* for a particular service. *Broker 1*, after determining that *Server 2* provides the service requested, forwards

TABLE 4.7

Components of the Broker Architectural Pattern

Component	Description
Client	Applications that use the services provided by one or more servers
ClientProxy	Component that provides transparency (at client) between remote and local components so that remote components appear as local ones
Broker	Component that mediates between client and server components
ServerProxy	Component that provides transparency (at server) between remote and local components so that remote components appear as local ones
Server	Provide services to clients; may also act as client to the broker
Bridge	Optional component for encapsulating interoperation among brokers

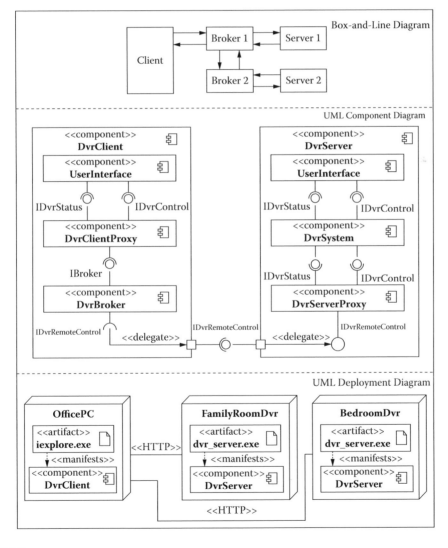

FIGURE 4.5

The broker architectural pattern.

the requests to *Broker 2*, which in turn forwards the requests to *Server 2*. Once the operations required for the particular service are executed, *Server 2* establishes a connection with *Broker 2* and supplies it with a response, which is forwarded to *Broker 1* and subsequently to the *Client*. This sequence highlights a major difference between client–server and broker architectural patterns: in the broker architectural pattern servers may also act as clients to the broker, whereas in client–server architectures roles are exclusive so that servers are never clients (Buschmann et al. 1996).

Consider the architectural design of the distributed digital video recording (DVR) system presented in the UML component diagram in Figure 4.5. In this example, two proxies are created to provide transparency at both client and server side. The *DvrClientProxy* component realizes the *IDvrStatus* and *IDvrControl* in a remote environment, while the *DvrServerProxy* realizes these interfaces in a local environment providing direct connection to the DVR computer. Therefore, both user interfaces at the client and server locations can be interchangeable, since they both interface with the *DvrSystem* component through well-defined methods provided by these interfaces. With these mechanisms in place, the broker system begins by initializing the DVR system to find appropriate servers and identify their provided services, as seen in Figure 4.6. Notice that in this example the optional bridge component identified in Table 4.7 is not used.

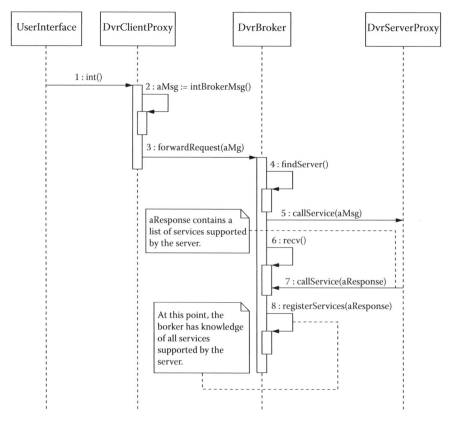

FIGURE 4.6
The broker architectural pattern—initialization.

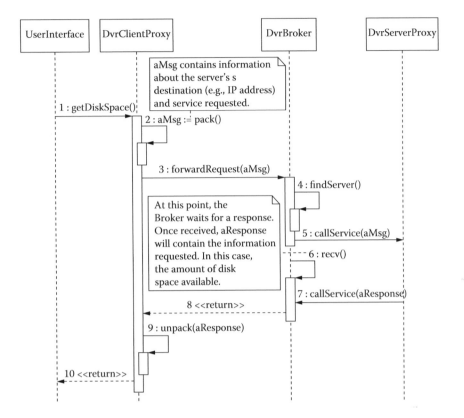

FIGURE 4.7
The broker architectural pattern—client operation.

As seen, once the system begins initialization an initialization message containing a request for services and client information is created and forwarded to the *DvrBroker* component, which finds appropriate servers and transmits the message for processing. At this point, the *DvrBroker* waits for a response, which contains the services provided by the particular server; these services are registered and become available to the client during system operation. Once the system is initialized, services from remote severs can be accessed through the broker, as seen in Figure 4.7. In this example, the client requests information about the DVR's available disk space. Notice that the client's *UserInterface* component, the *getDiskSpace()* interface method, can be called as if the DVR system were local to the client.

An important architectural design element for this system involves the deployment aspect of the DVR system. The logical view for architectural design does not convey enough information to fully provide the context for the operations that take place in the DVR system. Figure 4.5 provides a UML deployment diagram to add this context to the architectural effort. As seen, the system employs two DVR nodes, which manifest the *DvrServer* component identified in the UML component diagram. This means that the *getDiskSpace()* operation can be mapped to either *FamilyroomDvr* or *BedroomDvr* systems, all performed transparently from clients. That is, the call made to the *DvrServerProxy* to get service (i.e., *callService(aMsg)*) can be made to either node (i.e., *FamilyroomDvr* or *BedroomDvr*)

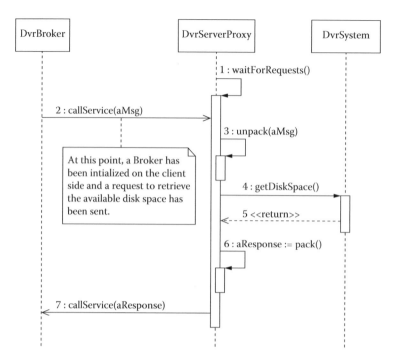

FIGURE 4.8

The broker architectural pattern—server operation.

transparently from clients, and the response is processed identically by the client. In similar fashion, many other nodes can be added to the system without affecting the client application. This provides additional flexibility when modifying the system to add more nodes. On the server side, messages received are processed as presented in Figure 4.8.

As seen, the *DvrServerProxy* interfaces directly with the *DvrSystem* to relay requests from clients and prepare responses for transmission back to one or more clients. In this case, once the *DvrServerProxy* receives a message, interprets it, and makes the *getDiskSpace()* operation call to the *DvrSystem* component, the *getDiskSpace()* operation encapsulates the details of the protocols required for the direct communication between the server component and the actual DVR computer. Once a response is received from the DVR computer, the *getDiskSpace()* returns with results from the disk space availability; these are packaged into a message and sent back to the broker as response for the client's requests. This process is repeated for all other services requested by clients.

In practice, there are numerous variations of architectural designs based on the broker architectural pattern. Some broker systems may have the broker component deployed on separate nodes from the client; others allow clients to communicate directly with servers in special cases; some rely on remote procedure calls (vs. the messaging approach presented here); and others rely on reactive models, where callback methods from registered components are invoked by the broker whenever an event is triggered. However, all broker systems typically benefit mainly from the flexibility provided by decoupling clients and servers. The quality attributes associated with broker systems are identified in Table 4.8.

TABLE 4.8

Qualities of the Broker Architectural Pattern

Quality	Description
Interoperability	Allows clients on different platforms to interoperate with servers of different platforms; also allows clients to interoperate (transparently) with multiple servers
Modifiability	Allows for centralized changes in the server and quick distribution among many clients
Portability	By porting the broker to different platforms, services provided by the system can be easily acquired by new clients in different platforms
Reusability	Brokers abstract many system calls required for providing communication between nodes; when using brokers, many complex services can be reused in other applications that require similar distributed operations

INTERACTIVE SYSTEMS

Interactive systems are systems that support user interactions, typically through user interfaces. When designing interactive systems, design alternatives concentrate on two main quality attributes: usability and modifiability. As stated before, usability refers to the quality goal that seeks to minimize the degree of complexity involved when learning or using the system. Usable systems are designed in such way that operators can quickly become proficient with the system; they also respond to user requests rapidly to support high interactivity requirements. A large portion of usability design takes place during the user interface design activity. Whereas usability is achieved mostly through user interface design, modifiability and interactive performance are mainly functions of the architectural logical design. To maximize modifiability and performance in interactive systems, the graphic user interface that represents the system data needs to be efficiently decoupled from the functional system core. By doing this, the functional core—which is typically stable since it is largely based on functional requirements—is separated from user displays, which are largely based on quality requirements. Since user interfaces are more likely to change and adapted to future versions of software systems, segregating them from the system core increases the modifiability of interactive systems. Examples of interactive systems include gaming systems, simulations, and Internet applications, where such systems need to respond to user requests rapidly and update the display so the user can interact appropriately. The mainstream architectural pattern employed in most interactive systems is the model–view–controller (MVC).

Model–View–Controller Pattern

The MVC architectural pattern is used in interactive applications that require flexible incorporation of human–computer interfaces. With the MVC, systems are decomposed into three main components that handle independently the system's input, processing, and output. By separating the system's output from its core processing functions, different representations of the system core can be easily supported. The main components present in the MVC architectural pattern are presented in Table 4.9.

TABLE 4.9

Components of the MVC Architectural Pattern

Component	Description
Model	Component that represents the system's core, including its major processing capabilities and data
View	Component that represents the output representation of the system (e.g., graphical output or console based)
Controller	Component (associated with a view) that handles user inputs

View and controller components work together as part of the user interface to accept user input and transform this input into format compatible with the model component. In some variants of the MVC, the responsibility of controllers and views are fused into one component. The relationship among the model, view, and controller components can vary depending on the application; however, at minimum, MVC designs provide relationships that allow changes in the model to be propagated to its view and, when necessary, to controllers. This way, MVC systems provide a systematic, flexible, and controlled approach for accepting system inputs and providing system outputs.

As an architectural pattern, MVC defines the interfaces required for the change propagation mechanisms among the model, view, and controller components. However, it does not (and should not) specify the details of how the change propagation mechanism is actually implemented. Details of such mechanisms are left to the detailed design activity, which can provide design patterns, such as the observer, to realize the intent of the MCV. As an architectural pattern, MVC designs should specify the components, their interfaces, and the nature of those interfaces to support system development. This fundamental difference provides a clear delineation between MVC and other detailed design patterns. Figure 4.9 presents a generic box-and-line design of the MVC architectural pattern. This diagram presents the MVC in its most connected form, in which bidirectional relationships exist among all components. However, many variants exist that customize relationships among components depending on the application.

Figure 4.9 also presents a UML component diagram for a hypothetical real estate housing market system that allows users to find properties for sale. The real estate system is based on the MVC architectural pattern and is composed of two views, each with their own controller and a model that contains all real estate information. The two views are designed uniquely for usability on a standard PC and large SMART board environment. Since the form factor of PC monitors and SMART Boards differ significantly, two different views are created for the system. Since the PC monitor is significantly smaller than the SMART board, the user interface created by the *PCView* component will cover the whole monitor screen and rely on speech recognition technology for its input mechanism. Since the SMART board provides larger space for viewing the software, the *SmartboardView* component provides more informative buttons and menu options to use the software. The SMART board version of the software relies on direct human touch interface or hand gesture recognition. For this reason, two different controller components—one that performs speech processing and the other for hand touch or hand gesture recognition—are designed.

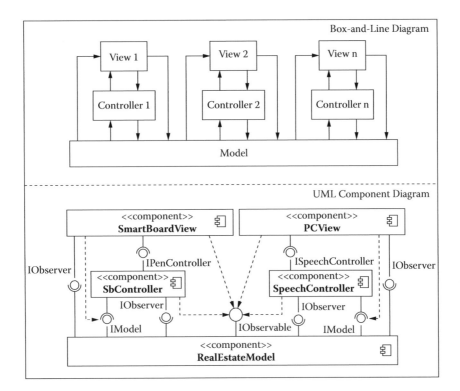

FIGURE 4.9
The model–view–controller architectural pattern.

When using the system on a PC, users can command the system using speech, such as "Find single family homes in Lakeland, Florida." Once this input is received through the PC's microphone, the speech controller transforms it into a command that is passed on the model using the provided *IModel* interface. Once the request is processed by the model component, it uses the *IObserver* interface to employ the change propagation mechanisms to let the *PCView* component—or any other view associated with the model—know that the request has been processed. At this point, the *PCView* component retrieves the data using the model's *IModel* interface and displays them to users. A similar approach is conducted in the SMART board version of the system. These sequences of operations for the MVC system are presented in Figure 4.10.

From this trivial example, the major advantage in the flexibility that MVC systems provide can be clearly examined. For example, consider the case where a more advanced speech processor is created. In this case, neither view nor model components need to be modified for this addition. This means that support for enhanced speech processing or new languages can be added to the real estate system without much effort. Similarly, other views for the same data can be incorporated easily to the system, for example, a view providing graphical descriptive or inferential statistics for housing markets based on the model's data. Finally, advanced computational features can be added to the real estate systems by adding faster search algorithms to the model component independently from both view and controller. This flexibility can be extended to distributed environments, such as

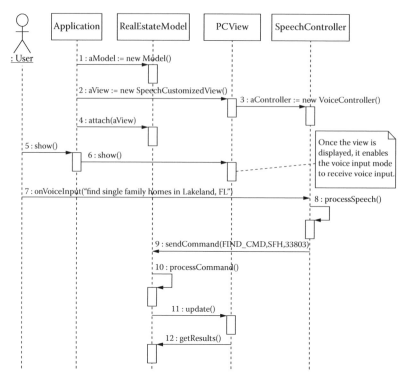

FIGURE 4.10

The sequence for searching for single-family homes in Lakeland, Florida.

TABLE 4.10

Qualities of the MVC Architectural Pattern

Quality	Description
Modifiability	Easy to exchange, enhance, or add additional user interfaces
Usability	By allowing easy exchangeability of user interfaces, systems can be configured with different user interfaces to meet different usability needs of particular groups of customers
Reusability	By separating the concerns of the model, view, and controller components, they can all be reused in other systems

Internet systems, where MVC architectures are very popular. Systems based on the MVC benefit from flexibility that allows them to evolve gracefully over time. The main quality attributes associated with MVC systems are presented in Table 4.10.

There are some variations of the MVC architectural pattern. One popular variation of designing MVC systems includes the fusion of views and controller components into one component. This variant was very popular in the 1990s as part of Microsoft's Document-View architecture integrated in the Microsoft Foundation Classes (MFC) Visual C++ environment. The Document-View architecture sacrificed exchangeability of the controller for simplicity. Other, more extensive variations include the process–abstraction–controller (PAC) architectural pattern (Qian et al. 2009). The PAC is an extension of the MVC, where systems are decomposed into agents, each containing a process, abstraction, and controller components arranged in hierarchical fashion.

Skill Development 4.3: Distributed MVC Real Estate System

Consider a distributed, Internet version of the MVC real estate system. Using pencil and paper, use UML ports and delegate relationships to modify the component diagram of Figure 4.9 to support the development of this system under the new environment constraints. Draw also a deployment diagram that shows how the system can be deployed on tablets and mobile phones. Feel free to modify the original MVC relationships and diagram to account for this new problem.

HIERARCHICAL SYSTEMS

Hierarchical systems are systems in which components can be structured in hierarchical fashion so that components exist at different levels of abstraction and each level addresses a particular concern of the software system. For each level identified in the hierarchical system, one or more components can be identified, each possibly branching downward to other components necessary to carry out a particular operation. Conceptually, components residing at higher levels of the hierarchy structure dispatch requests and rely on the services of those in lower levels of the hierarchy. In some cases, access to the services provided at the different levels can be unified and strictly controlled, therefore compartmentalizing them and increasing the reusability of their services. In other cases, the hierarchy structure is mapped conceptually to the processing of data, resulting in a set of functional cohesive components at appropriate levels of abstraction for creating modular systems. In any case, designing systems in hierarchical fashion typically leads to well-structured and modular systems. Two common architectural patterns for hierarchical systems are

- Main program and subroutine
- Layered

Main Program and Subroutine

The main program and subroutine architectural pattern is popular in systems that are designed using the structured (or functional) design strategy. In these systems, a main component (or program) contains the main data for the program, which is shared among components residing at lower levels of the hierarchy. Each level of the hierarchy represents refinements of the system, so that level n provides the main level; level $n + 1$ provides further refinements of services; $n + 2$ provides even further refinements, and so on. This process continues until the system is decomposed into an appropriate set of finer-grained components (or subroutines). To illustrate this concept, consider creating the logical architecture for a printer system, based on its data-flow diagram (DFD). When using a DFD, inputs and outputs are represented by boxes, data flowing through systems are represented by arrows, and data transformations are represented by circles, as presented in Figure 4.11. As seen, a

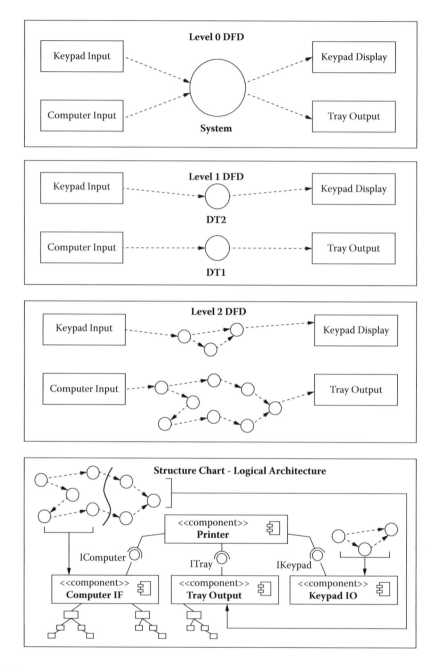

FIGURE 4.11
The main program and subroutine architectural pattern.

Level 0 DFD represents the initial context of the system. The input source 1 (IS1) represents a keypad for configuration of the printer, and the input source 2 (IS2) represents input from the computer that sends jobs to the printer. Two system outputs are presented: one to the printer's onboard display (OD1); and another for the paper printout (OD2). The initial context of the system (i.e., Level 0) design indicates that the system transforms two inputs to generate two different outputs. As the DFD is refined, a Level 1 DFD is produced to indicate that two

TABLE 4.11

Quality Properties of the Main Program and Subroutine Pattern

Quality	Description
Modifiability	By decomposing the system into independent, single-purpose components, each component becomes easier to understand and manage.
Reusability	Independent, finer-grained components can be reused in other systems.

distinct transformations are required: one for transforming data from the keypad input to the keypad display; and the other for transforming computer input into a printout. In the Level 2 DFD, two distinct flows of data are identified: one to generate printouts in black and white; and the other to generate printouts in color. In each flow, different transformations are required. This refinement is iteratively done, and once all transformations are identified they can be grouped into components to form the logical architecture of the system. In this example, the print manager (PM), which is the main program, consists of three independent components, which provide the subroutines identified based on the data transformations. A more detailed coverage of this approach is represented by Pressman (2010, p. 265).

The main components identified for the main program and subroutine architectural pattern include one main component, which stores all the data, and various, finer-grained, subcomponents that carry out detailed system operations. Systems based on this architectural pattern benefit mainly from its structured decomposing, such that independent, single-purpose components become easier to understand, manage, code, debug, and reuse. The main quality properties associated with the main program and subroutine architectural pattern are presented in Table 4.11.

Layered Pattern

The main program and subroutine architectural pattern leads to hierarchical structures that expand vertically and horizontally, with each level of the hierarchy containing one or more components that can interact with one or more components at lower-levels of the hierarchy. A more constrained form of hierarchical structure involves each layer having one main component—which can be composed internally of multiple components—that provides a unified interface for communicating with components residing immediately below in the hierarchy structure. This form of constrained collaboration of hierarchical architectures is captured with the layered architectural pattern. With the layered architectural pattern, the work performed to accomplish a system function is somewhat independent and more compartmentalized than in the main program and subroutine. It is used when systems can be decomposed into cohesive layers with a structured way of interfacing between layers. The layered architecture is widely used in systems software, such as an operating system's communication stack, where each layer is an abstraction of a major function of communication systems. Each layer also relies on services from other layers directly below to create communication packets and to provide quality of service, routing services, node-to-node communication, and transmission using varied physical layers. This way, rules can be imposed on the system's logical architecture to restrict access among components, therefore decreasing the system's coupling and increasing its modifiability and portability. That is, by compartmentalizing major system functions and controlling access to their services (via well-defined and stable interfaces), system modifiability and portability can be increased.

Consider the logical architecture of an environmental embedded monitor and control system capable of being remotely deployed to monitor and control other nodes in a system that provides environmental information. The system works by receiving a collection schedule that is used to activate and deactivate other nodes in the system, to control their operations, and to retrieve their collected data. Since the system is deployed in environmental areas where communication infrastructure may not be present, it uses satellite communications to receive collection schedules and to provide environmental information back to a central station, where it can be safely analyzed. Collection schedules are encrypted to provide additional level of security, which means that upon receipt the remotely deployed system needs to decrypt the messages and perform application-dependent logic to interpret and execute them. Once a collection schedule for a particular node in the system is executed, the system interfaces with the hardware to send appropriate commands to other collection nodes. The logical architecture for this system is designed using the layered architectural pattern, as seen in Figure 4.12.

The box-and-line design of Figure 4.12 presents a generic approach to designing layered software. It shows each independent layer collaborating only with the services of the layers immediately below. This way, replacing services at one layer does not affect the whole system. When applied to the environmental monitor and control system, the UML component diagram results in the one presented in Figure 4.12. As seen, the *SatcomLayer* component abstracts the services required to receive a monitor plan, which when received is passed down to the *SecurityLayer* component for decryption and further passed down the layered hierarchy for processing in the *ApplicationLayer*. Once environmental monitoring is activated, the *ApplicationLayer* component interfaces with the *HardwareComponent* to initiate activation of the external nodes. As seen, UML ports are used to show the boundaries of the remote monitor system, and the delegate label is used to indicate that the responsibility for fulfilling the required services is delegated to one or more components in the system. The main quality attributes associated with the layered architectural pattern are presented in Table 4.12.

Skill Development 4.4: Layered Architectural Pattern

Conduct an online search for the Open Systems Interconnection (OSI) reference model or TCP/IP model. Select one and explain how the layered architectural pattern applies to the selected model. Clearly identify each layer, their services, and how they interact with other layers in the system. Can you think of other system software that can be designed using the layered architectural pattern? Come up with such examples and then identify the layers that you would create and the services (and interaction with other layers) within the system.

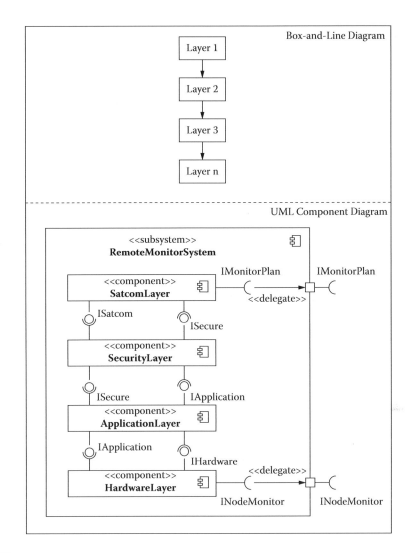

FIGURE 4.12

The layered architectural pattern.

TABLE 4.12

Quality Attributes Associated with the Layered Architectural Pattern

Quality	Description
Modifiability	Dependencies are kept local within layer components. Since components can access other components only through a well-defined and unified interface, the system can be modified easily by swapping layer components with other enhanced or new layer components.
Portability	Services that deal directly with a platform's application programming interface (API) can be encapsulated using a system layer component. Higher-level layers rely on this component for providing system services to the application; therefore, by porting the system's API layer to other platforms the systems become more portable.
Security	The controlled hierarchical structure of layered systems allows for easy incorporation of security components to encrypt or decrypt incoming or outgoing data.
Reusability	By compartmentalizing each layer's services, they become easier to reuse.

CHAPTER SUMMARY

During software architecture, designers spend a great deal of time devising architectural solutions that provide the necessary components and interfaces to achieve systems' requirements. At the architectural level, common patterns have emerged that describe the elements of the system and the quality characteristics of those elements. These patterns, also known as architectural styles, have emerged as the mainstream approach for achieving reuse of successful design solutions at the architectural level and are fundamental to the efficient creation of software architectures. Architectural patterns provide generic, reusable architectural solutions, documented in a way that can be easily understood and applied to new problems requiring similar architectural features. Decisions based on architectural patterns benefit from years of documented experience that highlights the solution approach to given problems, the benefits of these approaches, and the consequences of designing the system with a particular style.

Architectural patterns can be classified by the type of systems they support, such as data-centered, data-flow, distributed, interactive, and hierarchical systems. Examples of architectural patterns include blackboard, pipe and filter, client–server, broker, model–view–controller, main program and subroutine, and layered patterns. These patterns allow designers to efficiently conduct principled analyses of the layout of subsystems and components that need to communicate in the operational system. During the past decade, many styles and patterns for software architecture have been researched and published. Many of these patterns have been identified in pattern catalogue books; some of these are common design patterns in enterprise-level systems, while others address specific needs such as distributed systems. Identifying and designing using architectural patterns can improve the efficiency of the development process and the quality of the final system.

REVIEW QUESTIONS

1. What is an architectural pattern, and how does it differ from detailed design patterns?
2. List and explain the different types of systems discussed for which architectural patterns can be employed.
3. Are software architectures restricted to only one architectural pattern for its logical design, or can they include more than one architectural pattern? Explain with examples.
4. Can architectural patterns lead to direct translation to code? Explain.
5. Explain the following architectural patterns, and provide an example of a system (different from the one discussed in this chapter) appropriate for them. Explain how these patterns support particular quality attributes.
   a. Blackboard
   b. Pipe and filter
   c. MVC
   d. Layered

6. Compare and contrasts the following architectural patterns:
   a. Client–server vs. broker
   b. Layered vs. main program and subroutine
7. How can the pipe and filter architectural pattern enhance the performance of software systems?
8. How can the MVC enhance a system's modifiability, usability, and reusability?
9. How can the broker pattern enhance a system's interoperability?
10. How can the layered pattern support a system's security and portability?
11. Explain how using design elements from different architectural views can support the use of architectural patterns for providing a complete picture of an architectural design element.

CHAPTER EXERCISES

1. Find a computer using the Microsoft Windows operation systems and Microsoft Office Word. Perform a Google search on how to split the window horizontally of the particular version of Word that you are executing so that you can split a document horizontally into two windows that mirror each other. Position each window on the same document location, and begin typing in the topmost window. As you type, you should see the bottom window getting updated in real time to incorporate the newly entered text. Explain how architectural patterns can help achieve this capability. Provide specific examples of architectural patterns that can be used for this capability.
2. Using the UML tool of choice, create the logical design using patterns for a portable, interactive, and distributed software system. State your assumptions, and accompany your design with a rationale of why the particular patterns were selected and how they support the required quality attributes. Feel free to design around the patterns to provide other views and to present a whole picture of the system design.

REFERENCES

Alexander, Christopher, Sara Ishikawa, Murray Silverstein, Max Jacobson, Ingrid Fiksdahl-King, and Shlomo Angel. *A Pattern Language: Towns, Buildings, Construction.* New York: Oxford University Press, 1977.

Bass, Len, Paul Clements, and Rick Kazman. *Software Architecture in Practice*, 2d ed. Boston: Addison-Wesley, 2003.

Buschmann, Frank, Regine Meunier, Hans Rohnert, Peter Sommerlad, and Michael Stal. *Pattern-Oriented Software Architecture: A System of Patterns.* West Sussex, UK: Wiley, 1996.

Clements, Paul, Rick Kazman, and Mark Klein. *Evaluating Software Architectures.* Santa Clara, CA: Addison Wesley, 2001.

Pressman, Roger S. *Software Engineering: A Practitioner's Approach*, 7th ed. Belmont, CA: McGraw-Hill, 2010.

Qian, Kai, Xiang Fu, Lixin Tao, Chong-Wei Xu, and Jorge L. Diaz-Herrera. *Software Architecture and Design Illuminated.* Sudbury, MA: Jones & Barlett, 2009.

Taylor, Richard N., Nenad Medvidovic, and Eric M. Dashofy. *Software Architecture: Foundations, Theory, and Practice.* Hoboken, NJ: Wiley, 2009.

5

Principles of Detailed Design

CHAPTER OBJECTIVES

- Understand the role of detailed design within the software design phase
- Become familiar with detailed design tasks during software design
- Become familiar with the detailed design process
- Understand fundamental concepts of object-oriented concepts and principles for component designs
- Understand the role of documentation in software design and how to create a software design document

---

CONCEPTUAL OVERVIEW

The previous chapters presented the software architecture activity as a macrodesign approach for transforming software requirements into design elements that specify the main components and interfaces of software systems. This holistic black-box approach is essential for establishing the initial design and a framework of quality that guides and supports the detailed design and construction of software systems. During detailed design, the design process continues where software architecture leaves off for providing a white-box approach to design, where details left undefined and deferred to downstream designers are created to define the necessary details for fully specifying the internal structure and behavior of components identified during architecture. These detailed designs fill the gaps in the design and provide a complete picture of how the system achieves its functional requirements within the quality framework established by the software architecture. Detailed design decisions can significantly shape the system's quality properties (e.g., portability, performance, usability); therefore, they must exist within the bounds of the software architecture. In some cases, where modeling tools are used to generate code, detailed designs can also significantly impact the quality properties of the construction phase. Upon completion of the detailed design activity, the system's design is sufficiently complete so that it can be formally documented, reviewed, and approved by the system's stakeholders, which marks the end of the design phase.

WHAT IS DETAILED DESIGN?

The detailed design activity begins once the software architecture is specified, reviewed, and approved by all stakeholders in the project. During detailed design, logical components are refined and their interactions are modeled to verify the validity of their structural composition. The execution of the detailed design activity requires a shift from the macrodesign approach to the microdesign approach to further decompose and refine system components into one or more fine-grained elements, functions, and data variables required for supporting the internal structure and behavior of components that meet assigned roles during the software architecture activity. IEEE (1990, p. 26) defines detailed design as

1. The process of refining and expanding the preliminary design phase of a system or component to the extent that the design is sufficiently complete to be implemented.
2. The result of the process in 1.

Extending the IEEE definition, detailed design is both the process of refining the software architecture to reach a point where construction can begin and the result of such process. The detailed design activity is the last major design effort before the software construction phase. A fundamental difference between architectural and detailed design is that whereas the former is concerned mostly with defining the major components of the system and their interfaces, the latter is concerned with how these components realize their assigned responsibility. This suggests that architectural designs employ a holistic approach to software system design, which emphasizes system quality, while detailed design focuses on particular components within the system, which emphasizes the functional aspects of a system. This fundamental difference is essential in determining what and how work is performed during these activities. For example, whereas the component notation provides an appropriate mechanism for designing logical architectures, their level of abstraction is inappropriate for modeling detailed design elements. Therefore, in object-oriented systems, classes and interfaces become the major unit of design work. This, in turn, influences the type of analyses performed during both activities. The modeling and analyses that occur during architecture help answer the questions of what needs to be developed, and by themselves these models and analyses cannot be used to build directly a working software system. Detailed design goes deep into each component to define its internal structure and behavioral capabilities, and the resulting design leads to natural and efficient construction of software. Clements, Bachmann, Bass, Garlan, Ivers, Little, Nord, and Stafford (2002, p. 5) differentiate between architectural and detailed design as follows:

Architecture is design, but not all design is architecture. That is, many design decisions are left unbound by the architecture and are happily left to the discretion and good judgement of downstream designers and implementers. The architecture establishes constraints on downstream activities, and those activities must produce artifacts—finer-grained design and code—that are compliant with the archtiecture, but architecture does not define an implementation.

Detailed design is closely related to architecture and construction; therefore, successful designers (during detailed design) are required to have a full understanding of the system's requirements and architecture, design strategy, programming language, and methods and processes for software quality control. Detailed designers must also work closely with stakeholders (e.g., hardware team, test team, quality team, management) to provide designs that accommodate multiple concerns appropriate to the detailed design activity. This requires a holistic vision—different from that of the software architecture designer—to envision detailed designs and how they relate to requirements, architecture, and construction, as presented in Figure 5.1.

The conceptual model presented in Figure 5.1 shows interrelationships that detailed design elements have with other architectural or construction elements. In this context,

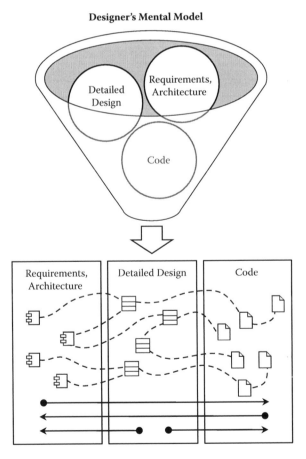

FIGURE 5.1
Context of detailed design activity.

detailed designs provide the essential structure that acts as bridge connecting the work performed during architecture and construction. Detailed designs need to incorporate design alternatives that support the requirements and quality attributes (e.g., testability, maintainability, modifiability) identified in previous phases and activities of the software engineering life cycle. When presented with requirements or concerns from other stakeholders, detailed designers are able to visualize designs that provide the required structural and behavioral capabilities for achieving those needs. As they work to shape new or existing designs, they are also capable of visualizing the executing code to help them formalize the design. When given code, such as the case during the maintenance phase, detailed designers are required to envision detailed designs or even reverse engineer the code into designs and to understand how both code and designs relate to the original software requirements. This mental model allows designers to understand the complex interdependencies that exist among these different life cycle phases and how requirements and quality attributes are achieved throughout the software project. Achieving such visions from designers helps in all aspects of designing high-quality, large-scale software systems.

KEY TASKS IN DETAILED DESIGN

It can be argued that the detailed design phase is where most of the problem-solving activities occur in software projects. Consider the case where formal design processes are followed so that the requirements phase is followed by the architectural design activity, which is followed by detailed design. In many practical applications, the architectural design activity defers complex problem solving to the detailed design activity mainly through abstraction. In some cases, even defining the requirements is deferred to the detailed design phase, leaving the detailed design activity as the gatekeeper for ensuring that the system's specification and design are sufficiently complete before construction begins. Deferring such problems to the construction phase is a recipe for failure, since this typically results in higher cost (Clements, Kazman, and Klein 2001). When done properly, detailed designs should provide a ready-made solution that eases the construction process. To achieve this during detailed design, designers must fully understand requirements assigned to components and architectural decisions deriving detailed design; they must design complex interfaces, identify design patterns, evaluate and validate detailed designs, generate code from the models, and establish policies for ensuring design synchronicity throughout the construction phase.

DETAILED DESIGN PROCESS

The detailed design process is carried out to identify how architectural components are designed with enough detail so that their implementation using programming languages can follow without much effort. Many process flows can be identified and used to carry out and manage detailed design activity, including iterative, sequential, and spiral (Pressman 2010). Regardless of the particular process flow selected for a given project, carrying out the detailed design activity requires the following fundamental tasks:

- Understanding the architecture and requirements
- Creating detailed design
- Evaluating detailed design
- Documenting detailed design
- Monitoring and controlling implementation

UNDERSTANDING THE ARCHITECTURE AND REQUIREMENTS

Unlike the software architecture activity, where the complete set of system requirements are evaluated and well understood, designers during the detailed design activity focus on requirements allocated to their specific components. In some cases, requirements can cross-cut several components; therefore, communication with other designers is essential to coordinating the design solution without duplicating work. Besides addressing requirements passed on from the architectural activity, it is also common during detailed design to derive new software requirements as knowledge of the system is enhanced throughout the detailed design activity. Derived requirements are requirements based on higher-level specifications created to address a finer-grained function or process during detailed design and construction. These requirements can help standardize operations for higher-level requirements identified in previous phases and activities of the project. Consider an embedded real-time software system broken down into five different major subsystem components, each executed on different target hardware and broken down further into numerous other components. During requirements, the functional capability to log events in the system is specified. To carry out this function of the system, a detailed design activity is done to create a common event logger so that all components in the systems rely on a standardized way for logging events in the system. Because of the resource-constrained environment of the particular embedded system, simply having one functional requirement to log events provides insufficient specification for the desired behavior. Consider the case where the event logger is designed to log all events in the system to a file without limits or policies to manage how events are stored, purged, and so forth. In such a resource-constrained environment, enforcing and verifying policies for such behavior is essential, since a large number of events, depending on the target resources, can slow or bring the system down. In such cases, deriving requirements that specify these policies (e.g., maximum number of events logged, event purge policy such as first-in, first-out (FIFO), last-in, last-out (LIFO)) provides essential items of verification for the system. These requirements are imposed not by customers but by the design team to enforce a desired capability of the software or process to develop the software. When conducting the detailed design activity, assigned requirements for the components have to be well understood, and, when appropriate, derived requirements need to be specified before construction begins.

Besides understanding requirements during detailed design, understanding and adhering to the software architecture are essential for building high-quality systems. The concept of design synchronicity was presented in Chapter 3 as the degree to which the software implementation conforms to its design. To maintain synchronicity throughout the development effort, all decisions made during detailed design must conform to the system's identified architecture. To achieve this, software processes must be in place for monitoring and controlling detailed designs throughout. Unmanaged deviations from the software architecture during detailed design and construction can reshape the properties of the system and affect its overall capability to meet requirements. Therefore, detailed designers need to work closely with each other and with software architects to ensure that their design choices are consistent with the overall system plan. This is especially true during maintenance phases, where deviations may occur long after the initial system design is devised.

CREATING DETAILED DESIGNS

After requirements and the software architecture are well understood, the detailed design of software components can begin. The detailed design consists of structural and behavioral designs required to specify components sufficiently so that they can be consistently constructed by one or more programmers. This entails various design tasks, including refining or creating components' interface design internal structure, and behavioral design; identifying design patterns; applying design principles; adopting naming conventions; and evaluating and documenting detailed designs. These are discussed in more detail throughout the following sections.

Interface Design

Interface design refers to the design activity that deals with specification of interfaces between components in the design (Sommerville 2010). Interface design can be focused on specifying the interfaces used internally within software components or externally across software components. In both cases, interfaces provide a standardized way for specifying how services are accessed and provided by software components. Interface design allows subsystems to be designed independently and in parallel; therefore, it is typically done first within the detailed design step.

External Interface Design

During the software architecture activity, externally visible interfaces are specified. The realization of these interfaces may involve much detailed design work before they can be used in construction. These may include a customized binary message definition,

Extensible Markup Language (XML) schemas and messages, or other interfaces required for specifying how components interact with other external components. Depending on the interface design effort, a formal interface document can be created and managed independently, similar to the requirements specification or design document. This document, known as the interface control document (ICD), is an important piece of documentation that serves as a written contract between components of the software system to specify how they will communicate. The ICD defines the important data and protocols used for communication between components, therefore providing developers during construction the required information needed to write the software.

Internal Interface Design

The Internal interface definition establishes policies for subsequent development in the software design. It provides a way for abstracting common operations so that problems during detailed design can be reasoned in terms of these interfaces, which provides a higher level of abstraction for specifying rules that apply to a larger set of entities that rely on them. In object-oriented systems, Unified Modeling Language (UML) can be used to create interface designs using class diagrams that include the <<interface>> stereotype in the name section of the class, as presented in Chapter 2. These help identify the major classes and functions that allow intercomponent communication and provide the rules of communication that must be followed by other classes that implement these interfaces during the detailed design activity.

Graphical User Interface Design

Visual designs have a major role in the success or failure of software systems. Systems that meet functional requirements but are not usable cannot succeed. During detailed-design, the initial Human Computer Interface (HCI) design identified during the software architecture activity is refined and the appropriate design for interfacing the Graphical User Interface (GUI) to the whole system is done. During detailed design, all aspects of the GUI—such as modes, navigation, visual designs (e.g., color, icons, fonts), response time and feedback, design modalities (e.g., forms, menu-driven), localization, internationalization, and general human–computer design principles—are fine-tuned.

Designing Internal Structure of Components

Component design is not restricted to object-oriented systems; however, the discussion and approach presented in this section and throughout the book focus on object-oriented systems. Other forms of component design can be employed based on the design strategy, such as the structured design strategy. In object-oriented systems, the internal structure of components is typically modeled using UML through one or more class diagrams. Component design refers to the detailed design task of defining the internal logical structure of components. That is, the internal data structures, algorithms, interface characteristics, and communication mechanisms of all components are all defined during component design. For this reason, component design provides the most significant mechanism for determining the functional correctness of the software system and allows for evaluating alternative solutions before coding begins.

A multitude of principles, guidelines, and patterns exist for creating quality component-level design. These principles guide engineers to make appropriate decisions when refining components into other components and classes and defining the relationships between them. The work produced during component design serves as strong indication of the functional success of the software system. Before these concepts can be understood, it is necessary to understand the basic concepts in component design of object-oriented systems. These include (Gamma et al. 1995):

- Classes and objects
- Interfaces, types, and subtypes
- Dynamic binding
- Polymorphism

Classes

The main unit of composition in object-oriented component design is the class. Chapter 2 introduced classes as modeling entities in UML class diagrams. However, before becoming efficient during component design, a clear distinction between classes and objects needs to be made. A class is a specification that defines the data and services used and provided by particular objects. There are two types of classes in object-oriented component designs, as presented in Table 5.1.

Concrete classes specify the data, services, and implementation of those services required for instantiating objects. Concrete classes provide complete information that supports instantiation of objects at run time that have state and behavior. On the other hand, abstract classes are special types of classes that contain one or more abstract methods, which have no implementation. Because abstract methods contain no implementation, abstract classes cannot be instantiated at run time. A special type of abstract class is one where all methods are abstract. These are equivalent to Java interfaces and the pure virtual classes in C++. As abstract classes, interfaces and pure virtual classes cannot be instantiated at run time. At first glance, it seems logical to think that classes that cannot be instantiated serve little to no purpose in software designs. However, these classes provide powerful mechanisms for creating elegant and reusable designs that can lead to increased maintainability, reusability,

TABLE 5.1

Types of Classes in Component Designs

Type	Description
Concrete	Ordinary class for specifying object's data and behavior
Abstract	Special class that contains at least one abstract method

and efficient software evolution. Abstract classes provide the means for designers to create contracts that dictate the use of interfaces throughout software designs. These contracts are enforced by compilers and are founded on the principles and concepts of interfaces, types, subtypes, dynamic binding, and polymorphism.

Interfaces, Types, Subtypes, Dynamic Binding, and Polymorphism

In a broad sense, an interface is the set of functions that specify the services provided by objects of a particular type. An interface method is simply one method that belongs to an object's interface. The concepts of types and interfaces are interrelated; that is, since an interface specifies the services provided by a particular type, it follows that a particular type refers to a particular interface. In popular object-oriented systems, the concept of types is used interchangeably with classes. A subtype refers to an interface that includes the interface of another type, referred to as its supertype (Gamma et al. 1995). This concept is reflected in object-oriented languages as inheritance. At design time, the concepts of interfaces, types, and subtypes are used to create software that is extensible at run time, mainly through the techniques of dynamic binding and polymorphism. Consider the specification of an interface using an abstract class, which, as discussed before, cannot be instantiated. In such cases, abstract classes are useful for defining the common set of services provided by a specific type. Through inheritance, one or more subtypes can be specified at design time to provide implementations for the defined interfaces, therefore creating concrete classes that share the same interface, as defined by the abstract class. By designing classes this way, different objects can be instantiated at run time to share the same interface but to provide completely different implementations (Gamma et al. 1995). Consider the type Shape with a single interface method named draw(). Now consider two other subtypes (inheriting from Shape), named Circle and Rectangle. By definition, since Circle and Rectangle are subtypes of Shape, then they share its interface, which in this example includes the draw() interface method. This scenario is easily designed in modern programming languages by specifying Shape as pure virtual class in C++ or interface in Java. Both Circle and Rectangle would be designed using a (UML) realization relationship with the Shape type. Since Circle and Rectangle are meant to be concrete classes, they both must provide an implementation for the draw() interface method; otherwise, they would both be abstract classes that cannot be instantiated. With this framework in place, portions of the software *at design time* can be specified using the Shape interface, which both Circle and Rectangle support. At *run time*, services specified by the Shape interface are carried out by the particular run-time object attached to the request, which could be objects of either Circle or Rectangle subtypes. This way, when calling upon the object's draw interface method, the software can behave differently at run time by drawing to the screen either a circle or a rectangle.

The mechanism for providing the run-time association between an object and an interface method is known as dynamic binding (Gamma et al. 1995). This allows objects of the same type hierarchy to behave differently at run time simply by associating the interface method call to the appropriate run-time instance. This capability is known as polymorphism.

Interfaces, types, subtypes, dynamic binding, and polymorphisms are essential to achieving efficient designs of components in object-oriented systems and are the fundamental mechanisms for achieving most object-oriented design principles and patterns.

Objects

Whereas classes are design-time entities, objects are run-time entities; that is, objects are the manifestation of classes and therefore occupy space and time during software execution. For classes to be of use in executing programs, objects have to be instantiated. Instantiation is the process of manifesting a class in the computer's memory; this manifestation is referred to as an object of that class. Therefore, one class can be manifested in the computer's memory as multiple objects, since we can instantiate a class numerous times. This concept is presented in the conceptual model presented in Figure 5.2.

As seen, the code in the main function of the `ProgramDriver` class instructs the compiler to instantiate three different objects of type `ListNode` type. In this example, the specification for objects of type `ListNode` is provided by the `ListNode` class and instantiation of objects of that class is done by employing the new keyword. When the compiled and built version of the code is executed, three different objects of the same class—together with the object of type `ProgramDriver`—will occupy some space in the computer's memory. These three objects of type `ListNode` occupy specific locations in memory and are addressable by their own memory address. This is possible because each object has its own identity. Notice also in the figure that the `ProgramDriver` object has links to the three different node objects, since it has variables holding the addresses to

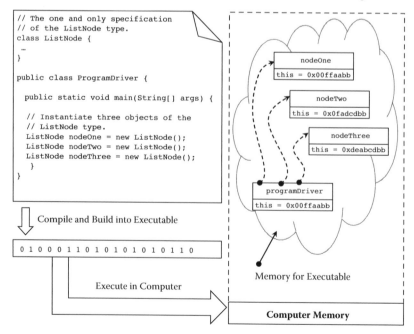

FIGURE 5.2
Conceptual model for classes and objects.

TABLE 5.2

Characteristics of Objects

Characteristic	Description
Attributes	The object's data
Behavior	The object's designed behavior, as specified by its public functions
State	The current state of the object, as defined by the values of its data
Identity	Their own individual memory address
Responsibilities	Two objects of the same class can be instantiated for specific purposes

these objects; therefore, `programDriver` can always access these objects through these variables (i.e., nodeOne, nodeTwo, nodeThree). Unlike classes, objects exist at run time and have specific characteristics such as the ones presented in Table 5.2 (Douglas 1999).

When designing at the component level, careful class specification is essential to allow objects at run time to behave in such a way that flexibility and reusability are added to the software. This in turn allows component designs to provide the means to allow the software to evolve gracefully over time and to become more reusable. Designing efficient component structures allows today's software to adapt to future technology or new system functionality. Therefore, when designing component-level software, careful attention has to be paid in the application of fundamental detailed design principles.

Design Principles for Internal Component Design

Several principles have been identified throughout the literature that help in making component-level design decisions, including

- The open–closed principle (OCP)
- The Liskov substitution principle (LSP)
- The interface segregation principle (ISP)

Open–Closed Principle

The OCP is an essential principle for creating reusable detailed designs. It promotes designs that allow changes to be made by extension of designs rather than by modification of existing code. The main idea behind the OCP is that code that works should remain untouched and that new additions incorporated to address new concerns should be extensions of the original work. The OCP was originally coined by Bertrand Meyer (1997) and states that software designs should be open to extension but closed for modification. At first glance, the OCP sounds contradictory since it promotes designs that are closed to modification. However, in the OCP context, being closed to modification does not mean that designs cannot be modified; it means that modifications should be made as extensions to the design, by adding new design and code instead of modifying existing working designs and code (Marin 2003). This is possible in object-oriented systems through the use of abstract classes and interfaces. Consider a gaming system that includes several types of terrestrial characters, which can roam freely over land, as shown in Listing 5.1.

Listing 5.1: C++ Code for the Gaming System

```cpp
// The terrestrial character.
class TerrestrialCharacter {

public:
  // Draw the character on the screen.
  virtual void draw() { /*Code to draw the terrestrial character.*/
}

  // Make the character run!
  virtual void run() { /* Code to make the character run.*/
};

// The game engine responsible for managing the game.
class GameEngine {

public:
  // Add the character to the screen.
  void add(TerrestrialCharacter* pCharacter) {

    // Display the character.
    pCharacter->draw();

    // Make the character move!
    pCharacter->run();
  }
};
```

As seen, the GameEngine class is designed with an interface method that accepts references (i.e., pointer) to objects that share the TerrestrialCharacter interface. When an object of type TerrestrialCharacter is passed into the addCharacter(...) method, the method draws it to the screen and calls the character's run() method, which activates the character to move over land in a random pattern. This design works fine for all kinds of terrestrial characters; however, it does little to support efficient addition of other types of characters to the game. This is true because the design of the GameEngine class relies on the interface of the concrete TerrestrialCharacter class. Consider the case where characters that move differently—for example, aerial characters or aquatic characters—are added to the gaming system design. In such cases, the addCharacter method needs to be modified to account for these new types of characters. Therefore, the design of the GameEngine class is not closed for modification. That is, the code inside the GameEngine class would have to change, which violates the OCP. To prevent this, the OCP promotes and relies on an indispensable design principle in object-oriented systems, which states that *software designs should rely on interfaces and not on implementations* (Gamma

---

Listing 5.2: C++ Code for the `Character` Interface

```cpp
class Character {

public:
  // Get the type of character.
  virtual string getType() = 0;

  // Draw the character on the screen.
  virtual void draw() = 0;
};
```

---

et al. 1995). Consider the addition of the `Character`* interface to the gaming system's design, as presented in Listing 5.2.

As seen, the `Character` class is abstract, as specified by the two pure virtual methods `getType()` and `draw()`. The character interface can be used to define interface methods that are common to all characters in the gaming system. With this interface in place, the aerial character is added to the design by implementing the `Character` interface, as presented in Listing 5.3.

Listing 5.3: C++ Code for the `AerialCharacter` Class

```cpp
class AerialCharacter : public Character {

public:
  // Get the type of character.
  virtual string getType() {

    // Return the type of character.
    return "aerial";
  }

  // Draw the character on the screen.
  virtual void draw() {

    // Code to draw the aerial character.
    cout<<"drawing aerial character!\n";
  }

  // Make the character fly!
  virtual void fly() {

    // Code to make the character fly.
    cout<<"character flying!\n";
  }
};
```

---

* For those of you interested in compiling the code, e.g., the Character code, you will need to include in your code appropriate libraries and namespace. In this case, to use the `string` type, you will need to include `<string>` and namespace `std` to compile the Character class. This approach is generally followed throughout the rest of the book.

Listing 5.4: C++ Code for Redesigned `TerrestrialCharacter` Class

```cpp
class TerrestrialCharacter : public Character {

public:
  // Get the type of character.
  virtual string getType() {

    // Return the type of character.
    return "terrestrial";
  }

  // Draw the character on the screen.
  virtual void draw() {

    // Code to draw the terrestrial character.
    cout<<"drawing terrestrial character!\n";
  }

  // Make the character run!
  virtual void run() {

    // Code to make the character run.
    cout<<"character running!\n";
  }
};
```

As seen, the `AerialCharacter` class implements both `getType()` and `draw()` in terms of aerial characters. The `AerialCharacter` class also specifies the interface method `fly()` to make the character fly in random patterns during the character's activation in the game. With the `Character` interface added to the design, the `TerrestrialCharacter` is now modified to implement the newly added interface so that anywhere in the design where objects sharing the `Character` interface are expected, both terrestrial- and aerial-type objects can be used. The redesigned `TerrestrialCharacter` class, which now implements the `Character` interface, is presented in Listing 5.4.

With this new framework in place, consider the redesign of the `GameEngine` from Listing 5.1, presented in Listing 5.5. Two major modifications have been made to the GameEngine design. First, the `add( )` method is modified to rely on the `Character` interface instead of on concrete classes; second, the code inside the `add( )` method now accounts for different types of characters. To support this new behavior, the `getType( )` method has been added to retrieve the type of the character at run time so that the code inside the `add()` method can determine whether to make characters run or fly, depending on their type. This fixes the problem of not being able to handle various types of characters with different movements. This is an improvement from the first design version; however, the design still violates the OCP. Anytime that a new character is added to the game, the

Listing 5.5: C++ Code for the `GameEngine` Class

```cpp
class GameEngine {

public:
   // Add a character to the game.
   void add( Character* pCharacter ) {

      // Draw the character on the screen.
      pCharacter->draw();

      // If aerial, make it fly, otherwise, make it run.
      if( pCharacter->getType() == "aerial" ) {

         // Downcast the pointer to an aerial character.
         AerialCharacter* pAerial = dynamic_cast<AerialCharacter*>
                              (pCharacter);

         // Assume a valid pointer and make the character fly!
         pAerial->fly();
      }
      else {

         // Downcast the pointer to a terrestrial character.
         TerrestrialCharacter* pTerrestrial =
                  dynamic_cast<TerrestrialCharacter*>(pCharacter);

         // Make the character run!
         pTerrestrial->run();

      } // end if statement.
   } // end add function.
};
```

`add( )` method needs to be modified to add another conditional statement to test for the new character and call the appropriate method to make the new character move. This is a direct effect of designs that violate the OCP. The gaming system's design is redesigned one last time to make it conform to the OCP, as presented in Listing 5.6. As seen, to make the design OCP-compliant, better abstractions are introduced to the `Character` interface, which now includes the `move( )` interface method.

A major design decision made in the redesign of the gaming system includes the addition of the `move()` interface method to the `Character` interface. This provides a higher level of abstraction that allows the design to appropriately abstract moving behavior for all characters in the system. By introducing a higher level of abstraction that is appropriate for characterizing the behavior required by characters (e.g., walk, run, swim, or fly), the design now allows the `GameEngine` class to rely on this abstraction to support multiple existing and future characters in the game, as seen in Listing 5.7.

Listing 5.6: C++ Code for the OCP-Compliant Gaming System's Design

```cpp
class Character {

public:
  // Draw the character on the screen.
  virtual void draw() = 0;

  // Make the character move.
  virtual void move() = 0;
};

// The aerial character.
class AerialCharacter : public Character {

public:
  // Draw the character on the screen.
  virtual void draw() { /* Code to draw the aerial character. */ }

  // Make the character fly.
  virtual void move() { /* Code to make the character fly! */ }
};

// The terrestrial character.
class TerrestialCharacter : public Character {

public:
  // Draw the character on the screen.
  virtual void draw() { /* Code to draw the terrestrial character. */ }

  // Make the character run.
  virtual void move() { /* Code to make the character run! */ }
};
```

With the redesign in place, the GameEngine can be used throughout to draw and activate all types of characters that share the Character interface, as seen in Listing 5.8.

Consider the addition of an aquatic character under this new gaming system's design. In the OCP-compliant case, the new character is added with new code, by implementing the Character interface. At run time, objects that share the Character interface can be passed into the GameEngine, which draws and activates the new character using the interface methods specified by the Character interface. The OCP-compliant design of the gaming system with all three supported characters is presented in Figure 5.3.

An important caveat to the OCP is that no design is 100% closed for modification. At some point, some code has to be readily available for modifications. The main idea of the OCP is to locate the areas of the software that are likely to vary and encapsulate them, so

---

Listing 5.7: C++ OCP-Compliant Design for the `GameEngine` Class

```cpp
// The game engine responsible for managing the game.
class GameEngine {

public:
  // Add the character to the screen.
  void add(Character* pCharacter) {

    // Display the character.
    pCharacter->draw();

    // Activate the character... make it move!
    pCharacter->move();

  } // end add function.
};
```

Listing 5.8: C++ Client Code that Uses the `GameEngine` Class

```cpp
// Create the main game engine.
GameEngine game;

// Create the aerial character object.
AerialCharacter aerialCharacter;

// Crete the terrestrial character object.
TerrestrialCharacter terrestrialCharacter;

// Add all characters to the game.
game.add(&aerialCharacter);
game.add(&terrestrialCharacter);
```

---

that variations required to account for particular behaviors can be compartmentalized and made interchangeable through polymorphism.

Skill Development 5.1: Open–Closed Design Principle

Using the IDE of choice, implement the OCP-compliant design presented in Figure 5.4. Create a test driver function that uses the `GameEngine` to add all three characters to the game. Once the code compiles and executes, design a fourth character and add it to the game. How do you think the OCP made the addition of the new character easy or hard? Explain.

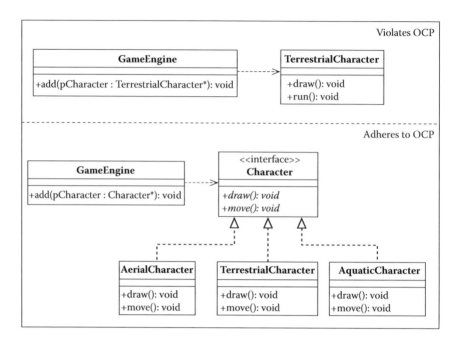

FIGURE 5.3

UML class diagrams for the OCP examples of the gaming system's design.

Liskov Substitution Principle

The OCP from the previous section provides guidance to design extensible systems by making designs open to extension but closed to modification. In some cases, it can be seen that adhering to the OCP alone does not guarantee correct designs or designs that lead to reusability throughout the system. To maintain the integrity of designs that adhere to the OCP, designs must honor any implied contract between base classes and the components that use them (Pressman 2010). This concept is captured by the LSP, which was originally proposed by Barbara Liskov. The LSP serves as basis for creating designs that allow clients that use derived classes to behave just as they would if they used the corresponding base classes (Liskov and Guttag 2000). The LSP requires not only that signatures between base and derived classes are maintained but also that the subtype specification supports reasoning based on the supertype specification (Liskov and Guttag 2000).

Consider the following implementation for a new `EntryLevelTerrestrialCharacter` in the gaming system. The new entry-level character inherits from the terrestrial character class, which provides the interface method `move()` and information about the semantics of the operation through pre- and postcondition specification, as presented in Listing 5.9.

As seen, `EntryLevelTerrestrialCharacter` implements the `move` method to make terrestrial characters fly, therefore providing a design that can adhere to the OCP but that violates the LSP, since the semantics of the `TerrestrialCharacter` are not maintained. Anywhere in the design where objects of type `TerrestrialCharacter` are called upon to move, the postconditions defined for this type specify that terrestrial characters will walk or run. Upon extending this design with its entry-level subtype, characters

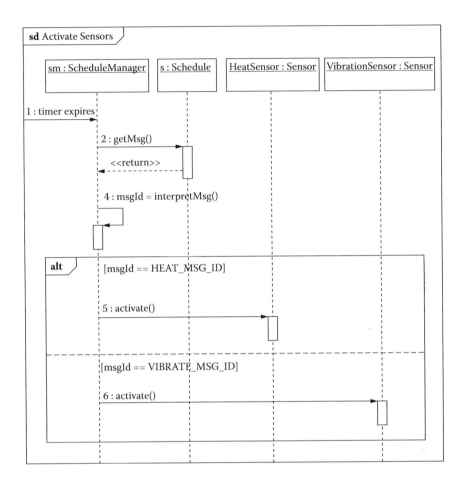

FIGURE 5.4
Sequence diagram during detailed design.

no longer walk but fly. When designing systems that adhere to the LSP, subtypes must conform both syntactically and semantically to their base types, so they can be replaceable at run time throughout the software execution.

Interface Segregation Principle

Well-designed classes should have one (and only one) reason to change. When this concept is violated, there is a strong indication that the interfaces provided by these classes are providing more information than they should, which makes designs harder to maintain and reuse. The SIP states that "clients should not be forced to depend on methods that they do not use" (Marin 2003). As example, consider incorporating into the gaming system a set of different types of enemy characters, each with specific capabilities for moving over land, under water, or over the air. In addition, a fourth type of enemy character is added to the system, which incorporates moving capabilities from all other enemy characters into the system (e.g., run, swim, and fly). To allow characters to be interchangeable at run time, these characters are designed initially with a common `EnemyCharacter` base class, as seen in

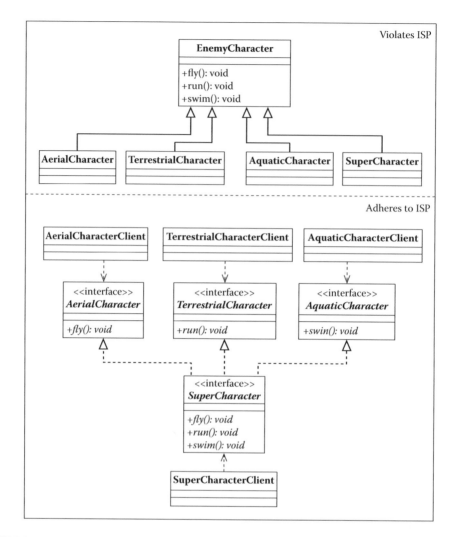

FIGURE 5.5

The interface segregation principle for the enemy character design.

the top part of Figure 5.5. Notice that since the SuperCharacter class requires behavior from all other enemy characters, the EnemyCharacter base class is designed to contain the implementations for all enemy characters in the system. This way, through inheritance, the SuperCharacter can reuse all behaviors. What is wrong with this design? For starters, the design violates the LSP, since only the SuperCharacter conforms both syntactically and semantically to the base type. However, of more interest is the fact that the interface for all other characters in the system has now been polluted with unnecessary methods. As enemy characters and capabilities continue to increase, so will the complexity of the EnemyCharacter interface, which in turn passes this complexity on to its derived types. Designs such as this, where clients or subtypes are forced to depend and maintain methods that they do not use, leads to designs that are hard to reuse and maintain.

The SIP implies that many client-specific interfaces are better than one general purpose interface. For example, consider the redesign presented in the lower part of Figure 5.5. As

Listing 5.9: C++ Implementation for `EntryLevelTerrestrialCharacter`

```cpp
class TerrestrialCharacter : public Character {

  // Pre-Condition: Character is drawn on screen.
  // Post-Condition: Character roams around randomly over land, either
  // walking or running.
  virtual void move() {

    //code to make the character walk or run.
  }
  // code here to implement all other interfaces.
};

class EntryLevelTerrestrialCharacter : public TerrestrialCharacter {

public:

  // Override move to make the character fly!
  virtual void move() {

    // code to make the character fly.
  }
  // Code here to implement all other interfaces.
};
```

seen, the bloated `EnemyCharacter` interface has been dissolved and many client-specific interfaces have been created. These interfaces are easier to maintain and reuse and lead to easier adherence to both OCP and LSP.

Programming Styles in Detailed Design

During detailed design, styles are used to provide a consistent approach for structuring code by specifying a standard for code elements, such as code formatting, naming conventions, documentation, and many other programming language-specific conventions. The application of styles is typically an activity that is emphasized during construction; however, due to the capabilities of today's modeling tools the application of styles is prevalent during the detailed design phase. For example, when modeling tools are used in software projects, the detailed design activity is where, for example, classes, variables, functions, function parameters, and return types are specified. When modeling tools are used to generate code, other construction styles such as formatting styles (e.g., spaces, bracket positioning) can also be specified. In all of these cases, styles are used to specify the way these elements appear in code in such way that it is consistent, readable, and therefore more maintainable. Programming styles provide the means for ensuring consistency in code when designs are transformed to code by different engineers.

Since programming styles are mostly programming language-specific, styles for one particular programming language may not apply to another programming language. However, some styles can be applied in a general fashion to a wide variety of modern programming languages, in particular those that share similar language characteristics, such as C++, Java, and C#. When creating detailed designs, the focus of programming styles can be placed on the following:

- Type names
- Function names
- Variable names

Type names are names selected for defining types in a programming language. Examples include classes, interfaces, structs, and enumeration. Type names are commonly specified using nouns and the *PascalCase* style. Type names that refer to collections can be pluralized to explicitly convey this information. Styles for interface names vary from most other type names. Popular styles for interface names include the use of nouns, adjectives, the letter "I" before the interface name, and a combination of all of these. Both the Java language and C# use nouns and adjectives when specifying interface names. In addition, the C# language employs the style of applying "I" before interface names. For custom-defined interfaces, Vermeulen, Ambler, Bumgardner, Metz, Misfeldt, Shur et al. (2000) recommend using nouns for interfaces that act as service declarations (e.g., Java's ActionListener) and adjectives for interfaces that act as description of capabilities (e.g., Java's Runnable). Examples of type name conventions are presented in Listing 5.10.

Function Names

Whereas type names typically use the *PascalCase* style in the naming convention, function names vary significantly between *PascalCase* and *lowerCamelCase* styles. Naming conventions for function names also vary among the software engineering community, with camps strongly supporting each side. This is largely due to the way in which different programming languages use styles for function names. For example, it is not uncommon for C++ programmers to support *lowerCamelCase* style, since every function name in the standard template library uses this style. The same is true about Java programmers. However, the C# programming language employs the *PascalCase* style for function names; therefore, programmers coming from Java or C++ background may tend to disagree with the C# convention. Consider, for example, the function calls for displaying text to the console in both Java and C#, as seen in Listing 5.11.

Notice how `pintnln` and `WriteLine` use different styles built into the Java and .NET frameworks, respectively. Ultimately, projects should adopt a style for the function naming convention that fits the project team and target programming language to maintain consistency. If in doubt, follow the convention provided by the target programming language.

Another characteristic of quality function names is how well they conform to all other parts of a function's signature. Function names should be chosen so that they relate

---

Listing 5.10: Example of Type Name Conventions

```cpp
// Class name for a single node.
class MobileNode {
};

// Class name for a collection of nodes, therefore name is
pluralized.
class MobileNodes {
  public:
    void addNode( int nodeId );
    void removeNode( int nodeId );
    MobileNode* getNode( int nodeId );
};

// Another example of a collection name in C++.
list<MobileNode*> mobileNodes;

// Custom-defined interface name in Java.
interface SampleInterface {
}

// Custom-defined interface name in C#.
interface ISampleInterface {
}

// Built-in interface name in Java
java.util.Observable

// Built-in interface name in C#
System.ICloneable;
```

---

accurately to the main intention of the function and its return type. Function names that accurately describe the function's intent can be referred as action-conforming functions. Alternatively, function names that do not are referred as action-contradictive; these are function names that do not accurately relate to the function's main intent. Examples of action-contradictive and action-conforming function names are presented in Listing 5.12.

Listing 5.11: Example of Both PascalCase and lowerCamelCase for Function Names

```
// Displaying text to the console in Java.
System.out.println("console message...");

// Displaying text to the console in C#.
System.Console.WriteLine("console message...");
```

Listing 5.12: Action-Conforming and Action-Contradictive Function Names

```
// Function 1 Purpose: Display validity to the console.
void isValid() {

  if( /*some condition*/ ) {
    cout<<"X is valid";
  }
  else {
    cout<<"X is invalid";
  }
}

// Function 2 Purpose: Display validity to the console.
void displayValidity() {

  if( /*some condition*/ ) {
    cout<<"X is valid";
  }
  else {
    cout<<"X is invalid";
  }
}

// Function 3 Purpose: Display element count number to the console.
void hasElements() {
  cout<<"Element count: 0";
}

// Function 4 Purpose: Display element count number to the console.
void displayElementCount() {
  cout<<"Element count: 0";
}

// Function 5 Purpose: Determine if a function has elements.
bool hasElements() {
  return true;
}
```

As seen in Listing 5.13, the identified purpose for Function 1 is to display validity status to the console; however, this is not evident by the choice of function name isValid. Furthermore, the use of "is" in front of function names typically implies the return of a Boolean value; therefore, clients may be more inclined to expect the function isValid() to provide information regarding the validity of an object by returning a Boolean value instead of displaying a message to the console. The function name of isValid is action-contradictive, since it does not accurately reflect the function's main intent, which is to display validity to the console. The function name is made action-conforming in

---

Listing 5.13: Type-Contradictive and Type-Conforming Function Names

```cpp
class Message {

public:

  // Function 5: Type-contradictive function!
  bool toString() {

    // Convert this object to a string.
    // return true if success, false otherwise.
  }

  // Function 6: Type-conforming function.
  string toString() {

    // Convert this object to a string.
    // return the string to the calling function.
  }
};
```

Function 2 by changing the name to more accurately reflect its purpose. Similarly, the action-contradictive name of Function 3 can be changed to action-conforming by changing it as presented in Function 4. In Function 5, the same name as in Function 3 is used with a different purpose. In this case, the name results in an action-conforming type, since the name accurately relates to the main intent of the function.

Type-conforming function names are those in which the function name relates and conform to the function return type. Function names that are inconsistent with the return type used are referred as type-contradictive. Examples of type-contradictive and type-conforming function names are presented in Listing 5.13.

In the case of Function 5, the name toString implies the return of a string value; however, the return type of the function is set to bool to determine if the conversion was successful. Users of this function may come to expect the function to return a string value; therefore, this function is type-contradictive. The type-conforming version of the function is presented in Function 6.

The last commonly accepted style for function names includes the use of verbs to properly describe actions in the code. In code, function names are abstractions of some action; therefore, the use of verbs as function names can result in code that maps accurately to mental models used to reason about the code, as seen in Listing 5.14.

Variable Names

The styles for variable names also include the use of *CamelCase*; however, unlike styles for type names, which are typically *PascalCase*, and unlike styles for function names, which

---

Listing 5.14: Example of Function Names Using Verbs

```
class Door {

public:

  void open(/*...*/) {
    // Open door.
  }

  void close(/*...*/) {
    // Close door.
  }
};
```

---

typically vary according to programming language, variable names (including parameter names) typically use the *lowerCamelCase* style. Two main reasons exist for preferring *lowerCamelCase* for variable names. First, the difference in styles can be used to differentiate between variables and types. Second, the *lowerCamelCase* style in variables can be used to differentiate between variables and constants, which typically use *PascalCase* or all uppercase, as seen in Listing 5.15.

As seen, two different styles are used for the constant max value. When the uppercase style is selected, compound words are separated using the underscore "_" character.

Listing 5.15: Example of Styles for Variable Names

```
class Receiver {

public:

  // The style use for case differentiates types from variables.
  void receive(Message* message) {

    // Prefix used to identify member variables.
    _message = message;
  }
private:
  Message* _message;
};

// Style 1 for a constant.
const int MaxValue = 10;

// Style 2 for a constant.
const int MAX_VALUE = 10;
```

In addition, Listing 5.15 presents a common style for identifying member variables, such as the _message variable. Identifying member variables can improve readability of code where function parameters use the same name as member variables. In such cases, a prefix or suffix can be used to clearly identify the member variable, especially in large member functions.

Modeling Internal Behavior of Components

Modeling interactions among entities designed during component design provides an efficient approach for visualizing complex interactions required for achieving a particular system function. This helps verify the component designs before construction begins. Sequence or communication diagrams can be employed to model *objects* representing instances of classes, or *roles* representing prototypical instances of other entities, such as classes (Booch, Rumbaugh, and Jacobson 2005). Both objects and roles can be connected to model the exchange of messages using links or connectors, respectively, to carry out a particular function of the design, typically as part of the system's functional requirements. During detailed designs, the majority of behavioral models include objects, since analyses are made with detailed information that is already been designed. In many cases, class diagrams are accompanied by one or more behavioral diagrams to provide a complete picture of the detailed design; both of these are reviewed and documented as part of the software design document. An example of a detailed sequence diagram is presented in Figure 5.5.

The sequence diagram from Figure 5.5 presents the behavioral modeling of objects belonging to three classes, namely, the ScheduleManager, Schedule, and Sensor classes. The sequence diagram—identified by the sd keyword and name Activate Sensors—uses the Frame notation, which provides the means to model combined fragments of interactions throughout sequence diagrams. Each interaction frame inside the sequence diagram can be classified using the operators presented in Table 5.3 (UML 2.3 Superstructure 2010).

The alt operator is used to denote a conditional statement, where more than one case is examined. The opt operator is employed when a single optional fragment exists in a sequence. When this occurs, the operations inside the fragment are either executed or not. This differs from the alt operator, which includes additional conditional statements. The loop operator specifies a repetition structure. The format of the loop operator is as

TABLE 5.3

Common Interaction Operators Used in Sequence Diagrams

Operator	Description
seq	Default operator that specifies a weak sequencing between the behaviors of the operands
alt	Specifies a choice of behavior where at most one of the operands will be chosen
opt	Specifies a choice of behavior where either the (sole) operand happens or nothing happens
loop	Specifies a repetition structure within the combined fragment
par	Specifies parallel operations inside the combined fragment
critical	Specifies a critical section within the combined fragment

follows: `loop (min, max)`, where min specifies the minimum bound of the loop and max represents the maximum bound of the loop. When these are omitted, then it implies that min = 0 and max = infinity. In these cases, the loop typically includes a separate inter-action constraint, called a Guard, which evaluates to true or false. The loop will continue only if the guard evaluates to true during execution regardless of the minimum number of iterations specified in the loop. The Guard interaction constraint is in the format of [<<constraint>>]. Guards can also be used in other interactions throughout sequence diagrams. For example, in Figure 5.5, a Guard is used to explicitly specify the condition used to determine alternate paths in the alt combined fragment.

Design Components Using Design Patterns

In Chapters 3 and 4, the concept of patterns was introduced with an emphasis on software architecture. During detailed design, a wide variety of design patterns exists for providing solutions to recurring problems in the form of structural designs for components. Design patterns are recurring solutions to object-oriented design problems in a particular context. When used effectively, they can help improve efficiency in the detailed design effort by providing high-quality reusable solutions that can be applied in many practical applications. To properly and consistently capture design patterns, detailed descriptions are required to identify the patterns, the problem that they solve, and their solution approach.

Designing high-quality object-oriented software is hard. Typically, designers of systems that evolve gracefully have time to develop their skills through years of experience. This experience gives designers the ability to identify classes with the right granularity, appropriate relationships among the classes, and inheritance hierarchies that are reusable and maintainable. Experience also allows designers to evaluate the effects of their design decision in the overall development of a working software system. The more we experience the design of systems, the more knowledge and skill we acquire to design better systems. Unfortunately, for novice designers, this experience can take years to acquire. Because detailed design entails a great deal of problem-solving skills, novice designers can spend much time trying to determine how to efficiently structure their designs in a way that the system can exhibit a certain level of quality. Fortunately, many of the common design problems—those recurring over and over in different systems—have been solved already and captured as design patterns. Design patterns are experience captured in a well-structured and consistent format; they provide blueprints that guide designers to solve specific problems by specifying important design characteristics, such as the classes that need to be created, their level of granularity, their relationships, and how all these classes and relationships work together to solve a problem. They provide this information in a generic sense, so that they can be reused many times over, in different software systems, without ever doing it the same way twice.

There are many benefits from studying and applying design patterns. First, they can help designers and programmers become more efficient. It is now common to find built-in support for design patterns in today's popular language frameworks, such as Java and the .NET framework. Therefore, knowing about design patterns can help programmers come up to speed quicker in these environments and enable them to quickly apply them to particular problems. In the work reported by Walter Tichy (2010), strong empirical evidence suggested that merely documenting design patterns can already lead to an increase in programmer productivity and reduce errors during maintenance tasks. Design patterns also help enhance communication during the problem-solving process by providing abstractions of problem-solving techniques. Tichy's work also shows evidence of *improvements in communication when team members shared design patterns knowledge.* In his work, it was noticed that *weaker designers catch up with more experienced ones when using patterns.* Design patterns also serve as starting point for the design (or redesign) effort of software components; therefore, they help reduce the time to design new systems. Finally, design patterns provide examples of the application of many object-oriented design principles; therefore, they can serve as practical methods for learning object-oriented design techniques.

Architectural versus Design Pattern

Before diving deeply into the topic of design patterns in the next chapters, it is important to make a clear distinction between (detailed) design patterns—the topic of the next two chapters—and architectural (design) patterns, which were covered in Chapter 4. As mentioned in Chapters 3 and 4, architectural patterns serve mostly at higher levels of abstraction to identify the major components and interfaces of the software system. Therefore, their application is too abstract to be translated directly to code. In contrast, design patterns are detailed solutions to particular problems that can be directly translated to code. Architectural patterns have a direct effect on the architecture of a software system and are associated to particular application domains (e.g., interactive systems), whereas design patterns are independent of a particular application domain (Buschmann et al. 1996). These differences should become evident in Chapters 6 and 7.

Classification of Design Patterns

When first studying design patterns, it is important to understand what each pattern does and how it does it. In the influential work presented by Gamma, Helm, Johnson, and Vlissides (1995), design patterns are classified based on purpose and scope. The purpose of a design pattern identifies the functional essence of the pattern; therefore, it serves as fundamental differentiation criteria between design patterns. Three different purposes are identified by the Gang of Four (GoF), including creational, structural, and behavioral. Creational design patterns are the ones that attempt to efficiently manage the creation or creational process of objects in a software system. A common characteristic of creational pattern is the presence of creational classes and product classes. In some cases, the creational and product classes are combined into one class. Creational patterns are overall known for abstracting the instantiation process of one or more objects. Structural design patterns are the ones that attempt to create larger structures from the composition of existing classes, objects, or other structures. Finally, behavioral design patterns are concerned with how classes and object interact, the variation of behavior, and the assignment of responsibility between objects. The purpose criteria apply to a large number of patterns; therefore, it serves well for classifying a large variety of design solutions.

While the purpose criteria of design patterns captures the overview of what the pattern does, the scope of a design pattern captures whether the design pattern primarily applies to classes or objects. Class patterns apply primarily to classes by defining the relationship between classes and subclasses, at compile time, via inheritance. Object patterns apply primarily to objects by defining the pattern's relationship between objects, at run time, via object composition. Since the relationships in object patterns are defined via object composition, they result in more dynamic designs and flexible designs. Since the large majority of design patterns rely on inheritance, it can be difficult to draw the line to differentiate between class patterns and object patterns. Furthermore, some design patterns can be applied in different ways, so that the same pattern can be classified as class pattern or object pattern, depending on the design implementation. Typically, the distinction between class patterns and object patterns becomes clearer after having experience with patterns for some time. When it comes to scope classification, the most efficient differentiation criteria lies in the focus that the design pattern puts on inheritance versus object composition. Design patterns that place focus on inheritance as key relationship for the pattern are classified as class patterns, whereas design patterns that place focus on object composition are classified as object patterns.

Purpose and scope can be used in combination to fully classify design patterns. For example, design patterns can be classified as class creational or object creational, class structural or object structural, or class behavioral or object behavioral. In addition to purpose, scope, and their combination, many other types of classification and domains have been identified throughout the years. Example of these include design patterns in real-time programming (Douglass 2002), patterns in web applications (Vora 2009), and patterns for parallel software (Ortega-Arjona 2010).

Documenting Design Patterns

Documenting design patterns in a consistent format is important to the dissemination of pattern knowledge. Although design patterns can be documented in many ways, the GoF identified 13 categories that can be used as standard for fully documenting design patterns. Together, these categories provide detailed information of existing design patterns and provide direction for documenting future patterns. In practical applications, well-documented patterns are important because they allow designers to quickly study a design pattern to determine its applicability in a particular scenario. Well-documented patterns also provide the means to compare patterns and evaluate important characteristics, such as consequences, that can help designers in selecting the best pattern for the problem at hand. The 13 categories for documenting patterns proposed by the GoF and their descriptions are presented in Table 5.4.

Chapters 6 and 7 provide throughout coverage of common design patterns used during the detailed design activity. For extensive coverage of design patterns, readers are encouraged to study the original design patterns book by the GoF (Gamma et al. 1995).

TABLE 5.4

Categories and Descriptions for Documenting Design Patterns

Category	Description
Name and classification	The unique pattern name that reflects the essence of the patterns and its classification
Intent	Describes the purpose of the pattern in such way that it is clear what types of design problems the pattern solves, what the pattern does, its rationale and intent
Also Known As	A list of alternate well-known names for the pattern
Motivation	An example scenario that serves as motivation for the application of the pattern
Applicability	Describes the situations, or design problems, that lend themselves for the application of the design pattern; provides examples of poor designs that can benefit from the pattern and ways for identifying these situations
Structure	Provides a structural (e.g., UML class diagram) view of the design pattern
Participants	List the classes and objects required in the design pattern and their responsibilities
Collaborations	Provides information about how the participants work together to carry out their responsibilities
Consequences	Describes the effects of the design pattern, good or bad, on the software solution
Implementation	Provides information and techniques for successfully implementing the design pattern
Sample Code	Provides sample code that demonstrates how to implement the design pattern in different programming languages
Known Uses	Provides examples of real systems that employ the design pattern
Related Patterns	Provides information about other design patterns that are related or that can be used in combination with the design pattern

DOCUMENT THE SOFTWARE DESIGN

Documentation of a project's software design is captured in the software design document (SDD), a document that contains the designs or plans of the software to be implemented. From the time the SDD is written in the design phase, it may be used by various stakeholders and until the end of the software life cycle. During the code and unit test phase, it may be referred to in order to construct the software, to develop unit test plans, or to write script files and driver code to automate the running of tests. System integrators may use the SDD in the system integration test phase to better plan integration activities, and maintainers will use and possibly have to update the SDD in the maintenance phase. To provide relevant information to the stakeholders, the SDD must contain certain items that document everything that goes into the design of the software. The proposed contents of an SDD are as shown in Table 5.5 (IEEE 2009).

Providing this SDD information is important not only to communicate the design to stakeholders but also to properly maintain the SDD to ensure the version stakeholders receive is current and consistent. The body section of the SDD contains architectural and detailed design elements, presented in a format specified by design viewpoints. Design viewpoints dictate the way design views are presented within an SDD, and each design view has exactly one design viewpoint to go along with it. The IEEE (2009) recommends each design viewpoint specification to contain (among others) the following information:

TABLE 5.5

Sections of the Software Design Document

Section	Description
Date of issue and status	Date of issue is the day on which the SDD has been formally released. Every time the SDD is updated and formally released, there should be a new date of issue.
Scope	Scope provides a high-level overview of the intended purpose of the software. It sets a limit as to what the SDD will describe and defines the objectives of the software.
Issuing organization	Issuing organization is the company that produced the SDD.
Authorship	Authorship pertains to who wrote the SDD and certain copyright information.
References	References provide a list of all applicable documents that are referred to within the SDD. If there is a certain technology that is used within the design, it is important to refer to the corresponding documentation on that technology, so it may be referenced. When reading the referenced documents, stakeholders may uncover inconsistencies in how the technology should be used and how it is used in the software design.
Context	Description of the context of the SDD.
Body	Body is the main section of the SDD where the design is documented. This is where stakeholders look to understand the software and how it is to be constructed.
Summary	
Glossary	A glossary provides definitions for all software-related terms and acronyms used in the SDD.
Change history	Change history is a brief description of the items added to, deleted from, or changed within the SDD.

- Viewpoint name
- Relevant design concerns
- Design elements (e.g., elements of design language)
- Analytical methods or other operations for supporting the view
- Viewpoint authorship or citation
- Patterns, heuristics, or other guidelines used in the creation of the viewpoint

The specification of design viewpoints can be done fully in the SDD or incorporated by reference (IEEE 2009). Once specified, viewpoints can be used throughout the SDD to document software designs. The SDD should also present the rationale for selecting the specific design viewpoint. Long after the design phase is complete, the SDD will be referred to several times during the software life cycle. Therefore, it is useful if the rationale for making certain design decisions is included in the SDD so developers can gain additional insight into why decisions were made for certain parts of the software design. Design rationale includes justification for choosing a particular design approach and can be found in commentary throughout the SDD. Examples of design rationale include design issues raised in response to design concerns of stakeholders, trade-offs evaluated, criteria used to make decisions, and design options considered (IEEE 2009). With this information, a sample table of contents for the SDD is provided in Table 5.6.

TABLE 5.6

Sample Table of Contents for the Software Design Document

1. Introduction
    1.1 Date of Issue
    1.2 Context
    1.3 Scope
    1.4 Authorship
    1.5 Change history
    1.6 Summary
2. Software Architecture
    2.1 Overview
    2.2 Stakeholders
    2.3 System Design Concerns
    2.4 Architectural Viewpoint 1
        2.4.1 Design View 1
    2.5 Architectural Viewpoint 2
        2.5.1 Design View 2
    2.6 Architectural Viewpoint *n*
        2.6.1 Design View *n*
3. Detailed Design
    3.1 Overview
    3.2 Component Design Viewpoint 1
        3.2.1 Design View 1
    3.3 Component Design Viewpoint 2
        3.3.1 Design View 2
    3.4 Component Design Viewpoint *n*
        3.4.1 Design View *n*
4. Glossary
5. References

Interface Control Document

The interface control document (ICD) is an important piece of documentation that serves as a written contract between components of the system software as to how they communicate. This document is usually intended to cover only the software components that are internal to the software development effort. Many times in software engineering, there exists a system in which two pieces of software need to communicate to share information or possibly to invoke function calls. For developers to write software, they need to know what to expect when asking for certain data or how to perform a particular action on another piece of software. A classic example of this is a client–server based system. The server may contain and manage certain data, or it may provide a set of actions that a client may invoke. An ICD is much like documentation on how to speak a particular language. If two pieces of software cannot speak the same language, they will not be able to communicate and a software system will not be able to work. ICDs can also be an important part of communication within a single component of a software system. For instance, the example in Figure 5.6 has two

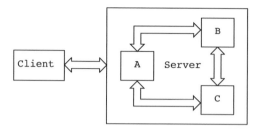

FIGURE 5.6
Conceptual model for system interfaces.

different kinds of interfaces. There is one interface between the client and server, and then there are several interfaces that are just internal to the server.

The server may be running three different processes, but it could be thought of as one cohesive component in the entire software system. These two different kinds of interfaces do not have to use the same kind of technology either. The interfaces described in an ICD can be either proprietary, such as a company-developed protocol using Extensible Markup Language (XML), or something standard such as Simple Network Management Protocol (SNMP) or Common Object Request Broker Architecture (CORBA). However, the descriptions of the data contents or what actions to take will surely be proprietary. To make an ICD effective, it must describe all the interfaces in as much detail as possible. ICDs can detail, for example, which data item on a server corresponds with what screen element on a GUI. Messages can also be formed in an ICD to detail all items coming back from a server to a client. It is much of this content that makes the bulk of an ICD. However, other documents may be referenced so that developers can get a better understanding of the communication process. For example, if a system uses SNMP, the ICD may reference the Request for Comments (RFCs) related to SNMP. This could further help a reader to understand certain parts of the software as related to communications.

Software Version Document

The software version description (SVD) is a document containing information about what is included in a software release, including different files, scripts, and executables. It also contains information about how to build the code, how to set up a computer that will host the software, and the software requirements for the host computer. The SVD is also an important document that tracks what changes have been made between different releases of software. It also details what problems might be encountered with a specific release of software and what problems have been fixed. Not every release of software is going to be perfect. Software can sometimes contain unfixed problems that go unidentified even after testing. These problems are then often noticed by the end users who report them to the software developers. To keep the customers satisfied, the software developers must fix the problems noted in the most recent release and issue a new release with the fixes. In other cases, changes are made to the design and code to create different versions of the software for different customers. When these modifications result in changes to the design, the SVD must document the appropriate steps to build software versions, which requires inclusion of the appropriate software design.

The SVD will often contain a section called the version description. It is in this section that the bulk of the material concerning the new release of software is documented. Even though this document may not be released to a customer, it could still prove to be very useful for internal tracking of different releases of software. The first section of the version description is the inventory of software contents. This part lists all the files, scripts, and executables that have gone into making the software build or are an output of the build process.

The section after the inventories of the materials released and software contents is the list of changes installed. As previously stated, these could either be fixes to problems identified in previous releases or entirely new capabilities. Installation instructions detail any necessary steps it takes to install the software to properly run on the host computers. The SVD also lists any potential problems that may be encountered when using the software or known and verified errors for which developers have yet to find a solution.

MONITOR AND CONTROL IMPLEMENTATION

Detailed design synchronicity is concerned with the degree of how well detailed designs adhere to the software architecture and how well software code adheres to the detailed design. Detailed designs provide a design structure carefully crafted to ensure desired characteristics of the software, such as reusability or maintainability. Typically, software engineers are good at respecting detailed design decisions early on in a project life cycle; however, as the development process continues, detailed designs are more prompt to deviations during construction. For any software architecture and detailed design to result in a successful system implementation, the construction phase must be synchronized with the software products resulting from both efforts. Therefore, the engineering team must ensure that detailed design decisions are enforced throughout the construction phase. Particular attention needs to be paid to design synchronicity when projects enter the maintenance phase or when new engineers are brought into the project. Similarly to achieving architectural design synchronicity, processes must be in place and enforced to ensure that overall design synchronicity is high.

CHAPTER SUMMARY

The detailed design activity begins after the software architecture is specified, reviewed, and approved by all stakeholders in the project. The detailed design activity corresponds to a microdesign view of the structure and behavior of the software system and is the last major effort before software construction begins. IEEE (1990) defines detailed design as "the process of refining and expanding the preliminary design phase of a system or component to the extent that the design is sufficiently complete to be implemented." That is, the process of refining the software architecture to reach a point where construction can begin. It is important to note that most of the detailed design activities deal directly with addressing functional requirements of the system. The detailed design process requires designers to understand the architecture and requirements before creation of detailed designs. Detailed design decisions can significantly shape the system's quality properties; therefore, they must exist within the bounds of the software architecture. In some cases, where modeling tools are used to generate code, detailed designs can also have significant impact on the quality properties of the construction phase. Once created, detailed designs can be documented together with architectural design to form the software design document, which is reviewed and approved before construction begins. The design document establishes the general framework of reference for all construction work; therefore, policies must be in place to maintain synchronicity between the design document and construction work. Upon completion of the detailed design activity, the system's design is sufficiently complete so that it can be formally documented, reviewed, and approved by the system's stakeholders, which marks the end of the design phase.

REVIEW QUESTIONS

1. What is detailed design, and how does it differ from architectural design?
2. Explain the relationship among requirements, architecture, detailed design, and construction.
3. What key tasks are performed during detailed design? Explain.
4. What steps are involved in the detailed design process?
5. What are derived requirements, and how do they play a role during detailed design?
6. What is the role of software architecture during detailed design? Can detailed design succeed without architecture? Explain.
7. Explain the concept of interface design during detailed design.
8. In object-oriented systems, what is the difference between a class and an object?
9. What is the difference between concrete and abstract classes?
10. Explain the following concepts:
    a. Interfaces
    b. Types and subtypes
    c. Dynamic binding
    d. Polymorphism
11. Compare and contrast the OCP, LSP, and ISP.
12. Why are programming styles important during detailed design? Give examples of some styles used during detailed design.
13. Explain the concepts of combined fragments, operators, and guards in interaction diagrams. Give an example of each.
14. What is the difference between architectural patterns and detailed design patterns?

15. What are the sections of the software design document? Explain each.

16. What is the interface control document, and why is it necessary in practical development efforts?

17. What is the version control document, and how does it relate to the software design?

CHAPTER EXERCISES

1. Create a class diagram and sequence diagram to design and validate the following system. The system will consist of a traffic light object that communicates with three light bulb objects. Each light bulb object cannot exist without the traffic light object. All light bulb objects have capabilities to turn green, yellow, and red. In fact, all light bulb objects are identical, except that they communicate with different light bulb hardware controllers to turn specific light bulbs on and off. All light bulb objects must support a turnOn(), turnOff(), and setColor(int color) method which will turn the light bulb on, off, and set the color, respectively. The system will use a custom timer object for managing the transition of the light bulbs and a sensor object to detect when cars arrived at the traffic light system. Both timer and sensor are part of the traffic light system but are also used in other sections of the system, so their lifetime is not controlled by the traffic light object. When the sensor object fires off, the traffic light object will activate the green light and the timer. When the timer expires, the traffic light object will deactivate the green light and activate the yellow light. It will also activate the timer again. When the timer expires, the traffic light system will deactivate the yellow light and activate the red light.

REFERENCES

Booch, Grady, James Rumbaugh, and Ivar Jacobson. *The Unified Modeling Langauge User Guide*, 2d ed. Addison-Wesley Professional, 2005.

Buschmann, Frank, Regine Meunier, Hans Rohnert, Peter Sommerlad, and Michael Stal. *Pattern-Oriented Software Architecture: A System of Patterns.* West Sussex, UK: Wiley, 1996.

Clements, Paul, Felix Bachmann, Len Bass, David Garlan, James Ivers, Reed Little, Robert Nord, and Judith Stafford. *Documenting Software Architectures.* Boston, MA: Addison Wesley, 2002.

Clements, Paul, Rick Kazman, and Mark Klein. *Evaluating Software Architectures.* Addison Wesley, 2001.

Douglas, Bruce P. *Doing Hard Time: Developing Real-Time Systems with UML, Objects, Frameworks, and Patterns.* Addison-Wesley Professional, 1999.

Douglass, Bruce P. *Real-Time Design Patterns: Robust Scalable Architecture for Real-Time Systems.* Addison-Wesley Professional, 2002.

Gamma, Erich, Richard Helm, Ralph Johnson, and John Vlissides. *Design Patterns: Elements of Reusable Object-Oriented Software.* Boston: Addison-Wesley, 1995.

IEEE. "IEEE Standard for Information Technology-Systems Design-Software Design Descriptions." 2009. http://ieeexplore.ieee.org/xpl/freeabs_all.jsp?arnumber=5167255.

IEEE. "IEEE Standard Glossary of Software Engineering Terminology." IEEE, 1990, p. 34.

Liskov, Barbara, and John Guttag. *Program Development in Java: Abstraction, Specification, and Object-Oriented Design.* Boston: Addison-Wesley, 2000.

Marin, Robert C. *Agile Software Development: Principles, Patterns, and Practices.* Upper Saddle River, NJ: Prentice Hall, 2003.

Meyer, Bertrand. *Object-Oriented Software Construction,* 2d ed. Upper Saddle River, NJ: Prentice Hall, 1997.

Ortega-Arjona, Jorge L. *Patterns for Parallel Software Design.* West Sussex, UK: Wiley, 2010.

Pressman, Roger S. *Software Engineering: A Practitioner's Approach,* 7th ed. Chicago: McGraw-Hill, 2010.

Sommerville, Ian. *Software Engineering,* 9th ed. Boston: Addison Wesley, 2010.

Tichy, Walter. *Making Software: What Really Works, and Why We Believe It.* Sebastopol, CA: O'Reilly Media, 2010.

"UML 2.3 Superstructure." Vers. 2.3. Object Management Group. May 2010. Available at: http://www.omg.org

Vermeulen, Allan, Felix Bachmann, Len Bass, David Garlan, James Ivers, Reed Little, Robert Nord, and Judith Stafford. *The Elements of Java Styles.* Cambridge, UK: Cambridge University Press, 2000.

Vora, Pawan. *Web Application Design Patterns.* Burlington, MA: Morgan Kaufmann, 2009.

6

Creational Design Patterns in Detailed Design

CHAPTER OBJECTIVES

- Understand the importance and role of creational design patterns in detailed design
- Identify, understand, and model common creational design patterns
- Become proficient in implementing models of creational design patterns
- Understand the benefits of creational patterns when implementing software systems

CONCEPTUAL OVERVIEW

During detailed design, software engineers spend a great deal of time devising component design solutions that fill in the gaps in architectural designs and provide the necessary internal design of components and their interfaces to achieve system functionality. At the detailed design level, common patterns in object-oriented designs have emerged that provide detailed design solutions to problems that recur many times over in different systems. A particular problem in these systems involves the efficient creation of objects so that concepts highlighted in previous chapters (i.e., interfaces, types, dynamic binding, and polymorphism) can be used effectively to generate reusable and maintainable software. Creational design patterns help identify problems that deal with creating quality detailed designs that are efficient in the creation of object in the system. They prescribe the classes required for their design solution and interrelationships required to support object creation. These patterns allow designers to quickly and systematically identify structural layouts of systems (or subsystems) and provide avenues for examining system interactions and quality evaluation within the operational system. This chapter explores several well-established creational design patterns and examines the problems they are designed to address, together with their exhibited quality attributes. Identifying and designing using creational design patterns can improve the efficiency of the development process and the quality of the final system.

CREATIONAL DESIGN PATTERNS

Creational design patterns are patterns for abstracting and controlling the way objects are created in software applications. They play a key role in the design of systems by making them independent of how objects in the system are created, composed, and represented (Gamma, Helm, Johnson, and Vlissides 1995). Therefore, parts of the system responsible for creating (or instantiating) objects do so through a common creational interface without knowledge of how the actual object or group of objects are created. In addition, by controlling the creational process with a common interface, enforcing creational policies becomes easier, therefore giving the system the ability to create product objects that share a common interface but vary widely in structure and behavior. Examples of creational patterns include the abstract factory, factory method, builder, prototype, and singleton.

ABSTRACT FACTORY

The abstract factory is an object creational design pattern intended to manage and encapsulate the creation of a set of objects that conceptually belong together and that represent a specific family of products. According to the Gang of Four (Gamma et al. 1995, p. 87), the intent of the abstract factory is to

> Provide an interface for creating families of related or dependent objects without specifying their concrete classes.

In the abstract factory pattern, the terms *family of products* or *family of objects* are used to denote a group of objects that belong together and therefore must be created together. When designing software that uses a group of objects that need to be created and used together, problems can arise when there is no consistent way for managing the creation of these objects. For example, consider two distinct families of computers: one representing standard computers made up of standard computer parts; and another representing advanced computers made up of advanced computer parts. Assume that the family of standard computers can be composed only of standard computer parts, such as a standard monitor, standard keyboard, and standard CPU, and that the family of advanced computers can consist only of advanced computer parts, such as an advanced monitor, advanced keyboard, and advanced CPU. When left unmanaged, designing software that instantiates both standard and advanced computers can be prone to various problems. First, there is the possibility that advanced computer objects can be created using standard products or vice versa, that is, standard computer objects created using advanced computer parts products. Moreover, without a standardized common interface identified for the different computer parts, the code inside the computer classes would be required to know about the correct computer parts type to use; therefore, the addition of new products or new product types would require changing the code inside the computer classes, a clear violation of the open–closed principle discussed in Chapter 5. These problems result in code that is hard to maintain and reuse. The abstract factory design pattern addresses these problems by encapsulating the creation of these families of products in such a way that they can be interchangeable at run time and by ensuring that products that belong to a specific group, or family, are instantiated together.

Problem

A computer store needs stand-alone software that keeps track of computer inventory, which includes computers and different computer parts made by different hardware manufacturers. The software for the computer store needs capabilities for displaying information about computer parts, including information from the manufacturer's site and various other sites that contain customer satisfaction reviews and other relevant information. Therefore, each computer part object needs to be capable of extracting information in real time from a list of predefined remote locations, of aggregating the information, and of providing this information upon request. Upon requesting the information for a particular computer, all computer part objects communicate over the network and find out the latest comments and statistics about a component from all predefined sources and make this information available to the requesting object. Initially, the store supports only two types of computers: standard computers and advanced computers, composed of standard and advanced computer parts (i.e., CPU, monitor, and mouse), respectively. Due to store policy, standard computers cannot be composed of advanced computer parts and advanced computers cannot be composed of standard computer parts. The software solution needs to provide a maintainable and modifiable design for creating these families of objects, to support easy addition of new families of computers, and to promote consistency with computer products.

Structure

The general and applied structure for the abstract factory design pattern is presented in Figure 6.1. As seen, the abstract factory is presented in general and applied form, and for simplicity the details of both abstract and concrete computer part classes are omitted in the applied form. The general structure of the abstract factory design pattern serves as a blueprint that depicts the participants and relationships required to design abstract factories; it presents the essence of the pattern, which needs to be fitted for the particular

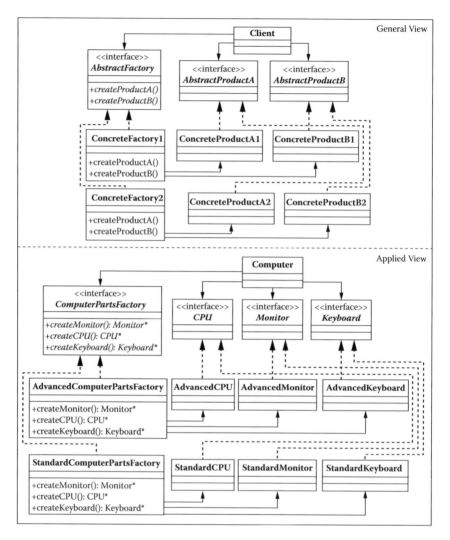

FIGURE 6.1
Abstract factory design pattern.

problem at hand. The applied view of Figure 6.1 presents an instantiation of the general structure for depicting the solution for the particular computer store problem, which consists of abstract products (e.g., monitor), concrete products (e.g., standard monitor), abstract creators (e.g., computer parts factory), and concrete creators (e.g., standard computer parts factory). These participants are interrelated via realization and association relationships. From this example, it should be evident how a new family of computer parts can be added to the design by adding the required pattern classes that make up the new family of computers.

Implementing the abstract factory design pattern can be confusing because of the number of classes required. However, when looking closely at the Unified Modeling Language (UML) diagram for the application view, it is evident that regardless of the number of computer factories or computer products, the structural relationship among these classes is always the same. This is true for all other patterns studied throughout this and other chapters. Therefore, a step-by-step approach can be taken to design abstract factories:

1. Design the product interfaces (e.g., CPU, monitor, keyboard).
2. Identify the different families or groups required for the problem (e.g., standard and advanced computers).
3. For each group identified, design concrete products that realize the respective product interface (e.g., standard monitor vs. advanced monitor) identified in Step 1.
4. Create the factory interface (e.g., `ComputerPartsFactory`). The factory interface contains n interface methods, where n is the number interfaces created in Step 1.
5. For each group identified in Step 2, create concrete factories that realize the factory interface created in Step 4.
6. Create the factory client (e.g., `Computer`) which is associated with both products and factory interfaces created in Steps 1 and 4, respectively.

Abstract factory designs contain two fundamental sets of class designs: products and factories. Once both products and factories portions of the design are complete, dynamic binding can be used at run time to allow the computer client to create different computer objects (e.g., standard vs. advanced computers) and use them throughout programs without actually knowing the specific type of the object. This way, adding other computer types to the system can be done by extending the design and not by modifying already working code.

Implementation

When studying the abstract factory (and all other design patterns), it is important that UML models are translated to code, compiled, and executed. When necessary, it is also helpful to step through the code with a debugger to keep track of dynamic binding throughout the software's execution. This provides additional insight and helps further the understanding of both concepts and benefits of using a particular design pattern. Once the structural design of the abstract factory is created, its translation to code is straightforward. Listing 6.1 presents the C++ implementation for the *ComputerPartsFactory* class.

As seen, the *ComputerPartsFactory* abstract class simply defines interface methods required for creating each computer part designed for the system. Therefore, there is a one-to-one relationship between interface methods and product interfaces. Since the code for the abstract factory interface is presented in C++, each interface method is defined as pure virtual, which includes the `virtual` keyword and is set to 0. In the Java programming language, the `ComputerPartsFactory` would be defined as a Java interface, using the `interface` keyword. Once the interface for the computer parts factory is established, all other concrete factories can be implemented to create products of specific computer types upon request. Consider the implementation for creating advanced computer parts, where the advanced computer part factory instantiates advanced computer products. The header file for the advanced computer parts computer factory is presented in Listing 6.2.

Listing 6.1: C++ Code for the Computer Parts Factory Interface

```cpp
// Computer parts factory interface.
class ComputerPartsFactory {

public:

  // Define the interface to create a monitor object.
  virtual Monitor* createMonitor(void) = 0;

  // Define the interface to create a keyboard object.
  virtual Keyboard* createKeyboard = 0;

  // Define the interface to create a CPU object.
  virtual Cpu* createCpu = 0;
};
```

Listing 6.2: C++ Header File for the Advanced Computer Parts Concrete Factory

```cpp
// Forward references
class Monitor;
class Keyboard;
class Cpu;

// Concrete advanced computer parts factory.
class AdvancedComputerPartsFactory : public ComputerPartsFactory {

public:

  // Create and return an advanced monitor.
  Monitor* createMonitor();

  // Create and return an advanced keyboard.
  Keyboard* createKeyboard();

  // Create and return an advanced cpu.
  Cpu* createCpu();
};
```

As seen, the `AdvancedComputerPartsFactory` realizes the `ComputerParts-Factory` interface by inheriting from it and defining concrete methods for each of its defined interface methods. Each interface method is implemented in terms of advanced computer parts, such that the `createMonitor()` method returns an instance of type `AdvancedMonitor`, the `createKeyboard()` returns an instance of type `AdvancedKeyboard`, and so on. This behavior is presented in the source file for the `AdvancedComputerParts` factory, as presented in Listing 6.3.

Listing 6.3: C++ Source File for the Advanced Computer Parts Concrete Factory

```cpp
#include "AdvancedComputerPartsFactory.h"
#include "AdvancedMonitor.h"
#include "AdvancedKeyboard.h"
#include "AdvancedCpu.h"

// Create and return an advanced monitor.
Monitor* AdvancedComputerPartsFactory::createMonitor() {

  // Caller is responsible for cleaning up the memory.
  return new AdvancedMonitor;
}

// Create and return an advanced keyboard.
Keyboard* AdvancedComputerPartsFactory::createKeyboard() {

  // Caller is responsible for cleaning up the memory.
  return new AdvancedKeyboard;
}

// Create and return an advanced cpu.
Cpu* AdvancedComputerPartsFactory::createCpu() {

  // Caller is responsible for cleaning up the memory.
  return new AdvancedCpu;
}
```

In Listing 6.3, it is assumed that the concrete products for the advanced computer parts factory have been defined. In fact, before any concrete computer parts factory code can be compiled, its parts need to be defined. Using this pattern, the implementation for the standard computer parts factory is similar to the advanced one, but instead of creating advanced concrete products it implements the creational methods in terms of standard computer parts products. Listings 6.4 and 6.5 present the generated code for the UML model of the standard computer parts factory together with its implementation. In a similar fashion, the creation of all other required computer parts factories in the system can be designed and implemented the same way.

The final piece of the abstract factory design pattern includes the factory client object. In this example, the client is a computer object that is composed of different computer part products. The concept employed in this example is that computers are composed of different computer parts; therefore, by configuring computer objects with computer parts factories they can delegate the creation of computer parts to run-time objects mapped using dynamic binding. This allows the creational code for computer objects to be open to extension but closed for modification. The header and source code for the Computer class are presented in Listings 6.6 and 6.7.

Listing 6.4: C++ Header File for the Standard Computer Parts Concrete Factory

```cpp
// Forward references
class Monitor;
class Keyboard;
class Cpu;

// Concrete standard computer parts factory.
class StandardComputerPartsFactory : public ComputerPartsFactory {

public:

  // Create and return a standard monitor.
  Monitor* createMonitor();

  // Create and return a standard keyboard.
  Keyboard* createKeyboard();

  // Create and return a standard CPU.
  Cpu* createCpu();
};
```

Listing 6.5: C++ Source File for the Standard Computer Parts Concrete Factory

```cpp
#include "StandardComputerPartsFactory.h"
#include "StandardMonitor.h"
#include "StandardKeyboard.h"
#include "StandardCpu.h"

// Create and return a standard monitor.
Monitor* StandardComputerPartsFactory::createMonitor() {

  // Caller is responsible for cleaning up the memory.
  return new StandardMonitor;
}

// Create and return a standard keyboard.
Keyboard* StandardComputerPartsFactory::createKeyboard() {

  // Caller is responsible for cleaning up the memory.
  return new StandardKeyboard;
}

// Create and return a standard CPU.
Cpu* StandardComputerPartsFactory::createCpu() {

  // Caller is responsible for cleaning up the memory.
  return new StandardCpu;
}
```

Listing 6.6: C++ Header File for the Computer Client

```cpp
// Forward references.
class ComputerPartsFactory;
class Monitor;
class Cpu;
class Keyboard;

class Computer {

public:
   // Constructor parameterized with a computer parts factory.
   Computer(ComputerPartsFactory* computerPartsFactory);

   // Display detailed information about the monitor.
   void displayMonitorInfo();

   // Display detailed information about the CPU.
   void displayCpuInfo();

   // Display detailed information about the keyboard.
   void displayKeyboardInfo();

   // Display computer cost.
   void displayCost();

   // All other computer methods.
   // Destructor needs to clean up memory.

private:
   Monitor* _monitor; // Pointer to the monitor interface.
   Cpu* _cpu; // Pointer to the Cpu interface.
   Keyboard* _keyboard; // Pointer to the Keyboard interface.
};
```

The key concept presented in Listing 6.6 is the reliance of the Computer class on four interfaces, namely, the ComputerPartsFactory, Monitor, Cpu, and Keyboard interfaces. This highlights a desirable attribute of component designs, which is to rely on interfaces instead of on concrete implementations. Together, these interface references (i.e., pointers) will hold the addresses of run-time objects that adhere to the particular interface. Therefore, upon creation, objects of the computer type will use these interface references to save the addresses of concrete products created by a particular computer parts factory object. The implementation code for this behavior is presented in Listing 6.7.

Once a concrete factory is passed into the constructor of the *Computer* class, the responsibility for creating each product is delegated to the factory object. This way, a *Computer* object can be created the same way for all computer types, simply by changing the factory

Listing 6.7: C++ Source File for the Computer Client

```cpp
#include "Computer.h"
#include "ComputerPartsFactory.h"
#include "Monitor.h"
#include "Cpu.h"
#include "Keyboard.h"

// Constructor
Computer::Computer(ComputerPartsFactory* computerPartsFactory) {

  // Delegate the creation of the monitor object to the Factory.
  _monitor = computerPartsFactory->createMonitor();

  // Delegate the creation of the keyboard object to the Factory.
  _keyboard = computerPartsFactory->createKeyboard();

  // Delegate the creation of the Cpu object to the Factory.
  _cpu = computerPartsFactory->createCpu();
}

// Display detailed information about the monitor.
void Computer::displayMonitorInfo() {

  // Display monitor's info.
  _monitor->displayInformation();
}

// Display detailed information about the CPU.
void Computer::displayCpuInfo() {

  // Display Cpu's info.
  _cpu->displayInformation();
}

// Display detailed information about the keyboard.
void Computer::displayKeyboardInfo() {

  // Display keyboard's info.
  _keyboard->displayInformation();
}

// Display computer cost.
void Computer::displayCost() {

  // Use all computer products to compute total cost and display it.
}
```

Listing 6.8: C++ Implementation of the Computer Store

```cpp
// Assume that the ComputerStore class has been defined and contains
// the method displayComputer and the member attributes used below.

// Method to display a computer's information.
void ComputerStore::displayComputer(string type) {

  // Determine which computer needs to be created.
  if( type.compare("standard") == 0 ) {

    // Create the standard computer factory object.
    computerPartsFactory = new StandardComputerPartsFactory;
  }
  else {

    // Create the advanced computer factory object.
    computerPartsFactory = new AdvancedComputerPartsFactory;
  }

  // Create the computer object using the appropriate factory.
  _computer = new Computer(computerPartsFactory);

  // Display the computer information, including its cost. This
  // information varies according to the factory object used to create
  // the computer.
  _computer->displayMonitorInfo();
  _computer->displayCpuInfo();
  _computer->displayKeyboardInfo();
  _computer->displayCost();

  // Do more stuff with the computer object here.
  // Clean up the all memory allocated when done.
}
```

---

that creates the products. Consider the code the computer store software that provides and manages inventory information using the ComputerStore class. Using the abstract factory design pattern, the implementation code for displaying computer information is presented in Listing 6.8. As seen, the display computer method is passed in a string to determine the type of computer to be displayed. Once the type is identified, the appropriate computer parts factory object is instantiated and passed into the constructor of the computer object. From this point forward, all operations called on the computer object are implemented in terms of the factory used to create its parts. Similarly, many different computer types can be supported by creating additional factories to parameterize computer objects with newly supported computer types.

When applying the abstract factory design pattern, depending on the problem, a large number of classes may be required, causing confusion to those who are new to the pattern. However, it is important to keep in mind that the core classes and relationships identified in the general structure of the pattern remain the same, regardless of the problem. That is, an abstract factory has one or more factory objects defined by an abstract factory interface and one or more products defined by one or more product interfaces.

Benefits

- Isolates concrete product classes so that reusing them becomes easier
- Promotes consistency within specific product families
- Adding new families of products, which requires no modification of existing code

---

Skill Development 6.1: Abstract Factory Design Pattern

Using the UML tool of choice, replicate the UML model presented in Figure 6.1 and generate code from the model. Using the Integrated Development Environment (IDE) of choice, fill in the gaps in the code generated using Listings 6.1 through 6.8 and compile and execute the software. Once the software executes, go back to the UML model and add a third factory, named `SpecialComputerFactory`, together with special computer products (e.g., `SpecialMonitor`, `SpecialKeyboard`, `SpecialCpu`). Repeat the code generation process, fill in the gaps of the new generated code, compile, and execute. When complete, explain the steps required to make this new modification and how the abstract factory design pattern made this change easy or hard.

FACTORY METHOD

The factory method design pattern is a class creational pattern used to encapsulate and defer object instantiation to derived classes. Structurally, the factory method can be modeled as a simplified version of the abstract factory design pattern, since both patterns require creator and product interfaces. However, unlike the abstract factory design pattern, in which the creator objects (i.e., factories) are responsible for instantiating a plurality of products that belong to a specific family type, creator objects in the factory method design pattern are responsible for the creation of a single product of specific type. Therefore, the creator interface for the factory method design pattern provides only one creational method, whereas the creator interface for the abstract factory design pattern provides two or more creational methods. In addition, unlike the abstract factory design pattern, the factory method design pattern defers object creation to subtypes that realize the creational interface; a relationship specified by inheritance, therefore, the factory method design pattern is classified as a class creational design pattern as opposed to an object creational design pattern. These fundamental differences are essential for understanding the difference between both patterns. According to the Gang of Four (Gamma et al. 1995, p. 107), the intent of the factory method is to

> Define an interface for creating an object, but let subclasses decide which class to instantiate. Factory Method lets a class defer instantiation to subclasses.

The factory method design pattern provides the ability for designers to model and implement code in terms of the factory method and product interfaces. The factory method design pattern is mainly characterized by one creational method, which is used to instantiate and return objects of a specified product interface. This creational method is made abstract at the factory base class so that objects of the factory base class cannot be directly instantiated. This is done to create a framework that allows the factory base class to define a series of operations that rely on the product interface; however, before executing operations, object creation is delegated to derived classes that are required to implement the factory (creational) method. This way, new derived factories can override the method to instantiate and return the appropriate product for the particular situation that is then used to carry out the operations specified in the factory base class. This way, through inheritance, new factories can be added to the design of the system to extend the factory base class without modifying its code. With the factory method in place, reasoning about application logic can be made in terms of the product interface and not on concrete products, therefore resulting in code that can be extended easily.

Problem

The computer store from the previous example has expanded its operations to have three different stores at different locations. Because of demographics at each location, particular types of computers are offered at specific locations. The computer store in Location 1 supports standard computers only, the computer store at Location 2 supports advanced computers, and the computer store at Location 3 supports a new type of special computer. The software system is now required to display information about computers carried at specific stores. Therefore, the software design requires modification so that the display of computer information is site-specific. A desired feature for the redesigned software is the ability to keep the logic code separate from specific types of computer stores so that future stores, carrying different computers, can be added to the system with minimal effort.

Structure

The generic and applied structure of the factory method design pattern is presented in Figure 6.2. As seen, the pattern requires both creational and product classes, similar to the abstract factory design pattern. However, unlike the abstract factory design pattern, creator classes in the factory method design pattern require only one creational interface

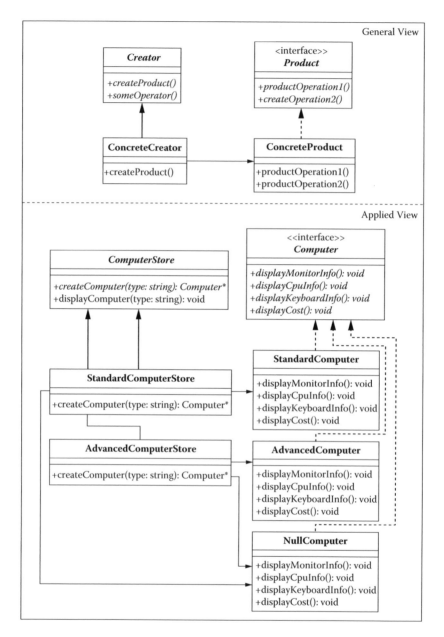

FIGURE 6.2

UML class diagram for the factory method design pattern.

method for creating products that share the same interface. Therefore, for each product in the system, the design incorporates concrete product and concrete creator classes.

A step-by-step approach to designing the factory method design patterns includes the following:

1. Identify and design the product interface (e.g., computer).
2. Identify and design the concrete products that realize the interface from Step 1 (e.g., StandardComputer, AdvancedComputer).

3. Design the factory base class (e.g., ComputerStore), which contains one abstract factory interface method for delegating product creation to derived classes. Product creation must conform to the interface defined in Step 1.
4. Design one or more concrete factories for each product identified in Step 2.

As seen in the applied version, a standard computer store capable of displaying computer information is added to the design. Displaying computer information is performed with the *displayComputer()* method that performs operations and requests services using the computer interface. Two creator classes have been added to the design: one for the standard computer store and another for the advanced computer store. As seen, each computer store is associated with the specific product that it supports. In addition, a *NullComputer* class is added to ensure that computer stores do not return *null* pointers to clients in the case that a requested computer is not supported by a particular computer store.

Implementation

Once the structural design is complete, translating it to code is straightforward. Listings 6.9 and 6.10 present the C++ implementation for the ComputerStore class.

As seen in Listing 6.10, the computer store displays a computer's information by relying on the computer product interface; therefore, once derived computer stores override the factory method to instantiate and return objects of the computer types supported in particular stores, the displayComputer() method will display the computer information according to the object bound to it at run time. Listing 6.11 presents the factory method code for a standard computer store.

Listing 6.9: Header File for the ComputerStore Class

```cpp
#include <string>

// Forward reference.
class Computer;

// The computer store creator class. This is an abstract class,
// therefore to instantiate computer stores, specific derived
// computer store classes are required.
class ComputerStore {

public:
    // The standard factory method for creating computer products.
    virtual Computer* createComputer(std::string type) = 0;

    // Method to display a computer's information.
    void displayComputer(std::string type);
};
```

Listing 6.10: Source File for the `ComputerStore` Class

```
#include "Computer.h"

// Method to display a computer's information.
void ComputerStore::displayComputer(string type) {

    // Delegate the responsibility of creating a computer object to
    // derived classes using the factory method.
    Computer* computer = createComputer(type);

    // Display the computer information, including its cost. This
    // information varies according to the factory object used to create
    // the computer.
    computer->displayMonitorInfo();
    computer->displayCpuInfo();
    computer->displayKeyboardInfo();
    computer->displayCost();

    // Do more stuff with the computer object here.
    // Clean up the pComputer and pFactory objects when done.
}
```

As seen, the implementation for the factory method for standard computer stores supports only standard computers. Internally, objects of type `StandardComputer` can use the abstract factory design pattern from Listings 6.4 and 6.5 to create the standard computer, which is common in many practical applications. To remain concise, this part of the problem is not presented in this example; however, to accomplish this, the design of the `StandardComputer` class would require an association with the `StandardComputerPartsFactory` from the previous section. With this association, the standard computer parts factory is used inside the `StandardComputer` object to create standard products, such as standard monitor, keyboard, and CPU. In many practical applications, both factory method and abstract factory design patterns are used in conjunction for providing extensible and reusable code. To support new products at the standard computer store, the factory method can be modified with different conditional statements for creating the new product; therefore, changes to support new products at a specific computer store are compartmentalized and do not affect all other computer stores.

Benefits

- Separates code from product-specific classes; therefore, the same code can work with various existing or newly created product classes.
- By separating the code, development becomes efficient, since different developers can work on the different parts of the project at the same time.
- By separating the code, it becomes easier to reuse and maintain specific parts of the code.

**Listing 6.11: Implementation of the Factory Method
for the Standard Computer Store**

```
// Implement the factory method.
Computer* StandardComputerStore::createComputer(string type) {

    // Pointer to a computer object.
    Computer* computer;

    // Determine which computer needs to be created.
    if( type.compare("standard") == 0 {

        // Create the StandardComputer. Clients are responsible for
        // cleaning up the memory for the computer object. Internally,
        // StandardComputer uses StandardComputerPartsFactory to create
        // a standard computer.
        computer = new StandardComputer;
    }
    else {

        // Create and return a null computer.
        computer = new NullComputer;
    }

    // Return the newly created computer object. Clients are responsible
    // for cleaning up the computer object.
    return computer;
}
```

Skill Development 6.2: Factory Method Design Pattern

Using the UML tool of choice, replicate the UML model presented in Figure 6.2 and generate code from the model. Using the IDE of choice, fill in the gaps in the code generated using Listings 6.9 and 6.11 and compile and execute the software. Once the software executes, go back to the UML model and add a third factory, `SpecialComputerStore`, that carries `SpecialComputers`. Repeat the code generation process, fill in the gaps of the new generated code, compile, and execute. When complete, explain the steps required to make this new modification and how the factory method design pattern made this change easy or hard.

BUILDER

The builder design pattern is an object creational pattern that encapsulates both the creational process and the representation of product objects. Unlike the abstract factory design pattern, in which various product objects are created all at once, the builder design pattern allows clients to control the (multistep) creational process of a single product object, allowing them to dictate the creation of individual parts of the object at discrete points throughout software operations. To accomplish this, the builder design pattern introduces a creator class (i.e., the builder) that species the (abstract) interface methods required to build a particular product. These methods are used to build parts of a product, and once all parts of the product are created (using the builder interface) clients can request the builder to return the created object as a whole. Since the creation of the product object is delegated to the concrete builder objects, the product's representation can vary according to the specific concrete builder creating the object. This provides added flexibility for managing the creational process and representation of products that is not present in other creational patterns. According to the Gang of Four (Gamma et al. 1995, p. 97), the intent of the builder is to

> Separate the construction of a complex object from its representation so that the same construction process can create different representations.

The idea of separating the process of constructing objects from their representations is essential when considering using the builder design pattern. Consider a client–server system consisting of three clients that work in a distributed fashion and report to a centralized server. The server can request status from all three clients, compile the status received into an object of the *Message* type, and forward it for further processing within the server system. In this scenario, the creational process of the *Message* object depends on receiving information from three different clients. Once information from the first client is received, the part of the *Message* object that contains information about this client can be created. Similarly, once information from the second and third clients is received, the parts of the *Message* object that require this information can be built. Once all parts of the *Message* object are built, the *Message* object can be forwarded to the rest of the system. In this example, two important characteristics should be noted. First, the *Message* object cannot be instantiated all at once; therefore, a finer-grained method of *Message* construction is required so that events occurring at discrete points in time can be used to build individual parts of the *Message* object. The second important, and perhaps more important, characteristic is the fact that the multistep process that allows for the construction of the *Message* object is the same, regardless of the representation of the *Message* object. In this example, the *Message* object can be forwarded within the server system using a binary format, Extensible Markup Language (XML), or any other custom-defined format. A major practical benefit can be gained by separating the construction process of objects from their representation. Since objects using the builder design pattern can be constructed one step at a time, complex algorithms necessary to create these objects can be separated from the actual construction of objects so that the same algorithms can be used to build different representations of an object. This results in code that can evolve to provide new representation of objects by adding new builder classes without modifying the code for the algorithm used for creating objects.

Problem

A company develops software to monitor and control custom-built hardware developed by a separate vendor. The equipment supports 100 different messages, defined using a custom-defined interface control document (ICD). Every time the messaging specification changes, the code that represents all 100 messages has to be changed manually. The company has decided to develop a message generator that reads the message specification document, finds the appropriate information for each message, and generates code to represent them. This way, once the ICD changes all the company has to do is regenerate the messages. Currently, the software for monitoring and control is developed in C++ so the message generator generates C++ code. However, the need for creating message libraries for both Java, C#, and other languages is being evaluated. This means that changes to the ICD will require message regeneration for all supported languages. The software company wants a design for the message generator that separates the algorithm for parsing the messaging specification from the code that generates classes for the messages in specific programming languages (e.g., C++, Java). This way, changes to the messaging specification will not affect the code that generates the messages in specific programming languages and vice versa; changes or addition to support new programming language generation will not affect the code that parses the messaging specification. To keep track of changes in the ICD and messaging libraries, the company also wants to keep history and statistics of code generation, such as build number, build date, number of methods generated, and number of classes generated.

Structure

The general and applied structural view of the builder design pattern for the message builder problem is presented in Figure 6.3. In the general view of the pattern's structure, notice that the association with the `Product` class and the method for returning the product are specified in the `ConcreteBuilder` class. In many practical situations, the products being built can have dissimilar interfaces, therefore making it difficult to add the interface method that returns the product in the `AbstractBuilder` base class and reducing flexibility in code. In the message builder example, since the products generated can be represented using the same interface, the method that returns the product (i.e., `getGeneratedProduct()`) is moved to the base class so that client code can reason about builders in terms of the `AbstractBuilder` interface and not based on concrete builders. The creational process is represented using the builder base class, which delineates the creational process using abstract interface methods. For each identified representation of the product, a class is created that inherits from the builder base class. These classes provide the specific creational details for their particular representation. Finally, builders are associated with the product class to generate the information required to build the product as a whole.

There are two main driving forces behind the application of the builder design pattern to the message builder problem. First, since messages are generated from a document, the

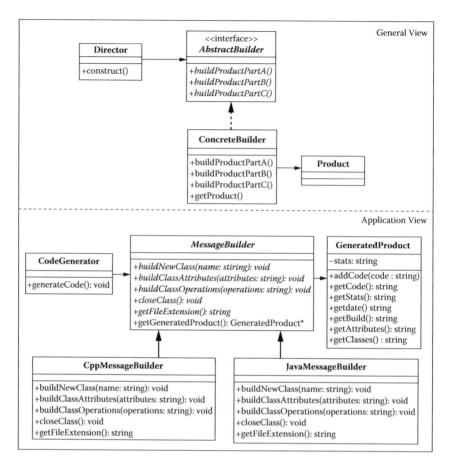

FIGURE 6.3
UML class diagram for the builder design pattern.

sections in the document that specify the parts of a particular message may be scattered throughout the document; therefore, the message object may not be able to be created all at once. Second, the processing of the ICD file is the same, regardless of the target programming language used for generating messaging code. This means that the same parsing algorithm can be used to identify the key document elements used for code generation, regardless of the target language. Once these characteristics are identified, a step-by-step approach can be used to design the builder design pattern. The steps for applying the builder design pattern are as follows:

1. Identify and design the product class (e.g., GeneratedProduct).
2. Identify the product's creational process and algorithm, and design a class for its execution (e.g., CodeGenerator). Each creational step (when necessary) must be made in terms of a standard product builder interface (instead of concrete product interface).
3. Using the knowledge acquired from Steps 1 and 2, design the builder interface, which specifies the parts that need to be created for the whole object to exist. These are captured as abstract interface methods that need to be implemented by derived concrete builders.

4. Identify and design classes for the different representations of the product (e.g., CppMessageBuilder and JavaMessageBuilder). These classes realize the interface from Step 3 in terms of the particular representations.

When using the builder design pattern, the representation of each object is encapsulated in one or more concrete builder classes; therefore, adding new representation can be done easily by extending the design and not modifying existing working code.

Implementation

Using the structural design from Figure 6.3, the implementation for the `MesageBuilder` class is presented in Listing 6.12. As seen, the purpose of this class is to specify the creational steps required for the generation of each message. Since messages in the ICD are generated as classes, the `MessageBuilder` has methods for creating new classes, adding attributes, adding methods, and generating code for closing classes (e.g., "};" in C++ and "}" in Java) and retrieving the extension used for the generated file. These interface methods serve as indication of the parts required to create a whole `GeneratedProduct` object. By separating these parts into multiple interface methods, the creational process can call upon them individually to create the product object at discrete points during software execution, when information becomes available.

Once the creational parts are identified and incorporated into the `MessageBuilder` base class, different derived classes can be implemented to provide the required object representation. Since this behavior is incorporated into the design using inheritance, the number of representations can be extended easily in future versions of the software. Listing 6.13 presents the code for the concrete message builder that generates C++ code for the messages.

For each creational method in the `CppMessageBuilder` class, the parameters passed in are processed and transformed to C++ code before adding it to the product being generated. The same process is used for any other language that needs to be supported, such as Java or C#. Finally, the algorithm for product creation is created and encapsulated using the `CodeGenerator` class. As seen, by varying the builder object passed to the code generator's constructor, message generation can occur in different languages, as presented in Listing 6.14.

Benefits

- The builder separates an object's construction process with its representation; therefore, future representations can be added easily to the software.
- Changes to the existing representation can be made without modifying the code for the creational process.
- The builder provides finer control over the construction process so that objects can be created at discrete points in time.

Listing 6.12: C++ Implementation of the MessageBuilder Class

```cpp
#include <string>

// Forward reference.
class GeneratedProduct;

class MessageBuilder {

public:
  // The interface method for building a new class.
  virtual void buildNewClass(string name) = 0;

  // The interface method for building class attributes.
  virtual void buildClassAttributes(string attributeList) = 0;

  // The interface method for building class operations.
  virtual void buildClassOperations(string operationList) = 0;

  // The interface method for closing a new class.
  virtual void closeClass() = 0;

  // The file extension for the target programming language.
  virtual string getFileExtension() = 0;

  // Return the generated product.
  GeneratedProduct* getGeneratedProduct() {

    return _codeProduct;
  }

private:
  // The product containing generated code and stats about code
  // generated.
  GeneratedProduct* _codeProduct;
};
```

Skill Development 6.3: Builder Design Pattern

Using pencil and paper, modify the UML class diagram for the message builder problem to include message generation using the C# programming language. Explain the steps taken and how the addition of the new program feature impacts the existing design. List the pros and cons of using the builder design pattern for this problem.

Listing 6.13: C++ Implementation for the Message Builder that Generates C++

```cpp
class CppMessageBuilder : public MessageBuilder {

public:

  // The interface method for building a new class.
  virtual void buildNewClass(string name) {

    // Generate code for creating a class using CPP style and the
    // name argument.

    // Once code is generated, add it to the product.
    getGeneratedProduct()->addCode(/*new C++ class code*/);
  }

  // The interface method for building class attributes.
  virtual void buildClassAttributes(string attributeList) {

    // For all items in attributeList, generate attributes using CPP
    // style and add them to the generated code.

    // Once code is generated, add it to the product.
    getGeneratedProduct()->addCode(/*C++ attributes*/);
  }

  // The interface method for building class operations.
  virtual void buildClassOperations(string operationList) {

    // For all items in operationList, generate operations using CPP
    // style and add them to the generated code.

    // Once code is generated, add it to the product.
    getGeneratedProduct()->addCode(/*C++ operations*/);
  }

  // The interface method for closing a new class.
  virtual void closeClass() {

    // Generate code to close a class in Cpp, and add it to the
    // generated code.

    // Once code is generated, add it to the product.
    getGeneratedProduct()->addCode("\n};\n\n");
};
```

Listing 6.14: C++ Implementation for the CodeGenerator

```cpp
class CodeGenerator {

public:

  // Constructor.
  CodeGenerator(MessageBuilder* pBuilder) : m_pBuilder(pBuilder) {
    // Assume a valid builder pointer. Notice that m_pBuilder is
    // initialized in the constructor's initialization list above.
  }

  // The interface method for building a new class.
  virtual void generateCode(string fileName) {

    // Open file for reading: fileName.
    while ( /* not end of file */) {

      // read next token in file.
      if( /*class name found*/) {

        // Assume that variable className holds the name.
        m_pBuilder->buildNewClass(className);

      } else if( /*attribute list found*/) {

        // Assume that attributeList contains the attributes
        m_pBuilder->buildClassAttributes(attributeList);

      } else if( /*operation list found*/) {

        // Assume that operationList contains the operations.
        m_pBuilder->buildClassOperations(operationList);

        // Close the class.
        m_pBuilder->closeClass();
      }

    } // end while( /* not end of file */)

    // Close file: fileName.

    // Create file using file extension from generated product object.
    // write(m_pBuilder->getGeneratedProduct()->getCode());
    // Close file.
    // logCodeGeneration(m_pBuilder->getGeneratedProduct());

  } // end generateCode(...)

private:
  MessageBuilder* m_pBuilder;
};
```

PROTOTYPE

The prototype design pattern is a class creational design pattern that allows clients to create duplicates of prototype objects at run time without knowing the objects' specific type. Previous creational design patterns, such as abstract factory and builder, required two distinct set of classes: one or more creational classes and one or more product classes to support the creational process. Unlike these, in which creator and product classes were separate, prototype objects are both creators and products. This characteristic allows them to support a generic interface for object creation while having the capability to access internal product data to create (deep) copies of prototypical objects. These copies are returned to clients and used independently from the original prototype object. According to the Gang of Four (Gamma et al. 1995, p. 117), the intent of the prototype design pattern is to

> Specify the kinds of objects to create using a prototypical instance, and create new objects by copying this prototype.

The prototype design pattern is typically used when clients need to duplicate products at run time without regarding how products are created or their specific concrete types. This allows copies from a variety of objects within the same class hierarchy to be created uniformly, which simplifies client code and adds flexibility to designs.

Problem

Consider the enemy component created for a gaming system. The detailed design of the enemy component includes a wide variety of enemy specifications defined for the game, each including different profiles and weapons. The game designers have identified the need to have each character provide a method for creating copies of themselves so that at any given point during the game a character clone can be made including identical energy level, weapons, and profiles. This functionality is required to develop an enemy registry of different `Character` subtypes to create and add enemies at any point during the game. Consider the initial proposed solution to the problem, as presented in Listing 6.15.

As seen, both *TerrestrialEnemyCharacter* and *AerialEnemyCharacter* have been designed to support an interface method for duplication of objects at run time. The problem with the code in Listing 6.15 is that clients are required to know about the specific concrete class to create a copy of each different character. Therefore, it is inefficient to design an enemy character registry that can be used throughout the game to create characters uniformly, since the creational process requires knowledge about the particular interface method for duplicating a run-time object. This decreases the design's flexibility, since it does not support object extension without code modification. That is, for every new type of enemy character, the enemy registry code for creating and adding characters

Listing 6.15: C++ Implementation for the Terrestrial and Aerial Enemy Characters

```cpp
// The character interface.
class Character {

public:
  virtual void attack() = 0;
  // Other methods such as defend, move, etc.
};

class TerrestrialEnemyCharacter : public Character {

public:
  // Method definitions for terrestrial attack, defend, etc.

  // Duplicate this object.
  TerrestrialEnemyCharacter* duplicateTerrestrial() {

    // Use the copy constructor to create a copy of this object and
    // return it.
    return new TerrestrialEnemyCharacter (*this);
  }
};

class AerialEnemyCharacter : public Character {

public:
  // Method definitions for aerial attack, defend, etc.

  // Duplicate this object.
  AerialEnemyCharacter* duplicateAerial() {

    // Use the copy constructor to create a copy of this object and
    // return it.
    return new AerialEnemyCharacter(*this);
  }
};
```

to the game needs to be modified for including the new character. This problem is presented in Listing 6.16.

As seen, the code required to create copies of enemy characters using the enemy registry with only two characters is quite large. Consider the case where 100 different enemy characters are designed for the gaming system. In such a case, the size of the function would increase significantly, since a conditional statement is required for each character. This problem can be solved easily by using a prototypical interface for creating copies that does not require clients—in this case, the function to create the enemy character—to know which object they are creating.

Listing 6.16: C++ Implementation of the Client that Creates New Enemy Character

```cpp
// Pre-Condition: A registry of 2 Enemy Characters has been created.
Character* createNextEnemyCharacter() {

  // Randomly pick the location of the next enemy character to be
  // created.
  int nextEnemyLocation = rand() % MaxNumberOfEnemies;

  // Make sure that nextEnemyLocation is within proper bounds.

  // Retrieve the character at the nextEnemyLocation.
  Character* pCharacter = enemyRegistry[nextEnemyLocation];

  // The enemy character to be returned.
  Character* pNewCharacter = 0;

  // Determine if the character located at nextEnemyLocation is
  // Terrestrial.
  if( dynamic_cast<TerrestrialEnemyCharacter*>(pCharacter) != 0 ) {

    // Terrestrial Character, downcast it so that the
    // duplicateTerrestrial method can be used to duplicate the
    // terrestrial character.
    TerrestrialEnemyCharacter* pTerrestrial =
              dynamic_cast<TerrestrialEnemyCharacter*>(pCharacter);

    // Create the copy. Clients are responsible for cleaning up memory
    // allocated for the copy.
    pNewCharacter = pTerrestrial->duplicateTerrestrial();
  }
  // Determine if the character located at nextEnemyLocation is Aerial.
  else if( dynamic_cast<AerialEnemyCharacter*>(pCharacter) != 0 ) {

    // Aerial Character, downcast it so that the duplicateAerial
    // method can be used to duplicate the aerial character.
    AerialEnemyCharacter* pAerial =
                dynamic_cast<AerialEnemyCharacter*>(pCharacter);

    // Create the copy. Clients are responsible for cleaning up memory
    // allocated for the copy.
    pNewCharacter = pAerial->duplicateAerial();
  }
  else {
    // Invalid Character.
    pNewCharacter = new InvalidEnemyCharacter;
  }
  // Return the newly created enemy character.
  return pNewCharacter;
}
```

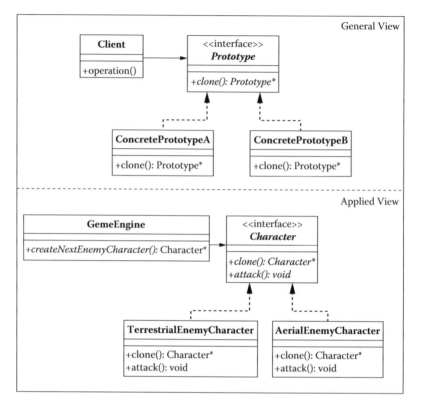

FIGURE 6.4
UML class diagram for the prototype design pattern.

Structure

The general and applied structural view of the prototype design pattern for the gaming system problem is presented in Figure 6.4. As seen, from the structural point of view the only thing required to implement the prototype design pattern is the addition of the clone interface method to the `Character` type. By adding the `clone()` method in the character interface, the behavior for creating character duplicates throughout the game is standardized and delegated to derived classes. Therefore, by deriving from this base class and implementing the clone interface, derived classes can abstract the process of creating a copy of themselves.

The driving forces behind this design are the ability of client objects to create duplicates of character objects without knowing the object's internal true composition and providing clients the ability to reason about character objects using the character interface. Once these characteristics are identified, applying the prototype design pattern is straightforward.

1. Identify and design the common interface that needs duplication. As part of the interface, the clone interface method needs to be specified.
2. Identify and design concrete products, which realize the interface created in Step 1.
3. For each concrete product created in Step 2, implement the clone method in terms of that particular concrete product.

**Listing 6.17: C++ Implementation of the Terrestrial Character
and New `Character` Interface**

```cpp
// The character interface.
class Character {

public:
  // Interface method for initiating an attack.
  virtual void attack() = 0;

  // Interface method for duplicating objects at run-time.
  virtual Character* clone() = 0;

  // Other methods such as defend, move, etc.
};

class TerrestrialEnemyCharacter : public Character {

public:
  // Method definitions for terrestrial attack, defend, etc.
  void attack() {

    // Display to the console the type of attack.
    cout<<"TerrestrialEnemyCharacter::attack()!\n";
  }

  // Duplicate this object.
  TerrestrialEnemyCharacter* duplicateTerrestrial() {

    // Use the copy constructor to create a copy of this object and
    // return it.
    return new TerrestrialEnemyCharacter (*this);
  }

  // Implementation of the clone interface method to duplicate a
  // terrestrial enemy character.
  Character* clone(void) {

    // Delegate duplication to existing method.
    return duplicateTerrestrial();
  }
};
```

Implementation

From the structural point of view, application of the prototype design pattern is straight-forward. In Listing 6.17, the `Character` interface is specified, which includes the `clone()` interface method. By specifying the clone method as a pure virtual method, derived classes are forced to provide an implementation before they can be instantiated. For simplicity (and to make the point clearer), the clone() method is implemented in terms of the previously existing duplicateTerrestrial() method from Listing 6.15. In a practical development effort, such a method is removed so that the clone method can directly create the object's copy.

As seen, the prototype's clone method results in a call to the copy constructor. In this example, the C++ default copy constructor is called upon to create a copy of the specific character object. However, careful attention must be in place when copying more complex objects. In these cases, where the default copy constructor is insufficient to provide a deep copy of the object, a specialized copy constructor must be provided. The same approach for creating duplicates is repeated for the AerialEnemyCharacter, as seen in Listing 6.18.

Once both TerrestrialEnemyCharacter and AerialEnemyCharacter implement the clone interface, the client code presented in Listing 6.16 is modified to randomly create enemy characters using prototypical instances that support the clone() method, as seen in Listing 6.19. By using the prototype design pattern, the original client function is reduced significantly. More importantly, the addition of new enemy characters or removal

---

Listing 6.18: C++ Implementation for the `AerialEnemyCharacter`

```cpp
class AerialEnemyCharacter : public Character {

public:

  // Implement the attack interface method for aerial characters.
  void attack(void) {

    // Display to the console the type of attack.
    cout<<"AerialEnemyCharacter::attack()!\n";
  }

  // Duplicate this object.
  AerialEnemyCharacter* duplicateAerial(void) {

    // Use the copy constructor to create a copy of this object and
    // return it.
    return new AerialEnemyCharacter(*this);
  }

  // Implementation of the clone interface method to duplicate a
  // aerial enemy character.
  Character* clone(void) {

    // Delegate duplication to existing method.
    return duplicateAerial();
  }
};
```

**Listing 6.19: C++ Code for the Client that Creates
New Characters Using the Prototype Interface**

```cpp
Character* createNextEnemyCharacter() {

  // Randomly pick the location of the next enemy character to be
  // created.
  int nextEnemyLocation = rand() % MaxNumberOfEnemies;

  // Make sure that nextEnemyLocation is within proper bounds.

  // Retrieve the character at the nextEnemyLocation.
  return enemyRegistry[nextEnemyLocation]->clone();
}
```

---

of existing characters will not affect the client's implementation. This provides added flexibility to support change in future versions of the gaming system.

Benefits

- Clients are shielded from knowing the internal structure of objects; therefore, adding products at run time is easier. This reduces the client's complexity.
- Reduced number of classes; instead of having two classes for object creation (i.e., creator and product classes), the prototype is both, therefore eliminating the need for one class for each product.

SINGLETON

The singleton design pattern is an object creational design pattern used to prevent objects from being instantiated more than once in a running program. It is meant to provide a design solution that enforces the conceptual representation of entities that must be singular within the problem domain. For example, consider the simulation of an operating system. In the operating systems domain, the simulation software may contain types (i.e., classes) for processes, threads, and so forth that can be instantiated multiple times to properly represent running programs within the simulation. In these cases, the multiple instantiation of these types is conceptually consistent with the problem domain. However, consider an entity type for singular items, such as the file system. In this case, for a typical operating system, it would be conceptually incorrect to have multiple file system object instances running within the simulation. Furthermore, if the simulation were to create two file systems by mistake, the results would not be reliable. In cases such as this one, the singleton design pattern can be used to enforce the policy that only one instance of the file system object is running at all times. According to the Gang of Four (Gamma et al. 1995, p. 127), the intent of the singleton is to

Ensure a class only has one instance, and provide a global point of access to it.

Since the singleton limits object creation to one instance, it is important that the one instance can be accessible through a standard method. Therefore, the singleton design pattern also provides a global point of access to it.

Problem

Consider an application that requires event-logging capabilities. The application consists of many different objects that generate events to keep track of their actions, status of operations, errors, or any other information of interest. A decision is made to create an event manager that can be accessed by all objects and used to manage all events in the system. Upon instantiation, the event manager creates an event list that gets updated as events are logged. At specific points during the software system's operation, these events are written to a file. To prevent conflicts, it is desirable that at any given time there is only one instance of the event manager executing.

Structure

The general and applied structural view of the singleton design pattern for the event manager is presented in Figure 6.5. As seen, from the structural point of view the singleton is the simplest design pattern, since it requires only one class. The driving force behind this

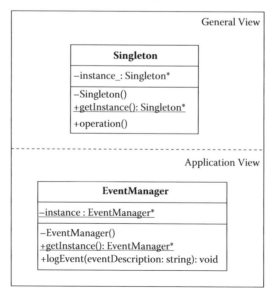

FIGURE 6.5
UML class diagram for the singleton design pattern.

design is the ability for clients to have global access to the event manager and the assurance that there is only one instance of the event manager at all times. Assuming a single-threaded application, these characteristics are typically a good indication for applying the singleton design pattern. To apply the singleton design pattern, a three-step approach is employed:

1. Set the visibility of the constructor to private.
2. Define a private static member attribute that can store a reference (or pointer) to the one instance of the singleton.
3. Create a public static `getInstance` method that can access the private constructor to instantiate objects of the singleton type and return it to clients.

When designing singletons, the class constructor needs to be specified as private to prevent clients from instantiating objects of the singleton type via the direct access to the constructor. Since access to the constructor is prohibited, the second step involves creating a method that can access the private constructor to instantiate objects of the singleton's type. This method needs to be a class method (i.e., static) so that it can be called at the class level without instantiating an object of the class. This is done by specifying the method as static with public visibility. Finally, a private static member attribute that can store a reference or pointer to the running instance of the singleton needs to be created to keep track of the one, and only one, instance of the singleton. This attribute is initially set to zero or null, and once a call to the `getInstance()` method is made the attribute is checked to determine if the instance of the singleton has been created. If it hasn't, the method instantiates it and returns it to the caller. After the first initialization process, further calls to the `getInstance()` method will fail the condition that determines that the attribute is null, therefore directly returning the existing singleton object.

Implementation

As specified before, the implementation of the singleton consists of three main steps. First, the visibility of the constructor needs to be private to prevent direct instantiation from clients. Next, a public class (static) member function must be created to provide clients with a globally accessible function for the singleton. Finally, the globally accessible function must instantiate the singleton object while enforcing that only one instance is created throughout program. The C++ implementation of the *EventManager* singleton class is presented in Listings 6.19 and 6.20.

Once the singleton design pattern is applied to the `EventManager`, client objects can use it easily via the standardized and globally accessible `getInstance()` method, as presented in Listing 6.21.

The singleton design pattern has been known to fail in multithreaded applications, resulting in the creation of more than one instance of the singleton. Therefore, its usage in these types of environments should be carefully evaluated before implementation.

Listing 6.19: C++ Header File for the EventManager Singleton

```cpp
#include <string>

class EventManager {

public:
  // The global point of access to the EventManager.
  static EventManager* getInstance();

  // The method that logs events.
  void logEvent(std::string eventDescription);

private:
  // Private Constructor.
  EventManager();

  // The one and only instance of the EventManager.
  static EventManager* _instance;
};
```

Listing 6.20: C++ Source File for the EventManager Singleton

```cpp
#include "EventManager.h"

// Initialize the instance_ static member attribute.
EventManager* EventManager::_instance = 0;

// The global point of access to the EventManager.
EventManager* EventManager::getInstance() {

  // Determine if an instance of the EventManager has been created.
  if( _instance == 0 ) {

    // Create the one and only instance.
    _instance = new EventManager;
  }
  return _instance;
}

// The method that logs events.
void EventManager::logEvent(std::string eventDescription) {
  // Code to log event.
}

// Private Constructor.
EventManager::EventManager() {
  // Intentionally left blank.
}
```

Listing 6.21: C++ Implementation for Client Objects Using the EventManager Singleton

```cpp
int main() {

  // Log events using the singleton event manager.
  EventManager::getInstance()->logEvent("log some event here");

  // Or store the pointer to log events later.
  EventManager* pEventManager = EventManager::getInstance();
  pEventManager->logEvent("log some event here");
}
```

Benefits

- The singleton provides controlled access to a single instance of a given type.
- It has reduced name space since it provides an alternative to global variables.
- It can be customized to permit variable number of instances.

CHAPTER SUMMARY

Creational design patterns are patterns for abstracting and controlling the way objects are created in software applications. They play a key role in the design of systems by making them independent of how objects in the system are created, composed, and represented. Therefore, parts of the system responsible for creating (or instantiating) objects do so through a common creational interface without knowledge of how the actual object or group of objects are created. In addition, by controlling the creational process with a common interface, enforcing creational policies becomes easier, therefore giving the system the ability to create product objects that share a common interface but that vary widely in structure and behavior. Examples of creational patterns include the abstract factory, factory method, builder, prototype, and singleton. This chapter explored several well-established creational design patterns and presented the problems they are designed to address, together with the benefits that each of the discussed patterns provides. Identifying and designing using creational design patterns can improve the efficiency of the development process and the quality of the final system.

REVIEW QUESTIONS

1. What are creational design patterns? What are they used for?
2. Compare and contrasts the following patterns:
   a. Abstract factory
   b. Factory method

   c. Builder

   d. Prototype

3. List and explain the benefits of applying the abstract factory design pattern.

4. What is the builder design pattern? List and explain the main features of the builder design pattern.

5. What particular problems are addressed by the builder design pattern?

6. What is the essential structural element required in the prototype design pattern?

7. Explain the steps required to implement the singleton design pattern? Are there any limitations to this pattern? Explain.

CHAPTER EXERCISES

1. A company is designing software for monitoring and controlling a custom-built system consisting of multiple hardware components (i.e., Equipment1, Equipment2, and Equipment3). Each equipment component provides unique status, unique commands, and specific interface for communicating, such as a Universal Serial Bus (USB), Serial, and Transmission Control Protocol/Internet Protocol (TCP/IP). Regardless of the communication type, each class representing an equipment must provide functionality to get specific status (e.g., getEquipmentOneStatus1, getEquipmentTwoStatus1) and send specific commands to the device (e.g., sendEquipmentOneCmd1, sendEquipmentTwoCmd1). The software provides a graphical user interface (GUI) that polls each hardware component for its status data and also provides means for sending commands to the components. Since hardware development is expected to take longer than the expected GUI development, management has decided to simulate the components so that GUI development and testing can move forward. That is, there are two streams of equipments: real equipment, composed of Equipment1, Equipment2, and Equipment3; and simulated equipments, composed of SimEquipment1, SimEquipment2, and SimEquipment3. Design this system using the abstract factory design pattern so that the GUI software can work the same way using real or simulated components, regardless of the type of component.

2. Your company develops software to monitor and control custom-built hardware developed by a separate vendor. The equipment supports 100 different messages, defined with the format specified in the following box. Every time the messaging specification changes, the code for all 100 messages has to change manually. To make things worse, your company supports two versions of the software, one in Java and one in C++, so these changes must be made to both versions. In addition, there are future plans for providing a messaging library in C# as well, based on the messaging specification. Clearly, there has to be a more efficient way to manage this process. Management has asked you, the design team, to come up with a design that separates the algorithm for parsing the messaging specification from the code that generates classes for the

messages in a specific programming language (e.g., Java or C++). This way, changes to the messaging specification will not affect the code that generates the messages in specific programming languages and vice versa; that is, changes or additions to support new programming language generation will not affect the code that parses the messaging specification. A sample of the messaging specification containing three messages is given to you so that you can propose a design that can improve the code generation process. Management would be thrilled if your design would support different generators (at run time) capable of producing the messages in different programming languages. That way, by swapping generators different programming languages can be supported. The generated code should provide get() and set() methods for all attributes.

Messaging Specification Sample

```
Name:PowerOnCmd;
Attributes:4;
byte:headerSize;
byte:msgId;
byte:sourceId;
byte:destinationId;
Operations:0;
Name:SelfTestCmd
Attributes:5;
byte:headerSize;
byte:msgId;
byte:sourceId;
byte:destinationId;
byte:testId;
Operations:0;
Name:SetDataCmd;
Attributes:6;
byte:headerSize;
byte:msgId;
byte:sourceId;
byte:destinationId;
byte:dataType;
byte:dataSize;
Operations:2;
byte*,getData,void;
void,setData,byte*;
```

---

3. Apply the builder design pattern to design this system.
4. Use the tool of your choice (e.g., rational rose, starUML, MS PowerPoint, Visio) to create the UML class diagram for the problem
5. Write code in C++ to demonstrate the implementation of your design. Your program must create files containing Java or C++ code for the generated messages, depending on the builder used.

6. Prepare a 10- to 15-minute PowerPoint presentation consisting of the following:
   a. Introduction to the problem
   b. Solution approach (UML class diagram)
   c. Presentation of the builder code
   d. Demo of the program
   e. Be ready to *state your assumptions* and to justify and defend all of your design decisions.

REFERENCE

Gamma, Erich, Richard Helm, Ralph Johnson, and John Vlissides. *Design Patterns: Elements of Reusable Object-Oriented Software.* Boston: Addison-Wesley, 1995.

7

Structural and Behavioral Patterns in Detailed Design

CHAPTER OBJECTIVES

- Understand the importance and role of structural and behavioral design patterns in detailed design
- Identify, understand, and model common structural and behavioral design patterns
- Become proficient in implementing models of both structural and behavioral design patterns
- Understand the benefits of important structural and behavioral design patterns

CONCEPTUAL OVERVIEW

As seen in the previous chapter, common patterns in object-oriented designs exist to provide detailed design solutions to problems that recur many times over in different systems. Beside the creational design patterns studied so far, other common and popular design patterns have been identified to address structural and behavioral problems commonly encountered in software applications. Structural and behavioral designs patterns help identify problems that deal with the structure and behavior of software designs; they prescribe the classes required for their design solution and interrelationships required to support object creation their behavior. These patterns allow designers to quickly and systematically identify structural layouts of systems (or subsystems) and provide avenues for examining the system's interactions and quality evaluation within the operational system.

This chapter explores several well-established structural and behavioral design patterns and examines the problems they are designed to address, together with the benefits they provide. Identifying and designing using these design patterns can improve the efficiency of the development process and the quality of the final system.

STRUCTURAL DESIGN PATTERNS

Structural design patterns are patterns that deal with designing larger structures from existing classes or objects at run time. They play a key role in the design and evolution of systems by allowing integration of new designs with existing ones, via object composition (i.e., object structural) or inheritance (i.e., class structural). Class structural design patterns identify the inheritance relationship necessary to create new interfaces or implementations that may be compatible with the older design structure. Object structural patterns provide the relationships required to create larger structures through object composition at run time, therefore providing more flexibility to extend the system at run time, which is impossible for class structural solutions. In both cases, by allowing designs to build on other existing structures, systems can be made interoperable by designing compatible interfaces for otherwise incompatible systems. Structural design patterns have also significant impact on the reusability and modifiability of systems. Examples of structural design patterns include the adapter, composite, and facade.

ADAPTER

The adapter design pattern is a class/object structural design pattern used to adapt an existing interface to another interface that is expected in a software system. It can be designed as both class structural, in which the major composition relationships are defined at compile time, and object structural, where structural object composition occurs at run time. In either case, the adapter design pattern allows systems with incompatible interfaces to work together, therefore increasing the reusability and evolution of software systems. According to the Gang of Four (Gamma, Elm, Johnson, and Vlissides 1995, p. 139), the intent of the adapter is to

> Convert the interface of a class into another interface clients expect. Adapter lets classes work together that couldn't otherwise because of incompatible interfaces.

Conceptually, adapters are used everywhere. For example, electrical adapters can be used to connect devices with incompatible interfaces, such as European plugs and American sockets. In gardening, adapters are used to connect water hoses with incompatible interfaces to extend their reach. In computer hardware, adapters are used to covert between many different interfaces, such as serial to Universal Serial Bus (USB). In software, the adapter concept is applied similar to adapters in the previous examples. Consider the graphical user interface (GUI) for an application to monitor and control a satellite communication system composed of several independent hardware devices. For each hardware device, complex GUI screens are designed to monitor and control each device. All screens rely on a class, named `HardwareDevice`, that provides methods (e.g., *string getStatusA(), string getStatusB()*) designed and developed assuming that commands and status for each device use the *string* type (in C++). When receiving the hardware devices from their manufacturers and the binary compiled library that provides monitor and control capabilities for each device, it is noticed that the class `ManufacturerHardwareDevice` (provided by the manufacturer) provides all functions for command and control using the *char** type or other nonstring type, which creates an incompatible interface between the existing GUI code and the library code. Since the code inside the library cannot be changed and changing the code for all screens (depending on the number of screens) may be impractical, the provided class in the binary library can be adapted using the adapter design pattern to fit the expected interfaces in the GUI software or vice versa.

Problem

Consider the completed gaming system discussed in Chapter 5, which includes the design and development for all 10 levels of a gaming system, including the design and implementation of all gaming characters. At each level, the core of the gaming system (i.e., *GameEngine)* uses the *Character* interface to add enemy characters to the game, making them move, defend, and attack using the `move()`, `defend()`, and `attack()` interface methods, respectively. Each character in the game implements the `Character` interface to provide specific behavior appropriate for the character and the level of the game. That is, depending on the character and the game level, the behavior for moving, defending, and attacking varies among characters. An online character developer has created a special character that is compatible with the game development's application programming interface (API) but not with the particular `Character` interface; that is, the special character designed by the online developer includes the following interface methods: `specialMove()`, `specialAttack()`, and `specialDefend()`. The special character is made available freely to the gaming community; however, the special character code can be downloaded and incorporated into other gaming systems only as a binary compiled library, which can be incorporated into the existing game. Since all levels of the game are complete, it is impractical to change the code in all places to detect the new special character and make different calls for moving, attacking, and defending; therefore, the adapter design pattern is required to adapt the special character's interface to the current character interface.

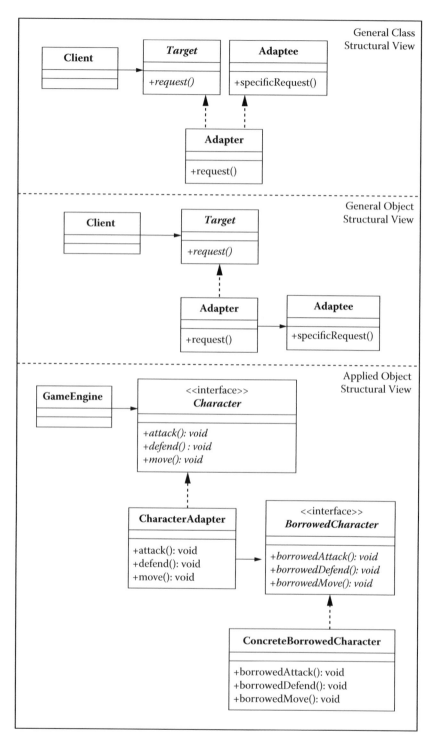

FIGURE 7.1

UML class diagram for the class/object structural adapter design pattern.

Structure

The general and applied structure of the adapter design pattern is presented in Figure 7.1. As seen, the adapter can be designed using multiple inheritance or object composition.

In the multiple inheritance version, the pattern's relationships between classes and subclasses are defined at compile time, via inheritance; therefore, this version is classified as class structural. When the adapter design pattern is designed using object composition, object relationships are defined at run time; therefore, the adapter design pattern in this case is classified as object structural. The object structural version of the adapter design pattern results in a more dynamic and flexible design; therefore, it is the recommended and followed approach for the gaming system. The step-by-step approach for designing the object structural adapter design pattern is presented as follows:

1. Identify the source and destination interfaces that need adapting in the new system (e.g., target and adaptee or character and SpecialCharacter).
2. Add a new class (e.g., adapter or AdaptedCharacter) in the design that realizes the target interface and implements it in terms of the adaptee's implementation. This requires a realization relationship between the adapter and target, and an association between the adapter and the adaptee.
3. In the new system, whenever objects that share the target interface are expected, it can now be possible to use the adapter objects created in Step 2.

The driving forces for applying the adapter design pattern are reusability and integration of code between two mature software structures. Under these conditions, changing the code to match either of the two software entities is impractical. Furthermore, access to the code for either software entity may not be possible; therefore, to reuse and integrate code from one entity to the other, the adapter is required. When this is the case, the adapter design pattern is easily applied by creating an adapter class that inherits from the target class. By incorporating new adapter objects that share the *Target* interface, clients can use them the same way they used original *Target* objects; however, these new adapter objects implement the *Target* functions in terms of the *Adaptee*, which is the object providing the new functionality under a different, incompatible interface.

Implementation

The implementation of the object structural adapter design pattern simply requires the creation of one class with two relationships—realization and association. In practical applications, the *Target* and *Adaptee* classes are typically part of larger mature and sable software structures. In this example, the *Target* and *Adaptee* classes are represented by the *Character* and *BorrowedCharacter* classes, as seen in Listings 7.1 and 7.2.

Listing 7.1: C++ Code for the `Character` Interface

```cpp
// The Target class.
class Character {

public:

  // Interface method for attack functionality.
  virtual void attack() = 0;

  // Interface method for defend functionality.
  virtual void defend() = 0;

  // Interface method for moving functionality.
  virtual void move() = 0;
};
```

Listing 7.2: C++ Code for the `BorrowedCharacter` Interface and `ConcreteBorrowedCharacter`

```cpp
// Interface for the borrowed character.
class BorrowedCharacter {

public:
  // Interface methods for the borrowed character.
  virtual void borrowedAttack() = 0;
  virtual void borrowedDefend() = 0;
  virtual void borrowedMove() = 0;
};

// Concrete borrowed character.
class ConcreteBorrowedCharacter : public BorrowedCharacter {

public:
  // Implementations for the BorrowedCharacter interface methods.
  void borrowedAttack() { /* attack code here... */}
  void borrowedDefend() { /* defense code here... */}
  void borrowedMove() { /* code to move here... */}
};
```

As seen, the interfaces for the `Character` and `BorrowedCharacters` are different; therefore, client code that expects objects with the *Character* interface cannot accept objects with the *BorrowedCharacter* interface even though conceptually, both objects do the same operations. To allow the existing code to process objects of the borrowed character type as if they were objects of the character type, a `CharacterAdapter` is required, as seen in Listing 7.3.

Listing 7.3: C++ Header File for the `CharacterAdapter` Class

```cpp
// Forward reference.
class BorrowedCharacter;

class CharacterAdapter : public Character {
public:
  // Constructor.
  CharacterAdapter(BorrowedCharacter* pCharacter);

  // Adapt the attack method.
  void attack(void);

  // Adapt the defend method.
  void defend(void);

  // Adapt the move method.
  void move(void);

private:
  // BorrowedCharacter that needs adapting to the Character interface.
  BorrowedCharacter* _borrowedCharacter;
};
```

As seen, the `CharacterAdapter` inherits from the `Character` to implement the realization relationship in C++. It is also associated with the `BorrowedCharacter` class via member attribute. To finalize the object adaptation, the newly created character adapter type is required to implement all interface methods defined by the character interface in terms of the associated borrowed character, as seen in Listing 7.4.

Once the adapter design pattern is applied, it is easy to use borrowed characters in the gaming system. Consider the method presented in Listing 7.5 for triggering character behavior in the `GameEngine` class.

As seen, this and other methods defined in the `GameEngine` class can now employ the adapter design pattern to accept character objects that comply with the character interface but provide behavior from the borrowed character. An example of client code used to activate a borrowed character in the gaming system is presented in Listing 7.6. As seen, the borrowed character is created and passed into the character adapter during its initialization through the constructor. From this point forward, the adapted character is used instead of the borrowed character to provide the new features to the game.

Benefits

- Allows classes with incompatible interfaces to work together, therefore increasing reusability and ease of code integration
- Provides a standard way for integrating a plurality of different types to existing software

Listing 7.4: C++ Source File for the `CharacterAdapter` Class

```cpp
#include "CharacterAdapter.h"
#include "BorrowedCharacter.h"

// Constructor.
CharacterAdapter::CharacterAdapter(BorrowedCharacter* pCharacter) {

  // For simplicity, assume a valid pointer.
  _borrowedCharacter = pCharacter;
}

// Adapt the attack method.
void CharacterAdapter::attack() {

  // Implement the attack functionality in terms of the
  // BorrowedCharacter.
  _borrowedCharacter->borrowedAttack();
}

// Adapt the defend method.
void CharacterAdapter::CharacterAdapter::defend() {

  // Implement the defend functionality in terms of the
  // BorrowedCharacter.
  _borrowedCharacter->borrowedDefend();
}

// Adapt the move method.
void CharacterAdapter::move() {

  // Implement the move functionality in terms of the
  // BorrowedCharacter.
  _borrowedCharacter->borrowedMove();
}
```

Skill Development 7.1: Adapter Design Pattern

Using the Unified Modeling Language (UML) tool of choice, replicate the UML model presented in Figure 7.1 and generate code from the model. Using the Integrated Development Environment (IDE) of choice, fill in the gaps in the code generated using Listings 7.1 through 7.6, and compile and execute the software. Create two additional classes: one that derives from the character class in which its methods are implemented to simply display some output to the console; and another adapter class that adapts another character with different interface methods for attacking, defending, and moving (e.g., slowAttack, slowDefend, and slowMove). Use the triggeredAction method to pass in (one at a time) objects of all the types created. Observe how the triggeredAction method accepts both objects of the original character interface and the new adapted objects (since they now all share the character interface). How does the adapter design pattern increase reusability, maintainability, and modifiability in such system?

Listing 7.5: C++ Code for the `GameEngine` Method to Trigger a Character's Actions

```cpp
class GameEngine {

public:
  // ...
  // Method to activate a character.
  void GameEngine::triggeredAction(Character* pCharacter) {

  // Activate the character and make it move randomly for a short
  // time.
  pCharacter->move();

  // Once the character stops moving, if being attacked, defend!
  pCharacter->defend();

  // Once the characters stops defending, if others characters are
  // detected, attack!
  pCharacter->attack();
  }
  // ...
};
```

Listing 7.6: C++ Code for Client Code in the Gaming System to Activate a Borrowed Character

```cpp
// Instantiate the game engine.
GameEngine engine;

// Create the borrowed character that needs adapting.
ConcreteBorrowedCharacter borrowedCharacter;

// Create the character adapter and pass in the borrowed character.
// From this point on, the adapterCharacter object can be used
// throughout the game engine as if it were a Character!
CharacterAdapter adaptedCharacter(&borrowedCharacter);

// Move, attack, and defend with the borrowed character's features!
engine.triggeredAction(&adaptedCharacter);
```

COMPOSITE

The composite design pattern is an object structural pattern that allows designers to compose (large) tree-like design structures by strategically structuring objects that share a whole–part relationship. Whole–part relationships are those in which a larger entity (i.e., the whole) is created by the composition of smaller entities (i.e., the parts). The key advantage of using the composite design pattern is that it provides a design structure that allows both whole and part objects to be treated uniformly; therefore, operations that are common to both type of objects can be applied the same way to both types of objects. According to the Gang of Four (Gamma et al. 1995, p. 163), the intent of the composite is to

> Compose objects into tree structures to represent part-whole hierarchies. Composite lets clients treat individual objects and composites of objects uniformly.

Many situations exist that require objects to be composed of many parts. However, in some specific instances, some problems require both objects and their parts to be treated uniformly. In the software domain, perhaps the most common example is seen in modern user interfaces, which contain both *Menu* and *MenuItem* objects. A *Menu,* in the graphical user interface context, is a mechanism of the software that allows users to select and activate features of the system. A *Menu* can also provide access to other *Menus* or *MenuItems* that can be selected to trigger software execution. Both *Menu* and *MenuItem* may contain functions to change their visible text, size, and background color or to handle events. Therefore, both must be treated uniformly. In this case, the composite design pattern can be used to create a flexible design structure that groups both *Menu* and *MenuItems,* that provides easy addition and removal of both *Menu* and *MenuItems* to the design structure, and that provides a uniform interface so that operations common to both can be easily performed using the composite interface. Although the composite design pattern is prevalent in examples such as this, its application can be found in numerous practical applications.

Problem

A wireless sensor system is remotely deployed to collect environmental information. The sensor system communicates via satellite to a central location, where a schedule of tasks (i.e., a mission plan) is created and sent over satellite communications. A mission plan is a composite message that contains one or more messages that command the sensor system to perform particular tasks. These messages contain information on how and when to perform particular tasks. Mission plan messages can be created with many different combinations of messages. Upon creating the mission plan message, it is sent to the wireless sensor system, which retrieves each message and message information from the mission plan and executes them to collect environmental data, store it, and send it back to the central location, as directed by the mission plan message. The sensor system is extensible and contains many capabilities provided by numerous sensors (e.g., temperature, vibration), still-shot camera, and video recording. To operate the sensor system, the operators at the central location are requesting a message generator capable of allowing them to easily create a mission plan message. The mission plan message may contain both primitive and composite messages. Numerous mission plan messages can be created to support different "missions," and it is expected that more sensing capabilities will be added in the future. Therefore, the design of the message generator must provide easy addition and removal of

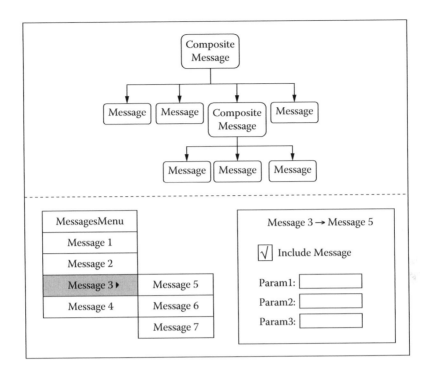

FIGURE 7.2
Message generator graphical user interface concept.

both messages and composite messages to a mission plan. A graphical representation of the message generator is presented in Figure 7.2.

As seen, the topmost composite message represents the mission plan message (or schedule). The message generator provides a series of menu items that allows operators to select a particular message, to configure its parameters, and to add it to the mission plan message. In this example, Message 3 is a composite message that can be configured to contain Messages 5, 6, and 7. Message 3 can also be configured individually and added to the mission plan. Both primitive and composite messages need to be treated uniformly, so that methods such as getId(), setId(), and toXml() can be supported by both types of messages.

Structure

The general and applied structure of the composite design pattern is presented in Figure 7.3. As seen, the general structure of the composite design pattern requires three main classes, the *Composite, Leaf,* and *Component* classes. The *Component* class defines the operations that are common to both *Composite* and *Leaf* objects, for example, print(), toXml(), getId(), setId(), etc., as shown in the Applied View portion of Figure 7.3. The component class also defines the methods specific to support the composite design pattern, namely, the add() and remove() methods. The add and remove methods are intended for use by composite objects and not by leaf objects; therefore, they must be specified as overridable methods with default implementation that indicates an unsupported operation.

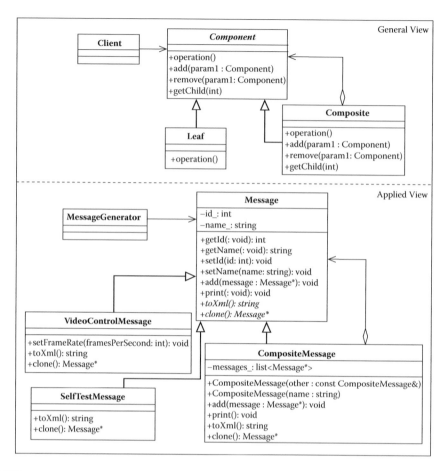

FIGURE 7.3
UML class diagram for the composite design pattern.

This means that if at any point during run time a leaf object is called upon to add or remove objects to the hierarchy, the default implementation for these methods is executed to reflect the unsupported requests. In many cases, a good alternative for the default implementation involves writing code that throws exceptions within the add and remove methods. On the other hand, composite objects that derive from the component base class are required to override the default implementation so that objects can be added and removed from the hierarchy. This way, when composite objects are bound dynamically at run time to a reference of the component type, the appropriate code for adding and removing objects is called, preventing the default implementation from being executed. The steps required to apply the composite design pattern include

1. Identify, understand, and plan the tree-like structure required for the system.
2. With the knowledge from Step 1, identify and design the component base class, which includes overridable methods common to both leaf and composite objects as well as methods specific to composite objects, which provide capability for adding and removing objects to the hierarchy.

3. For the methods specified in Step 2 for adding and removing objects to the hierarchy, implement default behavior that if not overridden will result in an exception or error message indicating an unsupported operation.
4. Identify and design the composite class, which overrides methods for adding and removing objects to the hierarchy. The composite class requires an internal data structure to store leaf nodes added to the hierarchy. In addition, the composite class is required to override all other operational methods identified in Step 2 to implement functionality in terms of the composite object and all of its contained leaf objects.
5. Identify and design the leaf class, which overrides operational methods specified in Step 2 to implement behavior in terms of the leaf object. Leaf objects do not override the add and remove methods identified in Step 2.
6. Identify and design the client that uses both composite and leaf objects.

In the message generator example, `add()` and `remove()` are used to add and remove both `CompositeMessage` and all other derived messages to the design structure (e.g., `VideoControlMessage`, `SelfTestMessage`). Therefore, to support the addition of new messages that provide control of future sensing capabilities, a new class that derives from the `Message` base class needs to be added to the message generator design. In addition, to support easy duplication of both types of messages, the prototype design pattern is incorporated into the message generator design so that message copies can be easily created throughout the application. This is reflected in the design with the addition of the `clone()` method to the `Message` class.

The driving forces behind the design include the ability to treat both individual messages and mission plan messages uniformly, so that the complexity of client code is minimized. The composite design pattern is also chosen to achieve design flexibility so that new messages can be created easily to support future systems' demands. The most influential step when applying the composite design pattern is the addition of the *add()* method in the *Component* base class. Once this method is created, composite objects override it to store the primitive objects contained by it.

Implementation

Most of the implementation work for the composite design pattern takes place in both the component and composite classes, which are represented in the message generator by the `Message` and `CompositeMessage` classes. Once these are created, other message classes that share the same Message interface can be added easily by deriving from the Message class. The implementation for the `Message` class is presented in Listing 7.7.

As seen, the `toXml()` and `clone()` methods are incorporated in the `Message` type interface. These methods are application specific and are not related to the composite design pattern. The `toXml()` method is added to enforce the policy that all messages in the system are required to provide implementation appropriate to convert the particular message data into Extensible Markup Language (XML) format. Other application-specific methods include the `getId()`, `setId()`, `getName()`, and `setName()`.

Listing 7.7: C++ Header File for the Message Class

```cpp
class Message {

public:

  // Method to retrieve the message's id.
  int getId() const;

  // Method to retrieve the message's name.
  string getName() const;

  // Method to set the message's id.
  void setId(int id);

  // Method to set the message's name.
  void setName(string name);

  // Method to add messages to a composite message.
  virtual void add(Message* message);

  // Method to display messages to the console.
  virtual void print();

  // Method to transform the contents of this message to XML format.
  virtual string toXml() = 0;

  // Duplicate Messages using the prototype design pattern.
  virtual Message* clone() = 0;

private:
  // The message's id.
  int _id;

  // The message's name.
  string _name;
};
```

The add(Message*) method is specific to the composite design pattern. Specifically, it gives composite classes the ability to add messages to their structure so that the whole–part relationship can be realized. Because this method is intended specifically for composite classes, it violates the Liskov substitution principle presented in Chapter 5. However, it provides the functionality necessary to support efficient solution to the problem; therefore, its usage can be easily justified during design reviews. To minimize the effects of this violation, careful attention needs to be paid when implementing the default behavior of the *add(Message*)* method in the *Message* base class. The easiest solution is to provide a base implementation that notifies the operator stating that the operation is not supported. That way, derived classes that do not support the add method would simply inherit the default

Listing 7.8: C++ Implementation for the `Add()` and `Print()` Methods of the `Message` Class

```cpp
#include "Message.h"
#include <string>
#include <iostream>

// Method to add messages to a composite message.
void Message::add(Message* message) {

  // The default implementation lets clients know that the operation
  // is unsupported. This behavior is inherited by Leaf classes, but
  // overridden by Composite classes.
  std::cout<<"Messages cannot be added to Leaf objects!\n";
}

// Method to display messages to the console.
void Message::print(void) {

  // The default behavior for displaying a message's information.
  // This behavior is inherited by Leaf classes, but overridden by
  // Composite classes.
  std::cout<<"Message "<<_name.c_str()<<", Id: "<<_id<<endl;
}
```

implementation. A more sophisticated approach includes writing code that throws an exception indicating that the operation is not supported. This way, calls to the add(Message*) method from leaf classes will result in exceptions that can explicitly notify developers of this unsupported operation. The default implementation for both the add() and print() methods is presented in Listing 7.8. Notice that the print method can be defined in the *Message* base class to display the message's information. This implementation is appropriate for leaf objects but not for composite objects; therefore, leaf objects can inherit this implementation without further changes.

The main difference between the CompositeMessage class and all other messages in the design is that the operations of the CompositeMessage need to support its contained messages. For example, the print() method needs to display the information of the composite message and all of its contained messages. Similarly, the CompositeMessage class needs to override the add(), toXml(), and clone() methods to appropriately support all of its contained objects. The CompositeMessage class is specified in Listing 7.9.

To support the addition of primitive messages in the composite structure, a C++ template list is used, so the implementation of the add(Message*) method simply pushes messages to the back of the list. By using a list, implementing the print() method is made easy since all it has to do is iterate through the list and call each of the message object's print() methods, as displayed in Listing 7.10.

Primitive objects of the message type are created by deriving from the *Message* base class and implementing all other application-specific required methods. For example, the *video*

Listing 7.9: C++ Header File for the `CompositeMessage` Class

```cpp
#include <list>
#include "Message.h"

class CompositeMessage : public Message {

public:

    // Copy constructor.
    CompositeMessage(const CompositeMessage& other);

    // Overloaded constructor to set the message's name.
    CompositeMessage(string name);

    // Destructor to clean up memory for messages in _message.
    virtual ~CompositeMessage();

    // Method to add messages to this Composite Message.
    void add(Message* message);

    // Override the print method to display all messages in _message.
    virtual void print();

    // Method to transform the contents of this message to XML format.
    string Message::toXml();

    // Create a duplicate of the Composite Message using the prototype
    // design pattern.
    Message* clone();

private:

    // The Messages that make up the Composite Message.
    list<Message*> _messages;
};
```

---

control message for the system is required to provide implementation for required *toXml()* and *clone()* methods and all other methods required to execute video control messages, such as the `setFrameRate()` method. An example of the `VideoControlMessage` implementation is presented in Listing 7.11. In similar fashion, all other messages in the system are created.

Once the `CompositeMessage` and primitive messages are designed and implemented, the client message generator can be implemented, as seen in Listing 7.12.

As seen, by using the composite design patterns message hierarchies containing both primitive and composite objects can be created easily simply by adding objects to the composite objects via the `add()` interface method. For example, the `powerOnMessage`, `selfTestMessage`, and `transmitStatusMessage`, all sharing the `Message` interface, are added to the composite message `initializeTaskingMessage`,

Listing 7.10: C++ Implementation of the Composite's `Add()` and `Print()` Methods

```cpp
// Add a message to the collection of messages in the Composite
// Message.
void CompositeMessage::add(Message* message) {

  // Add this message.
  _messages.push_back(message);
}

void CompositeMessage::print() {

  // Display the Composite Message's name and id.
  cout<<"\nComposite Message: "<<getName().c_str()
      <<", Id: "<<getId()<<endl;

  // Retrieve an iterator for the _messages collection.
  list<Message*>::iterator pIter = _messages.begin();

  // Iterate through the messages that make up this composite
  // message and display their info.
  for( unsigned int i = 0; i < _messages.size(); i++ ) {

    // Display the message's information and move the iterator to
    // the next position.
    (*pIter++)->print();
  }
}
```

which in turn is added to the composite message `missionPlanMessage`. Similarly, `collectionMessage`, which is a composite message, and `shutdownMessage`, which is a primitive message, are both added to the `missionPlanMessage` to create a full collection mission plan message. Once the whole message is created from its parts, the mission plan message can be used to display its content and convert all messages contained in the *missionPlanMessage* to XML before being sent out via the communication link. The sample output for the code in Listing 7.12 is presented in Listing 7.13.

Benefits

- Provides a design structure that supports both composite and primitive objects
- Minimizes complexity on clients by shielding them from knowing the operational differences between primitive and composite objects; clients that expect a primitive object will also work with a composite object, since operations are called uniformly on both primitive and composite objects
- Easy to create and add new component objects to applications

---

Listing 7.11: C++ Header File for the `VideoControlMessage` Leaf Class

```cpp
#include "Message.h"

class VideoControlMessage : public Message
{
public:

  // Constructor.
  VideoControlMessage(void);

  // Destructor.
  ~VideoControlMessage(void);

  // TODO: Specific video control methods.
  void setFrameRate(int framesPerSecond);
  // .
  // .
  // .

  // Method to transform the contents of this message to XML format.
  string toXml(void);

  // Duplicate the VideoControlMessage using the prototype design
  // pattern.
  Message* clone(void);
};
```

FACADE

The facade design pattern is an object structural pattern that provides a simplified interface to complex subsystems. By providing a simplified interface, the facade design pattern provides a higher level of abstraction that liberates clients from the responsibility of knowing the internal structure of various elements of the subsystem, which in turn reduces coupling and simplifies client code. Facade also shields clients from changes that occur in the subsystem; by having a standardized facade interface, the internal structure of the subsystem can vary without affecting clients. According to the Gang of Four (Gamma et al. 1995, p. 185), the intent of the facade design pattern is to

> Provide a unified to a set of interfaces in a subsystem. Facade defines a higher-level interface that makes the subsystem easier to use.

In most practical applications, components or subsystems are created to abstract a complex behavior that the system must provide. In these cases, executing a complex

Listing 7.12: C++ Implementation for the Message Generator and Sample Usage

```cpp
// Create the initialization primitive messages.
PowerOnMessage powerOnMessage;
SelfTestMessage selfTestMessage;
TransmitStatusMessage transmitStatusMessage;

// The message to task the system to initialize properly.
CompositeMessage initializeTaskingMessage("Initialize System");

// Add copies of the power on, self test, and transmit status messages
// to the initialize tasking composite message.
initializeTaskingMessage.add( powerOnMessage.clone() );
initializeTaskingMessage.add( selfTestMessage.clone() );
initializeTaskingMessage.add( transmitStatusMessage.clone() );

// Collection Control Messages.
TemperatureSensorControlMessage temperatureSensorControlMessage;
VideoControlMessage videoControlMessage;

// The message to task the system to collect information.
CompositeMessage collectionMessage("Information Collection");

// Add the temp. sensor and video control messages to the collection
// tasking composite message.
collectionMessage.add( temperatureSensorControlMessage.clone() );
collectionMessage.add( videoControlMessage.clone() );

// Shutdown Messages.
ShutdownMessage shutdownMessage;

// The message to task the system to complete Mission 1.
CompositeMessage missionPlanMessage("Mission 1 - Temperature
                                     and Video Collection");

// Add the messages to the initialize, collection, and shutdown
// messages to the mission plan composite message.
missionPlanMessage.add( initializeTaskingMessage.clone() );
missionPlanMessage.add( collectionMessage.clone() );
missionPlanMessage.add( shutdownMessage.clone() );

// Before sending message, verify its content.
missionPlanMessage.print();

// If content is valid, send the message through the system. Before
// being sent out through the communication link, a call to
// missionPlanMessage.toXml() is made to convert all of the
// message's content to XML format.
```

Listing 7.13: Sample Output for the Message Generator Problem

```
Composite Message: Mission 1 - Temperature and Video Collection, Id: 20

Composite Message: Initialize System, Id: 20
Message Power On Message, Id: 0
Message Self Test Message, Id: 1
Message Transmit Status Message, Id: 2

Composite Message: Information Collection, Id: 20
Message Temperature Sensor Control Message, Id: 3
Message Video Control Message, Id: 4
Message Shutdown Message, Id: 5

Press any key to continue . . .
```

---

subsystem behavior may require the combination of multiple function calls from multiple component and subsystem elements. For example, consider a software component that provides various elements and functionality for assessing the integrity of a particular computer. This component may contain elements responsible for particular items of interests, such as a file system element, memory element, and communication element. In this case, the facade design pattern can be used to abstract all elements in the subsystem by creating a method *testSystem()* that in turns calls upon the various elements of the subsystem in the appropriate order to evaluate the integrity of the system. This allows clients to be associated only with the facade and relieves them from knowing the internals of the integrity assessment component.

Problem

Consider the sensor system described as part of the message generator in the previous section. Upon field deployment, it is desirable to test the system's capabilities to ensure that the system works properly before engaging in autonomous operation. For this reason, a graphical user interface is required to monitor and control the system in the field during installation. A conceptual diagram of both subsystems and their interactions is presented in Figure 7.4.

The sensor subsystem consists of the following elements: *SystemManager*, *SerialComm*, *FileSystem*, *DataAnalyzer*, and *WirelessComm*. A typical set of operations to assess the integrity of the system would require clients to know about all subsystem elements—for example, opening the serial port, sending a collection message to the system manager, and opening the wireless communication link. This adds complexity to the developers of the UI subsystem, since they are required to know the details of the sensor subsystem. In addition, in many practical applications, the internals of subsystem are prone to change; therefore,

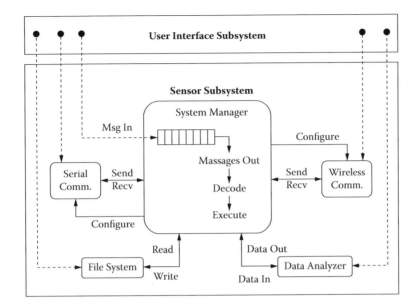

FIGURE 7.4
Conceptual diagram of wireless sensor system.

clients relying on the internal of subsystems must keep up with changes throughout development and maintenance phases. The designers of the sensor system wants an easy solution to shield UI subsystem developers from changes in the sensor subsystem—one that allows developers of the sensor subsystem to identify and set interfaces for the visible aspects of the sensor subsystem so that clients can rely on this interface, giving developers of the sensor subsystem the ability to change the internals of the subsystem without affecting clients.

Structure

The general and applied structure of the facade design pattern is presented in Figure 7.5. As seen, the facade provides functionality in terms of existing classes through a simplified interface. In most cases, a facade's functions will be implemented in terms of several functions from different subsystem classes. This prevents clients from depending on these internal subsystems; therefore, both complexity and dependencies on the client side are reduced.

Consider the set of operations required to retrieve sensor data, which may require opening communication links, testing the connections, and scheduling a collection message. These operations require interfacing with several components within the sensor subsystem. In such cases, the UI subsystem is required to know the details required to carry out all of these operations, which increases coupling and complexity of the UI. However, with the facade design pattern, an interface method, named `transmitSensorData()`, can be used to abstract all of the required operations to transmit sensor data, such as opening

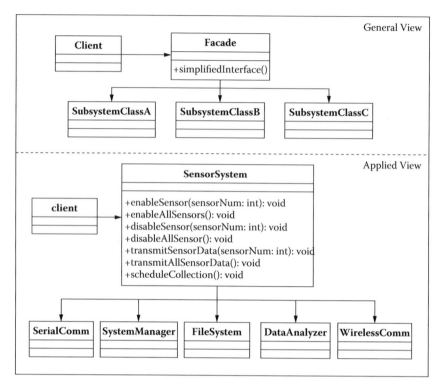

FIGURE 7.5
UML class diagram for the facade design pattern.

the serial connection, opening the wireless connection, testing both connections, and scheduling a collection message. A step-by-step procedure for applying the facade design pattern includes

1. Identify all components involved in carrying out a subsystem operation.
2. Create an ordered list of the operations required to execute the subsystem operation.
3. Design a facade class that includes an interface method to carry out the subsystem operation. The facade class has dependencies to all other subsystem components required to carry out the subsystem operation.
4. Implement the facade interface method by calling operations on one or more subsystem components, in the order identified in Step 2.
5. Allow one or more clients to access the objects of the facade type so that they can gain access to the subsystem operation. This creates a many-to-one relationship between external subsystems and the facade interface instead of many-to-many relationships.

The driving forces behind the facade are simplicity of client code and lower coupling. The facade design pattern can be simply applied by creating an additional facade class that provides simple functions summarizing the major external functions expected and required by clients.

Listing 7.14: C++ Implementation of One Method of the `SensorSystem` Facade

```cpp
void SensorSystem::transmitSensorData(int sensorNumber) {

    // Create an object for serial communications parameters.
    SerialParams params;
    params.setCommPort( SerialParams::COM_1 );
    params.setBaudRate( SerialParams::BR_9600 );
    params.setParity( SerialParams::PARITY_NO_PARITY );
    params.setByteSize( SerialParams::BYTE_SIZE_8 );
    params.setStopBits( SerialParams::STOP_BIT_ONE );

    // Retrieve pointer to the serial communication object.
    SerialComm* pSerialComm = SerialComm::getInstance();

    // Open the serial communication with the specified parameters.
    if( serialComm->open(params) ) {

        // Ready to communicate with collection nodes, now get ready for
        // transmitting the data via the wireless link.
        TcpConnection* pConnection = TcpConnection::getInstance();

        if( pConnection->open(TcpConnection::PORT_NUMBER,
                              TcpConnection::IP_ADDRESS) ) {

            // Schedule a collection message.
            SystemManager::getInstance()->scheduleMessage(/*...*/);
        }
        else {
            // Log TCP error here.
            // Close serial connection.

        } // end if( pConnection->open(...)
    }
    else {
        // Log serial connection error here.
    } // end if( serialComm->open(...)
} // end transmitSensorData function.
```

Implementation

Implementing the facade design pattern is straightforward, since it simply provides behavior in terms of other subsystems. An example facade method for transmitting sensor data is presented in Listing 7.14. As seen, many of the complexities associated with using the subsystem elements are hidden by the facade. By depending only on the facade, clients are shielded from unnecessary details required to perform the operation.

Benefits

- Shields clients from knowing the internals of complex subsystem, therefore minimizing complexity in clients
- Since the internals of the subsystem are prone to change, provides a stable interface that hides changes to internal subsystems, therefore making client code more stable
- Promotes weak coupling on clients; clients depend on only one interface instead of multiple interfaces

BEHAVIORAL DESIGN PATTERNS

Behavioral design patterns deal with encapsulating behavior with objects, assigning responsibility, and managing object cooperation when achieving common tasks (Gamma et al. 1995). Behavioral design patterns include many of the mainstream design patterns used in modern object-oriented frameworks and play a key role in the design of systems by making them independent of specific behavior, which is made replaceable with objects throughout these design patterns. Therefore, parts of the system responsible for performing some algorithm or behavior do so by relying on a common interface without knowledge of how the actual behavior or algorithm is carried out. In addition, by controlling the behavioral process with common interfaces, enforcing behavioral policies becomes easier, therefore giving systems the ability to create algorithms that share a common interface but that vary widely in behavior. Examples of behavioral patterns include the iterator and the observer.

ITERATOR

The iterator design pattern is an object behavioral pattern that provides a standardized way for accessing and traversing objects in a collection data structure. A collection data structure may consist of arrays, vectors, lists, or other custom-designed structures. The iterator design pattern works by abstracting the way each specific collection structure operates on the data so that clients are not required to have knowledge of the details of their internal structure. According to the Gang of Four (Gamma et al. 1995, p. 257), the intent of the iterator design pattern is to

> Provide a way to access the elements of an aggregate object sequentially without exposing its underlying representation.

By providing a standard interface and encapsulated methodology for accessing elements of a collection structure, client code becomes more consistent and easier to maintain, since changing the internal structure of the data collection structure does not affect the way client code interacts with the structure. Iterators are prevalent in software engineering; their presence can be found built-in in today's most common programming languages and frameworks, such as C++, Java, and the .NET framework.

Problem

A company's software system manages inventory, financials, and all other information available from its two store branches. Each store carries specific computer products appropriate for its location's demographics. During design, the software system is decomposed into several components, including two components for deferring and abstracting design information relevant to requirements for each computer store branch. The detailed design of each component is carried out separately by two different software engineers; this results in two different versions of data structures for managing and providing store product information. Now, anytime the software system is called upon to display information about store products, it is required to identify between the two store branches so that the correct implementation for accessing store information can be executed. This problem is encountered every time a new computer store branch is added to the system; therefore, a uniform and standardized method for accessing computer store products from different collection data structures is highly desirable. Consider the existing `ComputerProduct` code for the store's software system, as presented in Listing 7.15. The `ComputerProduct` is the product class for all products carried at all store branches, which includes simple or advanced computer products.

Consider the case where the designer of one computer store branch uses a list data structure to save computer products for the computer store branch carrying simple computer products. To retrieve the products from the simple computer store, a method is

---

Listing 7.15: C++ Specification of the `ComputerProduct` Type

```cpp
class ComputerProduct {

public:

  // Return the product's id.
  int getProductId();

  // Return the product's price.
  int getPrice() const;

  // Return the product's description.
  string getDescription() const;

  // Other methods here...
};
```

Listing 7.16: C++ Code for the `SimpleComputerStore` Class

```cpp
#include "SimpleProductList.h"

// Simple Computer Store
class SimpleComputerStore {

public:
  // Constructor.
  SimpleComputerStore() { /*Connect to DB and initialize all
                            products.*/ }

  // Computer store methods...

  // Return the computer products carried by the simple computer store.
  SimpleProductList* getProducts() {

    // Return the simple product list.
    return &_products;
  }

private:
  // The list of simple computer products.
  SimpleProductList _products;
};
```

---

provided, `getProducts()`, which returns a reference or pointer to the object of type `SimpleProductList`, as seen in Listing 7.16.

The second computer store, which carries advanced computer products, is designed to keep track of computer products using a custom-made list data structure for the advanced computer products class. This list provides a method `getProducts()` that returns a reference or pointer to a collection object of type `AdvancedProductList`, as seen in Listing 7.17.

As trivial as this problem may seem, it highlights problems in code that occur typically in software teams during practical applications. Different developers want to work with their own code, they may want to showcase their skills by developing a better collection data structure, or the lack of oversight in the design process results in work redundancy. This example presents the problem using two different (but almost similar) lists; however, in practical situations, the difference in design and implementation may involve significantly different approaches like arrays versus custom-defined lists versus library-specific lists, such as the C++ standard template library list. Lack of standardization in the way that computer stores access and traverse through their products creates complexity for clients. Consider the software system code for displaying computer product information from both stores, as presented in Listing 7.18.

Listing 7.17: C++ Code for the `AdvancedComputerStore` Class

```cpp
#include "AdvancedProductList.h"

// Advanced Computer Store
class AdvancedComputerStore {

public:
  // Constructor.
  AdvancedComputerStore() { /*Initialize all products.*/ }

  // Computer store methods...

  // Return a pointer to the advanced product list.
  AdvancedProductList* getProducts() {

    // Return the advanced product list.
    return &_products;
  }

private:
  // The computer products... in ProductList form.
  AdvancedProductList _products;
};
```

Notice that by having different methods to retrieve each product (i.e., `getSimple-Product` and `getAdvancedProduct`), the client code now requires a conditional statement to differentiate between the two store branches, which results in two versions of code for displaying product information. For each store added to the system, a new conditional statement is required to support the display of the new computer store branch.

Structure

The general and applied structure of the iterator design pattern is presented in Figure 7.6. The key to designing the iterator design pattern lies in the `Iterator` interface. As seen in the General View portion of Figure 7.6, the `Iterator` interface consists of the `first()`, `next()`, `isDone()`, and `currentItem()` interface methods. These methods specify the fundamental operations that need to be provided by iterator objects that implement the interface. Regardless of the collection data structure employed to store products, these interface methods can be used uniformly to traverse the items contained by the data structure. The `first()` method is used to return the first item in the collection; the `next()` method is used to move the current item to the next element of the list; the `currentItem()` method is used to return the product stored at the current location of the iterator; and the `isDone()` method is used to determine if there are more products to traverse in the collection item.

**Listing 7.18: C++ Code for the Centralized Server
Software to Display Computer Products**

```cpp
// Simple store.
SimpleComputerStore simpleStore;
ComputerProduct* pProduct = 0;
SimpleProductList* simpleStoreProducts = simpleStore.getProducts();

// Display simple store products.
for( int i = 0; i < simpleStoreProducts->size(); i++ ) {

  // Retrieve the product at index i.
  pProduct = simpleStoreProducts->getSimpleProduct(i);

  // Make sure pProduct is valid before using it!

  // Display product's information.
  cout<<"Product id: "<<pProduct->getProductId()<<endl
    <<"Product price: "<<pProduct->getPrice()<<endl
    <<"Product Description: "<<pProduct->getDescription().c_str()<<endl;
}

//Advanced store.
AdvancedComputerStore advancedStore;
AdvancedProductList* advancedProducts = advancedStore.getProducts();

// Display advanced store products.
for( int i = 0; i < advancedProducts->length(); i++ ) {

  // Retrieve the product at location i.
  pProduct = advancedProducts->getAdvancedProduct(i);

  // Make sure pProduct is valid before using it!

  // Display product's information.
  cout<<"Product id: "<<pProduct->getProductId()<<endl
    <<"Product price: "<<pProduct->getPrice()<<endl
    <<"Product Description: "<<pProduct->getDescription().c_str()<<endl;
}

// Repeat here for all other types of lists!
```

Also, in the General View of the iterator design pattern, the `Aggregate` interface specifies the method for instantiating and returning an iterator object. Clients use this object to traverse the collection using the iterator interface instead of the concrete aggregate object. This version of the iterator design pattern is the preferred version for new design efforts. However, in practice, the iterator can be designed differently from project to project, especially when existing code is in place. For example, in the Applied View of Figure 7.6, some

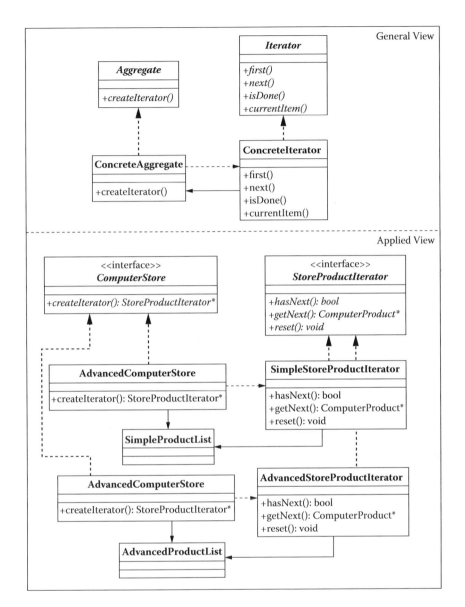

FIGURE 7.6
UML class diagram for the iterator design pattern.

of the iterator interface methods are omitted and the names are modified from the original pattern. In addition, each concrete aggregate class is designed as of two independent and existing classes in the system. This is necessary when code for the existing collection data structures (e.g., `SimpleProductList`) cannot be modified. When examined closely, the Applied View of Figure 7.6 consists of the same relationships and similar interface methods but are structured differently to account for the existing code. Similar variations of the iterator design pattern can be found in practice; therefore, modifying the iterator relationships to fit a particular problem is common. Notice, however, that if code for both `SingleProductList` and `AdvancedProductList` is available for modification, the design of these classes would take the place of the simple and advanced computer store from the Applied View of Figure 7.6 to match the general view of the design pattern.

In the applied version, the `hasNext()` method is specified to return true if the collection data structure has more elements for traversal; the `getNext()` interface method is used to move the iterator's pointer to the next element in the collection and return the product stored at that location; finally, the `reset()` interface method is designed to reset the collection index to the first item in the collection. Similar to the applied design for the computer store software, the iterator design pattern is applied in software systems with different interface methods to solve the original problem that the pattern describes.

Once the iterator is designed, the next key element of the design pattern involves designing the concrete iterators that provide a uniform level of abstraction for each collection structure (e.g., array, linked list) in the system. As seen in Figure 7.6, for each concrete iterator designed an association is made to the appropriate collection structure. This means that each iterator knows the specific interface methods provided by its associated collection structure so that it can use them to traverse and access its products. This way, when clients of the iterator call a method from the iterator interface (e.g., `getNext()`), the concrete iterator can carry out the request internally in terms of the collection structure's interface method, hiding these details from its clients. Therefore, regardless of the collection structure, clients of the iterator can always rely on the `Iterator` interface to traverse any collection structure supported by concrete iterators. This property of the iterator design patterns is desirable in many practical applications.

Finally, the iterator design pattern requires the design of the `Aggregate` interface which is manifested in the computer store problem as the `ComputerStore` interface. The importance of this interface is that it allows clients of the computer store to create iterators for traversing through the different store product items. As discussed earlier, the aggregate interface can be directly implemented by the class representing the collection structure or, if this code is unavailable, by another class that provides one more levels of abstraction, such as the `ComputerStore` in Figure 7.6. With this in place, clients rely on the `ComputerStore` interface to create and return an iterator without needing to know the particular type of store; once the iterator is returned, clients use the iterator interface to traverse through the products, therefore providing a design that relies fully on interfaces rather than concrete implementations. This results in flexible designs that can be modified and adapted easily to future demands. The step-by-step approach for applying the iterator design pattern is as follows:

1. Identify and design the `Iterator` interface.
2. For each class representing a collection data structure in the software system, design a concrete iterator and associate it with it. Implement the concrete iterator's methods in terms of the collection data structure.
3. Create the aggregate interface, which includes the interface method to create iterators.
4. For each class representing a collection data structure, implement the aggregate interface to instantiate and return a concrete iterator.

The driving forces behind the design are decreased complexity for clients and flexibility. By applying the iterator design pattern, clients are shielded from the internals of the collection data structure. This in turn provides flexibility by allowing new stores to be added easily or different existing iterators to be swapped without changes to the client code.

Implementation

The implementation of the iterator design pattern for the computer store system assumes that both collection data structures (i.e., simple and advanced lists) cannot be modified. Therefore, the aggregate portion of the pattern is split, as seen in Figure 7.6. The implementation of the iterator design pattern begins with the specification of the StoreProductIterator interface, as seen in Listing 7.19. This interface is designed

---

Listing 7.19: C++ Specification of the `StoreProductIterator` Interface

```cpp
// Forward reference.
class ComputerProduct;

// The base for all store product iterators.
class StoreProductIterator {

public:
  // Constructor.
  StoreProductIterator() : _position(0) { /*Intentionally left
                                             blank.*/}

  // Interface method for determining if more products are available.
  virtual bool hasNext() = 0;

  // Interface method for retrieving the next available product.
  virtual ComputerProduct* getNext() = 0;

protected:
  // Give access to derived classes for setting the iterator's
  // position.
  void setPosition(int position) { _position = position; }

  // Allow derived classes to retrieve the iterator's position.
  int getPosition(void) { return _position; }

  // Reset the iterator's position.
  void reset(void) { _position = 0; }

private:
  // The iterator's current position.
  int _position;
};
```

Listing 7.20: C++ Specification of the `SimpleStoreProductIterator`

```cpp
class SimpleStoreProductIterator : public StoreProductIterator {

public:
  // Constructor.
  SimpleStoreProductIterator(SimpleProductList* products);

  // Determine if more products are available.
  bool hasNext();

  // If more products are available, get the next one.
  ComputerProduct* getNext();

private:
  // Pointer to the simple computer product list.
  SimpleProductList* _products;
};
```

---

with simplicity in mind; therefore it contains two main methods for iteration, `hasNext()` and `getNext()`. There are many different ways iterators can be designed; in this case, if the method `hasNext()` returns true, a subsequent call to `getNext()` can be made to move the iterator to the next element and to retrieve the product stored at that location.

Once the `StoreProductIterator` interface is specified, each concrete iterator can be created. Listing 7.20 presents the specification of the `SimpleStoreProductIterator`, which is the iterator used for traversing through in the simple computer store, which stores computer products in a simple product list. Since this iterator is designed to work with the simple computer store, a `SimpleProductList` memory reference or pointer is passed to it in the constructor.

As expected, the interface methods for the `SimpleStoreProductIterator` type are implemented in terms of the `SimpleProductList` type, as seen in Listing 7.21. Of particular interest is the `getNext()` method, which encapsulates the specific call to `getSimpleProduct()` to retrieve a computer product.

The specification of the `AdvancedStoreProductIterator` is similar to the one presented in Listing 7.21 but is specific to the `AdvancedProductList` collection data structure. Therefore, implementation of the `AdvancedStoreProductIterator` is made in terms of this data structure, as seen in Listing 7.22.

To enforce the policy that all computer stores must support the iterator design pattern, a standard `ComputerStore` interface is specified, as seen in Listing 7.23.

Computer stores deriving from this interface must provide an implementation for the `createIterator()` method before they can be instantiated. This provides clients with a standard method for retrieving iterators from all computer stores. Listings 7.24 and 7.25 present the C++ implementation for both simple and advanced computer stores, respectively.

Listing 7.21: C++ Implementation for the `SimpleStoreProductIterator`

```cpp
#include "SimpleStoreProductIterator.h"
#include "SimpleProductList.h"

// Constructor.
SimpleStoreProductIterator::
    SimpleStoreProductIterator(SimpleProductList* products) {

  // For simplicity, assume a valid pointer.
  _products = products;
}

// Determine if more products are available.
bool SimpleStoreProductIterator::hasNext() {

  // The return value.
  bool isNextProductAvailable = false;

  if( getPosition() < _products->size() ) {

    isNextProductAvailable = true;
  }

  return isNextProductAvailable;
}

// If more products are available, get the next one.
ComputerProduct* SimpleStoreProductIterator::getNext() {

  // Temporary pointer to computer product.
  ComputerProduct* pProduct = 0;

  // Get the iterator's current position.
  int nextItem = getPosition();

  // Determine if there are more products.
  if( hasNext() ) {
    // Get the address of the next product and move the iterator's
    // position.
    pProduct = _products->getSimpleProduct(nextItem++);

    // Set the new position of the Iterator.
    setPosition(nextItem);
  }
  // Return the requested product.
  return pProduct;
}
```

Listing 7.22: C++ Implementation for the `AdvancedStoreProductIterator`

```cpp
#include "AdvancedStoreProductIterator.h"
#include "AdvancedProductList.h"

// Constructor.
AdvancedStoreProductIterator::
    AdvancedStoreProductIterator(AdvancedProductList* products) {

  // For simplicity, assume valid pointer.
  _products = products;
}

// Determine if more products are available.
bool AdvancedStoreProductIterator::hasNext() {

  // The return value.
  bool nextProductAvailable = false;

  if( getPosition() < _products->length() ) {
    nextProductAvailable = true;
  }
  return nextProductAvailable;
}

// If more products are available, get the next one.
ComputerProduct* AdvancedStoreProductIterator::getNext() {

  // Temporary pointer to computer product.
  ComputerProduct* pProduct = 0;

  // Get the iterator's current position.
  int nextItem = getPosition();

  // Determine if there are more products.
  if( hasNext() ) {
    // Get the address of the next product and move the iterator's
    // position.
    pProduct = _products->getAdvancedProduct(nextItem++);

    // Set the new position of the iterator.
    setPosition(nextItem);
  }
  // Return the requested product.
  return pProduct;
}
```

Listing 7.23: C++ Specification of the `ComputerStore` Interface

```cpp
class StoreProductIterator; // Forward reference.


// The interface for all computer stores.
class ComputerStore {

public:
  // The interface method to create an iterator.
  virtual StoreProductIterator* createIterator() = 0;
};
```

Listing 7.24: C++ Implementation for the Simple Computer Store

```cpp
#include "SimpleStoreProductIterator.h"
#include "SimpleProductList.h"


// Simple Computer Store
class SimpleComputerStore : public ComputerStore {

public:
  // Override the createIterator interface method to create the
  // appropriate iterator for simple computer stores.
  StoreProductIterator* createIterator() {

    // Create and return a simple store product iterator.
    return new SimpleStoreProductIterator(&_products);
  }

  // All other methods for simple computer stores.

private:
  // The simple product list.
  SimpleProductList _products;
};
```

With the iterator design pattern in place, the function to display computer products in the software system can be modified to work in terms of the iterator interface, as seen in Listing 7.26.

The software system can now display each store's product using a unified interface, as seen in Listing 7.27. This design supports adding new computer stores without much effort.

Listing 7.25: C++ Implementation for the Advanced Computer Store

```cpp
// Advanced Computer Store
class AdvancedComputerStore : public ComputerStore {

public:
  // Override the createIterator interface method to create the
  // appropriate iterator for advanced computer stores.
  StoreProductIterator* createIterator() {

    // Create and return an advanced store product iterator.
    return new AdvancedStoreProductIterator(&_products);
  }

  // All other methods for advanced computer stores.

private:
  // The advanced product list.
  AdvancedProductList _products;
};
```

Listing 7.26: C++ Implementation of the Display Function in the Centralized Software

```cpp
// Display the products using the iterator.
void displayProducts(StoreProductIterator* pIterator) {

  // Temporary pointer to hold a computer product.
  ComputerProduct* pProduct = 0;

  // Determine if there are more products to browse.
  while( pIterator->hasNext() ) {

    // Retrieve the next product.
    pProduct = pIterator->getNext();

    // Display the product's information.
    cout<<"\nProduct id: "<<pProduct->getProductId()<<endl
        <<"Product price: "<<pProduct->getPrice()<<endl
        <<"Product Description: "<<pProduct->getDescription().c_str();
  }
}
```

Listing 7.27: C++ Code for the Centralized Software to Create Iterators and Display Products

```cpp
// Simple store.
SimpleComputerStore simpleStore;

// Iterator for the simple store.
StoreProductIterator* pIterator = simpleStore.createIterator();

// Display the products using the iterator.
displayProducts(pIterator);

// Cleanup the simple computer store iterator.
delete pIterator;

// Advanced store.
AdvancedComputerStore advancedStore;

// The advanced store iterator.
pIterator = advancedStore.createIterator();

// Display the products using the iterator.
displayProducts(pIterator);

// Cleanup the advanced computer store iterator.
delete pIterator;
```

Benefits

- Provides a consistent way for clients to iterate through the objects in a collection
- Abstracts the internals of the collection objects so that if they change, clients do not have to change
- Allows client code to be extended easily; numerous iterators can be created to support different traversals from the same or different collection structure

Skill Development 7.2: Iterator Design Pattern

Using the UML tool of choice, create the design presented in the Applied View Section of Figure 7.6. Rename the aggregate interface method from ComputerStore to create *Product* Iterator. Make the appropriate modifications to both simple and advanced computer stores so that they work with the new interface method. Generate code from the model, and create a test driver code to verify the design. Once the code compiles and executes, describe how your design benefited from using the iterator design pattern.

OBSERVER

The observer design pattern is an object behavioral pattern that standardizes the operations between objects that interoperate using a one-to-many relationship. According to the Gang of Four (Gamma et al. 1995, p. 293), the intent of the observer is to

> Define a one-to-many dependency between objects so that when one object changes state, all its dependents are notified and updated automatically.

In many practical applications, a common design structure is required to support interaction between objects that monitor a common data source so that when changes occur in the data source the objects react appropriately. Consider a detailed design that supports the model–view–controller (MVC) architectural pattern from Chapter 4. In the MVC architectural pattern, once the data in the model component changes, all views must change as well. In cases such as the MVC, the observer design pattern provides the necessary structural interfaces to allow one or more views to register with the model component. Once registered, the observer design pattern provides the structural interfaces for executing a uniform change propagation mechanism for the model to notify all registered views of the recent changes. The observer design pattern is very popular and prevalent in today's modern languages and frameworks, such as Java (i.e., *Observable* and *Observer* interfaces) and .NET.

Problem

A local university is designing a system for weather-alert notification that allows students, faculty, and staff to receive notifications of class cancellations (due to weather) via e-mail, voice call, or SMS text messages. Other methods of notification may be added in the future. The system is based on the weather data decision engine that interfaces with several weather-related data sources, fuses the information, and automatically decides whether class cancellations are in effect. The university is interested in integrating the existing communication services (i.e., e-mail, SMS, and voice) with the decision engine so that these services can be triggered to initiate notification via their respective communication types. The design must be flexible so that other types of communication mechanisms can be added to the system in the future.

Structure

The general and applied structure of the observer design pattern is presented in Figure 7.7. The typical application of the observer design pattern includes one concrete subject and one or more concrete observers, as seen in the Applied View of Figure 7.7.

Each concrete observer is required to implement the update() interface method specified by the *Observer* interface. Similar to other design patterns, implementation of the observer design pattern varies depending on particular details of projects. Specifically,

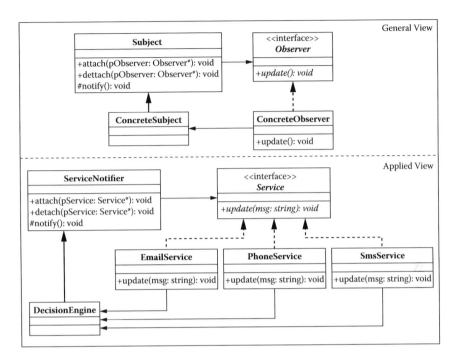

FIGURE 7.7
UML class diagram for the observer design pattern.

the implementation of the update method is typically seen in two common versions. One version includes passing as parameter the details of the change notification. Using this approach, concrete observers examine notification information using the update parameter and act accordingly. This is possible when the type of notification can be abstracted so that it provides a common interface for all other concrete observers. Another popular approach involves designing the update() method without parameters. Upon receiving change notification, concrete objects call a method of the concrete subject to retrieve the details of the notified change. Since the behavior for attaching, detaching, and notifying observers is the same, the Subject base class can specify and implement these methods, which are inherited by all other concrete subjects. The step-by-step approach for applying the observer design pattern includes

1. Design the subject interface and implement code for attaching, detaching, and notifying observer objects. The code for keeping track of observers can be done using linked-lists data structures.
2. For classes that manage information of interest to observers, inherit from the subject class created in Step 1.
3. Design the observer interface, which includes the abstract update interface method.
4. For all observers in the system, implement the observer interface, which requires implementing the update method.
5. At run time, create each observer and attach it to the subject. When changes occur, the subject iterates through its list of registered objects and calls its update method.

The driving force behind the application of the observer design pattern is flexibility. By applying the observer design pattern, future additions of services can be done automatically, therefore leading to software that is easy to maintain.

Implementation

Implinting the observer design pattern begins with the `ServiceNotifier` class, which serves as base class for the subjects. As seen, the methods to provide registration and notification services are implemented in terms of a C++ STL list, as presented in Listing 7.28.

With the registration mechanism in place, all services realize the `Service` interface to acquire notification capabilities. Listing 7.29 presents an example for the `EmailService` observer.

An example of the registration and notification mechanism is presented in Listing 7.30. As seen, many different observers can register with the `DecisionEngine` object to get notifications of weather alerts.

Benefits

- Flexibility for adding new services to the system
- Maintaining and modifying existing system services become easier because specific services are compartmentalized

---

Listing 7.28: C++ Code to Provide Registration and Notification to Observers

```cpp
// Provide the registration mechanism for all observers.
void ServiceNotifier::attach(Service* pService) {

  // Add this observer to the list of registered observers. Assume a
  // valid pointer.
  _services.push_back(pService);
};

// The trigger mechanism to notify all observers of class cancellation.
void ServiceNotifier::notify(string message) {

  // Get an Iterator that points to the beginning of the
  // observers_ list.
  list<Service*>::iterator pIter = _services.begin();

  // Iterate through the list of observers and notify them.
  for( int i = 0; i < _services.size(); i++ ) {

    // Pass the message along to all registered observers.
    (*pIter++)->update(message);
  }
}
```

Listing 7.29: C++ Code for the `Update()` Method of the `EmailService` Observer

```cpp
class EmailService : public Service {

  public:
  // Once the Observable object changes, it will call this method.
  void update(string message) {

    // Open file containing all users registered for email
    // notification. Open connection to the Email server.
    // For all registered clients, notify them via email.
  }

  // ...
};
```

Listing 7.30: C++ Registration and Notification Mechanism of the `WeatherDataObject`

```cpp
// Sends message as email.
EmailHandler emailHandler;

// Sends message as text message.
SmsHandler smsHandler;

// Translates message to speech and sends it via the voice interface.
VoiceHandler voiceHandler;

// Assume that the decision engine object is a singleton.
DecisionEngine::getInstance()->register(&emailHandler);
DecisionEngine::getInstance()->register(&smsHandler);
DecisionEngine::getInstance()->register(&voiceHandler);
```

Skill Development 7.3: Observer Design Pattern

Using the UML tool of choice, create the detailed component design of the MVC architectural design presented in Figure 4.9 using the observer design pattern. Generate code from the model, and create a test driver method to validate the design. Explain the differences between the MVC architectural pattern and the observer design pattern in this example.

CHAPTER SUMMARY

Structural and behavioral designs patterns help identify problems that deal with the structure and behavior of software designs; they prescribe the classes required for their design solution and interrelationships required to support object creation. These patterns allow designers to quickly and systematically identify structural layouts of systems (or subsystems) and provide avenues for examining the system's interactions and quality evaluation within the operational system. Structural design patterns are patterns that deal with designing larger structures from existing classes or objects at run time. They play a key role in the design and evolution of systems by allowing integration of new designs with existing ones, via object composition (i.e., object structural) or inheritance (i.e., class structural). By allowing designs to build on other existing structures, systems can be made interoperable by designing compatible interfaces for otherwise incompatible systems. Examples of structural design patterns include adapter, composite, and facade design patterns. Behavioral design patterns deal with encapsulating behavior with objects, assigning responsibility, and managing object cooperation when achieving common tasks. Behavioral design patterns include many of the mainstream design patterns used in modern object-oriented frameworks and play a key role in the design of systems by making them independent of specific behavior, which is made replaceable with objects throughout these design patterns. Therefore, parts of the system responsible for performing some algorithm or behavior do so by relying on a common interface without knowledge of how the actual behavior or algorithm is carried out. In addition, by controlling the behavioral process with common interfaces, enforcing behavioral policies becomes easier, therefore giving systems the ability to create algorithms that share a common interface but vary widely in behavior. Examples of behavioral patterns include the iterator and the observer. This chapter explored each structural and behavioral design pattern to present the problems they are designed to address together with the benefits they provide. Identifying and designing using these design patterns can improve the efficiency of the development process and the quality of the final system.

REVIEW QUESTIONS

1. What are structural design patterns? What are they used for?
2. Compare and contrasts the following patterns:
   a. Adapter
   b. Composite
3. What is the adapter design pattern? Explain its main benefits and features.
4. What is the composite design pattern? List and explain the main features of the builder design pattern.
5. Give an example each of both adapter and composite design patterns. Do not use the ones presented in the chapter.

6. Explain the steps required to implement the composite design pattern.

7. What is the facade design pattern? What does it do?

8. What are the essential structural elements required in the composite design pattern?

9. What are the main benefits of using the iterator design pattern?

10. What is the observer design pattern? Give one example of a particular software feature that you think is appropriate for applying the observer.

11. What are the essential elements required in the observer design pattern?

CHAPTER EXERCISES

1. You have been hired to work on a car testing utility class. The car testing utility class has one method with the following signature: void testCar(Car* pCar). As seen, the testCar function is designed to test objects of the type Car. The car interface supports the following methods: void enableCruise(), void openWindow(), void closeWindow(), and void accelerate(int mph). The test utility function is currently being used to test objects of type TypicalCar, which support all interface methods. However, the test utility is now needed to test objects of the new type RaceCar, however, the RaceCar type only supports the accelerateReallyFast(int mph) method. Use an appropriate design pattern to allow the RaceCar type to be used in the testCar utility function. Feel free to make any assumptions necessary to complete the design. The usage and output are presented below.

```
void testCar(Car* pCar)
{
    pCar->enableCruise();
    pCar->openWindow();
    pCar->closeWindow();
    pCar->accelerate(50);
}

// Sample output - if typical car passed in to the test utility
// function.
TypicalCar::enabling smart cruise control...
TypicalCar::opening 2 windows...
TypicalCar::closing 2 windows...
TypicalCar::accelerating fast to 50 mph...

// Sample output - if race car passed in to the test utility
// function.
ConcreteRaceCar::no cruise control available...
ConcreteRaceCar::no window available...
ConcreteRaceCar::no window available...
ConcreteRaceCar::accelerating really fast to 50 mph...
```

REFERENCE

Gamma, Erich, Richard Helm, Ralph Johnson, and John Vlissides. *Design Patterns: Elements of Reusable Object-Oriented Software*. Boston: Addison-Wesley, 1995.

8

Principles of Construction Design

CHAPTER OBJECTIVES

- Understand the importance and role of construction design
- Identify, understand, and apply table-based and state-based function design
- Identify, understand, and apply the general construction styles
- Understand how quality can be evaluated during construction design

---

CONCEPTUAL OVERVIEW

The transition from software design to construction should occur with minimal effort. In some cases, component designs provide enough detail to allow their transformation from design artifact into code easily; however, in other cases, a more fine-grained level of design detail is required. Construction design provides a form of design that closely resembles code so that complex operations can be planned and evaluated prior to implementation in code. Once the correctness of operations is verified, the construction design activity provides additional heuristics to enforce consistency in the code. Construction design provides the last form of design to create high-quality software operations that are correct, consistent, and efficient.

WHAT IS CONSTRUCTION DESIGN?

The idea of the detailed design phase is to manage complexity so that design artifacts can be translated to code with minimal effort. Even though significant attempts can be made during the detailed (component) design activity to create extensive designs, in most practical applications transitioning from the component design domain to code can still be daunting. Regardless of the amount of effort spent during the design phase, additional design efforts may still be required during construction to identify, plan, and manage the construction of complex operations. This form of construction design extends the work performed during detailed design to provide essential information that is used to generate correct, efficient, and consistent code. Construction design is the lowest level of detailed design that addresses the modeling and specification of function implementations. By designing complex operations, problem solutions can be evaluated, analyzed, and verified for correctness and efficiency before construction using programming languages. Construction design provides the means for evaluating problem solutions using a form of design that closely relates to code—that is, a form of design that models what the code does and how the code is specified.

Construction design can address problem solving from a dynamic (behavioral) perspective, which provides the description of operations (such as methods and functions) and the *internal details* and *logic* of each design entity (IEEE 2009). This approach involves graphical, tabular, or other methods to model and specify the internal structure of functions (e.g., operations, routines) so that the algorithms or flows required to carry out a function's intent are evaluated and clearly specified. The algorithm approach minimizes complexity during construction by providing a graphical method for specifying the details required by programmers to implement the function's code. A separate but closely related task performed when evaluating the quality of software construction deals with enforcing styles for establishing a consistent approach to structuring function implementations. These styles play a significant role in shaping the system's maintainability, complexity, and testability. Therefore, they are included as part of the construction design activity.

Construction design is not a new concept. In fact, there are many books covering construction design under different names. McConnell (2004) specifies five levels of software design, the lowest two of which deal with division of data and routines within classes and internal routine design. Similarly, Fox (2006) identifies a form of low-level design that fills the gap between detailed design and programming and deals with issues such as operation specification, including operation name, parameter types, and return types. Similarly, Meyer (1997) and Misfeldt, Bumgardner, Gray, and Xiaoping (2004) provide coverage of construction design.

WHY STUDY CONSTRUCTION DESIGN?

Construction design is about developing abstract models of the structure and behavior of the internal implementation of operations. From a behavioral perspective, construction design is important because it provides the means for evaluating different implementations for a particular function before committing to it. Behavioral designs at this level provide the means to evaluate a function's completeness, complexity, testability, and maintainability. They also provide the means for analysts to evaluate algorithms in regard to time–space performance and processing logic prior to implementation (IEEE 2009). Finally, since they provide a representation of the code through graphical and tabular ways, they increase collaborative evaluation efforts, since other members without knowledge of the particular programming language in use can evaluate the design and contribute to the solution. These collaboration efforts can lead to improvement in future phases, for example, the testing phase, where construction designs can be used to generate unit test cases, or the maintenance phase, where construction designs can be used to increase knowledge and understanding of the software behavior.

From the structural perspective (i.e., construction styles), construction design is important because it provides heuristics for establishing a common criterion for evaluating the quality of the structure of code, which directly affects code readability and thus maintenance. Code with low readability leads to higher maintenance costs, since it requires more effort to understand (Collar 2005). Construction styles are important during the design and construction phases so that code generation from design models can be done correctly. From a construction phase perspective, construction styles serve as a blueprint that ensures consistency among teams of developers. Finally, as mentioned before, during the testing and maintenance phase construction styles increase code readability and understanding, which can result in minimized cost during these phases.

BEHAVIORAL CONSTRUCTION DESIGN

Behavioral designs at the construction level are used to model complex logic that is unknown or difficult to understand. This way, details required to describe an operation can be discovered or evaluated without requiring code. The purpose of behavioral design is to model the dynamic aspects of code that makes up a particular function. Behavioral designs have been the topic of much research work in software engineering and are an integral part of all major software design strategies (e.g., structured and object-oriented designs). Behavioral designs provide the means for assessing the completeness, correctness, and quality of functions before actual implementation occurs and therefore are an essential activity for complex operations. Four major approaches to behavioral design at the construction level are flow-based designs, state-based designs, table-based designs, and programming design languages.

Flow-Based Designs

Flow-based designs provide a systematic methodology for specifying the logic of operations using a graphical approach. Two popular approaches for creating flow-based designs include flowcharts and Unified Modeling Language (UML) activity diagrams. Both work well for modeling the internal flow of routines because they can be defined using sequential process flows, loops, conditional statements, and other useful mechanisms needed to model complex business logic or complicated algorithms. UML activity diagrams provide powerful constructs for modeling complex logic at different stages of the software engineering life cycle; however, when applied toward modeling logic, activity diagrams provide similar features to flowcharts. Four important modeling constructs for flow-based designs are

- If statements
- Case statements
- Do while loop
- While loops

The common elements used to model flow-based designs using UML activity diagrams are presented in Figure 8.1, together with examples of modeling conditional and repetition statements.

State-Based Designs

Flow-based designs can be used to model operational logic by identifying the transitions from activity to activity required to perform an operation. However, in some cases the operational logic of a function or system is dictated by the different states that the system exhibits during its lifetime. That is, certain activities can be performed only when a system is in a particular state. When this occurs, the operational logic of a system can be modeled as a state machine using a (UML) state diagram. State diagrams are typically used to model the behavior of complete system. However, in many practical applications, state diagrams can be used to guide the logical design of one or more operations in the system. Consider the state design presented in Figure 8.2.

Figure 8.2 depicts the design of a software system that receives messages and performs operations based on the messages received and the system's state. That is, during the power-on initialization state, the system only reacts to the *GetStatus, SelfTest,* and the *SoftwareUpdate* message. Once the *SelfTest* message is received, the system transitions to the self-test state, where system capabilities are evaluated to determine the integrity of the system. Once the self-test state is complete, two transitions can occur; if the tests were successful then the system transitions to the operational state, and if any failures are encountered then the system enters a fault state, in which no commands can be executed. Once the fault state is complete, the system transitions to a power-down state, which allows the system to save all pertinent information to the file system before transitioning to the initialization (*Power On*) state.

Upon successfully execution of the self-test state, the system transitions to the operational state, where all messages in the system can be processed, including the *SelfTest* message and *ShutDown* message. As seen, the state diagram presents the state of the system, together with the transitions and the events that trigger each transition. Unlike the flow-based design

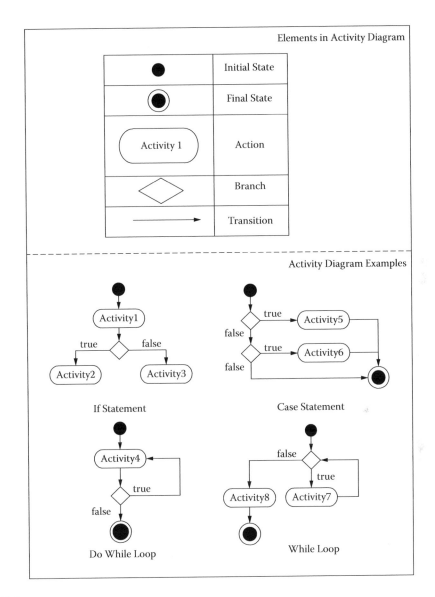

FIGURE 8.1
Flow-based logic design using UML activity diagrams.

approach in the previous section, the system's state-based designs show the flow of operations from state to state; it acts like a well-structured algorithm that is efficient, simple, adaptable, and understandable (Booch, Rumbaugh, and Jacobson 2005). It also presents the full operation of a complete system during its lifetime, which can be derived from the design. Consider the implementation of Listing 8.1, which implements the state machine.

Initially, the system is set to the *Power-OnState*; therefore, upon executing the code the `executePowerOnState()` method is called to process the received message and determines if a state change is required (or not), as seen in Listing 8.2. Listing 8.2 uses a message queue for retrieving messages received in the system.

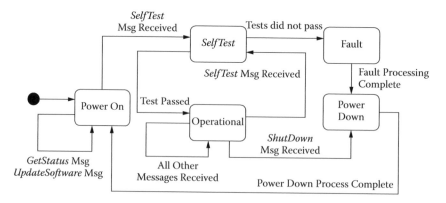

FIGURE 8.2

Example of a state design using UML state diagrams.

The source of the code presented in Listing 8.2 can be traced back to the state design presented in Figure 8.2. As seen, once the EmbeddedComponent is in the power-on state, it can execute the messages only for updating the software, retrieving the component's status, and executing a self-test. Messages containing different IDs cannot be executed in this state; therefore, upon receiving any other message the system logs an event and waits for the next message to be received. In a similar fashion, the code for all other states is implemented according to the state design, as presented in Listings 8.3 and 8.4.

As seen, once the EmbeddedComponent enters the self-test state, it executes the appropriate tests, and based on the tests results it sets the new system state to the operational or fault state, as defined in the state design. Assuming all tests are performed successfully, the EmbeddedComponent transitions to the operational state, where all messages can be received and processed by the EmbeddedComponent. The implementation for the operational sate is presented in Listing 8.4.

Table-Based Designs

Many times, the internal logic of routines is made up of complex conditional statements, each statement evaluating a condition (i.e., a cause) and providing some action (i.e., an effect) as a result. This can lead to an increasingly complex nesting structure that is error-prone, hard to read, and hard to maintain. In these cases, the logic design can be managed using a decision table (Hurley 1982). A decision table is a well-structured table that provides the means to formulate, evaluate, and improve the design of complex problems that deal with cause and effect. The format of decision tables is presented in Table 8.1.

Table 8.1 has four different sections. The first section is the *Condition* section, which contains a list of all of the conditions present in the decision problem. The second section is the *Action* section, which contains a list of all possible outcomes that can result from one or more conditions occurring. The third and fourth sections are found in matrix form, adjacent to the *Condition* and *Action* sections. The matrix adjacent to the *Condition* section indicates all possible combinations of conditions for the decision problem, while the matrix adjacent to the *Action* section indicates the corresponding actions. Combined, the

Listing 8.1: C++ Implementation of the State Design

```cpp
// The state machine's execute method.
void EmbeddedComponent::execute() {

  // Execute the state machine. _compnentState is a member variable
  // of the EmbeddedComponent class.
  switch( _componentState ) {

    case PowerOnState:
      // Execute in the power on state. When finished, allow the
      // executing function to determine if a state change is required
      // (or not) and set the state appropriately. This capability is
      // provided by executing functions in all other states.
      executePowerOnState();
      break;

    case SelfTestState:
      // Execute in the self test state.
      executeSelfTestState();
      break;

    case OperationalState:
      // Execute in the operational state.
      executeOperationalState();
      break;

    case FaultState:
      // Execute in the fault state.
      executeFaultState();
      break;

    case PowerDownState:
      // Execute in the power down state.
      executePowerDownState();
      break;

    default:
      // invalid state, log error.
      break;
  }
}
```

respective columns in both matrices provide a policy for decision making in the decision problem. Four types of decision tables are as follows (Hurley 1982):

- Limited-entry decision table (LEDT)
- Extended-entry decision table (EEDT)
- Mixed-entry decision table (MEDT)
- Hybrid-entry decision table (HEDT)

Listing 8.2: C++ Implementation of the PowerOn State

```cpp
void EmbeddedComponent::executePowerOnState() {

  // Assume messages are received and placed in a blocking message
  // queue. Therefore, the messageQueue.read call is a blocking call.
  Message* message = messageQueue.read(WAIT_FOREVER);

  // Retrieve the message's id.
  MessageIdType messageId = message->getId();

  // This state only processes three messages according to the state
  // diagram.
  if( messageId == UpdateSoftwareMsgId ) {
    // Cast message to an UpdateSoftwareMsg.
    // Retrieve the software image from the message and update
    // software.
  }
  else if( messageId == GetStatusMsgId ) {
    // Retrieve status from File System and return to client.
  }
  else if( messageId == SelfTestMsgId ) {
    // Cast message to a SelfTestMsg.
    // Retrieve the type of self test and change state.
    selfTestType_ = message->getTestType();
    _componentState = SelfTestState;
  }
  else {
    // Any other message received in this state results in an error.
    // Log the specific error here and do not change state.
  }
}
```

Limited-Entry Decision Table

The LEDT is the simplest type of decision table in which the condition section of the LEDT presents Boolean conditional statements. That is, the condition section of the LEDT presents features of the design problem that are either present or not, and their combined presence (or absence) triggers specific actions. Therefore, the condition entry section of the LEDT consists of Boolean values, such as true or false or yes or no, that can be used to define different policies in the decision problem. For example, consider the LEDT design for a function that computes discounts for the purchase of mobile phones. Two types of discounts are available, a store discount of $15 and a manufacturer discount of $30, as presented in Table 8.2.

Using the information specified in the LEDT from Table 8.2, the code for the function used to compute phone discounts can be easily implemented, simply by translating the information captured in the LEDT to code, as presented in Listing 8.5. The table name is

Listing 8.3: C++ Implementation of the SelfTest State

```cpp
void EmbeddedComponent::executeSelfTestState() {

  // No messages are processed during self test.

  // Perform either a simple, normal, or advanced test. Advanced tests
  // perform a complete test of the system, therefore they take
  // longer to complete.
  if( performTest(_selfTestType) ) {

    // Software and hardware are working properly. Log results and
    // change state to the operational state.
    _componentState = OperationalState;
  }
  else {
    // Faulty system software or hardware! Log results and change
    // state to the Fault state.
    _componentState = FaultState;
  }
}
```

Listing 8.4: C++ Implementation of the Operational State

```cpp
void EmbeddedComponent::executeOperationalState() {

  // Assume messages are received and placed in a blocking message
  // queue. Therefore, the messageQueue.read call is a blocking call.
  Message* message = messageQueue.read(WAIT_FOREVER);

  // Retrieve the message's id.
  MessageIdType messageId = message->getId();

  // Process messages according to the state diagram.
  if( /* messageId == x */ ) {
    // Process message x.
  }
  else if( /* messageId == y */ ) {
    // Process message y.
  }
  else if (/* ... */ {
    // ...
  }
  else {
    // Invalid message. Log error.
  }
}
```

TABLE 8.1

Fundamental Structure of Decision Tables

Condition	Condition Entry
Action	Action Entry

TABLE 8.2

Limited-Entry Decision Table for the Phone Discount Logic

Get Phone Discount	P1	P2	P3	P4
Store Discount	T	T	F	F
Manufacturer Discount	T	F	T	F
$15 Discount	x	x		
$30 Manufacturer Discount	x		x	
No Discount ($0)				x

used to name the function, and the two items in the conditional section of the table are translated as conditional statements in the code. The action portion of the table is used to determine the code executed when each of the conditional statements evaluate to true. For example, Policy 1 (P1) states that the $15 and $30 discounts are applied when both store and manufacturer discounts are active (as seen by the x's in the table). This behavior is seen in Listing 8.5.

Although such a simple problem hardly requires effort to design, it is valuable in pointing out several important characteristics of LEDTs. As seen, the condition section contains features that are either present or not for each policy defined in the problem. These conditions represent questions for determining the types of discounts (i.e., store or manufacturer discounts) that are in effect and the types of polices required for each possible combination of discounts. The condition entry section follows by providing answers to all possible combinations for the given problem. As seen, for an LEDT, the number of distinct elementary policies is 2^n, where n is the number of conditions in the condition section. In this example, where $n = 2$, there are four distinct policies. It is also evident that the fourth policy (P4) is never applied to the implementation presented in Listing 8.5. Therefore, this policy could have been left out of the decision table, since it represents not an action but the absence of one. Such policies that are left out of the decision table are referred to as *missing policies*. Finally, it can be seen that all policies result in a unique set of actions. When two or more policies result in identical actions, the actions are considered *redundant actions* and can be combined to simplify the decision table.

Extended-Entry Decision Table

Whereas the condition and action sections of LEDTs contain complete questions and actions, the condition and action sections of the EEDT are extended into the entry sections (i.e., upper-condition entry section and lower-action entry section) of the decision table. That is, in LEDTs, the condition section contained information that can be used to ask a

Listing 8.5: Implementation of the LEDT for the Phone Discount Function

```c
int getPhoneDiscount() {

  const int StoreDiscount = 15;
  const int ManufacturerDiscount = 30;

  // The total added phone discount.
  int phoneDiscount = 0;

  // Determine if the store discount applies.
  if( isStoreDiscountActive ) {

    // Apply the store's discount.
    phoneDiscount += StoreDiscount;
  }

  // Determine if the manufacturer discount applies.
  if( isManufacturerDiscountActive ) {

    // Apply the manufacturer's discount.
    phoneDiscount += ManufacturerDiscount;
  }

  // Return the total added phone discount.
  return phoneDiscount;
}
```

complete questions, such as, "Is there a store discount in effect?" In EEDTs, the condition and condition entry sections of the table are required to formulate a complete question, such as, "Is the customer a regular, preferred, or VIP customer?" Similarly, the action section must be combined with the action entry section of the decision table to formulate a complete action, such as "add a free car kit to the purchase." In addition, the number of possible values for each condition and action in EEDTs is not bounded to two. An example of the EEDT for the customer discount logic is presented in Table 8.3.

TABLE 8.3

Extended-Entry Decision Table for the Customer Discount Logic

Get Phone Discount	P1	P2	P3	P4	P5	P6
Customer type is	REG	REG	PRE	PRE	VIP	VIP
Credit score is	BAD	GOOD	BAD	GOOD	BAD	GOOD
Discount	$0	$15	$10	$25	$50	$100
Add a free	HOLSTER	CHARGER	BLUE TOOTH	CAR KIT	DATA PLAN	CAR KIT & DATA PLAN

As seen, customers can be of type regular (REG), preferred (PRE), or very important (VIP); therefore, the number of possible values for the type of customer condition is three. Also, actions can take on any form; the "X" used for denoting the presence or absence of actions in LEDTs cannot be applied in EEDTs. In this example, the number of possible values for the credit score condition is two, denoting good and bad credit scores. Finally, the number of distinct elementary policies in EEDTs is the product of all maximum numbers of possible values for each condition. In this example, this result in $3 \times 2 = 6$ policies (i.e., 3 for Condition 1 and 2 for Condition 2).

Mixed-Entry Decision Table

The MEDT combines features from both LEDTs and EEDTs. For example, consider a company that sells mobile phones of different kinds and with different promotional discounts based on the type of mobile phone. The software used to manage inventory and discounts uses a method to return the total discount that can be applied toward the purchase of a phone. The company carries three types of phones: a simple second-generation (2G) phone; an advanced third-generation phone (3G); and a special fourth-generation (4G) phone. Depending on the type of phone, different store discounts are applied toward the total purchase of the phone. For simple phones, when the manufacturer's discount is in effect a $30 discount can be applied, whereas when the store discount is in effect a $15 discount can be applied. When both discounts are in effect, a $45 discount can be applied toward the purchase of the phone. For advanced phones, a default store discount of $60 is always applied. In addition, when the manufacturer's discount is in effect an additional $50 is applied; when the store discount is in effect an additional $60 can be applied, since a free Bluetooth ear piece is included; and when all discounts are in effect all discounts can be applied toward the price of the phone. Finally, for special phones, a default discount of $120 is always applied. Additionally, discounts of $70, $180, or $370 (i.e., the sum of all discounts) can be applied toward the purchase of a special phone. The problem is formulated using the decision table presented in Table 8.4.

Using the information presented in Table 8.4, the construction of the function applying discounts to phone products can take place. Listing 8.6 presents the code for the phone type used in this problem. As seen, the phone type includes interface methods for returning a phone's type (i.e., simple, advanced, or special phone) and the particular discount that applies the phone type.

Using the phone type created, the code for the (*getPhoneDiscount*) function is presented in Listing 8.7. As seen, the code matches the table-based design presented in Table 8.4.

Table-Based Construction

Table-based construction is a technique for transforming table-based designs to code that is easy to maintain, read, and so forth. As seen, the resulting code for implementing the table-based design from Table 8.4 contains various conditional statements. Similarly, table-based designs can result in complex code that is hard to read and maintain. When

TABLE 8.4

Mixed-Entry Decision Table for the Phone Discount Logic

Get Phone Discount	Simple Phone Policies				Advanced Phone Policies				Special Phone Policies			
	P1	P2	P3	P4	P5	P6	P7	P8	P9	P10	P11	P12
Phone type is	S	S	S	S	A	A	A	A	SP	SP	SP	SP
Manufacturer discount	F	T	F	T	F	T	F	T	F	T	F	T
Store discount	F	F	T	T	F	F	T	T	F	F	T	T
$15 discount			x	x								
$60 discount					x	x	x	x				
$120 discount									x	x	x	x
$30 manufacturer discount		x		x								
$50 manufacturer discount						x		x				
$70 manufacturer discount										x		x
Bluetooth discount ($60)							x	x				
6-month data discount ($180)											x	x
No discount ($0)	x											

this occurs, table-based construction can be used to shift the complexity of logic to the problem's data structure. Consider the data structures in Listing 8.8 designed for the table-based design of Table 8.4.

As seen, the logic defined in Table 8.4 is now captured using data structures, through the `discounts` array. The discounts array consists of 12 different elements of the `Discount` type. Each index in the array represents one of the 12 policies defined during the table-based design from Table 8.4. For example, the element at index 0 of the discounts array contains the discounts defined by P1 of Table 8.4; the element at Index 1 contains the discounts defined by P2, and so on. With this framework in place, the code from Listing 8.7 can be reduced to the one presented in Listing 8.9, which drastically reduces the amount of code required to achieve the same operation.

Programming Design Language

Programming design language (PDL) is a form of pseudo-code used widely for designing internal function behavior. Its popularity stems from the use of natural languages—as opposed to computer languages or graphical techniques—to define the required behavior of functions. This results in detailed function designs that are easier to create, review, and translate to code. In addition, the usage of a natural language in PDL provides a "comments-first approach" to constructing code for any programming language. Therefore, PDL should be written without concern given to the target programming language and detailed enough that code can be generated with minimal effort.

PDL can be effectively employed using a top-down approach that first describes the general work performed by the function and then more specific operations within the function (McConnell 2004). The description of the general work performed by the function should

---

Listing 8.6: Implementation of the Phone Class to Support the Table-Based Design

```
// The different types of phones.
typedef enum{ SIMPLE_PHONE = 0, ADVANCED_PHONE = 1, SPECIAL_PHONE = 2}
PhoneType;

// The different types of discounts options.
typedef enum{ NO_DISCOUNT = 0,
  MANUFACTURER_DISCOUNT = 3,
  STORE_DISCOUNT = 6,
  COMBINED_DISCOUNT = 9} DiscountType;

// The Phone class.
class Phone {

  public:
    // Constructor.
    Phone(PhoneType type, DiscountType discountType) {

      _type = type;
      _discountType = discountType;
    }

    // Return the type of phone.
    PhoneType getType(){ return _type; }

    // Return the discount type for this phone.
    DiscountType getDiscountType() { return _discountType; }

  private:
    PhoneType _type;
    DiscountType _discountType;
};
```

---

include the function's intent, inputs, and outputs. Once the general purpose of the function is in PDL form, individual parts are elaborated in PDL form to provide complete design details for the function. When finished, the function's detailed PDL should result in the identification of operations that support the general description of the function. Therefore, PDL can be used as both design technique and effective documentation approach for functions and code within functions. An example of a detailed function design using PDL is presented in Listing 8.10.

There are many benefits of using PDL. First, PDL provides a programming language-independent technique for creating detailed function designs; therefore, collaborative efforts with all disciplines involved in the project can be achieved to provide complete reviews for the design of a function. That is, members from the systems, hardware, quality, and test groups can all chime in to help the function design meet the required capabilities

Listing 8.7: Implementation for the Phone Discount Function

```
int getPhoneDiscount(const Phone& phone) {
  int totalDiscount = 0; // The total computer discount.
  if( phone.getType() == SIMPLE_PHONE ) {
    if( phone.getDiscountType() == MANUFACTURER_DISCOUNT) {
      // Add $30 manufacturer's discount to totalDiscount.
    }
    else if( phone.getDiscountType() == STORE_DISCOUNT ) {
      // Add $15 store discount to totalDiscount.
    } else if( phone.getDiscountType() == COMBINED_DISCOUNT ) {
      // Add $30 and $15 to totalDiscount.
    }
    else { // No discount.
    }
  }
  else if( phone.getType() == ADVANCED_PHONE ) {
    // Add $60 default advanced phone discount to totalDiscount.
    if( phone.getDiscountType() == MANUFACTURER_DISCOUNT) {
      // Add additional $50 manufacturer's discount to totalDiscount.
    }
    else if( phone.getDiscountType() == STORE_DISCOUNT ) {
      // Add additional Bluetooth ear piece discount ($60) to
      // totalDiscount.
    }
    else if( phone.getDiscountType() == COMBINED_DISCOUNT ) {
      // Add additional $50 and $60 to totalDiscount.
    }
    else { // No additional discount.
    }
  }
  else if( phone.getType() == SPECIAL_PHONE ) {
    // Add $120 default special phone discount to totalDiscount.
    if( phone.getDiscountType() == MANUFACTURER_DISCOUNT) {
      // Add additional $70 manufacturer's discount to totalDiscount.
    }
    else if( phone.getDiscountType() == STORE_DISCOUNT ) {
      // Add additional 6 month data plan discount ($180).
    }
    else if( phone.getDiscountType() == COMBINED_DISCOUNT ) {
      // A additional $70 and $180 to totalDiscount.
    }
    else { // No additional discount.
    }
  }
  return totalDiscount; // Return the computed phone discount.
}
```

Listing 8.8: Table-Based Implementation for Computing Phone Discounts

```
struct Discounts {
    int smallStoreDiscount;            // For this example, it should be $15.
    int mediumStoreDiscount;           // For this example, it should be $60.
    int highStoreDiscount;             // For this example, it should be $120.
    int smallManufacturerDiscount;     // For this example, it should be $30.
    int mediumManufacturerDiscount;    // For this example, it should be $50.
    int highManufacturerDiscount;      // For this example, it should be $70.
    int bluetoothDiscount;             // For this example, it should be $60.
    int dataPlanDiscount;              // For this example, it should be $180.
};


// The discounts available for simple phones (SIM), advanced phones (ADV),
// and special phones (SPE), all accessible via discount keys (DK#).
Discounts discounts[] = {
    { 0,  0,   0,  0,  0,  0,  0,  0    }, // DK0,  SIM/ No discounts.
    { 0,  60,  0,  0,  0,  0,  0,  0    }, // DK1,  ADV/ Store's default discount.
    { 0,  0,   120,0,  0,  0,  0,  0    }, // DK2,  SPE/ Store's default discount.
    { 0,  0,   0,  30, 0,  0,  0,  0    }, // DK3,  SIM/ Manufacturer's discount.
    { 0,  60,  0,  0,  50, 0,  0,  0    }, // DK4,  ADV/ Manufacturer's discount.
    { 0,  0,   120,0,  0,  70, 0,  0    }, // DK5,  SPE/ Manufacturer's discount.
    { 15, 0,   0,  0,  0,  0,  0,  0    }, // DK6,  SIM/ Special store discount.
    { 0,  60,  0,  0,  0,  0,  60, 0    }, // DK7,  ADV/ Default & spec. store disc.
    { 0,  0,   120,0,  0,  0,  0,  180  }, // DK8,  SPE/ Default & spec. store disc.
    { 15, 0,   0,  30, 0,  0,  0,  0    }, // DK9,  SIM/ All applicable discounts.
    { 0,  60,  0,  0,  50, 0,  60, 0    }, // DK10, ADV/ All applicable discounts.
    { 0,  0,   120,0,  0,  70, 0,  180  } // DK11, SPE/ All applicable disc.
};
```

from different viewpoints. Another important benefit from using PDL is the reduction of commenting efforts. Since PDL is written at the construction design level, it provides full documentation of what the function does and the meaning of actions within operations; therefore, once code is generated PDL is turned into complete and meaningful programming-language comments for the function (McConnell 2004). Finally, using the PDL approach greatly benefits the documentation effort, especially when using documentation techniques that allow for the creation of software documentation from the comments in code (e.g., Javadoc). In these cases, PDL provides the process for creating, reviewing, and evaluating the function documentation, therefore increasing its quality.

SOFTWARE CONSTRUCTION USING STYLES

Construction styles are not about programming but about defining the rules or guidelines for everyone in the project for writing the source code for a computer program. Combined with the logic design, styles provide the final piece to generate high-quality and consistent

Listing 8.9: Table-Based Construction of the Phone Discount Function

```cpp
// The table-based version for retrieving discounts.
int getPhoneDiscount( const Phone& phone ) {

  // Compute the key for accessing the corresponding table row.
  int discountKey = phone.getType() + phone.getDiscountType();

  // Add all discounts associated with the discount key.
  int totalDiscount = discounts[discountKey].smallStoreDiscount +
                      discounts[discountKey].mediumStoreDiscount +
                      discounts[discountKey].highStoreDiscount +
                      discounts[discountKey].smallManufacturerDiscount +
                      discounts[discountKey].mediumManufacturerDiscount +
                      discounts[discountKey].highManufacturerDiscount +
                      discounts[discountKey].bluetoothDiscount +
                      discounts[discountKey].dataPlanDiscount;

  // Return the total discount.
  return totalDiscount;
}

// Create a simple phone with manufacturer's discount.
Phone phone(SIMPLE_PHONE, MANUFACTURER_DISCOUNT);

// Display the phone's discount.
cout<<"Total Phone Discount: "<<getPhoneDiscount( phone )<<endl;
```

implementations for programming problems. As a general principle, programming styles must provide rules that ensure consistency, simplicity, and clarity of code. Numerous styles have been proposed. Baldwin, Gray, and Misfeldt (2006) provide an extensive list of guidelines for formatting code using the C# programming language. Similarly, Misfeldt, Bumgardner, and Gray (2004) and Vermeulen, Ambler, Bumgardner, Metz, Misfeldt, and Shur (2000) presented equivalent work for the C++ and Java language. Besides the styles covered in Chapter 5, typical styles used during construction design include

- Formatting conventions
- Naming conventions
- Documentation conventions

Formatting Conventions

Common styles for formatting code include the use of white spaces, indentation, and bracket placement. White spaces can be used to separate keywords, parentheses, curly braces, binary operators, and commas (Baldwin et al. 2006) in such a way that the resulting code is consistent, easier to read, and easier to maintain. For example, consider the use of white spaces to separate keywords, parentheses, and curly braces in control flow statements.

Listing 8.10: Example PDL for a System's Event-Handling Capabilities

```
This function writes events occurring in the system to the event
console. Events are displayed together with their classification and
description, which are both provided by the client's calling func-
tion. In addition, the number of events received for each type of
event is computed and displayed in the event console. Events are
required to have id and description. The function returns a value
indicating success/failure of the operation.

Set the value of the function status to "failure"
Determine if the event id is valid

If the event id is valid
  Use the event id to determine the type of event

  Increment by one the counter that keeps track of the number of
  events logged of this type to reflect this newly received event.

  Write the event id, description, and event counter to the event
  console and set the return value to "success"

If the event id is not valid
  Set the event id to "unknown"
  Set the event description to "invalid event ..."
  Write the event id and description to the event console

Return the value of the function status
```

Listing 8.11 presents three different ways white space can be used. Adopt a consistent style for spacing elements, and follow it consistently in your organization. In the case of binary operators, which require two operands, it is suggested that a single space be used on both sides of the operator, when applicable, as seen in Listing 8.12. Another important place to apply white spaces in common languages, such as C++, Java, and C#, is after commas and semi-colons, which are delimiters, also demonstrated in Listing 8.12.

Indentation

Indentation is a simple way to improve program readability. Programs that do not apply indentation consistently can be hard to read. Similarly, programs that do not apply appropriate forms of indentation may result in inappropriately formatted text when viewing on different platforms. Indentation is typically employed by applying two white spaces—this varies per project—in front of one or more related program statements that need to be differentiated from other statements. However, the choice of number of white spaces must be defined by the project policy. For example, one or more statements related in code can be grouped by the

Listing 8.11: Styles for Whitespaces to Separate Keywords, Parentheses, and Curly Braces

```
// Style #1: White space after keyword.
if·(x)·{


}

// Style #2: White space after parenthesis and parameter.
if(·x·)·{


}

// Style #3: White space after keyword, parenthesis and parameter.
if·(·x·)·{


}
```

Listing 8.12: Styles for White Spaces in Binary Operators and after Commas and Semicolons

```
// White before and after binary operators.
int x·=·y·+·z;

// Using Style #2 of white spaces.
// White space after comma.
int x,·y,·z;

// White space after semicolon.
for( int i = 0;·i < maxSize;·i++ ) {


}
```

number of white spaces used in indentation. Consider the example presented in Listing 8.13, where conditional statements are indented consistently throughout the program.

An important thing to consider when applying indentation is the prevention of tab characters, since they are interpreted differently in different development environments (Misfeldt et al. 2004). This means that code that appears properly indented can look drastically different when viewed by other developers reviewing the code in a different environment. In today's popular code editors (e.g., MS Visual Studio and Eclipse), this problem can be easily solved by configuring the editor to replace tab characters with white spaces automatically on new or existing code. Another important characteristic highlighted by Listing 8.13 is the difficulty of matching opening and closing brackets in nested statements. This can lead to complex code that is hard to maintain. When encountered with a highly nested code statement in programming languages that use brackets, it is desirable to match closing brackets with opening ones, as seen in Listing 8.14.

Listing 8.13: Styles for White Spaces in Nested Statements

```
// Indentation of nested statements.
if( x == y ) {

··// Code here is appropriately indented with 2 white spaces.
··if( z == r ) {

····// Code here is appropriately indented with 4 white spaces.
····if( c == a ) {

······// Code here is appropriately indented with 6 white spaces.
····}
··}
}
```

Listing 8.14: Matching Closing and Opening Brackets in Nested Statements

```
void computeValue() {

  while( /*some condition*/ ) {

    for( /*some condition, iterate*/ ) {

      if( /*some condition*/ ) {

        switch( /*some condition*/ ) {
          // ...

        } // end switch
      } // end if
    } // end for
  } // end while
}
```

Brace Placement

Brace placement is another commonly used technique for formatting code. Styles for brace placement are applied in many languages for class definitions, function definitions, conditional and repetitive statements, and exception handlers. Two major styles include the application of the opening brace in-line or the application of the opening brace on a new line, aligned with the first character of the statement that controls the statements inside the braces. Regardless of the style applied for the opening brace, the closing brace is applied on a new line. Listings 8.15 and 8.16 present examples of both in-line and new-line styles, respectively.

Listing 8.15: In-line Bracket Placement Style

```cpp
// Inline brace placement style in C++ class definition.
class List {
  // ...
};

// Inline brace placement style in function definition.
void append() {
  // ...
}

// Inline brace placement style in conditional statements.
if( condition == true ) {
  // ...
}
else {
  // ...
}

// Inline brace placement style in loops.
while( condition == true ) {
  // ...
}
```

Naming Conventions

Naming conventions can help programmers develop models for differentiating different aspects of software programs and maintain consistency through software items. This can in turn result in code that is self-documented by the use of conventions applied consistently in the code. Naming conventions can be used to differentiate all elements that compose a software program; therefore, consistent use of naming style can help software teams to better understand the work done by each other. When applied consistently, styles can easily help software developers, testers, and maintainers understand the code and make assumptions about it based on the programming style.

A general naming convention that applies to all elements in a software program is the use of meaningful names. Meaningful names are ones that are complete and contextually correct. Naming conventions should lead to names that unambiguously and completely define the intent of the entity that they represent. Names should be chosen so that they clearly define entities so that they quickly become familiar to those who read and maintain the code. Failure to select meaningful names can result in code that is hard to understand, follow, and maintain. Examples of bad and good examples of meaningful names are presented in Listing 8.17.

Listing 8.17 presents several cases of good and bad names. Example 1 presents the choice of using rdo1 and rdo2 for names to describe two Radio objects. These names are incomplete and as a consequence can make the code hard to understand, debug, and

---

Listing 8.16: New-Line Bracket Placement Style

```cpp
// Newline brace placement style in C++ class definition.
class List
{
    // ...
};

// Newline brace placement style in function definition.
void append()
{
    // ...
}

// Newline brace placement style in conditional statements.
if( condition == true )
{
    // ...
}

// Newline brace placement style in loops.
while( condition == true )
{
    // ...
}
```

---

maintain. Example 2 shows the usage of the name xmit to abstract the transmission function of a radio object. Developers who are not familiar with this abbreviation of the word *transmit* may find it difficult to find the appropriate function call in the documentation to transmit a message. In addition, consider the case where the integrated development environment (IDE) supports the intellisense feature. In this case, developers would intuitively and without success type the letter *t* in hopes that the IDE would reveal a function name that somewhat relates to the transmission behavior required by the radio object. Example 3 presents the case where the name chosen is both incomplete and inappropriate for the program's context. That is, it is hard to determine the correct meaning of the code when using s and MaxAmount. This is mainly because s does not describe the entity being evaluated and MaxAmount can refer to multiple limits that relate to different properties (e.g., max salary, max number of items). These names are improved by making them complete and appropriate for the context. Finally, Example 4 presents an example of a contextually inappropriate name for an object of type DirectoryManager. In this case, objects of type DirectoryManager monitor a directory for cleanup. Once the directory reaches a specified threshold, objects of the DirectoryManger type would begin deleting files. The choice of name reaper and destroy are not appropriate for this context. Reaper and destroy seem more appropriate for a gaming context; therefore, the names are improved by replacing them to describe better the actions of these objects.

Listing 8.17: Styles for Naming Conventions

```
// Example 1:
// Incomplete variable names.
Radio rdo1;
Radio rdo2;

// Complete variable name.
Radio activeRadio;
Radio backupRadio;

// Example 2:
class Radio {
  public:
     // Incomplete function name.
     void xmit(Message* message);
};

class Radio {
  public:
     // Complete function name.
     void transmit(Message* message);
};

// Example 3:
// Incomplete and contextually inappropriate variable names.
if( s > MaxAmount ) {
  // s is ambiguous!
  // MaxAmount of what?
  // MaxAmount does not reflect the appropriate context!
}

// Complete and contextually appropriate variable names.
if( salary > MaxSalaryAmount ) {
  // ...
}

// Example 4:
// Contextually inappropriate names.
DirectoryManager reaper;
reaper.destroy();

// Contextually appropriate names.
DirectoryManager directoryManager;
directoryManager.deleteFiles();
```

Documentation Conventions

Similar to formatting and naming conventions, documentation conventions can also be (almost universally) applied to projects in different domains and with different programming languages. Documentation conventions deal with styles and specifications for what to document and how to document during construction. Generally, if the naming conventions are followed, comments should provide information that describes why an operation is written as opposed to what the operation is doing. In many cases, the actions performed by operations (or blocks of codes) can be inferred from the naming conventions or programming syntax; however, the reasons behind the choice of code cannot be inferred as easily. Therefore, comments should provide the reasons why code was written and, when necessary, what the code is doing.

Documenting Files

In software construction, files are units of cohesive work. In some architectural efforts, using the development view discussed in Chapter 3, systems are decomposed using files (and directories) as a main unit of system decomposition. Therefore, files should be well documented in a clear and concise manner so that clients of the file can understand the actions carried out by its contents. Depending on the language, files can contain one or more classes, one or more functions, or one or more variable, constant, or type definitions. In all cases, file documentation is necessary for managing the file throughout its lifetime. File documentation can vary from company to company or even from project to project within a same company. However, at a minimum, file documentation should contain header information that identifies the contents of the file, description, and original author. In addition, file documentation can include other important information, such as revision information (e.g., bug fixes or enhancements), classification (mostly for companies that write software for national security purposes) of the file's content, and any restrictions associated with the file's content. An example of file documentation is presented in Listing 8.18.

Documenting Functions

Similar to files, functions are units of work; however, they operate on a smaller scale. Therefore, their intent should be well documented in a clear and concise manner so that their clients can understand the actions carried out by the function's contents. Functions operate on a finer-grained context than files; therefore, their documentation should be specific to the work performed by the functions. Information such as classification and history can be deferred to the file's documentation. At a minimum, function documentation should contain information about its intent, parameters, and return values. In addition, it can include any pre- and postconditions applicable. An example of function documentation header is presented in Listing 8.19. As seen, an important relationship exists between PDL and function documentation. When using PDL, a comment's first approach is employed to designing code at the construction level. PDL generated as part of

---

Listing 8.18: Style for File Documentation

```
//*********************************************************************
// FILE:           MyFile.h
//
// DESCRIPTION:    This file contains the definition of class x.
//                 Class x is used in the system for ... Clients of
//                 this class are required to ...
//
// REVISION:       Revision 1.0
//
// CLASSIFICATION: Unclassified
//
// RESTRICTIONS:   None
//
// AUTHOR:         Joe Developer
//
// HISTORY:
//    PROBLEM #   INITIALS   DATE       DESCRIPTION
//-------------------------------------------------------------------
//    N/A         JD         1/1/2011   Initial Design and Code.
//    10          TAE        5/1/2011   Removed dead code.
//    ...         ...        ...        ...
//-------------------------------------------------------------------
//
//*********************************************************************
```

---

a particular function's behavior can be directly used to create the function's documentation. In Listing 8.19, PDL generated and presented in Listing 8.10 is used word for word in the function's documentation.

MINIMIZING COMPLEXITY IN CONSTRUCTION DESIGN

Construction design is an activity directly related to the construction phase. In some cases, construction design begins during the design phase and continues throughout the construction phase. This activity is heavily collaborative, since construction design represents parts of a whole system. Complexity encountered during construction design can be minimized through making use of standards (Abran, Moore, Bourque, and Dupuis 2005). The use of standards is an important part of the software development process. In the construction design activity, standards can be used to define common processes and practices for improving the efficiency of engineers. Standards can help designers become more efficient by allowing them to quickly understand, for example, complex data structures, complex messaging interfaces, and configuration management processes. They can also help minimize complexity by defining the basis for implementing construction designs that are

---

Listing 8.19: Style for File Documentation

```
//*********************************************************************
// METHOD:        EventLogger::log(EventId id, string description)
//
// DESCRIPTION:  This function writes events occurring in the system
//               to the event console. Events are displayed together
//               with their classification and description, which are
//               both provided by the client's calling function.
//               In addition, the number of events received for each
//               type of event is computed and displayed in the event
//               console. Events are required to have id and
//               description.
//
// RETURNS:      The function returns a boolean value indicating
//               success/failure of the operation.
//
// PRE-CONDITIONS:   ...
// POST-CONDITIONS:  ...
//
//*********************************************************************
```

---

simple and readable rather than clever (Abran et al. 2005). Some important standards that can be created for software projects include the software development plan, the software version document, the interface control document, and the programming style standard, as presented in Chapter 5.

QUALITY EVALUATION OF CONSTRUCTION DESIGN

The construction design activity is the last major design step performed before construction. Therefore, it provides the last opportunity to evaluate the quality of the system to be built. There are numerous project-specific quality characteristics (e.g., security, usability) that can be identified and evaluated for construction designs. However, at a minimum, the design's completeness, correctness, testability, and maintainability should be evaluated, since these generally apply to all software projects.

Completeness and correctness deal with the degree to which construction designs correctly meet the allocated requirements. Construction designs that are correct, but incomplete, complete but incorrect, or incomplete and incorrect—those that do not meet all requirements, are incorrect, or both—need to be addressed and resolved to maintain the envisioned software quality of the product. Completeness and correctness can both be evaluated through peer reviews, unit testing, and audits. In all of these activities, the use of checklists—one of the seven common tools of quality—is essential. In other cases, incomplete designs are the product of incomplete specifications. In these cases, construction designs can be further analyzed using prototypes for eliciting the required capabilities to complete the specifications and therefore the construction design.

Testability quality (in construction design) deals with the amount of effort required to test artifacts that are the result of construction design. On the other hand, a design's maintainability deals with the amount of effort required to maintain a tested artifact that is the result of construction design. Both testability and maintainability goals can be achieved in many ways, as determined by nonfunctional requirements of the project. A common approach for evaluating the testability and maintainability of construction designs includes the measurement of the design's cyclomatic complexity (McCabe 1976); therefore, testability and maintainability goals can be transformed into requirements that are based on the cyclomatic complexity. In addition, maintainability quality can also be evaluated by the compliance of the resulting implementation of construction design to the programming style defined for the project. Pressman (2010, p. 437) states that "source code and related work products must conform to local coding standards and exhibit characteristics that will facilitate maintainability." Therefore, evaluation techniques that enforce 100% compliance with local styles of programming must be in place.

Peer Reviews

Peer reviews are tasks that concentrate on verifying and validating designs and code (i.e., design reviews and code reviews, respectively). Peer reviews must be planned, organized, and conducted in such a way that a collective approval among all members of the project (with different disciplines) is reached. The main tasks are performed by technologically savvy engineers and domain experts that can verify and validate the items of review. In addition, the presence of an auditor (or software quality personnel) is required to inspect both processes and products. Finally, members of the software testing and maintenance team can contribute highly to the review of items.

A great deal of time during code review is spent evaluating code. In many practical situations, where requirements have been established to meet a specific programming style, it can be time-consuming to read code line by line to validate that the code meets the style's requirements. In these cases, the use of automated style checkers can provide significant benefits. Automated style checkers are tools that can be configured to enforce a specific style of programming. Some of the capabilities provided by automated style checkers include checks for numerous conventions. For example, the open-source CheckStyle 5.3 (2010) is a Java code auditor that can be incorporated into the Eclipse integrated development environment to enforce coding styles and identify areas of potential errors in code. Some of the capabilities included by CheckStyle include the following:

- Naming conventions of attributes and methods
- Formatting conventions
- Limit of the number of function parameters, line lengths
- Comments (Javadoc) for classes, attributes, and methods
- Presence of mandatory headers

- Good practices for class design
- Checks for duplicated code sections
- Checks cyclomatic complexity against a specified threshold
- Other multiple complexity measurements

Unit Testing

Ultimately, the quality of construction designs in terms of completeness and correctness is evaluated through unit testing. Therefore, as construction designs are created, so are unit tests. One or more unit test cases are essential for verifying and validating construction designs. A sample unit test case is presented in Table 8.5.

Cyclomatic Complexity

Cyclomatic complexity is a technique developed by McCabe (1976) that can be used for evaluating the quality of flow-based designs. It is a mathematical technique based on graph theory that provides a quantitative justification for making design decisions that lead to higher quality in terms of a design's maintainability and testability. The cyclomatic complexity computation allows designers to measure the complexity of flow-based operational designs by determining the complexity of the decision structure of operations instead of lines of code. In his original work, McCabe illustrated the correlation between intuitive complexity and the graph-theoretic complexity of several programming operations and showed that the complexity of an operation had less to do with physical size and more to do with the decision structure of the operation. By using this approach, the cyclomatic complexity provides not only a measurement of the complexity of flow-based designs but also a measurement of the maximum number of independent paths required to fully test the operation (Galin 2003). Therefore, cyclomatic complexity can be used to determine the maintainability (i.e., understandability) and testability of flow-based designs.

The cyclomatic complexity technique works by computing the cyclomatic number $v(G)$ of a graph G with n vertices, e edges, and p connected components, as seen in Equation 8.1.

$$v(G)=e-n+2p \tag{8.1}$$

For a strongly connected graph G—in which there is a path connecting any pair of arbitrary distinct nodes—the cyclomatic number is equal to the maximum number of linearly independent circuits (McCabe 1976). Therefore, flow-based designs can be associated with directed, strongly connected graphs that have unique entry and exit points, where each node can be reached from the entry node, and each node can reach the exit node. When this is the case, the graph is referred as the program control graph, and Equation (8.1) can be used to compute the cyclomatic complexity of the function, based on its flow-based design. For example, consider a UML flow-based design (i.e., activity diagram) constructed as a directed, strongly connected graph consisting of five activities (i.e., nodes) and six transitional arrows (i.e., edges), each activity accessible from the starting node and capable of reaching the exit

TABLE 8.5

Sample Unit Test Case Template

	Unit Test Case			

Unit test name:
Description:
Requirements:
Preconditions:

S	Operator Action	System Action	P/F	N
1	Operator enters invalid product data and clicks on the send button.	Detects invalid data and displays error message to the operator		
2	Operator enters valid product data and clicks on the send button.	Validates the data; retrieves server's Internet Protocol (IP) address and port number		
3		Opens a socket connection and send product request data to the server		
4		Waits a maximum of 3 seconds for a server response		
5		.		
		.		
6		Response received and product information is displayed		
7		Save response data in file system and ask user to search for another product		
8	Operator clicks the cancel button to finish searching for products.			

	Test Result Notes			

	Approval Signatures			

Software engineer:
Test engineer:
Quality auditor:

activity. In this case, the cyclomatic complexity of the design is $v(G) = 6 - 5 + 2(1) = 3$. In most cases, the value of $p = 1$ is expected, since p is the number of connected components in the graph. Given the characteristics specified for the program control graph (i.e., unique entry and exit points, all nodes reachable from the entry, and all nodes capable of reaching the exit node), all program control graphs will end up having only one connected component (McCabe 1976). However, in some cases, complexity may be evaluated as the combined complexity of several operations. Consider a parent operation that calls on several child operations; in this case, the complexity of the operation is the combined complexity of the parent's operation complexity and the complexity of all other child operations that are called within the parent. In these cases, p will equal the number of connected components in the parent and child operations, which can be equal to the number of operations (parent and child operations) being evaluated. It is important to note that when $p \neq 1$, the complexity measure will be equal to the summation of the individual complexities of each connected component, since complexity measures are additive.

Computing the cyclomatic complexity for large operations can be tedious; therefore, two simplification methods are available for easily computing the cyclomatic complexity of single-component graphs (i.e., $p = 1$). The first method allows for the computation of complexity in terms of a program's decision constructs, such as *if* statements, *while* loop, *for* loop, and *case* statements. Mills (1972) proved that the cyclomatic complexity (C) of a structured program meeting the control graphs requirements previously mentioned is equal to the number of conditions in the code (π) plus 1, as seen in Equation (8.2).

$$C = \pi + 1 \tag{8.2}$$

The number of conditions (π) can be easily measured as follows. Conditional statements, such as *if* statements, *while* loop, and *for* loop, all count as one unit of complexity. Compound conditional statements, such as *if x and y then z,* count as two complexity units, since without the connective *and* the condition would have to be specified as *if x then, if y then z* (McCabe 1976). Case statements, such as the switch statement in C++, Java, and C#, or other conditional statements containing multiple n branching statements are counted as $\pi = n - 1$ unit of complexity.

The second simplification approach allows for the visual determination of complexity via the program's control graph (i.e., flow-based design). This approach is based on the work of mathematician Leonhard Euler, who proved that for connected planar graphs—those without intersecting edges—the regions (r) of a graph can be computed using Equation (8.3), known as Euler's formula.

$$2 = n - e + r \tag{8.3}$$

A region is an area enclosed by arcs; therefore, given the characteristics of the program control chart, the number of regions enclosed by arcs, plus one that resides outside the graph, is equal to the cyclomatic complexity of the graph. All three methods for computing the cyclomatic complexity of a program control graph are presented in Figure 8.3.

The top-left corner of Figure 8.3 represents the program control graph designed using a (flow-based) activity diagram. As seen, the program control graph represents a case statement with five branches; therefore, the number of conditions (π) is equal to $5 - 1 = 4$ and the cyclomatic complexity, using Equation (8.2), is $C = 4 + 1 = 5$. This can be easily verified with Equations (8.1) and (8.3). For example, using Equation (8.1), the cyclomatic complexity is $v(G) = 10 - 7 + 2(1) = 5$.

The top-right corner presents the evaluation of complexity of a program control graph using the *regions* visual inspection. As seen, the number of regions of the planar graph is five; therefore, the cyclomatic complexity of the design is five. This can easily be verified by rearranging Equation (8.3) to solve for r, which results in $r = 9 - 6 + 2 = 5$. Finally, the bottom of Figure 8.3 presents a more complex program design, which includes 23 nodes

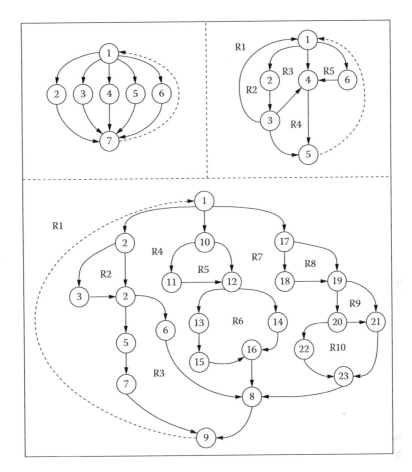

FIGURE 8.3
Cyclomatic complexity for three flow-based designs.

and 31 edges. By using the *regions* visual inspection, the complexity of the design can be evaluated quickly, which results in a complexity of 10. Since designs like this one involve a relatively large number of nodes and edges, it is a good idea to verify the complexity measurement using any of the other techniques presented. For example, using Equation (8.1), the complexity results in $v(G) = 31 - 23 + 2(1) = 10$.

An important consideration when evaluating quality in terms of cyclomatic complexity is the establishment of a threshold value for determining when the complexity of designs is acceptable. This threshold value can be used to create quality requirements for the software development process; for example, *the cyclomatic complexity of functions shall not exceed 10.* Typically, a value of 10 is acceptable, based on McCabe's (1976) work. Other studies have shown results similar to McCabe; for example, Casper Jones (2008, p. 415) reports the following:

> Empirical studies reveal that program with cyclomatic complexities of less than 5 are generally considered simple and easy to understand. Cyclomatic complexities of 10 or less are considered not too difficult. When the cyclomatic complexity is greater than 20, the complexity is perceived as high. When the McCabe number exceeds 50, the software for practical purposes becomes untestable.

Ultimately, a threshold value that makes sense for the project team (e.g., 10) should be selected and enforced throughout the design and construction phase, metrics should be collected and analyzed, and the threshold value should be reevaluated (for new projects) according to the results.

CHAPTER SUMMARY

The transition from software design to construction should occur with minimal effort. In some cases, component designs provide enough detail to allow their transformation from design artifact into code easily; however, in other cases, a more fine-grained level of design detail is required. Construction design provides a form of design that closely resembles code so that complex operations can be planned and evaluated prior to implementation in code. Once the correctness of operations is verified, the construction design activity provides additional heuristics to enforce consistency in the code. Construction designs are typically created using the following techniques: flow-based, state-based, table-based, and programming design language. Each method provides its own benefits; therefore, careful attention should be paid when selecting the appropriateness of construction designs in practical applications. The benefits acquired from designing complex functions and enforcing styles for consistency are essential to maintaining each system's envisioned quality.

REVIEW QUESTIONS

1. What is construction design, and why is it important?
2. List and explain common quality attributes that can be addressed during construction design.
3. Why are styles important during construction?
4. What are flow-based designs, and how do they relate to UML activity diagrams?
5. Describe the following elements of an activity diagram:
   a. Initial state
   b. Final state
   c. Action
   d. Branch
   e. Transition
6. What are state-based designs, and why are they important for construction design?
7. How are state-based designs typically translated to code?
8. What are table-based designs, and why are they important for construction design?
9. Compare and contrasts the following:
   a. Limited-entry decision table
   b. Extended-entry decision table
   c. Mixed-entry decision table

10. How are table-based designs used to decrease code's complexity and increase both readability and maintainability?
11. In decision tables, what are missing policies and redundant actions? How does identifying these help make more efficient tables?
12. What is programming design language, and what is the main benefit that it provides over other construction design methods?
13. How are construction styles used to decrease code's complexity and increase both readability and maintainability?
14. What are the main methods used for evaluating quality of construction designs?
15. List and explain an efficient method for enforcing styles during construction.
16. What is cyclomatic complexity? Name three different ways to compute the cyclomatic complexity of a function during construction design.
17. What is the relationship between cyclomatic complexity and software quality? Explain.

CHAPTER EXERCISES

1. Select a project of choice, and identify three different functions that can be designed using flow-based, table-based, and state-based design. Create the designs for these functions, and prepare a 5- to 10-minute presentation including designs, code, and justification.
2. Compute the cyclomatic complexity of the following code using all three methods:

```
switch( state ) {

  case ONE:

    // Perform activity.
    if( /*some condition*/ ) {
      // Perform activity.
    }
    else if( /*some condition*/ ) {
      // Perform activity.
    }
    else {
      // Perform activity.
    }
    break;

  case TWO:

    // Perform activity FIVE.
    break;
```

```
case THREE:

    // Perform activity FOUR.
    break;
default:

    // Intentionally left blank.
    break;
}
```

REFERENCES

Abran, Alain, James W. Moore, Pierre Bourque, and Robert Dupuis. *Guide to the Software Engineering Body of Knowledge—2004 Version—SWEBOK*. Los Angeles, CA: IEEE Computer Society Press, 2005.

Baldwin, Kenneth, Andrew Gray, and Trevor Misfeldt. *The Elements of C# Style*. Cambridge, UK: Cambridge University Press, 2006.

Booch, Grady, James Rumbaugh, and Ivar Jacobson. *The Unified Modeling Language User Guide*, 2d ed. Boston: Addison-Wesley, 2005.

Checkstyle 5.3. October 19, 2010. Available from: http://checkstyle.sourceforge.net/index.html (accessed March 11, 2011).

Collar, Emilio Jr. "An Investigation of Programming Code Textbase Readability Based on a Cognitive Readability Model." PhD thesis, University of Colorado at Boulder, 2005.

Fox, Christopher. *Introduction to Software Engineering Design: Processes, Principles, and Patterns with UML2*. Boston: Addison Wesley, 2006.

Galin, Daniel. *Software Quality Assurance: From Theory to Implementation*. Harlow, UK: Pearson Addison Wesley, 2003.

Hurley, Richard B. *Decision Tables in Software Engineering*. New York: Van Nostrand Reinhold, 1982.

IEEE. "IEEE Standard for Information Technology-Systems Design-Software Design Descriptions." 2009, p. 175.

Jones, Capers. *Applied Software Measurement: Global Analysis of Productivity and Quality*, 3d ed. New York: McGraw-Hill Osborne Media, 2008.

McCabe, Thomas J. "A Complexity Measure." *IEEE Transactions on Software Engineering* SE-2, no. 4 (1976): 308–320.

McConnell, Steve. *Code Complete*, 2d ed. Redmond, WA: Microsoft Press, 2004.

Meyer, Bertrand. *Object-Oriented Software Construction*, 2d ed. Upper Saddle River, NJ: Prentice Hall, 1997.

Mills, Harlan D. *Mathematical Foundations for Structured Programming*. Gaithersburg, MD: IBM Federal Systems Division, IBM Corporation, 1972.

Misfeldt, Trevor, Gregory Bumgardner, and Andrew Gray. *The Elements of C++ Style*. Cambridge, UK: Cambridge University Press, 2004.

Pressman, Roger S. *Software Engineering: A Practitioner's Approach*, 7th ed. Chicago: McGraw-Hill, 2010.

Vermeulen, Allan, Scott W. Ambler, Greg Bumgardner, Eldon Metz, Trevor Misfeldt, Jim Shur, and Patrick Thompson. *The Elements of Java Style*. Cambridge, UK: Cambridge University Press, 2000.

9

Human–Computer Interface Design

Jacob Somervell
University of Virginia, College at Wise

CHAPTER OBJECTIVES

- Understand the role that the computer interface plays in high-quality and successful software systems
- Describe how to address interface design and evaluation within the software development life cycle
- Provide usable guidance for evaluating designs

CONCEPTUAL OVERVIEW

To end users, the interface is the system. Most end users do not know, nor do they even need to know, about the underlying structure and implementation of the software system. They are concerned only with the interface presented to them and the capabilities provided by that interface. Consider the analogy of driving a car: the driver does not need to know anything about how an internal combustion engine works and how it is connected to the transmission to send power to the wheels, nor do they need to know about hydraulics and fluid dynamics of the braking system to actually drive a car. Indeed, mainly the driver needs to know that "D" means drive (assuming an automatic transmission), press gas pedal to go, press brake pedal to stop. The same concept applies to software systems. End users are concerned only with what they can do with the system and how they do it, not with how it works "under the hood." Hence, it is of vital importance to get the interface design sufficiently correct so that it serves users in an efficient and usable manner. This chapter shifts the focus away from the detailed under-the-hood approach to design to cover the essential human–computer design activity. The chapter focuses on providing valuable information on how to create effective and usable interfaces for software systems.

WHAT IS HUMAN–COMPUTER INTERFACE DESIGN?

So what does it mean to "get it right?" As part of the software design process, human–computer interaction (HCI) design must account for the user of the software. While designing the architecture and detailed design of software systems is essential for meeting most quality attributes, designing an efficient user interface that is understandable by the end user is paramount to the usability quality of all successful software systems. The most elegant, efficient, and high-quality architectural and detailed designs can be felled by a poor interface. In the context of HCI, interface design refers to the creation of the user interface. IEEE (1990, p. 80) defines the user interface as follows:

> An interface that enables information to be passed between a human user and hardware or software components of a computer systems.

For most software, this entails designing the graphical user interface (GUI). This involves selecting appropriate information presentation and interaction techniques for the various end-user classes (Rosson and Carroll 2002). More specifically this entails selecting appropriate information layouts, correct language, appropriate interface controls (e.g., radio buttons versus check boxes), and tying the detailed design to the various input mechanisms provided in the interface.

An essential task of the HCI design activity involves making sure that the interface provides appropriate means for using the system in an efficient manner. The best way to ensure an interface is sufficiently good is to iteratively improve the design through user testing. The implication is that there will be multiple iterations of a process that includes the following HCI design tasks:

- Creating a prototype of the system
- Having end users use that prototype in realistic ways
- Gathering data from these tests
- Redesigning the interface to address discovered problems

All of this work (choosing appropriate information representation and interaction methods) hinges on a thorough understanding of the users of the system. It is paramount to learn how the users typically perform similar actions and what their expectations of the new system may be. This information is gleaned through detailed requirements gathering and analysis and through significant user testing.

WHY STUDY HUMAN–COMPUTER INTERFACE DESIGN?

The HCI design activity is where general principles are applied to optimize the interface between humans and computers. Visual designs have a major role in the success or failure of software systems. Systems that meet functional requirements but are not usable cannot succeed. The major concerns of the HCI designs may include the evaluation and use of modes, navigation, visual designs, response time and feedback, and design modalities, such as forms and menu-driven. HCI designs directly influence the quality of any system and are essential to understanding and addressing the factors that affect the overall usability of the system. Many design principles and evaluation techniques exist to successfully design user interfaces. Therefore, understanding the techniques and tools for designing interfaces allows designers to become proficient in creating efficient interfaces. Providing an interface that allow users to accomplish their goals with the software, without unnecessary effort, is the ultimate goal of the user interface designer.

The "without unnecessary effort" clause is important. Consider a system that requires a date from the user, as presented on Iteration 1 of Figure 9.1.

The user interface could ask the user to type in the date in a text box. Without any extra information a user could type any of the following:

- Jan 1, 2011
- 1 / 1/ 11
- 1 - 1 - 11
- 1 January 2011

Which format was expected by the software? If the information typed by the user doesn't match the format, what happens? An error message? Program crash? The most flexible option involves allowing all of these and others as valid input and then correctly parsing the input to find the appropriate fields for month, day, and year from that input string. This is a nontrivial solution and does not help the user form a basis or understanding of the desired input. A simpler solution involves adding a label to the input box specifying the appropriate format (i.e., MM/DD/YYYY), as presented on Iteration 2 of Figure 9.1. This option works

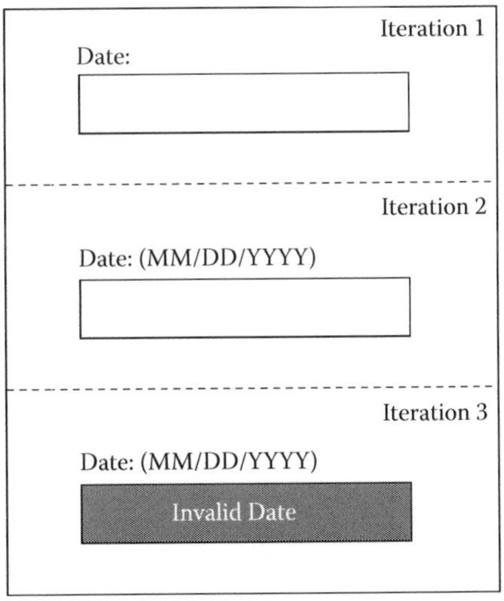

FIGURE 9.1
Simple data entry user interface.

fine and helps the user understand the expected formats for date objects, knowledge that can be leveraged in other software systems with similar requirements. Finally, to address input errors, error indicators in the interface are introduced to help guide the user to the correct input format, as presented on Iteration 3 of Figure 9.1. Typically, a red error indicator (e.g., as a background color on input boxes) is a passive way of accomplishing this.

Many other options for date input could be used instead, including drop-down lists, graphical mini-calendars for selecting the date, and spinners. Each of these options has been used with varying levels of success in various applications. Learning which method works for a specific software system requires end-user testing: create prototype systems or mock-ups with each design choice, have users complete realistic tasks using these systems, record information about the users' performance (e.g., speed, accuracy), and empirically determine the best design. This effort is significant and requires time and resources to accomplish correctly.

The point of this discussion is that the interface (the presented information to the user) plays a significant role in the utility of the software and the experience of the user. Carefully considering the user and the user's abilities when designing the interface can only increase the usability of the software system. Thorough testing of the design, with end users, is paramount to designing successful software systems.

So how do we go about involving the user in the process? One must spend time early in the software development life cycle identifying the user classes for the software. A user class is a set of users who share common tasks with the software. Consider a student information system that may be used by a university. Clearly, one class of user would be the students. Another obvious class would be the faculty. Other classes that might not be immediately obvious could include department chairs, registrar, advisors, enrollment management staff, and financial aid staff. There could be others. Furthermore, a single person could take on the characteristics of multiple classes. For example, a faculty member could also be an advisor and a department chair. Each of the user classes to which a user belongs contributes to the type of work that that user should be able to perform with the software.

After identifying the user classes, it is then necessary to hold requirements meetings with representatives of each user class. These meetings should elicit the tasks that the target user class should be able to do with the software as well as tasks that would be "nice" to have. Recall that these meetings would normally occur as part of the requirements gathering process in the overall software development life cycle, not as a separate activity, although it could be separate if needed. Similar to software architects, it is common for user interface designers to go back and forth between requirements and design, until the interface is sufficiently appropriate to accommodate the needs of users of each class.

Skill Development 9.1: Eliciting Needs from Different User Classes

Create a list of 10 questions you would ask a group of students about their expectations for a new student information system. Create a list of 10 questions you would ask a group of faculty about their expectations for the same system.

After learning about the typical interactions your user classes will have with the system, one can begin designing the user interface to meet those needs. One of the most challenging things for software engineers is to disconnect from the system they are designing and try to see the world through the eyes of the end user. It is tempting to simply design an interface that meets the needs of the engineer or developer (e.g., for testing, verification) instead of designing an interface that meets the needs of the end user. It is up to software developers to maintain a clear focus on the end user while developing the user interface for a system. The following sections provide specific information to aid the designer in focusing on the user.

GENERAL HCI DESIGN PRINCIPLES

Several design principles and heuristics exist for guiding user interface designers. According to Nielsen and Mack (1994), there are 10 major heuristics to follow when creating a user interface:

1. *Visibility of system status:* The interface should have some mechanism for showing where users are in their task.
2. *Match between system and the real world:* The interface should provide interaction techniques that mimic or model what is expected in the real world.
3. *User control and freedom:* The interface should support user exploration without fear of breaking anything. Undo and redo should be supported.
4. *Consistency and standards:* The interface should use, for example, language or wording that is consistent with users' expectations. Follow style guides and platform standards.
5. *Error prevention:* The interface should help users avoid mistakes. Always ask them when they initiate a destructive command.
6. *Recognition rather than recall:* The interface should support rapid and easy learning of the system and support recognizing features and their associated actions rather than relying on memorization of unique interface widgets.
7. *Flexibility and efficiency of use:* The interface should provide users with shortcuts or other accelerators. This helps the interface get out of the way of expert users while allowing novice users the opportunity to become more efficient.
8. *Aesthetic and minimalist design:* The interface should present only the necessary information and no more. Extra visual elements can distract from the important information.
9. *Help users recognize, diagnose, and recover from errors:* Error messages should be expressed in plain language (no codes), precisely indicate the problem, and constructively suggest a solution.
10. *Help and documentation:* Make sure the help and documentation is clearly available in the interface.

These 10 guidelines or heuristics are generic and open. This is intentional so that they can be applied across a large cross section of software systems. This generality can sometimes

FIGURE 9.2

Example calendar user interface.

lead to ambiguity and confusion on the part of the developer. More specific, heuristics can be useful when developing software for specific platforms or systems (Somervell and McCrickard 2005). However, the point is that there are some simple, straightforward things to consider when designing any user interface. More importantly, these 10 guidelines are focused on users and strive to keep them in control of the system: the system serves the user. Applying these rules in a specific application can help create an interface that users will find both useful and usable. Consider a popular online calendar application as presented in Figure 9.2.

In this particular calendar application, creating an appointment relies mostly on direct manipulation—directly clicking on the desired day, typing in a description, including time, and hitting the return key. This action is analogous to writing that information on a desk calendar or other paper calendar. It is exactly what users expect to be able to do with a calendar. In addition, there is a button ("Create event") that allows users to add appointments by filling in a form: some users may prefer this method of entry, especially for events that occur in the future, which would require navigation within the calendar to enter through the direct manipulation route. A new appointment is shown immediately in the day for which it is assigned.

Now consider the 10 guidelines in relation to this interface. In terms of system status this interface shows an entire month (or week or day) of appointments in the expected monthly format. A newly created appointment appears immediately within the day for which it occurs. Error conditions are displayed prominently in the top center of the display in red text. In terms of matching the real world, it clearly mimics the desktop calendar and heavily utilizes that metaphor. The form and layout closely resembles other calendar applications so consistency and standards are followed. Users can really commit no errors in the software, and any mistakes are easily corrected through undo or deletion capabilities. As a GUI application, there are no commands to learn and remember from usage to usage, and help is available through pop-up labels on hover. The design is minimal in that only the necessary information is shown with extra functionality available in submenus. Overall, this particular interface performs well with respect to Nielsen and Mack's (1994) heuristics.

This high-level analysis of the calendar application serves to illustrate a good interface and how a good interface will typically meet most of the general heuristics. Improvements to an interface will often revolve around one of the 10 areas described by these guidelines. However, these guidelines are just that: guidance. How does one go about starting the interface design process? How do we get a prototype of the system?

HUMAN–COMPUTER INTERFACE DESIGN METHODS

HCI sits at the intersection of design, science, and engineering (McCrickard, Chewar, and Somervell 2004). To create an effective interface, the designer must rely on information from psychology, sociology, graphic design, human factors and ergonomics, computer science, and mathematics (among a plethora of other specialty areas). This implies that designers work on or with a multidisciplinary team. Each of the aforementioned areas contributes to the design of the interface in some specific way—whether it be in leveraging the intricacies of the human information systems (e.g., visual, audible, haptic) through color choice, font choice, line width, and so forth or in leveraging the societal norms or customs of the target user class through, for example, wording, ordering of information, or icon design.

Getting Started

Almost all design activities, regardless of discipline, start with some form of brainstorming activity. There is no specific structure required or followed; the designer simply starts thinking about ways to solve a problem and then drawing or writing out descriptions of that solution. Often at this stage in design, the only technologies needed are kindergarten tools: pencils, paper, crayons, markers, scissors, tape. Some people prefer to work on a chalkboard or whiteboard and take pictures of the drawings for record keeping. In any case, the point is to capture ideas and thoughts on "paper" for later access.

It is interesting (but not surprising) to note that the majority of interfaces (electronic) are rectangular. We use rectangular paper, rectangular calendars, rectangular screens, and rectangular books. Humans like rectangles. Most of the interfaces you will design will be contained in rectangles. This fact can be leveraged when creating an interface. Furthermore, at least in North America, people read from left to right and from top to bottom. This is taught from early childhood when parents read to their children and trace their finger along with the words. Certainly by kindergarten, even before they know how to read, most children are trained to look at "readable" objects and materials at the top left and proceed to the right and down. This knowledge is used in interface design by placing prominent information in the upper left corner of the interface. Take a moment to examine your favorite program. Check out the interface and identify the type of information placed in the upper left quadrant. Most programs will have some important functionality located in that area of the interface. One notable exception is the Start menu in Windows operating systems (but it is still on the left). This type of understanding of the human element can help the interface designer create effective and usable interfaces.

Fidelity in Prototypes

Early design efforts generate low-fidelity prototypes of the system interface. Fidelity in this sense means the level of sophistication or realism in the interface (Virzi, Sokolov, and Karis 1996). Certainly a drawing of an interface on paper, done in pencil, would require lots of imagination on the part of end users or clients if they were to get a feel for the intent of the interface. More realism is needed when communicating design ideas to customers; perhaps screen shots or a simple presentation. Mostly working, high-fidelity prototypes are required for summative evaluations (Hix and Hartson 1993). The idea is that there is a spectrum of fidelity when it comes to designing prototypes. Low-fidelity prototypes are useful in early design for communicating and eliciting requirements from the client and end users. Medium-fidelity prototypes are useful for illustrating interaction sequences and specific design choices. High-fidelity prototypes are required for effective end-user testing. Each level of fidelity is useful to the designer and will likely be utilized during the interface creation process.

Skill Development 9.2: Low-Fidelity User Interface Design

Using only paper and pencil, draw an interface for a ticket purchasing kiosk. The hardware supports touch-screen interaction.

Low-fidelity prototypes are useful to the designer in the early stages for several reasons. They cost very little. Pencil and paper and other similar materials are cheap. The time and energy required to create a simple sketch of an interface are also negligible. Often, if the ideas come during the initial requirements gathering meetings, designers can create mock-ups on the spot to clarify ideas and get a better grasp of the customer's wants and needs. Low-fidelity prototypes can also be "thrown away" easily. Often designers simply crumple up a piece of paper and "start over" with the design. This is much more difficult and time-consuming when using higher-fidelity tools (e.g., commercial tools, integrated development environments, presentation software). Figure 9.3 presents an example of a low-

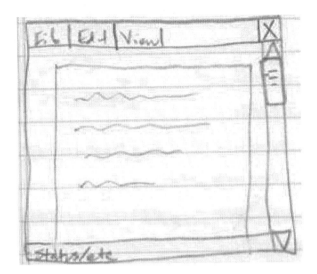

FIGURE 9.3
Low-fidelity prototype of a fictional document editor.

fidelity prototype of a fictional document editor, in which the major interface components are illustrated without any real details.

After identifying requirements and getting initial feedback from customers on early prototypes, designers must then work toward creating a more realistic prototype that can be used for specific testing. Interface design tools with drag-and-drop support for widgets like text boxes, labels, buttons, and other controls are highly useful for this phase. Most popular programming languages have graphical development environments with support for interface design. One popular example is Visual Studio, which has excellent support for C# and Visual Basic. Using these types of tools, and others, the designer then creates a more realistic prototype of the system, with either stubbed functionality or some "Wizard of Oz"* approach (Carroll and Aaronson 1998). In the high-fidelity prototype of the system all controls are functional and do what is expected of them so that it can be used for more extensive testing purposes. It is during this phase of creation that guidelines like the aforementioned heuristics can aid the designer in creating an interface that will be useful and usable. Style guides, system compatibility issues, and other external constraints must be followed and can impact the flexibility of the designer. Considerations such as these serve as input to the design process, and the resulting interface should meet as many of these constraints as possible.

Metaphors

Helping the end user learn and use a new interface requires thought and effort on the part of the interface designer. One highly used technique is the incorporation of metaphors in

---

* *The Wonderful Wizard of Oz* is a children's story by L. Frank Baum. In this story an all-powerful wizard turns out to be a normal man operating some sophisticated machinery behind a curtain. The relevance here is that the designers or testers "fake" the functionality for testing purposes.

the design. A metaphor is the application of a known, often real-world, object and its characteristics to an electronic interface. A classic example is the desktop metaphor used in all major operating system graphical shells (GUIs). Before computers became ubiquitous in the workplace, people sat at desks where all of the tools needed in their work were available within arm's reach. This work environment and management style was "copied" in the creation of the virtual desktop. People now rely on their graphical user interface to access all of the tools they need to get their work done. Learning this environment is straightforward and relatively simple for those familiar with a physical desk.

Other similar metaphors abound in electronic interfaces. Consider e-mail, which consists of a blend of two physical objects that are heavily used in interoffice communications: letters and memos. Most e-mail composition programs provide an interface that includes text entry areas for the recipient, copies, and subject—all requirements for most interoffice memos. E-mail also supports both formal and informal letter writing and copies the idea of sending a letter to someone. The e-mail–memo metaphor is readily understood by newcomers and easily mastered by those who have never dealt with the real-world counterparts: an all-around excellent use of a metaphor to aid the end user in learning and using a software system.

One must be mindful of overusing metaphors. While the benefits include ease of learning and ease of use, overapplication or too literal an application of a metaphor can limit the designer and prevent improvements. Take the classic calculator. A handheld calculator with basic functionality is simple and easy to use. Creating a calculator for use within an operating system is a normal thing, and many users employ the software calculator for various tasks. Figure 9.4 presents a simple software calculator interface.

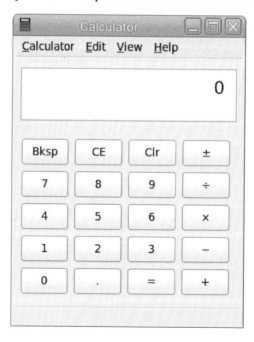

FIGURE 9.4
Simple software calculator.

Notice that the software version looks much like a handheld calculator. This is good for learning how the interface works and what is possible. A novice user can easily use the interface to perform simple calculations. However, the interface is a literal copy of the real-world interface and as such does not provide any extra features that might be expected in software, including selectable history, multiple storage areas (variables), and visualizations (like graphing or showing the equation that yielded the answer). In this case, the designers took the metaphor too far and restricted the utility of the program. Unfortunately, there are no hard-and-fast rules to tell when a designer has taken a metaphor "too far." The only way to discern this information is through beta testing or actual use. People will use a product and indicate functionality they would like to see in the product. Good designers try their best to anticipate that functionality, but that ability comes with experience.

Skill Development 9.3: Metaphors in User Interface Design

Describe three metaphors used on the popular social website Facebook (http://www.facebook.com).

Gestalt Principles

Another set of useful design guidance comes from perceptual psychology. Knowing how the human brain processes information should be high on the list of things with which an interface designer should be familiar. German psychologists described several principles of perception in the 1920s. They used the term *gestalt*, which means "whole," to illustrate how the human brain recognizes and organizes information. Take a moment to examine Figure 9.5. What do you see in the image on the left? Most people would describe it as a plus sign. Very few, if any, would describe it as two symmetric right angles sharing a common point. The image on the right shows the two right angles slightly separated for emphasis.

There are six major gestalt principles: proximity, similarity, closure, area, symmetry, and continuity (Rosson and Carroll 2002). Proximity relies on the fact that objects arranged close together are considered grouped together. Similarity simply means that objects that

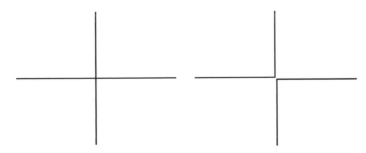

FIGURE 9.5
Illustration of continuity.

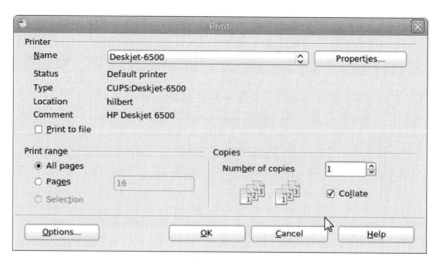

FIGURE 9.6
Common user interface for printer systems.

share visual characteristics (e.g., color, shape) will be considered as a group or as similar in functionality. Closure is the idea that humans try to organize things into closed figures. Area is similar to closure but with the extra emphasis on the fact that humans try to create the figure with the smallest area. Symmetry refers to the fact that humans often treat symmetric elements as part of the same figure or group. Finally, continuity refers to the human predisposition to see continuous contours or patterns.

Skill Development 9.4: Gestalt Principles in User Interface Design

Identify instances of the six gestalt principles in the interface presented in Figure 9.6.

Knowledge of the gestalt principles is useful in and of itself, but knowing how to utilize and capitalize on them for effective interface design requires extensive practice. In addition to the gestalt principles, there are some other useful design guidelines to consider. Consider white space in interface designs. White space is the area in a graphical display with no visual elements. White space becomes very important for helping the end user understand the graphical elements in a display. For example, tabs are often used for alignment purposes, and it is the extra white space between the columns in a tabbed display that allows users to perceive the data as columns, thus allowing them to more readily understand the presented information. Be generous with white space as it directly reinforces several of the gestalt principles. Simultaneously, be very careful about superfluous design elements. Anything extra in an interface that does not provide useful information has the potential to detract from the utility of the interface (Carroll 1990). Consider the interface in the previous skill development. All of the vertical and horizontal lines can be removed from the interface without detracting the utility or communication provided. Be careful about any graphical element. Whenever a graphical element is added to an interface, always ask the question, "Is this necessary?"

Reusing Earlier Designs

Sometimes interface designers do not need to start from scratch. Instead, they have access to similar products or have rough designs given to them. In these types of situations, interface designers are likely to work with designs that do need heavy modification to meet the unique needs of the new system. In such situations, designers need to rely on field studies and other empirical testing to identify areas for improvement. In other words, reusing an existing interface can sometimes reduce the design effort but will usually increase the testing effort.

EVALUATION OF HCI QUALITY

Before systems are deployed, significant efforts must be made to ensure that user interfaces are sufficiently complete, understandable, and efficient for providing users with systems that exhibit high quality in terms of usability. IEEE (1990, p. 80) defines usability as

> The ease with which a user can learn to operate, prepare inputs for, and interpret outputs of a system or component.

Therefore, evaluation of the HCI quality is essential during the design process. Several approaches can be taken when evaluating and minimizing the degree of complexity involved when learning or using the system, including usability testing, analytic testing, and empirical testing.

Usability Testing

At this point during the interface design process there should be some usable prototype of the interface that can be used for testing purposes. It is beneficial to understand testing and how to go about doing it. First, it should be noted that there are two classes of evaluation (Scriven 1967):

- Formative
- Summative

Formative evaluation occurs within the design process and focuses on alternatives and clarification. Summative evaluation occurs "after" the design process and focuses on assessing the result. Formative evaluation should be heavily utilized throughout the interface design process, iteratively improving the design. Summative evaluation should be utilized when a solid version of the interface is completed. (Note: this does not mean after the design is complete but rather when a version of the interface is considered ready for testing.) An easy way to distinguish between formative and summative evaluation is that formative evaluation is like the cook tasting the soup and summative evaluation is like the customer tasting the soup.

There are two main methods of user interface testing: analytic and empiric (Scriven 1967). Each can be used for both formative and summative evaluations. Analytic testing involves domain or usability experts analyzing an interface for design issues. Empirical testing (also known as user testing) involves representative end users performing realistic tasks with the interface. Each type of test reveals different information to the interface designer, and ideally both should be utilized in a mediated evaluation (Scriven 1967).

Analytic Testing

Analytic testing is often used earlier in the development process than empirical testing. The reason for this is that early in the interface design process there is usually no working system with which to test end users. Instead there are low- or high-fidelity prototypes. These prototypes can be examined by knowledgeable experts for compliance with, for example, design guidelines, style guides, and compatibility guides. The key result of an analytic evaluation is a subjective opinion about the interface. Multiple specific tests fall under the analytic umbrella: usability inspections, heuristic evaluations, and cognitive walkthroughs. Usability inspections are simply experts using the prototype in intended ways while ensuring usability guidelines are followed. Often these types of inspections have checklists or other guidelines (e.g., style guides) that are noted by evaluators. The end result is often a list of usability issues identified and sometimes rated by severity (how much an impact the issue might have on end users' ability to complete their task). Cognitive walkthroughs are an example of a usability inspection. In this specific type of inspection, experts are given a script to work through in an interface while looking for violations of usability guidelines and standards while assessing the interface for visual cues (Lewis, Polson, Wharton, and Rieman 1990). The goal is to identify aspects of the interface that detract from users' ability to complete their tasks with the system and to identify missing information that could be useful. The result of a cognitive walkthrough is a detailed listing of good and bad aspects of interfaces with respect to specific tasks.

Heuristic evaluation is similar to usability inspection whereas it involves multiple experts reviewing an interface with respect to a list of heuristics (see Nielsen's heuristics described earlier; Nielsen and Mack 1994). The difference is that the evaluator may be a representative stakeholder (e.g., developer, end user). Again, the result is a list of problems identified in the interface. These can be rated by severity. The interesting thing to note about this approach is the utility it brings. A few (3–5) experts can find about 80% of the usability issues in an interface with this method (Nielsen and Molich 1990). However, heuristic evaluation and all analytic methods suffer a major weakness: the results are mainly the opinion (albeit educated) of evaluators. Whether an identified issue will negatively impact real users of the system is unknown without further testing. This type of data is subjective and often holds less weight than objective data.

Empirical Testing

The opposite of subjective data is objective data, or empirical data. This type of data is highly respected because it is hard to argue about—it is factual data about the system of interest. Empirical testing provides this type of data to the designers. Unfortunately, empirical testing is difficult and expensive. Why? It costs time and money to set up and execute a good empirical study. Costs revolve around securing space, development time (of the tests), hiring participants, data collection, analysis, and reporting. Nonetheless, empirical testing is highly respected and should be utilized in the interface design process.

Many types of empirical testing can be used for interface evaluation: field studies, lab based experiments, and user surveys. The recorded data can vary from observations of use to survey responses to measured data from lab-based experiments. This data is objective, and the data itself is unquestionable. The issue with empirical data is the interpretation of the data and the validity of the setting from which the data came.

Field studies involve designers or design teams going into the field and observing the end users in their current work environment. Observations of work practices, data flow, and communication channels can provide insight for what to include in user interfaces. The raw data from a field study is typically not as useful as the analysis of the data through categorization or content classification (higher-level issues that caused the observed behavior). A major drawback of field studies is the cost involved. Significant time (and thus money) would need to be invested to fully understand the existing work environment. On projects with tight schedules, this type of evaluation may not be feasible. It is useful to note that field studies are highly useful for formative evaluations.

Lab-based studies are highly useful in usability evaluation (whether formative or summative). Often the prohibitive cost of doing field work implies testing should be done in a computer lab. In this situation the designers work with testers to create a testing environment with which to isolate and study specific aspects of an interface. Participants are brought into the lab environment and asked to perform the required tasks. In these settings, excellent data on usage can be collected. The major issue with lab-based studies comes from validity. Validity refers to how realistic the experiment happens to be—how well does the testing situation model the real-world situation? Are the participants representative of the real end users? Did the participants used in the test have more knowledge of this type of system than the average user? Would the participants be more distracted in their normal work environment? All of these questions and others take away from the utility of the data that comes from a lab-based study. Controlling for validity is difficult and time-consuming. Results should always be considered in light of any validity issues.

A specific type of lab-based study is the controlled experiment. If a specific design choice needs to be validated through experimental means, one can design an experiment to objectively determine the performance of competing options. Suppose a design team wants to determine which color scheme to use for a system display. The choices have been narrowed to black text on a white background or white text on a black background. Before determining the best approach, a criteria for evaluation needs to be in place. In other words, what does "best approach" mean? Does it mean faster reading times, higher reading comprehension, or less eye strain? We could actually study all three with a single experiment. In this situation, the read time, reading comprehension, and eye strain would be the dependent variables. The values obtained from the test participants are dependent upon the color scheme. This means that the color scheme is the independent variable, in this case with two levels: black on white and white on black.

There are many ways to design the actual experimental setting for this test. We could use a between-subjects design and have two separate sets of participants work with each level of the independent variable. Or we could use a within-subjects design and have the same groups of people read text with both color schemes. The latter choice would imply the need for two different sets of text, so that a person who reads a passage in white on black would not read the same passage in black on white but a different passage. We would need to account for the passage used in a within-subjects test because reading one passage before the other might influence the speed of reading or comprehension. We would also need to vary the order of the presentation of the white-on-black, black-on-white conditions: half of the participants would start with white on black first; the other half would start with black on white first. In all cases, we need to be concerned with the number of participants for our test. A good rule-of-thumb is 10 participants per condition (Scriven 1967). For our experimental setup (two levels of the independent variable and two passages to read) we would need $2 \times 2 \times 10 = 40$ participants. It should be clear that a within-subjects test requires more participants (if there are more conditions). Within-subjects tests are often more highly regarded with respect to the findings. The reason is that individual variability in the participants can be controlled for in a within-subjects test.

Skill Development 9.5: Designing Experiments for Empirical Testing

Design a between-subjects and a within-subjects experimental setup for determining whether direct entry or a drop-down list would provide faster input times for dates in a database form. In the direct-entry condition, invalid date formats are errors and cost an extra 3 seconds to correct. Identify the dependent and independent variables. Determine the number of participants required for each type of test (assume a minimal of 10 participants per condition).

Another way to gather empirical data is through user surveys. These can be stand-alone surveys or part of a lab-based experiment. The goal is to have end users comment on the system and their experiences. This type of data can be useful in identifying high-level usability issues as well as provide insight into how users will perform with the system. Depending on the type of data, it can be analyzed using statistical methods for concrete evidence for specific design choices. Often, survey results are used for categorization of the participants and aid in interpreting results.

CHAPTER SUMMARY

This chapter has provided high-level guidance for completing the human–computer interface design phase within system design. The main focus is users. It is the duty of the designer to keep users and their interests as the focus of the interface. The application of design guidelines, perceptual psychology, and sound scientific method are all used to provide and justify concrete interface designs that meet the needs of the users. It is on the shoulders of the designer to make sure the system is going to be easy to use, easy to learn, and enjoyable for the end user. Balancing these fundamental requirements with the various system requirements and functional constraints is the core of the interface designer's challenge.

REVIEW QUESTIONS

1. What is human–computer interface design?
2. What are the steps in the HCI design phase?
3. Why is the focus on the user so important to successful interface design?
4. What is a metaphor with regards to interface design?
5. What are the gestalt principles?
6. Why is white space so important?
7. What are the two major types of evaluations?
8. What are the two major evaluation methods?
9. Why are analytic methods typically cheaper and faster and empirical methods?
10. What is the difference between a between-subjects design and a within-subjects design?

CHAPTER EXERCISES

1. Using presentation software (e.g., PowerPoint, Impress), create a high-fidelity prototype of the ticket purchasing kiosk described in Skill Development 7.2. Fake the functionality by linking to different slides in your prototype.
2. Repeat Exercise 1 using a high-level graphical language (e.g., Visual Basic, Visual C#).
3. Analyze your favorite e-mail client with regards to Nielsen's 10 heuristics. Create a list of usability issues and rank them by severity.

4. Walk through the process of creating and sending an e-mail in your favorite e-mail client. Identify gestalt principles that are in use in the system. Identify improvements that could be made through the application of gestalt principles.

5. A common metaphor used for online shopping is the idea of a shopping cart. Thoroughly discuss the usage of this metaphor for your favorite online shopping system. Focus on how the similarities to the real world enhance the experience and how the differences detract from the experience.

6. Look up discount usability evaluation. Describe the process and identify whether it is more useful for formative or summative evaluation.

REFERENCES

Carroll, J. M. *The Nurnberg Funnell: Designing Minimalist Instruction for Practical Computer Skill.* Cambridge, MA: MIT Press, 1990.

Carroll, J. M., and P. Aaronson. "Learning by Doing with Simulated Intelligent Help." *Communications of the Association for Computing Machinery,* 1998: 1064–1079.

Hix, D., and H. R. Hartson. *Developing User Interfaces: Ensuring Usability Through Product & Process.* New York: John Wiley & Sons, 1993.

IEEE. "IEEE Standard Glossary of Software Engineering Terminology." 1990. http://ieeexplore.ieee.org/xpl/freeabs_all.jsp?arnumber=159342.

Lewis, C., P. Polson, C. Wharton, and J. Rieman. "Testing a Walkthrough Methodology for Theory-Based Design of Walk-Up-and-Use Interfaces." *Chi '90 Proceedings,* 1990, 235–242.

McCrickard, D. S., C. M. Chewar, and J. Somervell. "Design, Science, and Engineering Topics? Teaching HCI with a Unified Method." *Technical Symposium on Computer Science Education (SigCSE'04).* Norfolk, VA, 2004, 31–35.

Nielsen, J., and R. L. Mack. *Usability Inspection Methods.* New York: John Wiley & Sons, 1994.

Nielsen, J., and R. Molich. "Heuristic Evaluation of User Interfaces." *Proc. ACM CHI'90 Conference,* Seattle, 1990, 249–256.

Rosson, M. B., and J. M. Carroll. *Usability Engineering: Scenario-Based Development of Human–Computer Interaction.* San Franciso: Morgan Kaufmann, 2002.

Scriven, M. *The Methodology of Evaluation in Perspectives of Curriculum Evaluation.* Chicago, IL: Rand McNally, 1967.

Somervell, J., and D. S. McCrickard. "Better Discount Evaluation: Illustrating How Critical Parameters Support Heuristic Creation." *Interacting with Computers: Special Issue on Social Impact of Emerging Technologies* 17, no. 5 (September 2005): 592–612.

Virzi, R. A., J. L. Sokolov, and D. Karis. "Usability Problem Identification Using both Low- and High-Fidelity Prototypes." *Proceedings of ACM CHI '96,* British Columbia, Canada, 1996, 236–243.

10

Software Design Management, Leadership, and Ethics

Luis Daniel Otero
Florida Institute of Technology

CHAPTER OBJECTIVES

- Understand the definition and importance of software design management
- Describe various techniques to manage the software design phase
- Describe leadership in the context of design management
- Describe relevant ethics items from the software engineering code of ethics

CONCEPTUAL OVERVIEW

Software design is an essential phase of the software engineering life cycle. Conceptually, design is the process of transforming functional and nonfunctional requirements into models that describe a technical solution. This transformation process can be viewed as a complex decision problem that must be managed to ensure an effective use of resources to deliver quality products that meet requirements. It is regarded as a decision problem since there are many ways to design a software system, and software engineers must make design decisions to achieve the required goals of the software system in the most effective manner. Obviously, quality must be considered at every step of the design phase. The idea is that proper design efforts are expected to minimize the complexity of subsequent phases in the life cycle as well as the impact of requirements changes on the overall cost and schedule.

The objective of this chapter is to describe three major elements that are critical for the success of any major design project: management, leadership, and ethics. It is not intended to be a complete tutorial on any of these three elements. Instead, the chapter develops a design management framework that describes important concepts related to each element with the hope of facilitating the successful management of this complex phase. For this purpose, the chapter begins by describing the software design phase as a complex task that must be managed to achieve acceptable quality levels. Various project management techniques to monitor and control the resources that are responsible for the completion of design tasks are presented. The chapter then describes the relationship between management and leadership and highlights several leadership traits that are important for successful results. Finally, the chapter presents various ethic items from the Software Engineering Code of Ethics that are relevant to software design projects.

WHAT IS SOFTWARE DESIGN MANAGEMENT?

Griffin (2010, p. 5) defines management as "a set of activities—including planning and decision making, organizing, leading, and controlling—directed at an organization's resources (i.e. human, financial, physical, and information), with the aim of achieving organizational goals in an efficient and effective manner." Management plays a big role in software engineering projects. In the design phase, management refers to a set of activities required to efficiently create quality design artifacts, within schedule and budget constraints. This definition encompasses a broad set of activities that are particular to specific organizations. However, at the core of every organization's management activities, quality is a focal point.

WHY STUDY DESIGN MANAGEMENT?

In large-scale software projects, software design management is essential to plan, organize, staff, track, and lead the activities required to carry out successfully the software architecture and detailed design steps. Key to the success of software design management is an effective use of resources to achieve the various goals set forth for each main component in the design phase (i.e., software architecture, detailed design, and documentation). Therefore, software design management is needed to control/monitor the processes and resources necessary for completing quality design artifacts according to organizational goals.

THE CONCEPT OF QUALITY

Quality is a term that can be loosely defined as a performance measure for a service provided or a product produced, and it is relative to a particular stakeholder. For example, a personal website can be classified as high quality by the programmer that developed it and as low quality by user clients. That is, two stakeholders of the software system have different opinions regarding the quality of the product produced. Why? Because both of these stakeholders have different parameters by which they measure quality. For example, the programmer may perceive quality in terms of being able to use appropriate colors and organize the website to run on a particular web browser. On the other hand, a client using a different web browser may not see the website's organization and colors as intended, thus perceiving the website's quality as poor. Similarly, the quality of a software design can be assessed in various ways. However, from a management perspective, quality of software design tends to be evaluated in terms of cost and scheduling. Therefore, this chapter focuses on various project management techniques that can be used to keep the design artifacts within cost and schedule thresholds.

DESIGN MANAGEMENT FRAMEWORK

To efficiently and effectively manage the software design activities of a project, it is beneficial to view the design phase as a project itself. The managerial benefit of this approach is that project management techniques can be directly applied to the design phase. For example, the life cycle of the design phase can be represented with three stages similar to Figure 10.1. This life cycle represents a typical project pattern where contributions to a project's completion are relatively small during the initial and termination phases and significantly high during the implementation phase. Defining a life cycle structure for a project helps to decompose the project into its appropriate stages, where each stage can be managed individually.

There are two main objectives associated with the initial stage. The first objective is to achieve a clear understanding of the tasks to be accomplished and the resources that are necessary to successfully complete the tasks. The second main objective is to develop a plan to complete the project's tasks within schedule and budget constraints. Thus, the initial phase is

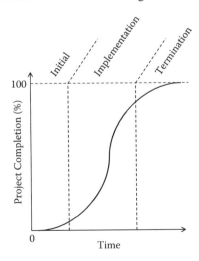

FIGURE 10.1
Project life cycle.

characterized by planning activities. Although some of the artifacts resulting from this phase (e.g., schedule) may be deliverables to clients, this phase is not viewed as contributing significantly to the percentage project completion. The implementation stage, on the other hand, is where most of the effort is employed and where most of the design project deliverables are achieved, including completed design documents. Therefore, the percent project completion is the highest during this stage. In the termination stage, key activities involve verification that everything is in place for a smooth transition into the code construction phase. Activities include, for example, making sure that the latest versions of the design documents are securely stored according to configuration management procedures, updating schedule and cost current values, reevaluating schedule and budget plans based on the resulting performance measures of the design phase, and communicating results to upper management. The design documents generated in this stage are critical for the robustness and maintainability of the software designed. However, the relative impact of this stage to project completion is not viewed as significant as that of the implementation phase. The key is that *each of these phases must be individually managed to ensure that all phases meet acceptable levels of quality and performance measures.* For example, an important outcome of the planning stage is a clear understanding of the tasks to be accomplished and the resources that are necessary to successfully complete the tasks. Various project management techniques exist to help achieve this outcome. Therefore, it is important to know how to apply these project management techniques to your particular design project, and go through a peer-review process* to ensure that the objectives of the planning stage are achieved. Performance measures in the planning stage are thoroughness (everything is considered), completeness (complete definition of plans), and accuracy of estimates. In the execution/implementation stage, quality is a function of a series of technical attributes of software designs. Managing during this stage is mainly a monitoring approach to make sure that the plan is being followed and to take corrective actions if necessary. Important factors that affect the effectiveness of managing these phases are leadership and good ethical conduct. Therefore, a design management framework composed of the following four main areas is proposed:

- Planning
- Execution/implementation
- Termination
- Leadership and ethics

PLANNING DESIGN EFFORTS

The planning stage is critical to the success of any major project. In a holistic view, planning exists to lay out a strong foundation for a successful project by clearly specifying the

---

* Peer reviews must be conducted throughout these stages to minimize the propagation of errors to subsequent stages and apply corrective actions.

tasks that must be completed, resources in terms of personnel skills required to complete each task and any hardware and software required, the durations of tasks, and the specific points within the project's life cycle phases where resources will be needed. Basically, planning establishes the directions to follow to complete the project and improve its probability of success. It is intended to facilitate future project accomplishments. The key functions in the project planning stage are *scoping* and *organizing*.

Scoping

Project scoping is the first key function of the planning stage. It involves two main activities: identify the tasks and develop the budget. The idea is to follow the divide and conquer paradigm to utilize a mechanism for identifying lower-level assignable activities that need to be completed. Then, expected costs for each activity are estimated to develop the budget. Two commonly used techniques for project scoping are the work breakdown function (WBS) and budgeting.

Work Breakdown Structure

In the project management point of view, a project begins as a statement of work (SOW), which mainly consists as the set of main objectives to be achieved. The SOW is decomposed into *tasks* where these tasks are decomposed into *subtasks* and subtasks into *work packages*. A management technique to represent, either graphically or in list format, a project modularized into task activities is called WBS. Also known as *hierarchical planning*, the WBS is a simple but powerful technique that helps to plan, clearly define, and organize the activities related to reach specific milestones and complete a project. Milestones are defined as specific events to be reached at specific points in time. For example, obtaining budget and schedule approvals for a project are typically considered important project milestones. Given that the major artifacts in the design phase are the main components of the design process, these are considered the main milestones. That is, the completion of the architecture design, detailed design, and documentation constitute the main project milestones of a design project. Therefore, the objective of a WBS in the design phase is to establish the work elements for each of these major milestones.

   Table 10.1 shows an example of a WBS for the design of a software application. This figure shows the managerial levels for each component. The top level is the design project itself. This level represents the overall objective to be achieved, which is to successfully complete the design phase. Then, this top level is decomposed into the three main milestones of the design phase, which are the development of architectural and detailed designs, and the completion of the design document. These tasks are direct sublevels of the design project; therefore they are labeled 1.1, 1.2, and 1.3. Each task is then decomposed into appropriate subtasks. For the architectural design task, two subtasks were identified: evaluation of alternative designs and selection of the final architectural design. Since these are sublevels of the architectural design task, they are labeled 1.1.1 and 1.1.2. Each of these subtasks is decomposed into appropriate work packages. For example, the evaluation of

TABLE 10.1

Example of a WBS for a Design Project

Outline Number	Task Name
1	Design project
1.1	Architectural design
1.1.1	Evaluate alternative designs
1.1.1.1	Prioritize objectives
1.1.1.2	Formal review of evaluations
1.1.2	Select architectural design
1.1.2.1	Make initial selection
1.1.2.2	Formal review to select final design
1.2	Detailed design
1.2.1	Evaluate alternatives
1.2.2	Select among alternatives
1.3	Documentation
1.3.1	Write architectural design documentation
1.3.2	Formal review (architecture design)
1.3.3	Final architectural design document
1.3.4	Write detailed design documentation
1.3.5	Formal review (detailed design)
1.3.6	Final architectural design document

alternative architecture designs was decomposed into prioritizing objectives and conducting formal evaluation peer reviews. Consequently, these two work packages were labeled as the four-level activities 1.1.1.1 and 1.1.1.2.

Evaluating the usefulness of a WBS is often more a matter of subjective assessments than not. We can define three criteria for this evaluation. The first criterion is called *scope accuracy*. That is, we need to agree that the WBS serves its overall objective of being a breakdown of the project into tasks, and nothing else. A WBS does not contain information regarding tasks' relationships such as task precedence or task durations, and it does not include personnel skills required for the completion of tasks. Instead, each element of a WBS represents an activity that consumes resources' time and effort. This brings us to the second criteria, *completeness*. The purpose of this evaluation criterion is to ensure that the WBS includes the complete set of tasks necessary to complete the project. The third criterion is *level of detail*. This criterion evaluates if the WBS breaks down the project's tasks into appropriate levels such that it facilitates the estimation of effort for each task.

Budgeting

Budgeting is the process of estimating the cost of a project. It is basically a forecasting problem, since cost is a function of various parameters that are uncertain, such as the number of resources required throughout the project, their cost, hardware and software equipment, inflation changes, and requirement changes. The accuracy of a budget is a function of the uncertainty of these individual cost parameters. For example, a budget for the construction of a house is expected to be more accurate than the budget for developing a complex software application. For the project of constructing a house, planners often have a very good idea of the resources that are needed, cost of permits, and so forth. For the software project, it becomes a more challenging task due to the level of uncertainty in key elements such as the number of software lines of code that it would take to develop the application, the number of software engineers required, and unknown learning curves for newer technology, to name a few. Compared with the house construction project, the typical error size for the estimation of cost parameters in software projects is much higher. Due to these uncertainties, monitoring and controlling activities must be enforced throughout the course of the project to determine any deviations from the plan (i.e., budget), and study the causes of these deviations (monitoring and control mechanisms will be discussed later in the chapter). As such, the budget serves as a baseline to compare differences between actual and estimated costs at any point in the life of a project.

Conceptually, a common strategy to develop a budget is to simply cost each element in the WBS. To accomplish this, elements are associated with *direct* and *indirect costs*. Direct costs are those that can be directly tied to the development of the design. The most often used direct costs are labor and equipment (i.e., hardware and software equipment). Indirect costs, on the other hand, include costs such as fringe benefits and administrative expenses.

One of the most significant and hard-to-estimate direct costs for each task is the cost of the staff that will be directly working on the completion of the task. The level of difficulty in developing accurate cost estimates related to task durations is a function of the complexity of the design project itself. Given that software projects are typically custom-made solutions to particular problems, tasks are considered nonrepetitive and often involve *learning rates*. This is particularly true for tasks that involve new technologies or the use of skills that the staff is unfamiliar with. Therefore, it is important to account for learning rates in the budgeting process.

It is important to understand that developing accurate budgets for design projects is often very difficult due to the complexity of the projects. Data from previous similar projects, as well as input from experienced personnel, are used as resources to prepare budgets. After the budget for a project is created and approved, it becomes more of a control mechanism for managers because it establishes the cost threshold for the entire project.

Organizing

Organizing is the second key function of the planning stage. It involves two main activities: responsibility assignments and scheduling. That is, after identifying and organizing the tasks in the scoping function with the WBS, the organizing function conducts task assignments, establishes task durations, and identifies any predecessors[*] for each task. Task durations are critical because they are an integral part of the monitoring and controlling mechanisms in the implementation stage. The next subsections describe various project management tools that are applicable for the organizing function.

---

[*] A predecessor is a task that must be completed before another task can begin.

Linear Responsibility Chart

An important outcome of the planning stage is to have a clear understanding of the roles that each staff member plays in the process of completing each element of the WBS. This can be viewed as a plan for task assignments. The goal here is to clearly identify the staff members that will be mainly responsible for each task and those that will serve as reviewers or support the task in any way. A project management tool that allows such outcome is called a *linear responsibility chart (LRC)*, which is a tabular representation of task assignments.

Table 10.2 shows an example of an LRC for a particular design project. This table clearly shows the staff members that are mainly responsible for each of the tasks and those that will be supporting the tasks in any way or acting as reviewers. Other than clearly establishing the responsibilities of each team member, having a clear understanding of task assignments is important for scheduling purposes. For example, finding skilled personnel to act as reviewers for a particular artifact (e.g., detailed design) later in the project's life cycle can become a challenging task because employees get regularly reassigned to new tasks. Therefore, it is beneficial to establish their roles with the design project early in the planning stage to minimize the probability of not having adequate reviewers and the chance of overrunning the schedule or compromising quality standards.

Scheduling with Gantt Charts and Network Diagrams

After task assignments, a key activity in the planning stage is *scheduling*. A basic function of the scheduling process is to determine task relationships in order to convert the WBS into an operating timetable. Scheduling helps to identify the critical project activities that cannot be delayed without delaying the overall project duration as well as those that will not affect the overall project duration if delayed. Furthermore, scheduling allows tasks to be ordered so that, for each task, preceding and subsequent tasks are easily identified.

Various project management techniques are used in scheduling. Two of the most common ones are Gantt charts and network diagrams. They are basically graphical representations of the logical flow between tasks (i.e., activities) and their durations. The Gantt chart technique is very simple to follow. Because of its simplicity, this approach is often used to show schedule and progress as well as to serve as a control and monitoring mechanism. The three basic parameters needed for a Gantt chart are tasks, their durations, and their predecessors and successors. These parameters are used to develop a graph that depicts the durations of tasks and their relationship. For example, consider a snapshot of a Gantt chart presented in Figure 10.2 from the Microsoft Project software package. The left-hand side of this figure shows the list of tasks from a WBS with expected duration, start date, and finish date. It also shows any predecessor for each task. For example, the predecessor to evaluate detailed design alternatives (WBS #1.2.1) is to have selected a final architectural design (WBS #1.1.2.2). On the right-hand side, we can see the actual Gantt chart showing predecessors of tasks and their durations. We can see, for example, that the documentation for the architectural design can be started as soon as the architectural design passes a formal review and the detailed design is ready to begin.

TABLE 10.2

Example of a Linear Responsibility Chart

Outline #	Task Name	Staff_1	Staff_2	Staff_3	Staff_4	Staff_5
1	Design project					
1.1	Architectural design	1	2			3
1.1.1	Evaluate alternative designs	1	2			
1.1.1.1	Prioritize objectives	1	2			
1.1.1.2	Formal review of evaluations			1	3	3
1.1.2	Select architectural design	1				
1.1.2.1	Make initial selection	1				
1.1.2.2	Formal review to select final design	1		2	3	3
1.2	Detailed design				1	3
1.2.1	Evaluate alternatives			2	1	
11.2.2	Select among alternatives			2	1	3
1.3	Documentation					
1.3.1	Write architectural design documentation	1	2			
1.3.2	Formal review (architecture design)	1			3	3
1.3.3	Final architectural design document	1		3		
1.3.4	Write detailed design documentation	2			1	3
1.3.5	Formal review (detailed design)	2			1	3
1.3.6	Final detailed design document			3	1	3

Legend:
1 = Primary responsibility
2 = Support development role
3 = Review role

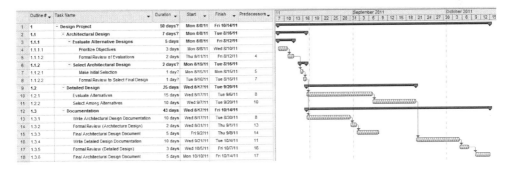

FIGURE 10.2
Snapshot of Gantt chart from Microsoft project.

Similar to Gantt charts, network diagrams are also graphical representations of logical flow among tasks, describe task durations, and need the same three basic parameters: tasks, their durations, and their predecessors and successors. Moreover, network diagrams are used to show additional important information such as *critical paths, earliest* and *latest completion times,* and *slack times.* We will use information from the WBS from Table 10.1 to explain the activity-on-node (AON) network diagram technique. First, we need estimates for task durations. Estimating accurate task durations is often a very complex endeavor. One common approach is to estimate minimum, maximum, and most likely duration

TABLE 10.3

Task Durations for the Three-Level Tasks Described in the WBS

	Time (Days)					
Outline #	Minimum (*a*)	Most Likely (*m*)	Maximum (*b*)	Immediate Predecessors	Expected Time (*ET*)	Variance (σ^2)
1.1.1	3	5	13	—	6	2.78
1.1.2	1	2	9	1.1.1	3	1.78
1.2.1	8	15	22	1.1.2	15	5.44
1.2.2	5	10	21	1.2.1	11	7.11
1.3.1	5	10	21	1.1.2	11	7.11
1.3.2	1	2	9	1.3.1	3	1.78
1.3.3	3	5	13	1.3.2	6	2.78
1.3.4	5	10	21	1.2.2; 1.3.3	11	7.11
1.3.5	1	2	9	1.3.4	3	1.78
1.3.6	3	5	13	1.3.5	6	2.78

times. Table 10.3 gives an example of task durations for the three-level tasks described in the WBS. For each task, this table shows an estimated minimum duration, *a*, a most likely duration, *m*, and a maximum duration, *b*. These three parameters are used to calculate the expected time, *ET*, of each task. *ET* durations are calculated using the beta distribution[*] with Equation (10.1) because of its simplicity and flexibility. A key benefit for having three estimates for task durations is that we can use them to develop variance calculations, which can then be used to estimate the probability of completing the project within a specific time. The variance of the duration of a task is calculated using Equation (10.2).

$$\text{Expected Time} = \frac{a + 4m + b}{6} \tag{10.1}$$

$$\text{Variance} = \left(\frac{b-a}{6}\right)^2 \tag{10.2}$$

Figure 10.3a shows the resulting network diagram from the information described in Table 10.3. Notice the inclusion of start and end nodes. These two extra nodes are included to make the network easier to follow. The network diagram clearly shows the predecessors for each.

After estimating task durations and variances, the next step is to calculate the critical path. A path is any combination of nodes from the start node to the last node. For example, our network diagram shows the following two paths:

- Path 1: (1.1.1) – (1.1.2) – (1.2.1) – (1.2.2) – (1.3.4) – (1.3.5) – (1.3.6)
- Path 2: (1.1.1) – (1.1.2) – (1.3.1) – (1.3.2) – (1.3.3) – (1.3.4) – (1.3.5) – (1.3.6)

Using the expected times from Table 10.3, the expected duration of the first path is 55 days. The expected duration of the second path is 46 days. The critical path is the one with

---

[*] For a refresher on elementary statistics, please refer to books such as Pelosi and Sandifer (2003).

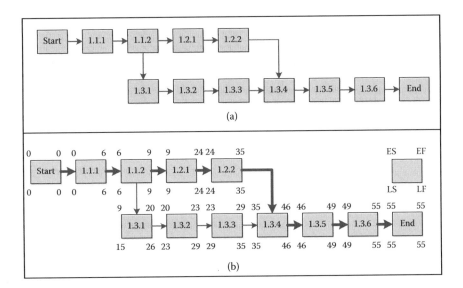

FIGURE 10.3
AON network diagram.

the longest duration; hence, the critical path for this problem is Path 1. The critical path is shown in Figure 10.3b with heavy lines. Identifying the critical path of a project is important because it pinpoints the activities that cannot be delayed without delaying the entire project. That is, if any of the activities along the critical path get delayed, the entire project will be delayed. Identifying the critical path also marks the activities that can be delayed without affecting the project duration. These activities are the ones outside of the critical path.

After calculating the critical path, the next step is to calculate earliest and latest times for activities to start and finish. That is, we need to calculate the earliest time that we can begin each activity and the earliest time that the activity can be completed. We denote these terms as *earliest start (ES)* and *earliest finish (EF)* times. Similarly, we calculate the latest time that we can begin each activity and the latest time that the activity can be completed. We denote these terms as *latest start (LS)* and *latest finish (LF)* times. The difference between the LS and ES of an activity is called the *slack time* for the activity. Because activities along the critical path cannot be delayed without delaying the entire project's duration, only noncritical path activities can have slack times.

To calculate earliest times, we move from the start node to the other nodes. Logically, the first activity (i.e., node 1.1.1) begins at time 0. Therefore, the ES for activity 1.1.1 is 0, and its EF time is its expected time duration (6 days). Any immediate subsequent activity can start as early as activity 1.1.1 ends. Therefore, the ES of activity 1.1.2 is 6 days, and its EF is 9 days, which is the sum of its ES and expected time duration. Similarly, the ES of activity 1.3.1 is 9 days, and its EF is 20 days. In cases where an activity has more than one predecessor, the largest EF time of the predecessors becomes the ES time of the activity. For example, activity 1.3.4 has two predecessors: 1.2.2 (with an EF time of 35 days) and 1.3.3 (with an EF time of 29 days). Since activity 1.3.4 can be started only when both of its predecessors are complete, its earliest possible start time is 35 days.

To calculate latest times, we move from the last node to the start node. The LF time for activities in the critical path is the same as their EF times. Similarly, the LS time for critical activities is the same as their ES. For noncritical activities such as 1.3.3, this is not the case. If this activity finishes at its EF time of 29 days, activity 1.3.4 (i.e., its successor) will still be unable to start because it needs to wait for activity 1.2.2 to finish at day 35. Therefore, activity 1.3.3 can actually finish as late as day 35 and not affect the critical path duration of the project. Consequently, the LF time for activity 1.3.3 is 35 days, and its LS time is 29 days, which is its LF minus its expected time duration of 6 days. Activity 1.3.2 can finish as late as the LF time of its successor 1.3.3. Therefore, its LF time is 29 days, and its LS time is 26 days. When the earliest and latest times for each activity are completed, it can be easily seen that only the noncritical activities (i.e., 1.3.1, 1.3.2, and 1.3.3) have slack times. The total allowable slack time for these activities is 6 days. This means that, for example, if a slack time of 5 days is used in activity 1.3.1, then only one of the remaining noncritical activities can be delayed by 1 day. If, for example, a slack time of 6 days is used in activity 1.3.1, then the network will have two critical paths. This means that in this case noncritical activities 1.3.2 and 1.3.3 will become critical activities (i.e., no slack times).

Probability of Time to Completion

In our network diagram example from the previous section, expected task durations were calculated based on estimates of minimum, average, and maximum durations using the beta distribution. The other obvious option is to overlook these three parameters and estimate a single average task duration instead. This option tends to be troublesome for decision makers since it does not explicitly consider a range of possibilities (e.g., max/min values), and accurate estimates of task durations with a single parameter seem unlikely. Consequently, setting values for these three parameters—instead of one estimate—alleviates the estimation process for decision makers. Another benefit from using these three parameters is that we can use them to develop variance calculations and then use the variances to estimate the probability of completing the project within a specific time.

To estimate the probability of completing a project by a particular time period, we use the *cumulative standard normal distribution* to obtain Z-values.[*] The standard normal distribution is a normal distribution with a mean equal to zero and a standard deviation equal to one. A Z-value represents the number of standard deviations from the mean (either to the right or to the left of the mean) of the standard normal distribution.

The critical path contains the activities that establish the duration of a project. We basically use the expected completion times of the critical activities and their variances to determine the probability of completing the critical path activities by a deadline. Before we continue, it is worth mentioning that there is an assumption that must be made when using the standard normal distribution to make our probability estimates. The assumption is that the durations of each activity in the critical path are statistically independent of each other. In other words, they must be independent random variables. This allows us

---

[*] Again, for a refresher on elementary statistics, please refer to books such as Pelosi and Sandifer (2003).

to invoke the *central limit theorem* (CLT) to find the mean and standard deviation of the project duration, which is basically the sum of each activity in the critical path. The CLT says that the sum of independent and identically distributed (iid) random variables forms a normal distribution as the number of random variables increases. In our case, we treat the project duration as the sum of the critical path activities (i.e., iid random variables); therefore, by virtue of the CLT, we can assume that the project duration is normally distributed. Armed with the CLT, we can use the standard normal distribution to make estimates about the probability of completing the project by a certain time.

First, we need to transform (sometimes called "normalize") the estimated project duration time into a Z-value using Equation 10.3

$$Z = \frac{D - EPT}{\sqrt{\sigma_{EPT}^2}} \qquad (10.3)$$

where

Z = the number of standard deviations of a standard normal distribution
D = the desired completion time (usually in days) of a project
EPT = expected project completion time (this is the critical path duration)
σ_{EPT}^2 = the variance of the critical path

Regarding the variance parameter (and refreshing some statistics concepts), if the random variables in a set are independent of each other, then the sum of the variances of the individual random variables equals the variance of the entire set. Since we assume that the critical path activities are independent of each other, the sum of their variances corresponds to the variance of the expected project duration.

After calculating the Z-value, we find the probability of completing the project by a certain time using a cumulative normal distribution table similar to the one found in Table 10.4. In this table we can find the probability associated with a Z-value. For example, assume that a design project has an expected critical path duration of 75 days, with a critical path variance of 36 days. We would like to know the probability of completing the project in 85 days. Using Equation (10.3), we calculate a Z-value of 1.67. Then, we go to Table 10.4 and find the probability to be 0.9525 (go down the left column until 1.6, then across to the right until column 0.07). This means that there is a 95.25 percent probability of finishing the design project in 85 days, given the variance in the expected project duration time.

Skill Development 10.1: Negative Z-Value

Assume that a design project has an expected critical path duration of 75 days, with a critical path variance of 36 days. We would like to know the probability of completing the project in 65 days. As you will see, the resulting Z-value will be a negative number. How do you get its associated probability from Table 10.4, which gives you only positive Z-values? *Hint*: Remember that the standard normal distribution has a symmetrical shape around the mean and that its area under the entire bell-shape curve equals 1.

TABLE 10.4

Probabilities of the Cumulative Standard Normal Distribution

Z	0.00	0.01	0.02	0.03	0.04	0.05	0.06	0.07	0.08	0.09
0.0	0.5000	0.5040	0.5080	0.5120	0.5160	0.5199	0.5239	0.5279	0.5319	0.5359
0.1	0.5398	0.5438	0.5478	0.5517	0.5557	0.5596	0.5636	0.5675	0.5714	0.5754
0.2	0.5793	0.5832	0.5871	0.5910	0.5948	0.5987	0.6026	0.6064	0.6103	0.6141
0.3	0.6179	0.6217	0.6255	0.6293	0.6331	0.6368	0.6406	0.6443	0.6480	0.6517
0.4	0.6554	0.6591	0.6628	0.6664	0.6700	0.6736	0.6772	0.6808	0.6844	0.6879
0.5	0.6915	0.6950	0.6985	0.7019	0.7054	0.7088	0.7123	0.7157	0.7190	0.7224
0.6	0.7258	0.7291	0.7324	0.7357	0.7389	0.7422	0.7454	0.7486	0.7518	0.7549
0.7	0.7580	0.7612	0.7642	0.7673	0.7704	0.7734	0.7764	0.7794	0.7823	0.7852
0.8	0.7881	0.7910	0.7939	0.7967	0.7996	0.8023	0.8051	0.8079	0.8106	0.8133
0.9	0.8159	0.8186	0.8212	0.8238	0.8264	0.8289	0.8315	0.8340	0.8365	0.8389
1.0	0.8413	0.8438	0.8461	0.8485	0.8508	0.8531	0.8554	0.8577	0.8599	0.8621
1.1	0.8643	0.8665	0.8686	0.8708	0.8729	0.8749	0.8770	0.8790	0.8810	0.8830
1.2	0.8849	0.8869	0.8888	0.8907	0.8925	0.8944	0.8962	0.8980	0.8997	0.9015
1.3	0.9032	0.9049	0.9066	0.9082	0.9099	0.9115	0.9131	0.9147	0.9162	0.9177
1.4	0.9192	0.9207	0.9222	0.9236	0.9251	0.9265	0.9279	0.9292	0.9306	0.9319
1.5	0.9332	0.9345	0.9357	0.9370	0.9382	0.9394	0.9406	0.9418	0.9430	0.9441
1.6	0.9452	0.9463	0.9474	0.9485	0.9495	0.9505	0.9515	0.9525	0.9535	0.9545
1.7	0.9554	0.9564	0.9573	0.9582	0.9591	0.9599	0.9608	0.9616	0.9625	0.9633
1.8	0.9641	0.9649	0.9656	0.9664	0.9671	0.9678	0.9686	0.9693	0.9700	0.9706
1.9	0.9713	0.9719	0.9726	0.9732	0.9738	0.9744	0.9750	0.9756	0.9762	0.9767
2.0	0.9773	0.9778	0.9783	0.9788	0.9793	0.9798	0.9803	0.9808	0.9812	0.9817
2.1	0.9821	0.9826	0.9830	0.9834	0.9838	0.9842	0.9846	0.9850	0.9854	0.9857
2.2	0.9861	0.9865	0.9868	0.9871	0.9875	0.9878	0.9881	0.9884	0.9887	0.9890
2.3	0.9893	0.9896	0.9898	0.9901	0.9904	0.9906	0.9909	0.9911	0.9913	0.9916
2.4	0.9918	0.9920	0.9922	0.9925	0.9927	0.9929	0.9931	0.9932	0.9934	0.9936
2.5	0.9938	0.9940	0.9941	0.9943	0.9945	0.9946	0.9948	0.9949	0.9951	0.9952
2.6	0.9953	0.9955	0.9956	0.9957	0.9959	0.9960	0.9961	0.9962	0.9963	0.9964
2.7	0.9965	0.9966	0.9967	0.9968	0.9969	0.9970	0.9971	0.9972	0.9973	0.9974
2.8	0.9974	0.9975	0.9976	0.9977	0.9977	0.9978	0.9979	0.9980	0.9980	0.9981
2.9	0.9981	0.9982	0.9983	0.9983	0.9984	0.9984	0.9985	0.9985	0.9986	0.9986
3.0	0.9987	0.9987	0.9987	0.9988	0.9988	0.9989	0.9989	0.9989	0.9990	0.9990
3.1	0.9990	0.9991	0.9991	0.9991	0.9992	0.9992	0.9992	0.9992	0.9993	0.9993
3.2	0.9993	0.9993	0.9994	0.9994	0.9994	0.9994	0.9994	0.9995	0.9995	0.9995
3.3	0.9995	0.9995	0.9996	0.9996	0.9996	0.9996	0.9996	0.9996	0.9996	0.9997
3.4	0.9997	0.9997	0.9997	0.9997	0.9997	0.9997	0.9997	0.9997	0.9998	0.9998
3.5	0.9998	0.9998	0.9998	0.9998	0.9998	0.9998	0.9998	0.9998	0.9998	0.9998

Establish Change Control Policy

Managing the design of software systems is often a very complex endeavor, especially when changes to the design occur after the design has successfully gone through peer reviews. Even a small design change can result in system failures if not managed appropriately. To avoid major problems later in the project, it is critical that a formal change control process gets adopted early in the planning phase. A change control process also serves to ensure the

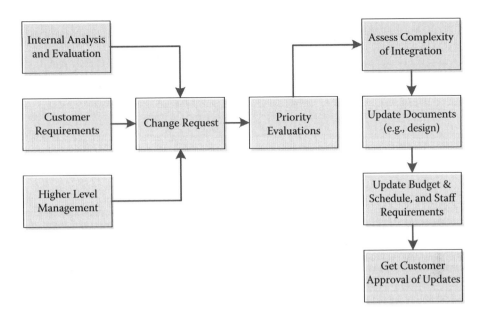

FIGURE 10.4
Example of a change control process.

technical integrity of the design in the presence of changes. Figure 10.4 shows an example of a change control process. Here, a change request is submitted to the change control authority, which in many cases corresponds to the project manager, the design lead, or the group that makes the final decision on the status and priority of a change. The request is then evaluated based on technical merit, complexity of integration, and potential side effects. From these assessments, the request is assigned a change priority. Developers then take their initial design documents through another round of formal reviews to obtain updated estimates for the budget, schedule, and staffing. Finally, updated design documents and schedule estimates must then be approved by the customer since they represent changes to the original estimates.

IMPLEMENTATION PHASE

During the implementation stage, the main managerial activities are monitoring and controlling that the design project activities are being accomplished according to the plan (i.e., schedule and budget). Monitoring and controlling mechanisms exist to identify any deviations from the plan and to ensure that these deviations get corrected in a timely manner in order to avoid major future problems. Appropriate project management tools for this phase are Gantt charts and *earned value management* (EVM). Recall that in our earlier discussion on Gantt charts, we mentioned that they are a useful mechanism to manage progress within the design phase. Since we have already covered Gantt charts in the previous section, we will limit our discussion only to earned value management.

Earned Value Management

Earned value management (EVM) is an important project management technique to determine the progress of tasks based on the value of the work currently completed versus the work that was expected to be completed at that particular time. The term used to define the dollar amount of the work currently completed is called *earned value* (EV), which is calculated by multiplying the percentage work completed times the planned total cost of the work when completed. Therefore, a key factor is to accurately estimate the percentage of work completed, which can be hard to do because of the complexity of tasks and the high degree of subjectivity that is typically involved. Furthermore, workers tend to inflate the percentage of work completed to give the perception that work is progressing smoothly for the completion of the task. Portraying a false sense of work completion is very dangerous for a project and can result in significant schedule and budget overruns. Knowing that the percent completion of a task at a particular point in time is lower than expected provides managers the opportunity to implement corrective actions to mitigate the risks of not completing the task within established cost and schedule constraints. There are various ways to estimate percentage completion. Meredith and Mantel (2009) provide a rough set of guidelines that can be used to help in the estimation process, which are briefly described in Table 10.5.

Armed with EV calculations for each task (i.e., each element in the WBS), we can examine deviations to cost and schedule and then establish a dollar amount to these deviations. The terms used to define current deviations to schedule and cost are called *schedule variance* (SV) and *cost variance* (CV). SV is calculated as the difference between the EV and the *planned value* (PV), which is the cost/value of the work that was expected to be completed at that point in time of the schedule. CV is the difference between the EV and the *actual cost* (AC), which is the amount of money that was spent on the work currently completed. Two other important measures are the *cost performance index* (CPI) and the *schedule performance index* (SPI). The CPI value is calculated as the ratio of EV to AC. This measure can be used to estimate the projected cost to complete some work. The SPI value is calculated as the ratio of EV to PV. This measure can be used to estimate the projected time to complete some work. Table 10.6 provides a brief description of the EVM parameters defined so far as well as *budget at completion* (BAC), *estimate cost to complete* (ETC), and *estimate at completion* (EAC). Table 10.7 shows the equations for the parameters. Notice

TABLE 10.5

Some Guidelines for Estimating Percentage Completion of a Task

Approach Name	Brief Description
50–50	Assumes 50% task completion as soon as the task begins, and 100% completion when the task is completed
0–100 percent	Assumes 0% until the task gets fully completed
Critical input use	Percent completion is a function of how much of a critical input is used versus its overall expected total to be used
Proportionality	Assumes work completion as the proportion of actual time (or cost) spent over the total time (or cost) planned for the task to be completed

TABLE 10.6

EVM Definition of Parameters

Parameter	Description
EV	Also called *budgeted cost of work performed* (BCWP), it is the dollar amount of the work currently completed
AC	Also called *actual cost of work performed* (ACWP), it represents the amount of money that was spent on the work currently completed
PV	Also called *budgeted cost of work scheduled* (BCWS), it represents the value of the work that was expected to be completed at that point in time of the schedule
CV	Describes the difference between the value of work completed and the actual cost spent to complete it
SV	Describes the difference between the value of work currently completed and the cost of the work that was expected to be completed
CPI	Describes the current cost efficiency of the work (CPI < 1 means over budget; CPI > 1 means under budget; CPI = 1 means right on budget)
SPI	Describes the current schedule efficiency of the work (SPI < 1 means behind schedule; SPI > 1 means ahead of schedule; SPI = 1 means right on schedule)
BAC	Total budget for the project
ETC	Represents the estimated cost remaining to complete the project
EAC	Represents the total cost of the entire project

TABLE 10.7

Equations for EVM parameters

Parameter	Equation
EV	$EV = (\% \text{ work completed}) * \text{planned cost for the work}$
CV	$CV = EV - AC$
SV	$SV = EV - PV$
CPI	$CPI = EV/AC$
SPI	$SPI = EV/PV$
ETC	$ETC = (BAC - EV)/CPI$
EAC	$EAC = ETC + AC$

that the EV parameter is present in all of these calculations. This highlights the importance of establishing accurate estimations of percent work completion, which is the key factor used to define EV.

Let's show the implementation of the EVM equations discussed so far through an example. Assume the following scenario:

Sara is managing a software design project composed of 10 tasks. Each task was estimated to cost $1,000; therefore, BAC = $10,000. Each task was estimated to be completed in a month; therefore, the total planned duration for the project was estimated to be 10 months. Since each task is expected to have the same cost and duration, the completion of an individual task represents 10% completion of the design project. In the current fifth month, only three tasks have been fully completed at a cost of $4,000. Sara needs to provide upper management with current progress status.

TABLE 10.8

Example EVM Parameters

Parameter	Calculation
EV	0.3 * $10,000 = $3,000
CV	$3,000 – $4,000 = -$1,000
SV	$3,000 – $5,000 = -$2,000
CPI	$3,000/$4,000 = 0.75
SPI	$3,000/$5,000 = 0.6000
ETC	($10,000 – $3,000)/0.75 = $9,333
EAC	$9,333 + $7,000 = $16,333

In this scenario, Sara can use the set of equations from Table 10.7 to present upper management with a complete progress status of the project. EV is calculated to be $3,000 given that the three tasks completed represent 30% of the project, and the budget for the entire project is $10,000. To calculate SV, we use a PV of $5,000 because each task was budgeted at $1,000 and five tasks should have been completed in the fifth month. Table 10.8 shows the calculations for the rest of the EVM parameters. These results clearly show that the project is over both budget and schedule estimates. The CPI index, for example, shows that only $0.75 of earned value was received for every dollar actually spent. The EAC shows an estimated $6,333 over budget amount. These alarming values give Sara and upper management the opportunity to implement risk mitigation policies to either get the project to its budgeted path or at least attempt to minimize losses.

Skill Development 10.2: Estimating Project Completion via Simple Simulation

Estimating the percent completion of tasks is not an exact science. In fact, we can say that estimated values of percentage completion are uncertain and therefore can be treated as random variables from assumed probabilistic distributions. An example of a probabilistic distribution is the uniform distribution, which is a continuous distribution where possible events (within a lower and upper bound) have the same probability of occurrence. This distribution is expressed as $U(a, b)$, where a and b denote lower and upper limits, respectively. In the example related to Table 10.8, assume that the costs for the tasks are considered random variables. More specifically, assume that the estimated costs for Tasks 1, 3, 5, 7, and 9 can be modeled with the following distribution: $U(\$700, \$1,300)$. Similarly, assume that the estimated costs for Tasks 2, 4, 6, 8, and 10 can be modeled with the following distribution: $U(\$800, \$1,200)$. In a spreadsheet (e.g., Microsoft Excel), simulate 10 values for the cost of each task. What is the average cost of the project using simulation? Are there any benefits from using simulation modeling for project cost estimation? *Note:* In Excel, to model a $U(a, b)$ random variable, type the following function in an empty cell: = a + (b – a)*RAND(). Remember that it is critical to begin with the "=" sign.

TERMINATION STAGE

During the termination stage, key activities involve verification that everything is in place for a smooth transition into the code construction phase. Activities include, for example, making sure that the latest versions of the design documents are securely stored based on configuration management procedures, updating schedule and cost current values, reevaluating schedule and budget plans based on the resulting performance measures of the design phase, and communicating results to upper management.

LEADING THE DESIGN EFFORT

Without a doubt, leadership plays a key role in the success or failure of complex projects. As such, it is necessary to cover important concepts related to leadership in the design effort. It is important to mention that the field of leadership is one that has been researched by academicians and practitioners for many years. Therefore, there is an extensive body of knowledge and literature related to this field. The purpose of this section is to highlight some key leadership concepts that are relevant to our study of software designs. A significant part of the material covered in this section was gathered from Lussier and Achua (2010); therefore, readers are referred to this work for more detailed explanations of leadership concepts.

Personality Traits and Leadership

Traits are personal characteristics that help to describe a person. For example, someone who has the ability to communicate well with others and start friendly conversations with unknown people can be said to have a highly sociable trait. Someone who works hard and tends to go the extra mile to complete assigned tasks can be said to possess an achievement trait. The combination of traits that a person has defines that person's *personality*, and personality significantly affects our decisions. For example, a highly sociable person with an achievement trait is expected to make decisions such as volunteering to make presentations to clients. Given that a good decision-making ability is a major part of being an effective leader, it is important to understand the relationship among traits, personality, decision making, and leadership.

Personality Dimensions

Researchers have identified five personality dimensions to categorize groups of traits. The idea behind this is to be able to classify someone's personality into one of these dimensions. The five dimensions are *agreeableness, surgency, adjustment, conscientiousness,* and *openness to experience.* Although called by different names by various researchers, we will refer to Lussier and Achua (2010) and call them the *Big Five Model of Personality.*

The agreeableness dimension contains traits that are related to getting along with people. Individuals who are strong in agreeableness are friendly, sociable, and compassionate. The surgency dimension, on the other hand, corresponds to personalities that are dominant (i.e., want to be in control), enjoy competition, and are willing to confront others, among other things. Individuals who are weak in surgency are typically followers. The adjustment dimension is related to emotional stability. Individuals who are strong in this dimension are considered stable people who are in control of themselves, are positive minded, and react well under pressure. Those who are weak in adjustment are considered unstable and typically are characterized by being negative and performing poorly under pressure. The conscientiousness dimension contains traits related to achievement. Basically, individuals who are strong in this dimension are those who are willing to work extra hours and make sacrifices to reach the assigned objectives. Last but not least, the openness to experience dimension is related to individuals who are flexible to change, are open-minded, and attempt enjoy trying new things. Understanding these dimensions is important because researchers have found varying degrees of correlations between leadership and each of the five personality dimensions. For example, Judge, Ilies, Bono, and Gerhardt (2007) analyzed over 70 prior studies to determine correlations among the five personality dimensions and leadership. The results of this study showed that the surgency dimension was the highest with a 0.31 correlation. This means that traits corresponding to surgency can be used, to some extent, to describe leadership. The second highest was conscientiousness with a 0.28 correlation, followed by openness to experience with 0.24 and agreeableness with 0.08.

Traits of Effective Leaders

As already stated, personality dimensions are defined by groups of traits and can provide an understanding of leadership in individuals. A different approach to studying personality dimensions is to investigate common individual traits that effective leaders possess, without grouping traits into personality dimensions. Some of the most important traits are presented in Table 10.9.

Ethical Leadership

Ethics can be defined as a set of moral principles that facilitates the process to distinguish between right and wrong behavior. Research has shown that ethical behavior positively correlates with leadership effectiveness (Veiga 2004). Furthermore, it is well-known that one of the best ways to lead is by example. Therefore, an ethical leader sets the tone for employees to conduct themselves in an ethical manner. However, being an ethical leader can be very challenging because of the risk of rejection or loss associated with ethical decisions. A few things can be done to overcome this challenge, one of which is to focus on a higher purpose while going through the decision process that involves moral behavior. For example, assume that the design lead of a major top secret software project is approached

TABLE 10.9

Traits of Effective Leaders

Principle	Description (Trait's Characteristics in a Person)
Dominance	This trait describes a person who wants to be a manager and takes control. Successful leaders with this trait are not overly bossy and avoid the bullying style.
High energy	This trait describes a positive-minded person who works hard to achieve objectives and is good at taking initiative.
Integrity	This trait describes a person who is highly ethical and trustworthy.
Flexibility	This trait describes a person who can adapt well to new and different situations.
Self-confidence	This trait describes a person who trusts his or her judgment, initiatives, intelligence, and ideas. This is not to be confused with arrogance.
Stability	This trait describes a person who is able to control emotions and act well under pressure.
Intelligence	This trait describes a person who possesses a high cognitive ability to solve problems and make decisions.
Sensitivity to others	This trait describes a person who focuses on the feelings of others and strongly considers them.

by a foreign citizen with a proposition to sell the software design and other important documents to an enemy country. If focused on the safety of the people (i.e., the higher purpose), then ethical values will provide the answer of not accepting the offer and reporting the foreign person to the authorities. Another approach that can be taken to overcome the challenges associated with ethical decisions is to find support from other ethical people (e.g., friends, family, coworkers). To help employees distinguish between ethical and unethical activities, most companies have their own internal documents that describe the expected ethical behavior from employees. It is very important for leaders to conform to these guidelines and discuss them with employees.

Power

Leading is about influencing others. The potential influence that leaders have over others is called *power*. The word *potential* means that it is actually the perception of power, and not the power itself, that influences followers. The two main sources of power are position power and personal power. *Position power* is related to hierarchical position levels. More specifically, higher hierarchical levels mean higher potential power. Therefore, the president of a software company has more potential power than any other employee in the company because of position power. Position power is important because it allows managers to influence employees to reach planned objectives. There are various types of position power. An example of one is called the *reward power*. This type of power gives managers the ability to influence employees with something of value to them, namely, performance evaluations. Employees will be influenced to complete their corresponding assignments because of their manager's reward power to provide good performance evaluations. Another type of position power—related to reward power—is called *coercive power*. The coercive power basically says that managers have the ability to influence others by the idea of punishment and withholding of rewards. Following the same example, employees can be influenced to complete their corresponding assignments because of their manager's coercive power to provide bad performance evaluations and withhold salary increases.

Personal power relates to the potential influence that a person's behavior has to influence others. Being positive, assertive, and hard-working are some of the characteristics that increase personal power. As with position power, there are also various types of personal power. One example is the *expert power*. This type of power is based on the ability to influence others based on a leader's skill and knowledge. For example, being an expert in developing architectural designs will influence others to follow the expert. The expert power of an individual gets stronger as people with similar expertise levels become fewer. Another type of personal power is called connection power. *Connection power* refers to the ability of a person to influence others because of the person's relationships with influential people.

KEY LEADERSHIP SKILLS

Various skills are important to leadership. Some of these skills include communication, networking, motivation, and negotiation. These are described in the following subsections.

Communication Skills

Good communication skills are essential for effective leadership. Various researchers (see, e.g., Li and Liu 2010; Simkin 1996) have mentioned that a high percent of a managers' time is spent in communications. As already mentioned, leadership is about influencing others. Leaders can influence and establish productive relationships with others through communication. Truly effective communication occurs when the information passed is equally and fully understood by all parties. One way to achieve effective communication is to plan in advance the message that needs to be conveyed. To achieve this, the goal of the message needs to be clearly understood. Also, it is important to think about the best timing to convey the message, how the message will be delivered (e.g., oral, written), and where (e.g., company's auditorium, employee's office).

One type of communication is *oral communication*. To become an effective oral communicator can be challenging and often takes much practice. One way to become effective is to have a process in place so that focus can be placed in the individual elements of the process. Lussier and Achua (2010) describe a five-step process for effectively sending oral messages. The first step is to develop a rapport. This means to try establishing a good relationship with the receiving party and begin small conversations related to the message. The second step is to clearly state the objective of the message. This is crucial as it helps the receiver to understand what the message is expected to accomplish before the details of the message are transmitted. This will engage the receiver's mind to focus on the message to be received. The third step is to actually transmit the message. The fourth step is to perceive the receiver's understanding of the message. It is important that the message was well understood; otherwise, its objectives were not achieved. This can be accomplished by asking direct questions or reading the receiver's expressions. When convinced that the message was understood, the final step of the process is to get a commitment from the receiver. This is unnecessary if the goal of the message is to merely inform. However, if the goal is to influence the receiver to accomplish a task (e.g., design document), then a commitment from the receiver to complete the task is necessary. For this, the leader must be convinced that the receiver is capable of completing the task by its deadline. When a commitment from the receiver is received, the leader must follow up to make sure that the task is being accomplished. If not, the leader can make use of the *power* concept to persuade the receiver to complete the task.

Another type of communication is *written communication*. This type of communication is now more important than ever, and it is mainly attributed to e-mail technology. Today, people around the world communicate with each other via e-mails, and e-mailing between managers and employees is almost always the preferred type of written communication.

The key elements for effective written communication are content and structure. That is, the message must be structured in such a way that the information it intends to transmit (i.e., content) is clearly described and the flow of information is smooth and easy to follow. As with oral communication, it is critical for the communicator to clearly understand the intended objective of the message before writing it. One way to do this is to make an outline with the main points that need to be transmitted. Making an outline also helps to establish an appropriate flow for the message, which is necessary for a clear understanding of it. Another way to improve message flow is to avoid including unnecessary information. Messages must be kept short, simple, and to the point.

A final point on written communication is that we must understand that writing is a skill. As such, it takes effort (e.g., reading books on proper grammar) and practice to become good at it. One way to improve this skill is to have others review your work so that you can learn from their feedback. It is important to keep in mind that editing and rewriting are often necessary actions to ensure the quality of messages. With continued advances in technology, the value of becoming an effective writer is becoming more and more important to leadership. Consider, for example, the relatively recent technology of social networking and electronic chatting rooms, which allow real-time written communication between parties around the world.

Networking Skills

Networking can be defined as a skill that focuses on building relationships with others through effective communications. Thus, communications and networking skills are closely related to each other. Networking is particularly important for leadership because it facilitates the process of meeting objectives. As with any skill, networking can be improved with practice.

Motivation Skills

It can be safe to say that there exists a positive correlation between employees' motivation levels and their productivity. Therefore, the ability to motivate others to work hard to achieve particular project goals is a major part of being a leader. For various decades now, motivation

TABLE 10.10

Types of Needs and Activities to Meet Them

Type of Need	Activities to Meet the Needs
Physiological	Adequate salaries
	Allowance of breaks
	Adequate working conditions
Safety	Safe working conditions
	Salary increases (considering inflation)
	Fringe benefits
Social	Social activities that conform to individual behavior
	Team-building retreats
	Team sports
	Lunch gatherings
Esteem	Raises based on performance
	Awards
	Public recognition
	Participation in decision making
Self-actualization	Skill development activities
	Promotions
	Increase control of an employee's task

has been an area of investigation to many researchers. Various theories have been developed to describe a set of motivational factors that significantly affect individuals' behavior. The general benefit sought from these research studies was that identifying and understanding these factors would provide leaders with necessary resources to positively influence and inspire employees to successfully complete their tasks.

One of the motivational theories developed is called the *hierarchy of needs theory* (Lussier and Achua 2010). This theory describes five types of needs through which employees are motivated. Table 10.10 shows the five types and provides some of the activities that can help meet the particular needs associated with each type.

Negotiation Skills

Negotiation skills are an important part of any management job. Good negotiators are capable of leading by looking out for the best interests of the people that they are leading. There are many research studies related to negotiations, some of which have resulted in guidelines that can help to improve a person's negotiation skills. One such set of guidelines, called *principled negotiation*, was developed by Fisher and Ury (1991). Principled negotiation is composed of four guidelines. The first one is to *separate the people from the problem*. This principle helps to keep the focus on the problem at hand rather than on interpersonal issues. The second guideline is to *focus on interests rather than positions*. This principle helps to keep the focus of the negotiation on the interests of people rather than their positions. The third guideline is to *generate options before trying to reach an agreement*. This principle promotes creativity and reminds the negotiating parties to brainstorm to find potential solutions that can be brought to the negotiation. The fourth guideline is to *insist on using objective criteria*. This principle promotes decision making based on reasonable standards rather than on subjective ones.

ETHICS IN SOFTWARE DESIGN

Software engineers must abide to the highest possible standards when developing software systems to make the software engineering profession beneficial and highly respected. Engineers have the responsibility to public welfare, including health and safety. The IEEE-CS/ACM organizations developed a Software Engineering Code of Ethics (SECE) (IEEE 2010) as the standard set of ethical guidelines that engineers must adhere to. This code contains the principles shown in Table 10.11.

As seen, these principles collectively ensure that professionals in the software engineering field adhere to high levels of ethical conduct. In one way or another, all of these principles can be directly related with the design of software systems. The SECE provides a very clear set of guidelines for each principle. Following is a brief description of some of these principles, as well as their specific guidelines from the SECE.

Public and Product Principles

The public principle is the first principle included in the SECE (Table 10.12). Basically, this principle states that professionals in the software engineering field must take responsibility for their own work and must ensure that their work positively affects the public good. The product principle (Table 10.13) states, among other things, that professionals must strive for high quality within acceptable cost and schedule thresholds.

TABLE 10.11

Principles of Ethics in Software Engineering

Principle	Description
Public	Software engineers shall act consistently with the public interest.
Client and Employer	Software engineers shall act in a manner that is in the best interests of their client and employer consistent with the public interest.
Product	Software engineers shall ensure that their products and related modifications meet the highest professional standards possible.
Judgment	Software engineers shall maintain integrity and independence in their professional judgment.
Management	Software engineering managers and leaders shall subscribe to and promote an ethical approach to the management of software development and maintenance.
Profession	Software engineers shall advance the integrity and reputation of the profession consistent with the public interest.
Colleagues	Software engineers shall be fair to and supportive of their colleagues.
Self	Software engineers shall participate in lifelong learning regarding the practice of their profession and shall promote an ethical approach to the practice of the profession.

Source: IEEE Computer Society, Software Engineering Code of Ethics and Professional Practice. 2010.

TABLE 10.12

Guidelines Concerning the Public Principle

No.	Guideline Description
1.01	Engineers must accept full responsibility for their own work.
1.02	Moderate the interests of the software engineer, the employer, the client and the users with the public good.
1.03	Approve software only if they have a well-founded belief that it is safe, meets specifications, passes tests, and does not diminish quality of life, diminish privacy or harm the environment. The ultimate effect of the work should be to the public good.
1.04	Disclose to appropriate persons or authorities any actual or potential danger to the user, the public, or the environment, that they reasonably believe to be associated with software or related documents.
1.05	Cooperate in efforts to address matters of grave public concern caused by software, its installation, maintenance, support or documentation.
1.06	Be fair and avoid deception in all statements, particularly public ones, concerning software or related documents, methods and tools.
1.07	Consider issues of physical disabilities, allocation of resources, economic disadvantage and other factors that can diminish access to the benefits of software.
1.08	Be encouraged to volunteer professional skills to good causes and contribute to public education concerning the discipline.

Source: IEEE Computer Society, Software Engineering Code of Ethics and Professional Practice. 2010.

Judgment Principle

Although maintaining integrity in professional judgment should be implicitly under-stood for every principle in the SECE, a high level of individual integrity is so impor-tant that the code explicitly included it into a single principle, the judgment principle (Table 10.14). Making decisions that conform to the highest ethical levels can be very challenging at times; therefore, the integrity and moral values of a person play a major role when making judgment calls.

Management Principle

The management principle is of particular relevance to this chapter. Therefore, Table 10.15 outlines the guidelines included for software engineering managers in the code of ethics.

CHAPTER SUMMARY

This chapter presented an introduction to software design management. In particular, this chapter focused on describing three major elements that are critical for the success of any major design project: management, leadership, and ethics. In doing so, the chapter developed a design management framework that describes important concepts related to each element with the hope of facilitating the successful management of this complex phase.

TABLE 10.13

Guidelines Concerning the Product Principle

No.	Guideline Description
3.01	Strive for high quality, acceptable cost and a reasonable schedule, ensuring significant tradeoffs are clear to and accepted by the employer and the client, and are available for consideration by the user and the public.
3.02	Ensure proper and achievable goals and objectives for any project on which they work or propose.
3.03	Identify, define and address ethical, economic, cultural, legal and environmental issues related to work projects.
3.04	Ensure that they are qualified for any project on which they work or propose to work by an appropriate combination of education and training, and experience.
3.05	Ensure an appropriate method is used for any project on which they work or propose to work.
3.06	Work to follow professional standards, when available, that are most appropriate for the task at hand, departing from these only when ethically or technically justified.
3.07	Strive to fully understand the specifications for software on which they work.
3.08	Ensure that specifications for software on which they work have been well documented, satisfy the users requirements and have the appropriate approvals.
3.09	Ensure realistic quantitative estimates of cost, scheduling, personnel, quality and outcomes on any project on which they work or propose to work and provide an uncertainty assessment of these estimates.
3.10	Ensure adequate testing, debugging, and review of software and related documents on which they work.
3.11	Ensure adequate documentation, including significant problems discovered and solutions adopted, for any project on which they work.
3.12	Work to develop software and related documents that respect the privacy of those who will be affected by that software.
3.13	Be careful to use only accurate data derived by ethical and lawful means, and use it only in ways properly authorized.
3.14	Maintain the integrity of data, being sensitive to outdated or flawed occurrences.
3.15	Treat all forms of software maintenance with the same professionalism as new development.

Source: IEEE Computer Society, Software Engineering Code of Ethics and Professional Practice. 2010.

TABLE 10.14

Guidelines Concerning the Judgment Principle

No.	Guideline Description
4.01	Temper all technical judgments by the need to support and maintain human values.
4.02	Only endorse documents either prepared under their supervision or within their areas of competence and with which they are in agreement.
4.03	Maintain professional objectivity with respect to any software or related documents they are asked to evaluate.
4.04	Not engage in deceptive financial practices such as bribery, double billing, or other improper financial practices.
4.05	Disclose to all concerned parties those conflicts of interest that cannot reasonably be avoided or escaped.
4.06	Refuse to participate, as members or advisors, in a private, governmental or professional body concerned with software related issues, in which they, their employers or their clients have undisclosed potential conflicts of interest.

Source: IEEE Computer Society, Software Engineering Code of Ethics and Professional Practice. 2010.

TABLE 10.15

Guidelines Concerning the Management Principle

No.	Guideline Description
5.01	Ensure good management for any project on which they work, including effective procedures for promotion of quality and reduction of risk.
5.02	Ensure that software engineers are informed of standards before being held to them.
5.03	Ensure that software engineers know the employer's policies and procedures for protecting passwords, files and information that is confidential to the employer or confidential to others.
5.04	Assign work only after taking into account appropriate contributions of education and experience tempered with a desire to further that education and experience.
5.05	Ensure realistic quantitative estimates of cost, scheduling, personnel, quality and outcomes on any project on which they work or propose to work, and provide an uncertainty assessment of these estimates.
5.06	Attract potential software engineers only by full and accurate description of the conditions of employment.
5.07	Offer fair and just remuneration.
5.08	Not unjustly prevent someone from taking a position for which that person is suitably qualified.
5.09	Ensure that there is a fair agreement concerning ownership of any software, processes, research, writing, or other intellectual property to which a software engineer has contributed.
5.10	Provide for due process in hearing charges of violation of an employer's policy or of this Code.
5.11	Not ask a software engineer to do anything inconsistent with this Code.
5.12	Not punish anyone for expressing ethical concerns about a project.

Source: IEEE Computer Society, Software Engineering Code of Ethics and Professional Practice. 2010.

The chapter described the software design phase as a complex task that must be managed in order to achieve acceptable quality levels. Various project management techniques were presented. These included techniques for planning such as work breakdown structures, linear responsibility charts, and network diagrams for scheduling. It also included a description of earned value management as a tool for determining the progress of tasks based on the value of the work currently completed versus the work that was expected to be completed at that particular time. The chapter also described the relationship between management and leadership, highlighted several leadership traits that are important for successful results, and presented various ethic items from the Software Engineering Code of Ethics that are relevant to software design projects.

REVIEW QUESTIONS

1. What is software design management, and why is it important?
2. Why is it important to view the software design phase as a project?
3. What are the phases of the software design phase?
4. What are the managerial objectives of the planning stage?
5. What project management tools can be used to manage the planning phase of a software design project? Briefly explain them.
6. What project management tools can be used to manage the implementation phase of a software design project? Briefly explain them.

7. What is the importance of a change control process?
8. Why is estimating the percent completion of a task so important in earned value management?
9. What are the four guidelines described in the chapter to estimate percent work completion?
10. What are some of the traits of effective leaders?
11. How do management and leadership relate to each other?
12. Explain the concept of power and how it can influence others.
13. What are the key leadership skills described in the chapter?
14. How do ethics and leadership relate to each other?

CHAPTER EXERCISES

1. The following table contains task durations for a project.

Task ID	Time (Days)			Immediate Predecessors
	Minimum (*a*)	Most Likely (*m*)	Maximum (*b*)	
A	10	22	38	—
B	3	7	12	A
C	11	25	44	B
D	11	24	42	B
E	4	9	17	B, C
F	2	5	9	D, E
G	4	8	14	F
H	11	24	43	G

a. Construct an AON network diagram and identify the critical path. What is the duration of the critical path?
b. What is the probability that the project gets completed by 85% of the critical path duration?

2. The following table contains expected duration times and expected cost for the set of tasks corresponding to a major design project that Dr. Christian Daniel is managing.

Task ID	Expected Duration (Months)	Expected Cost ($)	Task Predecessor
1	1	1,500	—
2	2	3,000	1
3	1	1,500	2
4	2	3,000	3
5	1	1,500	4
6	2	3,000	5
7	1	1,500	6
8	2	3,000	7

a. Assume a scenario where at the end of the seventh month five tasks have been completed at a cost of $11,500. Use the EVM equations to understand and show the current status of the project. Also, based on this scenario, what is the EAC value?

b. Assume a scenario where at the end of the sixth month two tasks have been completed at a cost of $8,500. Use the EVM equations to understand and show the current status of the project. Also, based on this scenario, what is the EAC value?

c. Assume a scenario where at the end of the tenth month seven tasks have been completed at a cost of $14,500. Use the EVM equations to understand and show the current status of the project. Also, based on this scenario, what is the EAC value?

REFERENCES

Fisher, R., and W. Ury. *Getting to Yes,* 2d ed. New York: Penguin Books, 1991.

Griffin, Ricky W. *Management,* 10th ed. Mason, OH: South-Western Publications, 2010.

IEEE Computer Society. "Software Engineering Code of Ethics and Professional Practice." 2010. Available at http://www.computer.org/portal/web/certification/resources/code_of_ethics.

Judge, T. A., R. Ilies, J. E. Bono, and M. W. Gerhardt. "Personality and Leadership: A Qualitative and Quantitative Review." *Journal of Applied Psychology* 87, no. 4 (2002): 765–768.

Li, Mei Yan, and Ying Zong Liu. "Study on Line Managers' Competence-Based Abilities of Performance Management." *Applied Mechanics and Materials* 40–41 (2010): 820–824.

Lussier, Robert, and Christopher Achua. *Leadership: Theory, Application, & Skill Development,* 4th ed. Florence, KY: Cengage Learning, 2010.

Meredith, Jack, and Samuel Mantel. *Project Management: A Managerial Approach,* 7th ed. Hoboken, NJ: John Wiley & Sons, 2009.

Nebus, J. "Building Collegial Information Networks: A Theory of Advice Network Generation." *Academy of Management Review* 31, no. 3 (2006): 615–637.

Pelosi, Marilyn K., and Theresa M. Sandifer. *Elementary Statistics: From Discovery to Decision.* Hoboken, NJ: John Wiley & Sons, 2003.

Simkin, Mark. "The Importance of Good Communication Skills on 'IS' Career Paths." *Journal of Technical Writing and Communication* 26, no. 1 (1996): 69–78.

Veiga, J. F. "Special Topic Ethical Behavior in Management, Bringing Ethics into the Mainstream: An Introduction to the Special Topic." *Academy of Management Executive* 18, no. 2 (2004): 37–38.

Index